Building Writing and Gramm___
Skills for School and Beyond!

GRAMMAR
for Writing

Grades 9-12

Welcome to Grammar for Writing

Grammar for Writing is designed for today's secondary school students. It offers a complete course in grammar, usage, and mechanics—with an emphasis on writing—intended to help build the communication skills needed in a rapidly changing world and to help students **excel on standardized tests**.

The program takes the "mystery" out of grammar and helps develop better and more confident writers.

Grammar for Writing illustrates how the rules of grammar, usage, and mechanics—the conventions of standard English—can help students develop writing that is not just **"correct" but powerful and persuasive**, too.

Grammar for Writing has been designed with today's students in mind. Grammar rules are presented and explained in a clear and simple manner so that students can grasp them quickly and **apply them to their writing immediately.**

"Researchers agree that it is more effective to teach punctuation, sentence variety, and usage in the context of writing than to approach the topic by teaching isolated skills."

Beverly Ann Chin

AUTHORSHIP

A broad-based team of experienced curriculum specialists and professional writers, working under the direction of Beverly Ann Chin, professor of English at the University of Montana and past-president of the National Council of Teachers of English (NCTE), developed the new *Grammar for Writing* series to help prepare today's secondary students to be effective writers in school, on writing assessments, on standardized tests, in college, and in the workplace.

Sadlier-Oxford has assembled the tools, strategies, and resources necessary for meeting many and varied student needs.

Program Features

NEW Standardized-Test Practice Unit

- Practice in SAT and ACT formats
- Full-length Practice Test

Composition Unit

- Complete coverage of the writing process
- Workshops in essential types of writing, including a **NEW** Workshop on **Writing a Timed Essay**
- **NEW** lessons on **sentence-level writing skills** that help students develop fluency

Grammar, Usage, and Mechanics Units

- Complete coverage of key topics
- Abundant exercises, with emphasis on cooperative learning activities
- Flexible lesson format
- Chapter openers featuring engaging photos and examples of actual student writing
- Applications of grammar skills to writing, revising, and editing tasks
- **NEW Test-Taking Tips** link grammar lessons to standardized-test practice items
- **NEW Connecting Writing and Grammar** exercises provide writing prompts for essays
- Revising and Editing worksheets
- Chapter Reviews and Cumulative Reviews

ONLINE COMPONENTS
www.grammarforwriting.com

- For students, portfolio writing projects linked to Grammar, Usage, and Mechanics chapters
- **NEW** for students, **standardized-test practice with grammar feedback**

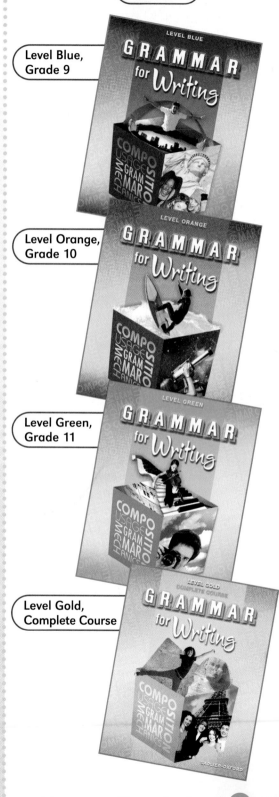

NEW!

Level Blue, Grade 9

Level Orange, Grade 10

Level Green, Grade 11

Level Gold, Complete Course

- **Writing Process and Strategies**

- **Forms and Models of Good Writing**

- **NEW Sentence-Level Skills**

- **NEW Timed Essay Writing Lesson**

Focus on Writing

Types of Writing

Help students focus on purpose and audience.

Lesson 4.3
Composition

Expository Writing:
Compare and Contrast Essay

Enriching Your Vocabulary

To understand the meaning of the adjective *indomitable*, you need to know the meaning of its two parts. The prefix *in-* means "not." The verb *domitare* is Latin for "to tame." Thus, *indomitable* means "incapable of being tamed." We all admire a person who faces a crisis with *indomitable* courage.

When you **compare**, you identify the way two or more subjects, or topics, are alike. When you **contrast**, you identify differences between subjects. Here are parts of an essay about two Civil War generals.

Grant and Lee: A Study in Contrasts
an excerpt by Bruce Catton

¹When Ulysses S. Grant and Robert E. Lee met in the parlor of a modest house at Appomattox Court House in Virginia, on April 9, 1865, to work out the terms for the surrender of Lee's Army of Northern Virginia, a great chapter in American life came to a close, and a great new chapter began. . . .

[*Most of Catton's essay analyzes how the two generals differ. Catton discusses Lee first. Lee had an aristocratic Virginia background, he believed in a society ruled by landowners, and he was intensely loyal to the South. Then Catton contrasts the same three features in Grant. Grant had a working-class Western background, he believed in a democratic society where anyone can achieve wealth and power through hard work, and he was fiercely loyal to the Union. Then Catton continues as follows.*]

²Yet it was not all contrast, after all. ³Different as they were—in background, in personality, in underlying aspiration—these two great soldiers had much in common.

⁴Each man had, to begin with, the great virtue of utter tenacity and fidelity. ⁵Grant fought his way down the Mississippi Valley in spite of acute personal discouragement and profound military handicaps. ⁶Lee hung on in the trenches at Petersburg after hope itself had died. ⁷In each man there was an indomitable quality . . . the born fighter's refusal to give up as long as he can still remain on his feet and lift his two fists.

⁸Daring and resourcefulness they had, too, the ability to think faster and move faster than the enemy. ⁹These were the qualities which gave Lee the dazzling campaigns of Second Manassas and Chancellorsville and won Vicksburg for Grant.

¹⁰Lastly, and perhaps greatest of all, there was the ability at the end to turn quickly from war to peace once the fighting was over. ¹¹Out of the way

Summarizes differences and begins discussion of similarities

Claims both men had tenacity and fidelity and gives examples

Claims both were daring and resourceful and gives examples

States most important similarity

62   Chapter 4 • Writing Workshop

Level Blue, p. 62

Level Blue, p. 63

Expository Writing:
Compare and Contrast Essay

Conclusion: restatement of thesis statement

him more than the part he played in their brief meeting in the McLean house at Appomattox. ¹⁶Their behavior there put all succeeding generations of Americans in their debt. ¹⁷Two great Americans, Grant and Lee were very different, yet under everything very much alike. ¹⁸Their encounter at Appomattox was one of the great moments of American history.

Critical Thinking   After you read the compare and contrast essay, answer the questions below.

1. Reread the introduction and the conclusion of the essay. What do you think the author's purpose is?

2. Name the ways Catton says the two generals are alike. What proof, or support, does he give?

Lesson 3.1
Composition   **Varying Sentence Beginnings**

➡ For variety, begin some of your sentences with a subordinate clause.

Lesson 7.3 provides practice in beginning sentences with different phrases. Subordinate clauses give you another tool for varying sentence beginnings. Here is the same idea expressed in a number of ways.

ORIGINAL	Giacomo Puccini died in 1924 before he finished the last act of his opera *Turandot*.
PREPOSITIONAL PHRASE	**In 1924,** Giacomo Puccini died before he finished the last act of his opera *Turandot*.
PARTICIPIAL PHRASE	**Not yet finished with the last act of his opera *Turandot*,** Giacomo Puccini died in 1924.
ADVERB CLAUSE	**Before he finished the last act of his opera *Turandot*,** Giacomo Puccini died in 1924.
NOUN CLAUSE	**That Giacomo Puccini died in 1924,** before finishing the last act of his opera *Turandot*, meant that another composer had to finish it.

Level Blue, p. 36

Authentic Passages set high standards and help model effective writing.

Annotations help students recognize essential elements of good writing.

Critical Thinking opportunities sharpen students' awareness of sound writing techniques.

Sentence-Writing Techniques offer students illustrations and practice in strengthening their personal styles.

Steps in Prewriting, Drafting, Revising, and Editing outline clear, easy-to-follow strategies. ▼

Graphic Organizers help students visualize, organize, and draft. ▼

Level Blue, p. 10

Lesson 1.3
Composition

Revising

▸ When you **revise**, you shape your draft into its almost-final form.

At this stage in the writing process, you try to make your written thoughts clearer. You may need to add new information, cut words or sentences, change the order of sentences and paragraphs, and replace weak words with stronger ones.

REVISING STRATEGIES

When you revise, you look for ways to eliminate problems with ideas and unity, organization and coherence, sentence variety, and word choice. To begin revising, try this four-step strategy. Reread your first draft four separate times, concentrating on only one of the issues below with each reading.

1. **Ideas and Unity** Can you summarize your main idea(s)? (In a narrative, you need to ask yourself whether you can summarize the event or events rather than the main idea or ideas.) Do you have enough supporting details or too many? Will adding or cutting details improve your draft? Do you need more background information? Is everything relevant, or related, to your main idea(s), or have you wandered off track?

2. **Organization and Coherence** Does the opening sentence grab the reader's attention? Can you improve your draft by moving paragraphs? by moving sentences? Is information presented in a logical order, an order that makes sense to the reader? Would adding transition words help? Does the last sentence bring closure to the writing?

3. **Sentence Variety** Have you varied the beginnings, lengths, and structure of your sentences? Would some sentences sound better combined?

4. **Word Choice** Is ... audience? Do tec... you delete unnec... words, and replac... an overworked w... express the same ...

Enriching Vocabul...

Narrare, Latin ... make known o... gives us the n... *narrative* (stor... narration). A w... may win critic... for her exciting ... narratives.

Writing Model

TOPIC: Car safety
What kinds of things do they look for during car inspections? Do they check tires? How? How often do you need to take a car in for an inspection? I'd better keep up regular maintenance. Maintenance. Of what? Of seat belts? What's to maintain? Doesn't matter. Point is to wear seat belts? Why? Dumb question...

Writing Model

Level Blue, p. 11

Level Blue, p.15

Writing a Timed Essay

Essay questions on standardized tests measure your ability to generate ideas relevant to a specific topic and to present those ideas clearly and logically in an appealing style, while applying the conventions of standard written English. You are asked to do all of this within a limited amount of time.

On a standardized test, you will find essay topics, also called "prompts," usually presented in one of these two ways:

Agree or Disagree. This type of prompt provides you with one or two quotations or a brief paragraph. You are directed to write an essay explaining whether you agree or disagree with the prompt. You are asked to develop and support your position with examples, facts, statistics, observations, or personal experience.

Solve a Problem. This type of prompt provides you with an issue or problem that needs solving. You are asked to propose a possible solution in an essay in which you develop and support your point of view with examples, facts, statistics, observations, or personal experience.

The writing prompt below is similar to one you might find on a standardized test. After the prompt, you will find one writer's essay in response to it.

> Consider the following issue. Then write an essay as directed.
>
> A former Secretary of Education remarked that if his son had approached him and said, "You promised to pay for my tuition at [a prestigious university]; how about giving me $50,000 instead to start a little business?" he might have thought it a good idea.
>
> **Assignment:** Do you agree or disagree? Write an essay in response to this issue. Develop and support your position with ideas, facts, and examples gained from your reading, observations, or personal experience.

Although the idea of starting a business rather than continuing your education through college may sound appealing, I believe that the plan is short-sighted. Furthering your education is not only important, it is essential for ourselves, our families, and communities. Studying at a university provides an excellent opportunity to learn more about who we are as we explore the world of ideas around us. We encounter new views in classes and in clubs and student organizations. We have opportunities to see plays, films, and art exhibits. In such a rich learning atmosphere, we are exposed to ideas that

Lesson 4.6
Composition

TEST-TAKING TIP
Most standardized test essays are scored from 6 (highest) to 1 (lowest).

Expresses position on the topic in thesis statement

Timed Essay Writing is a skill students must practice to succeed on standardized tests and in other real-world situations. ◀

Chapter 4 • Writing Workshops **83**

Level Blue, p. 83

visit **www.sadlier-oxford.com** T5

Focus on Skills: Grammar and Usage

Using Object Pronouns

Lesson 11.2 Usage

Object Pronouns

SINGULAR	PLURAL
me, you, him, her, it	us, you, them

Use an **object pronoun** when the pronoun functions as the direct object (DO), indirect object (IO), or object complement (OC) of a sentence or a clause.

      IO   IO   DO
My father gave Dolores and **me** the keys to the car.
      DO
We thanked **him** for the keys.
      DO   DO OC
The family counselor made **you** and **me** us.

Use an object pronoun when the pronoun functions as the object of a preposition (OP) in a sentence or clause.

      OP   OP
Dad handed the keys to Dolores and **me**.
  OP OP
For both of **us**, driving Dad's car was a big responsibility.

P.S. Don't become confused by the many terms that include the word *object*. Just get a general sense of how an object differs from a subject.

See **Grammar,** Lesson 6.6, for more on direct and indirect objects and Lesson 6.8 for more on object complements.

EDITING TIP
Avoid this common error: "between you and I." Always say or write, "between you and me."

EXERCISE 3 Choosing the Correct Pronoun

Underline the pronoun in parentheses that correctly completes each sentence.

1. Every actor in his heart believes everything bad that's printed about (he, him). —Orson Welles
2. There is nothing which (we, us) receive with so much reluctance as advice. —Joseph Addison
3. Everything intercepts (we, us) from ourselves. —Ralph Waldo Emerson
4. A man in passion rides a horse that runs away with (he, him). —Thomas Fuller
5. We shape our buildings; thereafter, they shape (we, us). —Winston Churchill

STEP BY STEP
To decide whether to use a subject pronoun or an object pronoun:
1. Decide what function the pronoun performs in the sentence.
2. If the pronoun is a subject or a predicate nominative, use the subject pronoun.
3. If the pronoun is a direct object, an indirect object, an object complement, or the object of a preposition, use the object pronoun.

Chapter 11 • Using Pronouns **233**

Level Gold, p. 233

Essential Concepts focus on principles students must apply to write correctly.

Cross References extend and reinforce students' knowledge.

PS Features add perspective to sharpen understanding of key principles.

Step by Step Features are targeted mini-lessons offering alternative strategies.

Examples of Conventions help guide student practice and writing.

Writing Hints make connections between conventions and real writing situations.

Enriching Your Vocabulary features help build word banks for students as they study and write.

Adverb Clauses

Lesson 8.3 Grammar

An **adverb clause** is a subordinate clause that functions as an adverb. It modifies a verb, an adjective, or another adverb.
    Because the school bus broke down, Jeff missed first period.
    [modifies the verb *missed*]
    I am three years older **than she is.**
    [modifies the adjective *older*]
    Tamiko left for work ten minutes earlier **than she usually does.**
    [modifies the adverb *earlier*]

Look for the introductory words listed at the right. Often (but not always), they signal the beginning of an adverb clause and at such times they are called **subordinating conjunctions**.

In an **elliptical adverb clause**, some words are omitted. In the following examples, the bracketed words are understood.
    Julio is older **than Sheila [is]**.
    I'm more worried about the math test than you are [**worried about the math test**].
    Have you ever met anyone as confident as **Andrew [is]**?

Subordinating Conjunctions

after	so that
although	than
as	though
as long as	unless
as soon as	when
as though	whenever
because	where
before	wherever
even though	whether
if	while
since	

WRITING HINT
When you use an adverb clause at the beginning of a sentence, follow it with a comma. If you use an adverb clause at the end of a sentence, you do not need to use a comma before it.
If you're outdoors in a thunderstorm, find shelter right away.
Find shelter right away **if you're outdoors in a thunderstorm.**

EXERCISE 5 Identifying Adverb Clauses

Underline each adverb clause in the following sentences.
Hint: Not every sentence contains an adverb clause, and some have more than one.

1. Whenever lightning strikes, it is always accompanied by thunder.
2. Thunder occurs when lightning heats the air and causes it to expand rapidly.
3. Even though thunder sounds scary, it poses no danger.
4. A person who is struck by lightning receives a severe electric shock.
5. Because light travels much faster than sound, you can see lightning before you hear the thunder.
6. If you count the seconds in the interim between the lightning and thunder, you can judge the distance of the source of the lightning.
7. When you see lightning and hear thunder at the same time, watch out because the lightning is very close.

Enriching Your Vocabulary
Interim comes to us unchanged in form from the Latin adverb meaning "meanwhile." In English the noun means "the time between." The word is also an adjective meaning "temporary" or "coming between two points in time."

Chapter 8 • Clauses **149**

Level Blue, p. 149

Revising and Editing Worksheets appear throughout—to build analytic skills and reinforce grammar and usage through revision.

Chapter 5
Grammar
Revising and Editing Worksheet

Improve the following draft by revising for ideas, organization, word choice, and sentence variety. After revising, edit the draft for errors in spelling, capitalization, punctuation, and usage. Write your revised and edited version on a separate piece of paper. Compare your changes with those of a writing partner.

¹It has been absent for nearly four hundred years. ²Now Shakespeares' Globe Theatre has been resurrected. ³Drawing on lots of scholarly research and archaeological evidence. ⁴Using Elizabethan building techniques, they have re-created the Globe. ⁵They've done it authentic. ⁶The process has been an adventure from the start. ⁷They had fund-raising nightmares, lawsuits, an[d ...]... arguments. ⁸They had other disasters, too. ⁹But the result is a [...] would make Shakespeare hisself proud.

¹⁰A brewery is where the original Globe Theatre once was. ¹¹[...] bank of the Thames River in London. ¹²The bank is on the sout[...] is two hundred yards away. ¹³Like the original, it has no roof. ¹⁴[...] timbered walls, there are three tiers of wooden benches. ¹⁵Thes[...] open yard and a platform stage. ¹⁶On the stage, plays are perform[...] back then.

¹⁷All fifteen hundred seats were filled when a performance o[...] V opened the Globe's first season. ²⁰The first season was 1997. ²¹Richard Olivier directed. ²²He is the son of Sir Laurence Olivier. ²³Sir Laurence Olivier was famous. ²⁴The Globe production was pure Elizabethan: All the roles were performed by men wearing costumes from that time.

²⁵The new Globe is the focus of a big-deal center that will eventually include a multimedia resource library, a bunch of buildings for education, places to eat and shop, and a three-hundred-seat indoor theater that is a copy of a 1617 design. ²⁶The cost of the entire project is about $45 million. ²⁷It cost about $900 to build the Globe in 1599.

136 Chapter 5 • Parts of Speech

Level Gold, p. 136

Connecting Writing and Grammar feature shows how writing and revising can be taught and connected through grammar principles.

CONNECTING
Writing & Grammar

Refer to **Composition**, Lesson 4.3, for more on writing persuasively.

Write What You Think

In many cultures, the traditional view is that the kitchen is a woman's domain. However, many of the world's most skilled and renowned chefs are men. Whose responsibility do you think it is to cook for a family? How do you account for the great number of leading male chefs? Write a persuasive paragraph putting forth your views. Support them with reasons and evidence. When you finish revising and editing, underline all the subjects of your sentences once and the verbs twice.

Level Gold, p. 146

Test-Taking Tips identify principles of grammar AND point students to relevant grammar and usage standardized-test items.

Editing Tips help students avoid pitfalls by calling attention to common errors and other possible problems.

EDITING TIP

Don't forget to use *-d* or *–ed* endings with *used* and *supposed* before an infinitive.

She **used to be** in our class.

Were you **supposed to get** the cake?

Level Gold, p.197

TEST-TAKING TIP

Examples of faulty parallelism often appear on standardized tests. When a sentence has a series of subjects, verbs or verb phrases, or other related structures, make sure they each have the same grammatical form. See item 8 on page 335.

Level Gold, p. 187

- **USE as a complete course or as a handbook**

- **DEVELOP students' reference skills**

- **NEW practice in STANDARDIZED-TEST FORMAT**

- **NEW Online Grammar Feedback for help with standardized-test items**

- **NEW practice writing TIMED ESSAYS**

Versatility + Comprehensiveness = TOTAL SUPPORT

The design and organization of *Grammar for Writing* facilitates a wide variety of instructional needs and styles:

Instructional Uses	Key Features and Support
As a complete course	• Detailed steps: all stages of the writing process • Full treatment: all principles of grammar, usage, mechanics • Graphic organizers to illustrate and guide • NEW Chapter: Sentence-level writing skills
As a reference tool during instruction	• Concise lesson numbering for easy access • Composition models by professional writers and student writers • Critical Thinking, Tips, and Editing features
As a handbook for independent and group learning	• Step-by-step features to guide writing and study • Annotations to explicate key concepts • Revision guidance, models, and practice • Writing Hints and other Tips
As review and practice for tests	• Simulations and practice items • NEW timed essay writing (Writing Workshop) • NEW Test-Taking Tips • NEW Practice Tests in standardized format • NEW Online Grammar Feedback

With Ancillary Support...

- **Resources for writing across the curriculum**
- **Writing process guidelines**
- **Chapter and cumulative reviews**
- **Online activities and support**

Features of Annotated Teacher's Edition

- On-page answers and annotations
- Strategies for grammar instruction
- Ideas and prompts for student writing
- Assessment rubrics for evaluating writing
- Strategies to connect grammar to writing
- Online support

Purposes of Writing

Help students see that there are many reasons for writing, now and in the future. Basically, these can be broken down into three categories: personal writing (self-expression), real-life writing, and writing for school.

Personal Writing

Writing as self-expression began to be emphasized in the mid-1960s, when teachers introduced journals, freewriting, and other kinds of personal writing into the classrooms. James Moffett (1973) saw self-expressive modes of writing as a way of engaging student writers, even those with limited English proficiency. Everyone has stories to tell, and ideas and feelings to communicate.

Journals/Diaries Encourage students to start a special notebook in which they record ideas and experiences. They might also include a list or description of "things I like"; or they can tape into their notebook excerpts from articles, poems, songs, cartoons/comic strips, photos, and ads that they find appealing. Over the course of months, such a journal becomes a rich source of topic ideas and details. Remind students to include in these journals or diaries only those things they are willing to share with their classmates.

- **Writing Logs** Prewriting notes, ideas for writing topics, proofreading

logs, reflections on their writing experiences

- **Reading Logs** A record of books they have read and their comments, questions, and responses; responses to particular stories and poems, novels, essays
- **Learning Logs** A record of important ideas and concepts they have learned

Sketchbooks Some students may want to create a sketchbook. They might sketch people, places, objects, and events from memory or direct observation. Encourage them to express what they have sketched in words, too. They might write on the back of a sketch or, if they are using a looseleaf notebook, interleave sketches and written descriptions.

Creative Writing Encourage students to write original poems and stories in conjunction with their study and discussion of literature genres. These may be individual, partner, or group efforts. Share finished works in class—on bulletin boards, in oral readings, or in a class newsletter or literary magazine. Tell students who are interested in creative writing to look for student writing contests and magazines (print and electronic) that publish student writing.

Real-Life Writing

Experienced teachers know that students are motivated when they write for a real-life purpose and a specific audience. Here are just a few of the real-life writing situations students may engage in.

Forms, Applications, Résumés Students must follow directions and develop the ability to summarize and express ideas clearly and concisely.

All Kinds of Letters Some letters are social (thank-you notes, friendly letters, and pen-pal letters) and chatty. Others are business letters (order letters, complaint letters, letters to the editor) and formal. Students need to write in the appropriate form and language.

Research As part of their research projects, students may write letters requesting information or interviews. They may need to write letters of acknowledgment and thanks.

E-mail Students may write formal e-mail messages (requesting information, asking questions of an expert) and informal messages to friends and family. They need to learn the "netiquette"—the accepted conventions for writing e-mail messages.

Persuasion Students express and support their opinions when they write letters to the editor, proposals for solving a school or community problem, and letters to elected representatives. The Write What You Think exercises throughout the Pupil's Edition give them repeated practice in writing for persuasive purposes.

Work At work, students may write letters, memos, and reports. Their writing must communicate ideas clearly and concisely.

Writing for School

Students know how important writing skills are in all their classes. Here are just a few of the reasons to write in school.

Reports In history, science, math, and other classes, students are asked to research, organize, and communicate ideas in written and oral reports.

Paragraphs Paragraph practice helps students gain skill in expressing and developing their ideas. (See Chapter 2 for lessons devoted to developing paragraph-writing skills.) In the mini-context of writing a single paragraph, students develop all of the following:

- a natural voice
- flow (sentences that read smoothly in a sequence)
- organization and coherence (ideas that are easy to follow)
- unity (ideas and supporting details that stick to a topic).

Essays By 9th grade, students should be applying their paragraph-writing skills to longer papers. (See Chapter 4, the "Writing Workshops.") Encourage students to write as much as they need to in order to express what they want to say.

T34   T35

Level Blue, pgs. T34 and T35

... and Specialized Checklists for Instruction

- Editing and Proofreading Checklist
- ELL Checklist

Editing and Proofreading

As previously mentioned, this series separates the revising task (which focuses on ideas and unity, organization and coherence, sentence variety, and word choice) from the editing task (which focuses on grammar and usage). Proofreading is the stage of the writing process when students look for mechanical errors in spelling, punctuation, and capitalization. These checklists provide references both for the teacher and the student.

Editing Checklist

- ☐ Is every sentence grammatically complete (not a fragment or a run-on)? *Lessons 6.1 and 6.3*
- ☐ Do subjects and verbs agree in number and gender? *Chapter 10*
- ☐ Are the correct forms of pronouns used? *Chapter 11*
- ☐ Does each pronoun clearly refer to an antecedent? *Lesson 11.5*
- ☐ Are verb tenses used consistently, unless there is good reason to vary them? *Chapter 9*
- ☐ Are the correct forms of irregular verbs used? *Chapter 9*
- ☐ Are the correct forms of plural nouns and the comparative forms of adjectives and adverbs used? *Chapter 5*

Proofreading Checklist

- ☐ Is every word spelled correctly? Check a dictionary if you're unsure. *Chapter 16*
- ☐ Have homonyms been confused (*their* instead of *there*, for example)? *Chapter 16*
- ☐ Do proper nouns and proper adjectives begin with capital letters? *Chapter 15*
- ☐ Does every sentence begin with a capital letter and end with an end punctuation mark? *Chapter 13*
- ☐ Are commas used correctly in all of their many uses? *Chapter 13*
- ☐ Is dialogue punctuated correctly? *Lesson 14.5*

Resources

In the classroom, students should have access to several copies of a good college dictionary and a dictionary-style thesaurus.

T41

Level Blue, p.T41

Grammar for Writing and ELL		
Target Area in English	**Comment**	**Grammar for Writing Treatment, Level Blue**
ADJECTIVE CLAUSES	Forming and positioning adjective clauses cause problems for speakers of Asian languages, of Arabic and Hebrew, and even of Latin-based languages.	Lesson 8.2
ARTICLES	ELL students often leave out the article before a singular count noun.	Lesson 5.4
CAPITALIZATION	Arabic, Chinese, and Hebrew do not use capital letters; Dutch and German capitalize some forms of the second-person pronoun; German caps all nouns.	Chapter 15
HOMOPHONES	Speakers of Asian languages in particular may be confused by the concept of words sounding alike but having different meanings.	Commonly Confused Words
NEGATION	Multiple negation is common in French and Russian, among other languages.	Lesson 12.3
PLURALS	Some Asian languages have no plural forms for nouns.	Lesson 5.1, Chapter 10, Lesson 16.4
PREFIXES AND SUFFIXES	These word parts are absent in Asian languages.	Lesson 16.3
PREPOSITIONS	English distinguishes between in and on; Spanish uses en for both.	Lessons 5.6 and 7.1
SILENT LETTERS	There are no silent letters in Spanish.	Chapter 16
SUBJECTS, DOUBLE	Some languages add personal pronouns as suffixes or prefixes, leading ELL speakers to say, "Maria she is pretty."	Lessons 6.2, 6.4, 11.1
TENSES	• Certain English verbs don't work in the present progressive, but ESL students may say or write, "I am knowing the answer." • In some languages, time is not signaled by word endings but rather by words that native English speakers would call adverbs.	Lessons 5.3 and 9.4
WORD ORDER	• In some languages, word order determines the part of speech. For example, the verb is the last word in sentences in Turkish, Korean, and Japanese. • In Russian, subject and object may switch places without affecting meaning.	Lessons 6.2, 6.6, 6.7

T43

Level Blue, p. T43

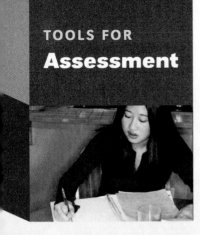

Ongoing ▶ Assessment in the Student Edition

- Chapter reviews
- Cumulative reviews of units

Chapter 9 REVIEW
Usage

EXERCISE C Using Verb Tenses

Change the italicized verbs to the verb tense specified in parentheses. You may look back at the charts on page 169. Write your answers on a separate piece of paper.

1. The twins always *wear* different outfits. (past)
2. Nora *make* lasagna at least once a week. (presen...)
3. Next year, everyone *sing* the school song before...
4. A committee *plan* the picnic. (past perfect prog...)
5. I *hope* you would call. (past progressive)
6. Jason *put* out the candles before we *go* to sleep.
7. Blanca *catch* the pass. (past)
8. Everyone *eat*, so no one *be* hungry. (present per...)
9. Sondra *grow* more spinach next year. (future pr...)
10. Leslie *worry* about her algebra final. (present pe...)

EXERCISE D Revising and Editing a Para...

Edit the paragraph below for correct verb usage. U...
possible. Decide whether the paragraph should be...
verb tenses consistent. Make any other changes th...
paragraph.

¹Homes of all different shapes, materials, and ki...
scrape, or nest in the dirt, is built by pressing their...
terns. ²Their eggs were sat on constantly by Arctic...
the ground by burrowing owls, bee-eaters, penguin...
have been made by woodpeckers and flickers to se...
the top of very tall poles or trees, large nests are co...
nests are created by hummingbirds. ⁴Bits of plants...
the cup nest by hummingbirds. ⁵Mud is shaped int...
swallows. ⁶Large mud mounds on the ground are...
swallow nests look like an apartment house under...

176 Chapter 9 • Using Verbs

Level Blue, p. 176

Cumulative Review
Chapters 5-8 CUMULATIVE REVIEW Grammar

EXERCISE A Identifying Parts of Speech

In the space above each numbered item, identify the part of speech of each underlined word in the sentences below. Use these abbreviations:

N = noun	ADJ = adjective	CONJ = conjunction
PRON = pronoun	ADV = adverb	INTER = interjection
V = verb	PREP = preposition	

        INTER
EXAMPLE Alas, this is the last day of vacation.

1. She found an old letter between the pages of the photo album.
2. Look, here is the list of e-mail addresses you asked for.
3. Has anyone been looking for me?
4. The restaurants usually close for the summer.
5. Neither Scott nor Tomás wants the job.

EXERCISE B Writing Complete Sentences

Revise and edit the following paragraph to correct sentence fragments and run-on sentences and to eliminate wordiness.

¹Old Faithful is a geyser in Yosemite National Park in Wyoming, it erupts regularly. ²Usually about every sixty-five minutes. ³Like other geysers, Old Faithful is a hot spring. ⁴A geyser is a fissure, or crack, in the earth's surface. ⁵Connected to a water supply far below the surface. ⁶Geysers shoot steam and boiling water high into the air. ⁷Old Faithful, about 150 feet into the air. ⁸And about eleven thousand gallons of water each time. ⁹The word *geyser* comes from the name of a specific geyser in Iceland, it means "gusher." ¹⁰Geysers are found in Iceland, New Zealand, and the western United States.

EXERCISE C Identifying Phrases

On the blank before each numbered item, identify each underlined phrase by writing one of these abbreviations in the space provided:

PREP = prepositional phrase	INF = infinitive phrase
PART = participial phrase	APP = appositive phrase
GER = gerund phrase	

EXAMPLE   _APP_ Mr. Haas, the band teacher, plays the cello and bass.

_____ 1. You'll find the hammer in the bottom drawer of the desk.

Chapters 5–8 • Cumulative Review **159**

Level Blue, p. 159

SAT Practice: Identifying Sentence Errors

🖥 **ONLINE COMPONENTS**
www.grammarforwriting.com

Directions: In each item, one of the underlined words d...
contain an error in grammar, usage, word choice, or idio...
error, choose the underlined part that must be changed to...
sentence correct, and fill in the corresponding oval. If the...
no error, fill in oval E. In selecting answers, follow the re...
standard written English.

Example

One of the really <u>difficult</u> problems that people every...
          A
<u>must contend</u> with <u>are</u> preserving <u>their</u> food supply. N...
  B   C   D

The correct choice is **C**. The subject of the sentence...
requires a singular verb such as *is*, not *are*.

1. The myth of Daedalus and Icarus are one of the most...
                A
myths; it is the story of a boy who ignores his father's...
     C   D

2. My best choice, I decided, is to vote for the incumbent...
     A   B
because he is the unequivocally favorite. No error
         C   D   E

3. Neither she nor her parents prefers rock-and-roll music...
    A   B
music Jessica plays when she's practicing her flute les...
            D

4. Everyone in the marching band is responsible for his...
             A   B
instrument, so when Kevin lost his tuba, he had to pay...
        C   D

288 Standardized Test Practice

Level Blue, p. 288

ACT Practice

🖥 **ONLINE COMPONENTS**
www.grammarforwriting.com

DIRECTIONS: You will find two reading passages in the left column and questions in the right column. In each of the passages, some words and phrases are underlined with a number underneath. The numbers refer to the questions at the right. Most questions ask you to choose the answer that best expresses the idea in standard written English or in the style of the passage. If you think the original wording is best, choose answer A, "NO CHANGE."

Other questions, indicated by a small number in a box, ask questions about the passage as a whole or about a particular section of the passage.

For each question, choose what you think is the best answer, and fill in the corresponding oval at the bottom of the page. Sometimes you will need to read several sentences beyond the numbered point in the passage to answer the question correctly.

Passage I

Homer's *The Iliad*

[1]

Not many details is known about
               1
Homer, the ancient Greek poet. He is said
to have been a blind man living in the
eighth century B.C. and the author of two
great epics, *The Iliad* and *The Odyssey*.
Literary scholars speculate that Homer was
one of ancient Greece's many <u>rhapsodes, they</u>
                      2
<u>were storytellers</u> who moved from town to
town reciting the much-loved tales of
gods and heroes.

[2]

[3] Scholars believe that the war
actually did take place during the twelfth

1. **A.** NO CHANGE
    B. have been known
    C. are known
    D. was known

2. **F.** NO CHANGE
    G. *rhapsodes*, storytellers
    H. *rhapsodes*, and they were story-tellers
    J. *rhapsodes*, being that they were storytellers

1. Ⓐ Ⓑ Ⓒ Ⓓ   **2.** Ⓕ Ⓖ Ⓗ Ⓙ

302 Standardized Test Practice

Level Blue, p. 302

◀ Plus NEW Preparation for High Stakes Tests

- Writing a timed essay
- Standardized Practice Tests
- Test-Taking Tips on student pages
- Standardized-test items in SAT and ACT formats
- Explications of sample test items

Assessment in the Teacher's Edition

- Rubrics for evaluating students' writing
- Diagnostic Tests
- Mastery Tests

Writing Portfolios

The movement for performance assessment has gained strength over many years. Today, writing portfolios, an essential part of performance assessment, are part of most English classrooms. Writing portfolios give students tangible evidence that their efforts pay off. The portfolios can be made available for review by students' new teachers in subsequent terms.

Many teachers have students create two different kinds of writing portfolios:

- **A works-in-progress portfolio** For every finished piece of writing, students include prewriting notes, outlines, early drafts, revised drafts, and even a brief reflection on their writing experience. Students may also include journals, sketches, logs, and notes about their reading.

- **A best-efforts portfolio** This portfolio shows only the *finished pieces of writing*, examples of what students think are their best writing efforts.

Teacher-Student Conferences

An integral part of performance assessment is teacher-student conferences. One-on-one conferencing helps you assess performance and motivates students to raise their own standards.

Test Booklet

For every Level of *Grammar for Writing*, a separate Test Booklet is available for purchase. The Test

Booklet contains a separat[e] every chapter as well as a [ ] Test and a Mastery Test. It[ ] standardized test formats: [ ] recognition and error corr[ ]

Here is an example of an e[ ] nition question from the L[ ] Mastery Test.

Directions: Fill in the circ[ ] sentence that contains an e[ ]

1. Ⓐ Ⓑ Ⓒ Ⓓ

  A. He and I are on the s[ ] paper together.

  B. Of the two of them, s[ ] best skater.

  C. Just between you and [ ] band needs work.

  D. Michel or Suki are rep[ ] our grade at the conf[ ]

Diagnostic Test

A four-page Diagnostic Test[ ] the beginning of each Test [ ] You may use this test at the[ ] ning of the school term to [ ] students' strengths and we[ ] Each question on the Diagn[ ] is devoted to a single prob[ ]

Tallying class results will als[ ] grammar, usage, and mecha[ ] that the class as a whole nee[ ] and review. Use the Diagno[ ] scores and the errors on stu[ ] batch of papers to decide w[ ] book lessons to use with th[ ] class and which lessons sh[ ] reserved for individuals or s[ ]

Level Blue, p. T47

A Rubric for Writing Performance Levels	
	The student's writing
LEVEL 6	• consistently pursues a strong central purpose across a complex range of ideas, skillfully engages the reader, and shows exceptional insight into the subject • includes main ideas that are developed comprehensively and are supported with a variety of logical reasons and detailed examples • is skillfully organized • shows distinctive style through skillful and expressive use of vocabulary, phrasing, and sentence structure • demonstrates essentially error-free control of grammar, punctuation, capitalization, and spelling
LEVEL 5	• consistently pursues a central purpose, holds the interest of the reader, and shows insight into the subject • includes main ideas that are developed and supported by a variety of reasons and examples • is effectively organized • shows emerging style through the effective use of vocabulary, phrasing, and sentence structure • consistently demonstrates the accurate use of grammar, punctuation, capitalization, and spelling
LEVEL 4	• shows a consistent purpose, communicates to the reader, and connects to the writer's knowledge of the subject • includes main ideas that are organized, developed, and supported by reasons and examples • shows suitable vocabulary, phrasing, and sentence structure • generally demonstrates the accurate use of grammar, punctuation, capitalization, and spelling
LEVEL 3	• shows a purpose but may be inconsistent in communicating to the reader or connecting to the writer's knowledge of the subject • includes main ideas that may be organized or partially developed and supported by some reasons and examples • may show imprecise use of vocabulary, phrasing, and sentence structure • includes some errors in the use of grammar, punctuation, capitalization, and spelling
LEVEL 2	• attempts to connect the writer's knowledge to the subject and may not show a purpose • is typically brief, unorganized, and underdeveloped • may include frequent errors in the use of grammar, capitalization, punctuation, and spelling
LEVEL 1	• is too brief or disorganized to communicate to the reader • may not connect the writer's knowledge to the subject • typically includes many errors in the use of grammar, capitalization, and spelling

Performance Levels, 1994. Reprinted with permission from the California Department of Education.

T46

Level Blue, p. T46

And More Teacher Assessment Tools Online

- Portfolio project ideas with assessment suggestions and instructional guidelines
- Hyperlinks to student writing and publishing Web sites
- Lists of creative ways for students to publish their writing

Empower Students and Teachers with Online Support Tools

Grammar for Writing Interactive Online Study Guides

Supplement the SAT and ACT practice provided in the Student Text of *Grammar for Writing* with self-scoring online study guides. These guides:

- **test students' abilities with four key skills needed for standardized tests such as the SAT and ACT:**
  - Identifying Sentence Errors
  - Improving Sentences
  - Improving Paragraphs
  - ACT practice
- **can be accessed by students at any time and from any computer with an Internet connection.**
- **score students' responses automatically and provide immediate answer rationale.**
- **are available for each grade level (9–12).**

ONLINE COMPONENTS
www.grammarforwriting.com

Also Available Online...

Internet Activities
with writing prompts and cross-curriculum projects help reinforce the concepts of each chapter.

Hyperlinks
to fascinating Web sites offer information on real-world topics.

Sadlier-Oxford : Grammar For Writing

Sadlier-Oxford
1.800.221.5175

student activity center

Grammar for Writing:
Blue Level — Chapter 1

Give Me Your Tired...

The immigration experience is as old as the colonies and as recent as today. Have you ever wondered why people have come to the United States or what they have left behind? What happened to those immigrants?

"I lift my lamp beside the golden door . . . ." An immigrant family watches as their ship approaches the Statue of Liberty and a new life (ca. 1900).

Your Assignment

Sadlier-Oxford : Grammar For Writing

Sadlier-Oxford
1.800.221.5175

student activity center

Grammar for Writing:
Green Level — Chapter 12

Shipwrecks and Undersea Treasures

Imagine that you are a writing an educational video about a salvage vessel's attempt to find the treasures aboard a sailing ship that sank in a storm 200 years ago. An old, tattered map has led the crew to the site of the shipwreck. At the bottom of the sea, there's a treasure chest waiting to be discovered. You've brought your scuba gear and cameras to record the divers as they search for the doubloons, reales, and jewels that once graced the necks of Spanish royalty. Will they find the treasure?

Your Assignment

Plus, password-protected supplemental Answer Keys for teachers! Use Access Code TTYUMDNJKF.

ONLINE COMPONENTS
www.grammarforwriting.com

Content Overview: Tools for Writing Effectively and Correctly

	COMPOSITION		GRAMMAR		
	Writing Workshops		Parts of a Sentence	Phrases	Clauses

Composition — Writing Workshops: The Writing Process · Writing Paragraphs · Writing Essays · Combining Sentences · Narrative Writing · Persuasive Writing · Expository Writing · Writing About Literature · Research Paper · Writing a Timed Essay · Workplace Writing

Grammar — Parts of a Sentence: Parts of Speech · Complete Sentences · Subjects and Predicates · Sentence Fragments and Run-ons · Direct and Indirect Objects · Predicate Nominatives and Adjectives · Object Complements

Grammar — Phrases: Prepositional Phrases · Participial and Gerund Phrases · Infinitive Phrases · Appositive Phrases

Grammar — Clauses: Independent and Subordinate Clauses · Adjective and Adverb Clauses · Noun Clauses · Sentence Structures

Level Blue — Grade 9

Level Orange — Grade 10

Level Green — Grade 11

Level Gold — Grade 12

KEY

■ = Lesson(s) dedicated to listed topic

USAGE

Using Verbs				Agreement		Using Pronouns			Using Modifiers		
Regular and Irregular Verbs	Verb Tenses	Active Voice	Mood	Person and Number, Compound Subjects	Other Agreement Problems	Subject and Object Pronouns	Who or Whom?	Agreement with Antecedents	Degrees of Comparison	Double Negatives	Misplaced and Dangling Modifiers

MECHANICS

Punctuation							Capitalization				Spelling		
End Marks and Abbreviations	Commas and Nonessential Elements	Compound Sentences and Phrases	Colons and Semicolons	Italics	Quotation Marks and Dialogue	Apostrophes and Other Marks	Titles, Proper Nouns, and Adjectives	Organizations, Religions, School Subjects	Historical Events, Documents, Periods	Calendar Items, Brand Names	Spelling Rules	Prefixes and Suffixes	Noun Plurals

TEST PRACTICE

Standardized Test Practice			
SAT Formats	ACT Format	Practice Test	Online Practice

New Edition

SADLIER-OXFORD

GRAMMAR
for Writing

Ensures student success in school and beyond with:

- **Tools for writing effectively**
- **Tools for writing correctly**

Provides teacher support tools including:

- **Assessment**
- **Implementation guidelines**
- **Online resources**

LEVEL BLUE
GRADE 9

GRAMMAR
for *Writing*

Sadlier-Oxford
A Division of William H. Sadlier, Inc.
New York, New York 10005-1002

Printed in the United States of America

Teacher's Edition: ISBN: 978-0-8215-0229-7
Student Edition: ISBN: 978-0-8215-0219-8
23456789/10 09 08 07

CONTENTS

Introduction T20–T21

Features and Benefits of *Grammar for Writing* T22–T23

"The Role of Grammar in Improving Students' Writing,"
   by Beverly Ann Chin T24–T29

Why Grammar? T30–T31

The Writing Process T31–T33

Purposes of Writing T34–T36

Step-by-Step Revising, Editing, and Proofreading T37–T41

Using *Grammar for Writing* with
   English Language Learners T42–T43

Assessment in *Grammar for Writing* T44–T48

ONLINE COMPONENTS
www.grammarforwriting.com

Now available at www.grammarforwriting.com

• For teachers, a password-protected supplemental Answer Key.

• For students, standardized-test practice with grammar feedback, and port-folio writing projects linked to Grammar, Usage, and Mechanics chapters.

• For more information about *Grammar for Writing* Online Components, see page T48.

NOTE

The Student Text for Level Blue (Grade 9) of *Grammar for Writing* is available in a softcover edition and in a hardcover edition. This Teacher's Edition is intended to accompany both editions of the Student Text. Students may, with the teacher's permission, write in the softcover texts, but are directed in the Dear Student letter in the hardcover edition not to write in those texts.

Introduction to Level Blue

The second edition of *Grammar for Writing* has been prepared with two goals in mind: first, to preserve and improve upon those key elements of the program that have proved so successful in the first edition; and, second, to introduce important new features to make it more current and effective as preparation for the grammar and writing strands of standardized tests.

As its name clearly suggests, the *Grammar for Writing* program is based on the principle that the primary purpose of grammar instruction is to improve student writing. Students are encouraged to view grammar not as a list of rules that must be memorized for their own sake but as a valuable tool that can help them develop their writing and communication skills—skills that will help ensure success not only in school and on tests but also in the workplace.

Level Blue (grade 9) of *Grammar for Writing* provides a full year's work—all the grammar and writing that students need to know—plus assignments and exercises to fill the school year. Used together with a literature program and literature-based writing assignments, this book gives you a powerful component to a complete language arts program.

Grammar for Writing helps students prepare for standardized testing.

With recent changes to the SAT, ACT, and PSAT, grammar and writing skills have become more critical than ever to success on these key college-entry exams. In the new edition of Level Blue, several new features have been introduced to address this new emphasis on grammar and writing.

The Composition unit has a new chapter on sentence-level writing skills and a writing workshop devoted to writing a timed essay.

The Table of Contents for the Grammar, Usage, and Mechanics units indicates (with asterisks) those topics most commonly assessed on standardized tests, and scattered through the text are new Test-Taking Tips, which help students make the connection between the grammar they are learning and the form in which that grammar is typically assessed on a standardized test.

Furthermore, a whole new section of practice in standardized-test formats has been added to Level Blue; and interactive online practice with grammar feedback is now available to students at the new *Grammar for Writing* Web site, www.grammarforwriting.com.

Grammar for Writing helps students meet the standards for writing.

In the Composition unit and throughout the text of Level Blue, students learn to express and develop their ideas effectively and correctly. In Chapter 4's Writing Workshops, students proceed step-by-step through the writing process as they write for a variety of audiences and for different purposes. Students are also given ample opportunities to revise and edit samples of poor writing. They use sentence-combining strategies to improve the flow of their writing; they correct errors in grammar, usage, and mechanics.

Use *Grammar for Writing* with a variety of schedules.

At the beginning or end of a class period, students can work on mini-lessons (the teaching text and exercises). Or you might go over the teaching text in class and assign the exercises to be started in class and finished as homework. Students can also meet in writing groups or with partners to work on both cooperative learning exercises marked by the "Working Together" label and on-going writing projects, such as the exercises in Chapter 4. Students can meet regularly in writing groups and in writing-partner sessions.

If the whole class shows repeated weakness in one grammar concept (say subject-verb agreement), set aside a block of time to go over the appropriate lesson(s) carefully. Assign the exercises as group, partner, or individual work, and meet as a class or in small groups to compare exercise answers.

Use *Grammar for Writing* with students of varying ability levels.

Exercises can be done individually by students or cooperatively with partners or in small groups. You might pair LEP (Limited English Proficiency) students with more proficient students to create an informal tutoring-buddy system. Give mainstreamed ELL (English Language Learner) students many opportunities to *hear* standard English used correctly. You might have them read aloud corrected exercise sentences and paragraphs, for example, and use small-group activities to give ELL students speaking and listening practice.

Grammar for Writing improves students' critical thinking skills.

The many "Write What You Think" exercises in Level Blue give students practice in developing arguments on real-life issues. Students strengthen their persuasive skills by giving logical reasons and relevant evidence to support their opinions.

Features and Benefits of *Grammar for Writing*

Throughout Level Blue, *Grammar for Writing* honors its commitment to teach the fundamentals of grammar in the context of and for the purpose of writing. The following charts itemize how both the Composition unit and the Grammar, Usage, and Mechanics units incorporate features that help today's students express their thoughts effectively and correctly.

Unit: Composition	
Feature	**Benefit**
WRITING PROCESS	Students are guided through prewriting, drafting, revising, editing, proofreading, and publishing stages.
EFFECTIVE WRITING	Students are provided with instruction and practice in essay-, paragraph-, and sentence-level strategies and skills.
WRITING WORKSHOPS	Students realize that regardless of what they write, they can *always* apply the multistage writing process.
COOPERATIVE LEARNING EXERCISES	Students learn that *every* writer needs an editor; students learn that a writing prompt may stimulate many different responses.
Modes of Writing	**Benefit**
NARRATIVE	Students tell a story—a fictional or true narrative. They use steps, critical events, or chronological order.
EXPOSITORY	Students explain or inform; state the main idea. They use facts, examples, quotations, statistics, and definitions presented in a logical order.
PERSUASIVE (AND TIMED ESSAY)	Students learn to convince a reader. They write a thesis statement, support their argument, use persuasive language.

Units: Grammar, Usage, Mechanics	
Feature	**Benefit**
SUCCINCT INSTRUCTION	Students receive clear and concise explanations and examples of grammar concepts.
WRITE WHAT YOU THINK	Students get ongoing practice in persuasive and expository writing; students are encouraged to apply grammar to their writing.
TEST-TAKING TIPS	Students are given advice about and pointed to examples of grammar concepts that commonly appear on standardized tests.
WRITING HINTS	Students learn that the end purpose of grammar, usage, and mechanics is applying those skills to paragraphs and essays.
EDITING TIPS	Students get advice in how to apply grammar skills to improve their writing.
STEP-BY-STEPS	Students think in an orderly way about complex grammar and usage concepts.
P.S. NOTES	Students begin to recognize that some rules and definitions are more important than others.
REVISING AND EDITING WORKSHEETS	Students get opportunities to see that all drafts need revising and editing; students apply their grammar and writing skills.
REVIEWS	Students receive reinforcement, in chapter and cumulative reviews, of concepts and skills they have been presented in lessons and units.
PRACTICE IN STANDARDIZED-TEST FORMATS	Students gain confidence in their ability to answer grammar and usage items in standardized tests; students are better prepared for the essay section of standardized tests.
ENRICHING YOUR VOCABULARY	Students develop vocabulary skills by being exposed to words used in context.
ONLINE COMPONENTS	Students have access to interactive practice in standardized-test formats, with grammar feedback; students have access to portfolio writing projects.

The Role of Grammar in Improving Students' Writing

by Beverly Ann Chin

Grammar is the sound, structure, and meaning system of language. All languages have grammar, and each language has its own grammar. People who speak the same language are able to communicate because they intuitively know the grammar system of that language—that is, the rules of making meaning. Students who are native speakers of English already know English grammar. They recognize the sounds of English words, the meanings of those words, and the different ways of putting words together to make meaningful sentences.

However, while students may be effective speakers of English, they need guidance to become effective writers. They need to learn how to apply their knowledge of grammatical concepts from oral language to written language.

Effective grammar instruction shows students what they already know about grammar, and it helps them use this knowledge as they write. By connecting their knowledge of oral language to written language, teachers can demystify abstract grammatical terminology so that students can write—and read—with greater competence and confidence.

What Does Research Say About Grammar and the Teaching of Writing?

Strong research evidence suggests that the most beneficial way of helping students improve their command of grammar in writing is to use students' writing as the basis for discussing grammatical concepts. Researchers agree that it is more effective to teach punctuation, sentence variety, and usage in the context of writing than to approach the topic by teaching isolated skills (Calkins, 1980; DiStefano and Killion, 1984; Harris, 1962).

As students revise and edit their writing, teachers can provide grammar instruction that guides students in their attempts to identify and correct problems in sentence structure and usage. For example, if a teacher sees that many students are writing sentences containing misplaced modifiers, the teacher can present a minilesson on this concept using examples from student writing. The teacher can have students edit their own and each others' drafts for this problem.

Integrating grammar instruction into the revising and editing process helps students make immediate applications, thus allowing them to see the relevance of grammar in their own writing.

To What Specific Aspects of Writing Does Grammar Contribute?

Because writing is a complex activity for many students, teachers should focus on the grammatical concepts that are essential for the clear communication of meaning.

Research on the teaching of grammar since the early 1900s shows that grammar instruction that is separate from writing instruction does not improve students' writing competence (Braddock and others, 1963; Hillocks, 1986). In addition, research indicates that the transfer of formal grammar instruction to writing is not applicable to larger elements of composition. Through detailed studies of students' writing, Shaughnessy (1977) concludes that the best grammar instruction is one that gives the greatest return for the least investment of time. Shaughnessy advocates four important grammatical concepts: the sentence, inflection, tense, and agreement. She recommends that teachers encourage students to examine grammatical errors in their own writing. She also cautions teachers not to overemphasize grammatical terminology to the detriment of students' ability to understand and apply the concepts.

Weaver (1998) proposes a similar approach to teaching grammar in the context of writing. She writes, "What all students need . . . is guidance in understanding and applying those aspects of grammar that are most relevant to writing." In a chart as reproduced here, Weaver proposes five grammatical concepts that enable writers to show improvement in sentence revision, style, and editing.

A minimum of grammar for maximum benefits

1. Teaching concepts of subject, verb, sentence, clause, phrase, and related concepts for editing
2. Teaching style through sentence combining and sentence generating
3. Teaching sentence sense through the manipulation of syntactic elements
4. Teaching both the power of dialects and the dialects of power
5. Teaching punctuation and mechanics for convention, clarity, and style

(Weaver, 1998, pp. 21–23)

Rather than striving to teach all grammatical concepts to all students, teachers should prioritize and provide instruction on the grammatical elements that most affect their students' ability to write effectively. Teachers should also be sensitive to individual students' readiness to learn and apply grammatical concepts.

How Does Sentence-Combining Improve Writing?

Sentence combining is the strategy of joining short sentences into longer, more complex sentences. As students engage in sentence-combining activities, they learn how to vary sentence structure in order to change meaning and style. Numerous studies (Mellon, 1969; O'Hare, 1973; Cooper, 1975; Shaughnessy, 1977; Hillocks, 1986; Strong, 1986) show that the use of sentence combining is an effective method for improving students' writing. The value of sentence combining is most evident as students recognize the effect of sentence variety (beginnings, lengths, complexities) in their own writing.

Hillocks (1986) stated that "sentence combining practice provides writers with systematic knowledge of syntactic possibilities, the access to which allows them to sort through alternatives in their heads as well as on paper and to choose those which are most apt" (150). Research also shows that sentence combining is more effective than freewriting in enhancing the quality of student writing (Hillocks, 1986).

Hillocks and Smith (1991) show that systematic practice in sentence combining can increase students' knowledge of syntactic structures as well as improve the quality of their sentences, particularly when stylistic effects are discussed as well. Sentence-combining exercises can be either written or oral, structured or unstructured. Structured sentence-combining exercises give students more guidance in the ways to create the new sentences; unstructured sentence-combining exercises allow for more variation, but they still require students to create logical, meaningful sentences. Hillocks (1986) reports that, in many studies,

sentence-combining exercises produce significant increases in students' sentence-writing maturity.

Given Noguchi's (1991) analysis that grammar choices affect writing style, sentence combining is an effective method that helps students develop fluency and variety in their own writing style. Students can discover sentence variety, length, parallelism, and other syntactic devices by comparing their sentences with sentences from other writers. They also discover the decisions writers make when they revise sentences for their effect on readers.

Teachers can design their own sentence-combining activities by using short sentences from student writing or other appropriate sources. For example, teachers who notice many choppy sentences in students' writing can place these sentences on an overhead for all their students to read. Teachers can then ask different students to combine orally the short sentences in a variety of ways. As students share their different sentence combinations, their teacher can show students how they are naturally applying grammatical concepts such as clauses, phrases, modification, conjunctions, appositives, antecedents, and verb forms.

By participating in oral and written sentence-combining activities, students discover the relationships among meaning, sentence structure, usage, and punctuation. When presented as a revising strategy, sentence combining activities help students identify short, choppy sentences in their own writing, leading them to combine their ideas in more fluid and sophisticated ways. As students generate more complex sentences from shorter sentences, they discover how the arrangement of phrases and clauses affects meaning and their readers.

What Strategies Can Teachers Use to Teach *Grammar for Writing*?

Grammar instruction is most naturally integrated during the revising, editing, and proofreading phases of the writing process. After students have written their first drafts and feel comfortable with the ideas and organization of their writing, teachers may wish to employ various strategies to help students see grammatical concepts as language choices that can enhance their writing purpose.

For example, teachers can help students revise for effective word choices in a writing conference. As the teacher and student discuss the real audience(s) for the writing, the teacher can ask the student to consider how formal or informal the writing should be. The teacher can remind the student that all people vary their level of language (formal to informal) in oral conversations, depending on their listeners and the speaking context. The teacher can then help the student identify words that change the level of formality of the writing.

Teachers can help students revise boring, monotonous sentences by having a partner read aloud the writing to the student writer. As the partner reads the writing aloud to the writer, both the partner and the writer can recognize when too many sentences begin with "It is" or "There are." Both the partner and the writer can discuss ways to vary the sentence beginnings. After the writer revises the sentences, the partner can read the sentences aloud, and both can discuss the effectiveness of the revision.

Teachers can help students edit from passive voice to active voice by presenting a minilesson. In editing groups, students can exchange papers and look for verbs that often signal the passive voice, such as "was" and "been." When students find these verbs, they can read the sentence aloud to their partners and discuss whether the voice is passive and, if so, if the sentence might be strengthened with an active-voice verb. The student writer can decide which voice is most effective and appropriate for the writing purpose and audience.

Teachers can help students become better proofreaders through writing groups. Based on the writing abilities of students, teachers can assign different proofreading tasks to specific individuals in each group. For example, one person in the group can proofread for spelling errors, another person for agreement errors, another person for fragments and run-ons, and another person for punctuation errors. As students develop increasing skill in proofreading, they can become responsible for more proofreading areas. Collaborating with classmates in writing partner groups helps students improve their own grammar skills as well as understand the importance of grammar as a tool for effective communication.

As teachers integrate grammar instruction into writing instruction, they should use the grammar terms that make sense to the students. By incorporating grammar terms naturally into the processes of revising, editing, and proofreading, teachers help students understand and apply grammar purposefully to their own (student) writing. Strategies such as writing conferences, partnership writing, grammar minilessons, and peer response groups are all valuable methods for integrating grammar into writing instruction.

How Does the Teaching of Grammar Relate to the National Content Standards for Students?

The National Council of Teachers of English and the International Reading Association (1996) published *Standards for the English Language Arts*, which defines "what students should know and be able to do with language" (p. 1). While the twelve content standards are presented as a list, they are closely intertwined and emphasize the complex interactions among language skills. Standards 4, 5, and 6 most directly address students' ability to write.

Standard 4: "Students adjust their use of spoken, written, and visual language (e.g., conventions, style, vocabulary) to communicate effectively with a variety of audiences and for different purposes" (p. 3).

Standard 5: "Students employ a wide range of strategies as they write and use different writing process elements appropriately to communicate with different audiences for a variety of purposes" (p. 3).

Standard 6: "Students apply knowledge of language structure, language conventions (e.g. spelling and punctuation), media techniques, figurative language, and genre to create, critique, and discuss print and nonprint texts" (p. 3)

According to the standards:

By closely observing students' writing processes and carefully reading their work, teachers can see which aspects of language structure are giving students trouble and help them learn these concepts through direct instruction and practice. It is also important for students to discover that grammar, spelling, and punctuation are useful not only in the context of fixing problems or mistakes; they can be studied effectively in a workshop context in which students work together to expand their repertoire of syntactic and verbal styles. When students connect the study of grammar and language patterns to the wider purposes of communication and artistic development, they are considerably more likely to incorporate such study into their working knowledge (p. 37).

The national content standards for English language arts are based on professional research and the best classroom practices. While the standards acknowledge the importance of grammar concepts, they clearly recommend that students learn and apply their knowledge of grammar for the purpose of effective communication. By embedding grammar instruction into writing instruction, teachers can positively affect students' actual writing skills.

References

Braddock, R., Lloyd-Jones, R., & Schoer, L. *Research in Written Composition.* Urbana, IL: National Council of Teachers of English, 1963.

Calkins, L. M. "When Children Want to Punctuate: Basic Skills Belong in Context." *Language Arts* 57 (1980): 567–73.

Cooper, C. "Research Roundup: Oral and Written Composition." *English Journal* (1975): 64, 72.

DiStefano, P. & Killion, J. "Assessing Writing Skills Through a Process Approach." *English Education* 16, no. 4 (1984): 203–7.

Harris, R. J. "An Experimental Inquiry into the Functions and Value of Formal Grammar in the Teaching of Written English to Children Aged Twelve to Fourteen." Ph.D. diss., University of London, 1962.

Hillocks, G., Jr. *Research on Written Composition: New Directions for Teaching.* Urbana, IL: ERIC Clearinghouse on Reading and Communication Skills and the National Conference on Research in English, 1986.

Hillocks, G., Jr., & Smith, M. "Grammar and Usage." In *Handbook of Research on Teaching the English Language Arts*, edited by J. Flood, J. M. Jensen, D. Lapp, & J. R. Squire, 591–603. New York: Macmillan, 1991.

Mellon, J. C. *Transformational Sentence-Combining: A Method for Enhancing the Development of Syntactic Fluency in English Composition.* NCTE Research Report No. 10. Urbana, IL: National Council of Teachers of English, 1969.

National Council of Teachers of English and the International Reading Association. *Standards for the English Language Arts.* Urbana, IL: National Council of Teachers of English, 1996.

Noguchi, R. R. *Grammar and the Teaching of Writing: Limits and Possibilities.* Urbana, IL: National Council of Teachers of English, 1991.

O'Hare, F. *Sentence-Combining: Improving Student Writing Without Formal Grammar Instruction.* Urbana, IL: National Council of Teachers of English, 1973.

Shaughnessy, M. P. *Errors and Expectations: A Guide for the Teacher of Basic Writing.* New York: Oxford University Press, 1977.

Strong, W. *Creative Approaches to Sentence Combining.* Urbana, IL: ERIC and the National Council of Teachers of English, 1986.

Weaver, C. *Lessons to Share on Teaching Grammar in Context.* Portsmouth, NH: Heinemann, 1998.

Why Grammar?

The definitions of grammar vary. In this series, the term *grammar* means not only the description of parts of speech and parts of a sentence but also the topics often labeled usage and mechanics.

The questions about whether to teach grammar—and, if so, how—have confronted secondary-school English teachers for years. From the 1960s through the 1980s, university-level scholarship argued against formal grammar instruction. But teachers at middle school and high school levels had to face several unsettling realities that have surfaced in the wake of this argument.

- Some students—even native English speakers—have not mastered the conventions of standard written English.
- Some students are not scoring well on standardized tests that require recognizing and correcting sentence-level errors.
- Some parents have demanded that schools teach their children writing skills that will get them into college, land them better entry-level jobs, and advance them in a chosen career.

In this age of raising standards, it is the philosophy of this series that all students need to know and use the conventions of standard English. To accomplish this goal, students need thorough and coherent teaching and practice. The random coverage of grammar in integrated literature anthologies is not sufficient to help students meet the standards.

How to Engage Students in the Study of Grammar

The following suggestions will help improve the study of grammar in secondary-school classrooms.

Tell Students Why They Are Using *Grammar for Writing*

To succeed in high school, on tests, in college, and in the workplace, students must be able to use conventions of standard English. They are learning skills and habits to last a lifetime. In jobs that require them to deal with the public (such as customer service representatives, sales personnel, and professional jobs), employees need to be able to use standard English. Companies require that their employees write and speak correctly because they represent the company. In business letters, memos, and e-mail, employees must express themselves according to the conventions of standard English.

Acknowledge That Students Already Know Grammar

Native speakers of English start speaking at a very early age. They learn where to place which words. *Grammar for Writing* helps students get around the spots that give most of us writers trouble. Students will be more open to embarking on a study of grammar if they realize there really is a limited number of concepts to deal with (see the 10 listed in the box below) in order to improve their writing.

"P.S." Feature

The little P.S. feature that appears in many lessons reassures students that they don't need to memorize or remember all of the terms in the lesson. It tells them which terms are important—and why.

Ten Key Grammar Concepts

1. subject-verb agreement
2. verb forms and tenses
3. pronoun-antecedent agreement
4. pronoun reference and case
5. degree of modifiers
6. positioning of modifiers
7. run-on sentences and fragments
8. spelling
9. punctuation
10. commonly confused words

The Writing Process

The writing process movement dates back to the early 1970s, when Donald Murray published his article, "Teaching Writing as a Process Not a Product." Faculty members at the University of New Hampshire (including Donald Murray, Donald Graves, Lucy Calkins, Nancie Atwell, and Thomas Newkirk) gave the writing process movement a home, training teachers and reporting on writing process theory in action. "Children want to write," Donald Graves wrote in 1983 (*Writing: Teachers and Children at Work,* Heinemann). "They want to write the first day they attend school." Today, the writing process movement dominates English classrooms from kindergarten through college.

Writing Workshops

At the core of the writing process are minilessons, peer response groups, and writing workshops (see Chapter 4). In a writing workshop, students complete a sustained writing activity in stages that involve planning, drafting, and revising. Prewriting (the planning stage) and revising (the improving stage) are most heavily emphasized.

You will find a writing workshop in each of the lessons in Chapter 4 of the Level Blue book. All of these workshops deal with the following common types of writing that students are asked to do throughout their school career:

Writing Workshops

- Narrative Writing: Autobiographical Incident (pp. 52–56)
- Persuasive Writing (pp. 57–61)
- Expository Writing: Compare and Contrast Essay (pp. 62–67)
- Writing About Literature: Analyzing Fiction (pp. 68–73)
- Expository Writing: Research Paper (pp. 74–82)
- Writing a Timed Essay (pp. 83–86)

How to Use Them These writing workshops are flexible and can be used in different ways to meet your classroom needs. With the whole class, you might read and discuss the professional model and go over the Strategies for Writing that appear in each workshop. Notice that in each workshop the exercises take students step-by-step through the writing process. By the time they complete all of the exercises, students will have completed a finished piece of writing of the type specified in the workshop. Students may work in small groups or with partners to talk about the critical thinking questions following the model and to give each other feedback on the exercises. If you prefer, students can work through the exercises individually—in class or as homework.

Writing Groups Try to make the writing groups heterogeneous, with a mixture of students of different ability levels. You might even try to have a mix of different learning styles in each group. A comfortable number for a writing group is four to six students. ELL students who are mainstreamed into regular English classes will benefit from speaking/listening interactions with members of their small writing groups.

Using the Writing Process

Emphasize to students that the writing process is not the same for everyone. Some students like to outline carefully; others just plunge ahead from rough notes and start writing. Some begin writing with a title and introduction; others find it easier to start with the body and write an introduction and conclusion later.

Explain also that the process is recursive; that is, students can return to an earlier stage to gather more information, for example. Or they may try out a topic and find that it just doesn't work, so they discard that topic and start over again in the topic selection process. Some teachers require students to do several drafts, revising each one. Others focus on just one draft. Many teachers do not separate revising and editing; they consider all the tasks to be revising.

Steps in the writing process may have different names, but basically it goes like this:

The Writing Process	
Steps	**Tasks**
PREWRITING	■ Use brainstorming, freewriting, class discussion, newspaper articles, clustering and other graphics, listing, and *5W-How?* questions to generate topic ideas. ■ Choose and limit topic. ■ Gather details, information; do research, if needed. ■ Organize details (make an outline). ■ Specify purpose and audience.
DRAFTING	■ Put prewriting notes into sentences and paragraphs. ■ Draft thesis statement (main idea of paper). ■ Draft attention-grabbing title and introduction. ■ Draft strong conclusion.
REVISING	■ Read draft for coherence, unity, content. ■ Writing partners comment on draft. ■ Consider writing partners' comments. ■ Do additional drafts (second, third, fourth).
EDITING AND PROOFREADING	■ Check for sentence completeness. Find and correct errors in subject-verb agreement, verb forms, pronoun usage, and other errors in grammar and usage.
PROOFREADING	■ Find and correct errors in mechanics: spelling, punctuation, capitalization. ■ Utilize writing partner proofreading.
PUBLISHING	■ Find a way to share writing with intended audience.

Resources

Atwell, Nancie. *In the Middle: Writing, Reading, and Learning with Adolescents.* Portsmouth, NH: Boynton/Cook, 1987.

Merriam-Webster's Collegiate Dictionary, 11th ed. Springfield MA: Merriam-Webster, 2003.

Powell, David. *What Can I Write About? 7000 Topics for High School Students.* Urbana, IL: National Council of Teachers of English, 1981.

Random House Roget's Thesaurus. New York: Ballantine, 2001.

Strunk, William, Jr. and E. B. White. *The Elements of Style,* 4th ed. New York: Longman, 1999.

Purposes of Writing

Help students see that there are many reasons for writing, now and in the future. Basically, these can be broken down into three categories: personal writing (self-expression), real-life writing, and writing for school.

Personal Writing

Writing as self-expression began to be emphasized in the mid-1960s, when teachers introduced journals, freewriting, and other kinds of personal writing into the classrooms. James Moffett (1973) saw self-expressive modes of writing as a way of engaging student writers, even those with limited English proficiency. Everyone has stories to tell, and ideas and feelings to communicate.

Journals/Diaries Encourage students to start a special notebook in which they record ideas and experiences. They might also include a list or description of "things I like"; or they can tape into their notebook excerpts from articles, poems, songs, cartoons/comic strips, photos, and ads that they find appealing. Over the course of months, such a journal becomes a rich source of topic ideas and details. Remind students to include in these journals or diaries only those things they are willing to share with their classmates.

- **Writing Logs** Prewriting notes, ideas for writing topics, proofreading logs, reflections on their writing experiences
- **Reading Logs** A record of books they have read and their comments, questions, and responses; responses to particular stories and poems, novels, essays
- **Learning Logs** A record of important ideas and concepts they have learned

Sketchbooks Some students may want to create a sketchbook. They might sketch people, places, objects, and events from memory or direct observation. Encourage them to express what they have sketched in words, too. They might write on the back of a sketch or, if they are using a looseleaf notebook, interleave sketches and written descriptions.

Creative Writing Encourage students to write original poems and stories in conjunction with their study and discussion of literature genres. These may be individual, partner, or group efforts. Share finished works in class—on bulletin boards, in oral readings, or in a class newsletter or literary magazine. Tell students who are interested in creative writing to look for student writing contests and magazines (print and electronic) that publish student writing.

Real-Life Writing

Experienced teachers know that students are motivated when they write for a real-life purpose and a specific audience. Here are just a few of the real-life writing situations students may engage in.

Forms, Applications, Résumés Students must follow directions and develop the ability to summarize and express ideas clearly and concisely.

All Kinds of Letters Some letters are social (thank-you notes, friendly letters, and pen-pal letters) and chatty. Others are business letters (order letters, complaint letters, letters to the editor) and formal. Students need to write in the appropriate form and language.

Research As part of their research projects, students may write letters requesting information or interviews. They may need to write letters of acknowledgment and thanks.

E-mail Students may write formal e-mail messages (requesting information, asking questions of an expert) and informal messages to friends and family. They need to learn the "netiquette"—the accepted conventions for writing e-mail messages.

Persuasion Students express and support their opinions when they write letters to the editor, proposals for solving a school or community problem, and letters to elected representatives. The Write What You Think exercises throughout the Pupil's Edition give them repeated practice in writing for persuasive purposes.

Work At work, students may write letters, memos, and reports. Their writing must communicate ideas clearly and concisely.

Writing for School

Students know how important writing skills are in all their classes. Here are just a few of the reasons to write in school.

Reports In history, science, math, and other classes, students are asked to research, organize, and communicate ideas in written and oral reports.

Paragraphs Paragraph practice helps students gain skill in expressing and developing their ideas. (See Chapter 2 for lessons devoted to developing paragraph-writing skills.) In the mini-context of writing a single paragraph, students develop all of the following:

- a natural voice
- flow (sentences that read smoothly in a sequence)
- organization and coherence (ideas that are easy to follow)
- unity (ideas and supporting details that stick to a topic).

Essays By 9th grade, students should be applying their paragraph-writing skills to longer papers. (See Chapter 4, the "Writing Workshops.") Encourage students to write as much as they need to in order to express what they want to say.

Writing for Tests With recent changes to such standardized tests as the SAT, ACT, and PSAT, students are now required (or, in the case of the ACT, are given the option) to write a timed essay. Students are graded on how well they accomplish a writing task in the given time frame. They must formulate, develop, organize, and express their ideas in a limited time. The skills they learn in practicing paragraph development (Chapter 2) and in the Writing Workshops, especially the one devoted to the skills needed to write a timed essay, will stand them in good stead on essay tests.

Writing for a Wider Audience

Within the context of school, students have many opportunities to use their writing for a real purpose and audience.

- school paper (articles, letters to the editor, critical reviews)

- literary magazine or classroom newsletter of students' creative writing

- speeches for school-wide campaigns (elections, assemblies, rallies)

- scripts (school radio broadcasts and theater productions)

- press releases and publicity (school events and productions)

Writing Across the Curriculum

Writing-across-the-curriculum programs began in the late 1960s with several researchers at the University of London Institute of Education. They proposed that writing should be an essential part of students' learning in all classes, not just in English, from kindergarten through university level. In some American schools, this policy manifests itself by encouraging teachers in all subject areas to give writing assignments, which they then help their students carry out according to the writing-process paradigm with, at times, advice from English-teacher colleagues. In other American schools, writing across the curriculum remains the purview of the language arts department in hopes that students' interest will be sparked with a variety of writing opportunities.

Step-by-Step Revising, Editing, and Proofreading

Many of your students would probably be happy turning in their first draft as a final paper. Help them to understand that the revising, editing, and proofreading stages in the writing process raise the standards for their own writing. What they learn from repeated practice in revising and editing sticks: Over the course of a year, students produce better-organized, better-witten first drafts based on what they have learned through revising and editing.

Note that this series distinguishes between revising and editing—two steps that many teachers lump together as revising. We have separated these steps because it is hard for students to look critically at a piece of writing and see everything at once:

- **Revising** is concerned with ideas and unity, organization and coherence, sentence variety, and word choice (see the four-step strategy for revising on p. 15).
- **Editing** involves correcting mistakes in grammar and usage.
- **Proofreading** refers to checking for errors in spelling, capitalization, and punctuation.

Self-Editing

Encourage students to let their first draft sit a while so they can approach it with "fresh eyes." Before they share their drafts with one or more writing partners, encourage them to do a round of self-editing. They can use the Revising and Editing checklists (see pp. T39–T41), which you can give them as handouts at the beginning of the year. They can also refer to the four-step process outlined in Lesson 1.3.

Writing Partners

In the days before **writing partners**, teachers spent a lot of their evenings marking up student papers with red pen or pencil. Students working with writing partners not only helps lighten teachers' paper load; it is also one of the most powerful tools of the writing process. Whether students comment on each other's papers in **writing groups** or one on one with writing partners, they develop skills and strategies that transfer to their own writing:

- They learn what to look for in evaluating a draft.
- They learn to ask questions about organization and ideas.
- They learn from others' approaches to the same assignment.
- They even learn to be tactful in expressing their comments.

Try to have students work with writing partners as soon as they have had a chance to do some self-evaluation of their first draft—so writers don't lose momentum. If margins are at least an inch on either side, writing partners may write comments directly on their own copy (printed or photocopied) of the draft. In some classrooms, drafts are posted on a local area network (LAN). Students might write their comments directly under the draft or even e-mail their comments to the writer.

Forming Writing Groups

Writing process expert Nancie Atwell reports that in her classes she lets students choose the classmate or classmates they think can help them on the part of a paper they are struggling with at the time. "In the writing workshop," she says, "small groups form and disband in the minutes it takes for a writer to call on one or more other writers, move to a conference corner, share a piece or discuss a problem, and go back to work with a new perspective on the writing" (*In the Middle: Writing, Reading, and Learning with Adolescents*, p. 41).

You may want to organize students into groups that stay together for several weeks or throughout the time devoted to one writing workshop. Such stable groups work well with block scheduling and with ongoing projects. Students get to know and trust each other as they try out topic ideas, discuss specific writing problems, and share their drafts and revisions. The same group might work together on a writing project—for example, a compare and contrast paper. Think of having a writing group do speaking/listening and media projects, too: perhaps a panel discussion with a question-and-answer period on a problem or issue that the group researches, or maybe a multimedia project.

Writing Partner Checklist

Depending on your class, you might use a brief writing partner checklist like the following; or the longer, more detailed checklists that follow:

Brief Writing Partner Checklist

What Are the Strong Points?
- What are the best parts of the paper?
- What has the writer done especially well?

What Are the Weak Points?
- What parts of the paper need more work?
- Do you have any questions about the paper?
- Can you make any specific suggestions for improving the writing?

Revising in Greater Depth

Here is a much more detailed Revising Checklist, one that students may refer to in revising their own work and when commenting on each other's papers. You might want to produce another version of this checklist (and the editing and proofreading ones as well) for students to refer to throughout the year. This checklist applies to expository writing, the kind of writing that students are most often asked to do in school (a comparison and contrast essay, for example, or a critical review). In addition, see the boxed revising questions on p. T40, which refer specifically to persuasive, narrative, and descriptive writing.

Revising Checklist

Purpose and Audience
❑ How well does the writing accomplish its intended purpose?

❑ Do you have unanswered questions? What are they?

❑ Are the language and details appropriate for the intended audience?

Ideas and Unity
❑ What is the main idea? Is it clearly and directly stated?

❑ How well does the writer develop the main idea and major points? Are there enough supporting details?

❑ Would the writing be improved by dropping or by adding information? Where?

❑ Would adding details make the writing more interesting? Where? What kind of details would you suggest?

Organization and Coherence
❑ How well can you follow the writer's ideas?

❑ Would a different organization help?

❑ Do any parts of the draft stray from the main idea?

❑ Do transitions help the reader follow ideas?

Sentence Variety
❑ Can unnecessary words, details, and sentences be dropped?

❑ Do sentences read smoothly? Can some be combined?

❑ Do sentence lengths, beginnings, and structures vary?

Word Choice
❑ Does the writing sound natural? Are technical terms defined or explained?

❑ Is the word choice appropriate for the intended audience?

❑ Are words used precisely? If not, can you find vague, overused words that should be replaced? Would vivid verbs and specific nouns improve the writing? Where?

❑ Are the sentences overloaded with modifiers or prepositional phrases?

❑ Do you spot any clichés?

Title
❑ Does the title capture the reader's interest? Does it accurately reflect the paper's content?

Introduction and Conclusion

❑ Does the introduction make you want to read more? What suggestions can you make for improving it?

❑ Does it introduce the topic and the main idea?

❑ Does the conclusion end the essay logically? You may want to offer students variations on writing partner checklists from time to time. One option is to generate mode-specific checklists such as the ones below or even assignment-specific checklists. (See also the discussion of rubrics on pp. T45–T46.)

Mode-Specific Checklists	
CHECKLIST FOR PERSUASIVE WRITING	❑ Is the writer's opinion clearly stated? ❑ Does the writer give at least two reasons to support that opinion? ❑ Are the reasons themselves supported by convincing evidence (facts, statistics, examples, anecdotes, quotations, and so on)? ❑ Do you understand what the writer wants the reader to do? ❑ Has the writer persuaded you? Why or why not?
CHECKLIST FOR NARRATIVE WRITING	❑ Does the introduction make you want to read more? ❑ Does the writer *show* characters in action and let you hear what they say, or does the writer simply *tell* you about characters? ❑ Does the writing include sensory details? ❑ Are the writer's comparisons relevant and illuminating? ❑ Has the writer used specific nouns and vivid verbs (especially alternatives for *said*)? ❑ Is the ending satisfying?
CHECKLIST FOR DESCRIPTIVE WRITING	❑ Can you picture the setting? ❑ Does the writing include specific sensory details? ❑ Are the comparisons fresh? ❑ Does the organization of details (for example, proceeding from near to far, left to right, or top to bottom) make sense? ❑ Does the description establish an overall mood? What is it?

Editing and Proofreading

As previously mentioned, this series separates the revising task (which focuses on ideas and unity, organization and coherence, sentence variety, and word choice) from the editing task (which focuses on grammar and usage). Proofreading is the stage of the writing process when students look for mechanical errors in spelling, punctuation, and capitalization. These checklists provide references both for the teacher and the student.

Editing Checklist

❑ Is every sentence grammatically complete (not a fragment or a run-on)? *Lessons 6.1 and 6.3*

❑ Do subjects and verbs agree in number and gender? *Chapter 10*

❑ Are the correct forms of pronouns used? *Chapter 11*

❑ Does each pronoun clearly refer to an antecedent? *Lesson 11.5*

❑ Are verb tenses used consistently, unless there is good reason to vary them? *Chapter 9*

❑ Are the correct forms of irregular verbs used? *Chapter 9*

❑ Are the correct forms of plural nouns and the comparative forms of adjectives and adverbs used? *Chapter 5*

Proofreading Checklist

❑ Is every word spelled correctly? Check a dictionary if you're unsure. *Chapter 16*

❑ Have homonyms been confused (*their* instead of *there*, for example)? *Chapter 16*

❑ Do proper nouns and proper adjectives begin with capital letters? *Chapter 15*

❑ Does every sentence begin with a capital letter and end with an end punctuation mark? *Chapter 13*

❑ Are commas used correctly in all of their many uses? *Chapter 13*

❑ Is dialogue punctuated correctly? *Lesson 14.5*

Resources

In the classroom, students should have access to several copies of a good college dictionary and a dictionary-style thesaurus.

Using *Grammar for Writing* with English Language Learners

Variously called ESL (English as a Second Language) students, EFL (English as a Foreign Language) students, nonnative speakers, English language learners (ELL), and multilingual writers, students for whom English is not a first language give you a chance to raise everyone's consciousness about the respect that all languages and dialects deserve. Here are some strategies for giving ELL students a chance to talk about languages and demonstrate what languages other than English sound and look like:

- Conduct an informal survey at the beginning of the term, asking students

  - What other languages do you speak, read, and write besides English?

  - What language(s) do you speak at home?

  - What language(s) besides English have you studied in school? How well do you speak it? Write it? Read it? Understand it when it is spoken to you?

  - How did you learn the rules for forming sentences in your first language? In the other language(s)?

- Give native English speakers a chance to hear the sounds of other languages by asking ELL students to translate into their native language and orally deliver conversational sentences based on the following English ones:

  – Hi. My name is _____.

  – I am _____ years old.

  – My hobbies are _____.

  – The kind of music I like best is _____, and _____ is one of my favorite songs.

  – Good-bye for now.

- Ask ELL students to identify ways in which their first language differs from English. Encourage them to talk about what is giving them the most trouble in learning to speak and write English.

Strategies for ELL Students

The following table identifies some of the difficulties ELL students may have with English. It lists chapters and lessons from *Grammar for Writing* Level Blue to which you can direct these students.

Grammar for Writing and ELL		
Target Area in English	**Comment**	***Grammar for Writing* Treatment, Level Blue**
ADJECTIVE CLAUSES	Forming and positioning adjective clauses cause problems for speakers of Asian languages, of Arabic and Hebrew, and even of Latin-based languages.	Lesson 8.2
ARTICLES	ELL students often leave out the article before a singular count noun.	Lesson 5.4
CAPITALIZATION	Arabic, Chinese, and Hebrew do not use capital letters; Dutch and German capitalize some forms of the second-person pronoun; German caps all nouns.	Chapter 15
HOMOPHONES	Speakers of Asian languages in particular may be confused by the concept of words sounding alike but having different meanings.	Commonly Confused Words
NEGATION	Multiple negation is common in French and Russian, among other languages.	Lesson 12.3
PLURALS	Some Asian languages have no plural forms for nouns.	Lesson 5.1, Chapter 10, Lesson 16.4
PREFIXES AND SUFFIXES	These word parts are absent in Asian languages.	Lesson 16.3
PREPOSITIONS	English distinguishes between *in* and *on*; Spanish uses *en* for both.	Lessons 5.6 and 7.1
SILENT LETTERS	There are no silent letters in Spanish.	Chapter 16
SUBJECTS, DOUBLE	Some languages add personal pronouns as suffixes or prefixes, leading ELL speakers to say, "Maria she is pretty."	Lessons 6.2, 6.4, 11.1
TENSES	■ Certain English verbs don't work in the present progressive, but ESL students may say or write, "I am knowing the answer." ■ In some languages, time is not signaled by word endings but rather by words that native English speakers would call adverbs.	Lessons 5.3 and 9.4
WORD ORDER	■ In some languages, word order determines the part of speech. For example, the verb is the last word in sentences in Turkish, Korean, and Japanese. ■ In Russian, subject and object may switch places without affecting meaning.	Lessons 6.2, 6.6, 6.7

Assessment in *Grammar for Writing*

The *Grammar for Writing* series has assessment built right in. In this age of assessment and accountability, you will want some ongoing measures of how well students are doing in the course of the term. The series offers the following different types of assessment in each Pupil's Edition and Test Booklet:

Objective Evaluation

- **Chapter Reviews** In each book, Chapter Reviews help students review the grammar, usage, and mechanics concepts learned in the preceding lessons. Each review is broken down into exercises that focus on one lesson or one particular grammar, usage, or mechanics problem.

- **Cumulative Reviews** At the end of Chapters 8, 12, and 16, a two-page Cumulative Review covers the preceding chapters in that section. Use these Cumulative Reviews as mastery tests or diagnostic tests depending on your classroom needs.

- **Standardized Test Practice** A new section of test practice has been added to Level Blue. This section consists of practice in three SAT test formats and one ACT test format, followed by a 16-page practice test. Test-Taking Tips scattered through lessons in Level Blue refer students to test items in this section and help students see the way that grammar skills are assessed on these tests.

- **Online Test Practice** New to the second edition of *Grammar for Writing* is an interactive online component that provides students with further practice in standardized test formats, and that offers grammar feedback to help students recognize the grammar skills being assessed. Students may access these online study guides at www.grammarforwriting.com.

Lightening the Paper Load

Consider letting students help you in scoring objective tests. Have students exchange papers and score them as you go over answers in class; ask for volunteers to give the answers. A whole-class discussion of test items gives students a chance to ask questions and reinforce understanding.

Evaluating Responses to Writing Exercises

Grammar for Writing includes many writing exercises that cannot be scored objectively, such as the exercises in the Composition unit (Chapters 1, 2, 4), as well as the exercises based on notes, exercises with paragraphs needing revision, and the Revising and Editing Worksheets in the Grammar, Usage, and Mechanics sections. It is up to you to decide whether—and how—to grade these writing exercises or simply to check that students have completed them.

Revising and Editing Worksheets

These one-page themed exercises are examples of weak or incorrect writing. Students are directed to work individually or with a partner or group to improve the writing. Typically, instructions ask students to correct errors covered in the preceding lessons and to combine sentences and eliminate fragments and run-ons. *There is no single correct answer to any of the revision exercises in the Pupil's Edition.*

What students will learn from these exercises—especially by comparing their revisions and edits with those of their classmates—is that there are many workable solutions to writing problems and many different ways to communicate the same idea. This empowering insight should make students more confident as they revise and edit their own writing.

It is impossible to give students' work on the Revising and Editing Worksheets a percentage score; they contain many errors and invite many ways to revise and edit. Also, remember that students may be working with partners or a group, so the final result is a shared effort. If you feel you must record a number score, try judging the revisions on a 1–4 scale (with four being "excellent"). Give students points for each of the following criteria, and then find the average score.

The revised and edited version:

- communicates ideas and information clearly.
- is made up of complete sentences (no fragments or run-ons) that read smoothly and naturally.
- has no errors related to the chapter content.
- has no (or very few) errors in grammar and usage.
- uses punctuation correctly.
- spells words correctly.

Rubrics for Evaluating Students' Paragraphs and Essays

You can measure students' original writing using the rubrics on p. T46, which help to identify students' performance levels. Note that the rubrics are generic (they apply to all types of essays) and are based on a six-point scale. (You may find that in your classroom a four-point scale, beginning at Level 4, is more suitable.)

At the beginning of the term, share these (or your own) rubrics with students as a handout that they can keep in their notebooks. Let students know exactly what your standards are, so that they know what to aim for. You might also give students copies of essays from unidentified writers as an example of each level of performance. Reading and discussing these sample essays will clarify for students what you expect of them.

A Rubric for Writing Performance Levels

	The student's writing
LEVEL 6	■ consistently pursues a strong central purpose across a complex range of ideas, skillfully engages the reader, and shows exceptional insight into the subject ■ includes main ideas that are developed comprehensively and are supported with a variety of logical reasons and detailed examples ■ is skillfully organized ■ shows distinctive style through skillful and expressive use of vocabulary, phrasing, and sentence structure ■ demonstrates essentially error-free control of grammar, punctuation, capitalization, and spelling
LEVEL 5	■ consistently pursues a central purpose, holds the interest of the reader, and shows insight into the subject ■ includes main ideas that are developed and supported by a variety of reasons and examples ■ is effectively organized ■ shows emerging style through the effective use of vocabulary, phrasing, and sentence structure ■ consistently demonstrates the accurate use of grammar, punctuation, capitalization, and spelling
LEVEL 4	■ shows a consistent purpose, communicates to the reader, and connects to the writer's knowledge of the subject ■ includes main ideas that are organized, developed, and supported by reasons and examples ■ shows suitable vocabulary, phrasing, and sentence structure ■ generally demonstrates the accurate use of grammar, punctuation, capitalization, and spelling
LEVEL 3	■ shows a purpose but may be inconsistent in communicating to the reader or connecting to the writer's knowledge of the subject ■ includes main ideas that may be organized or partially developed and supported by some reasons and examples ■ may show imprecise use of vocabulary, phrasing, and sentence structure ■ includes some errors in the use of grammar, punctuation, capitalization, and spelling
LEVEL 2	■ attempts to connect the writer's knowledge to the subject and may not show a purpose ■ is typically brief, unorganized, and underdeveloped ■ may include frequent errors in the use of grammar, capitalization, punctuation, and spelling
LEVEL 1	■ is too brief or disorganized to communicate to the reader ■ may not connect the writer's knowledge to the subject ■ typically includes many errors in the use of grammar, capitalization, and spelling

Performance Levels, 1994. Reprinted with permission from the California Department of Education.

Writing Portfolios

The movement for performance assessment has gained strength over many years. Today, writing portfolios, an essential part of performance assessment, are part of most English classrooms. Writing portfolios give students tangible evidence that their efforts pay off. The portfolios can be made available for review by students' new teachers in subsequent terms.

Many teachers have students create two different kinds of writing portfolios:

- **A works-in-progress portfolio**
  For every finished piece of writing, students include prewriting notes, outlines, early drafts, revised drafts, and even a brief reflection on their writing experience. Students may also include journals, sketches, logs, and notes about their reading.
- **A best-efforts portfolio** This portfolio shows only the *finished pieces of writing*, examples of what students think are their best writing efforts.

Teacher-Student Conferences

An integral part of performance assessment is teacher-student conferences. One-on-one conferencing helps you assess performance and motivates students to raise their own standards.

Test Booklet

For every Level of *Grammar for Writing*, a separate Test Booklet is available for purchase. The Test Booklet contains a separate test for every chapter as well as a Diagnostic Test and a Mastery Test. Items take standardized test formats: error recognition and error correction.

Here is an example of an error recognition question from the Level Blue Mastery Test.

Directions: Fill in the circle for each sentence that contains an error.

1. Ⓐ Ⓑ Ⓒ Ⓓ
   A. He and I are on the school paper together.
   B. Of the two of them, she is the best skater.
   C. Just between you and me, our band needs work.
   D. Michel or Suki are representing our grade at the conference.

Diagnostic Test

A four-page Diagnostic Test appears at the beginning of each Test Booklet. You may use this test at the beginning of the school term to determine students' strengths and weaknesses. Each question on the Diagnostic Test is devoted to a single problem area.

Tallying class results will also reveal the grammar, usage, and mechanics skills that the class as a whole needs to learn and review. Use the Diagnostic Test scores and the errors on students' first batch of papers to decide which textbook lessons to use with the whole class and which lessons should be reserved for individuals or small groups.

Mastery Test

Use the four-page Mastery Test to assess the progress students have made during the term. You might plan to hold brief individual conferences with each student to discuss the student's work as a whole and to identify those skills that still need work. Students whose Mastery Test scores indicate that they are still having trouble (with subject-verb agreement, for example) might work together in small groups to review appropriate lessons and to go over the exercises together. You might ask these students to create their own exercise items in the style of exercise items in the Pupil's Edition. For example, a pair of students working together might write ten sentences that test knowledge of subject-verb agreement. Exercise writers can then exchange exercises with another team and work together to answer the exercise questions. Finally, both teams (writers and exercise takers) can get together to see if their answers agree.

Chapter Tests

Most Chapter Tests are four pages; a few are two pages long. The Chapter Test focuses entirely on concepts taught in the chapter lessons. In addition to error recognition and error correction items in a standardized-test format, many Chapter Tests end with a writing prompt. Four-page tests may also contain a paragraph to be revised.

Writing Prompts

These are a variety of writing exercises that are similar to the Write What You Think exercises in the Pupil's Edition. Students are asked to express an opinion on a topic or issue related to the content of a preceding exercise. They don't need any additional information to express and support an opinion.

Paragraph Revision

Some of the four-page Chapter Tests contain paragraphs that students are to revise. These are similar to the revision exercises found in the Pupil's Edition.

Test Booklet Answer Key

A separate Answer Key is provided with each package of Student Test Booklets.

Online Components

Now available as an online component, teachers can find a password-protected supplemental Answer Key. Go to www.grammarforwriting.com and enter the teacher access code TTYUMDNJKF. Students, too, will find online components there. They include additional standardized-test practice with grammar feedback and portfolio writing projects linked to Grammar, Usage, and Mechanics chapters.

LEVEL BLUE

GRAMMAR
for Writing

Senior Series Consultant
Beverly Ann Chin
Professor of English
University of Montana

Series Consultant
Frederick J. Panzer, Sr.
English Dept. Chairman, Emeritus
Christopher Columbus High School
Miami, FL

Series Consultant
Charlotte Rosenzweig, Ed. D.
English Dept. Chairperson
Long Beach High School
Long Beach, NY

Series Editor
Phyllis Goldenberg

Sadlier-Oxford
A Division of William H. Sadlier, Inc.
New York, New York 10005-1002

Reviewers

John Manear
English Dept. Chair
Seton-La Salle High
   School
Pittsburgh, PA

Cary Fuller
English Teacher
Rye Country Day
   School
Rye, NY

Galen Rosenberg
English Dept.
   Coordinator
Los Altos High
   School
Los Altos, CA

Helen Gallagher
English Dept. Chair
Maine East High
   School
Park Ridge, IL

Rose F. Schmitt
Education
   Consultant
Melbourne, FL

Carolyn Waters
Language
   Arts/Reading 7–12
   Supervisor
Cobb County School
   District
Marietta, GA

Roxanne Hoblitt
English Dept. Chair
Belgrade High School
Belgrade, MT

Dr. Muriel Harris
Former Writing Lab
   Director
English Dept.
Purdue University
West Lafayette, IN

Thomas C. Anstett
English Dept. Chair
Lincoln-Way East
   High School
Frankfort, IL

Patricia Stack
English Teacher
South Park High
   School
South Park, PA

Mel Farberman
Former Assistant
   Principal
Supervision–English
Cardozo High School
Bayside, NY

Wanda Porter
Former English Dept.
   Head
Kamehameha
   Secondary School
Honolulu, HI

Donna Fournier
English Dept. Chair
   and Teacher
Coyle Cassidy
   Memorial High
   School
Taunton, MA

**Katherine R.
Wilson**
Secondary English
   Coordinator, K–12
North Penn School
   District
Lansdale, PA

Student Writers

Damian Acosta
Coral Gables, FL

Jonathan Dewbre
Dallas, TX

Hugh Field
San Diego, CA

Leslie Harrell
Grosse Pointe
   Farms, MI

Anna Markee
Tacoma, WA

Leslie Miller
Pottsville, PA

Mandy Kiaha
Kamehameha, HI

Greg Ruttan
Lake Oswego, OR

Dorothy Schardt
Darien, IL

Emma Sheanshang
New York, NY

Sarah Swenson
The Woodlands, TX

**Peter
Tanpitukpong**
Wilmington, DE

Joshua Vinitz
Queens, NY

Acknowledgments

Every good faith effort has been made to locate the owners of copyrighted material to arrange permission to reprint selections. In several cases this has proved impossible.

Thanks to the following for permission to reprint copyrighted materials.

Excerpt re Arthur Ashe from *Boys Will Be*, by Bruce Brooks. Copyright © 1993 by Bruce Brooks. Reprinted by permission of Henry Holt and Company, LLC.

"The Cuban Missile Crisis," by Leslie Porter. From *A Student Guide to Writing a Research Paper*. Reprinted by permission of the author.

Excerpt from *Days of Grace*, by Arthur Ashe and Arnold Rampersad. Copyright © 1993 by Jeanne Moutoussamy-Ashe and Arnold Rampersad. Reprinted by permission of Alfred A. Knopf, Inc.

"Ending Child Hunger," by Bob Dole and George McGovern. From *The Washington Times*, January 13, 2006. Reprinted by permission of the authors.

"Grant and Lee: A Study in Contrasts," by Bruce Catton. From *The American Story*, edited by Earl Schenck Miers, in *The Bedford Reader*. Copyright © 1956 by the U.S. Capitol Historical Society.

Excerpt from "Hemingway's Ancient Mariner," by Carlos Baker. Reprinted with permission of Scribner, an imprint of Simon & Schuster Adult Publishing Group. From *Ernest Hemingway: Critiques of Four Major Novels*, edited by Carlos Baker. Copyright © 1962 by Charles Scribner's Sons. Copyright renewed © 1990 by Brian A. Baker, Elizabeth Baker Carter, and Diane Baker Wagner.

Credits

Cover Art and Design
William H. Sadlier, Inc. and Studio Montage

Cover Photos
Shutterstock/Galina Barskaya: boy jumping; Stephen Troell: Statue of Liberty.
Getty Images/Photodisc Green/Glen Allison: St. Louis Arch; Taxi/Antonio Mo: 3 girls.

Interior Photos
Neal Farris: 107 *left*, 127, 143 left, 257.
Getty Images/Altrendo Images: 257 *background*; The Image Bank/David Allan Brandt: 151 *background*; The Image Bank/Darren Robb: 205; Photo Alto/Patrick Sheandell O'Carroll: 20; Photodisc Blue/Diane Macdonald: 87 *background*; Photodisc Green: 239; Photodisc

Green/Glen Allison: 221 *background*; Photodisc Red/Donovan Reese: 8 *background*; Taxi/Antonio Mo: 35.
Imagestate/Ethel Davies: 51 *background*.
NASA: space shuttle: 177.
PictureQuest/Banana Stock: 177.
Punchstock/Digital Vision: 143 *background*; Photodisc: 107 *right*, 191, 271 *background*; Rubberball: 87.

Shutterstock/Mukhin Maxim Anatolyevitch: 177 *background*; Galina Barskaya: 143 right, 221, 271; Bryan Brazil: 20 *background*; Alan Freed: 107 *background*; Eli Mordechai: 239 *background*; Brian Morrison: 205 *background*; Mike Norton: 191 *background*; Newton Page: 127 *background*; Stephen Troell: 35 *background*; Simone van den Berg: 51 *background*.
Veer/Fancy Photography: 8.

ISBN: 978-0-8215-0219-8
23456789/10 09 08 07

Dear Student:

As a student, you are being challenged to write correctly and effectively not only in your English classes but also in your social studies, science, and history classes. If you have taken a standardized test recently or are preparing to take one soon, you know this only too well. The writing and grammar sections of such tests as the SAT, the ACT, and the PSAT are more critical and more demanding than ever.

Grammar for Writing has been written with the demands of these tests especially in mind. In the **Composition Unit**, for example, you will find a new **Writing Workshop** devoted to writing a timed essay of the kind that is now being called for on standardized tests. A new section of **grammar and usage practice** in standardized-test formats has been added to the book as well. You will also see a new feature called **Test-Taking Tips** sprinkled through the Grammar and Usage Units. These tips, which appear in lessons covering the skills most often assessed on standardized tests, will help you see how the conventions and rules of grammar play out in the multiple-choice formats of these tests.

Of course, there are reasons to speak and write well other than to score well on standardized tests. People judge you by the way you write and speak. Your use of English is evaluated in the writing you do in school, on job and college applications, and in many different kinds of careers.

No textbook can make writing easy. Good writers work hard and revise their work often to find just the right words to move their audience. Consequently, in *Grammar for Writing* you will find many exercises called **Write What You Think**. These exercises are designed to help guide you in developing clear, logical arguments to persuade people that your opinion is right. These exercises will sharpen your thinking as well as your writing skills.

No one has to prove that writing is important—it just *is*. But writing can always be improved, and the best way to improve it is to learn and practice the skills and strategies in this book. *Grammar for Writing* presents the rules of grammar as simply as possible; whether you are merely refreshing your memory or learning the concepts for the first time, you'll be able to understand the rules and *apply* them to your writing.

All of the skills you learn and practice in this book—grammar, writing, thinking—will last you a lifetime.

Good Luck!
The Authors

CONTENTS

COMPOSITION

CHAPTER 1 **The Writing Process** **8**
Lesson 1.1 Prewriting: Gathering Ideas 9
Lesson 1.2 Organizing the Ideas and Drafting 13
Lesson 1.3 Revising 15
Lesson 1.4 Editing and Proofreading 18

CHAPTER 2 **Writing Effective Paragraphs and Essays** **20**
Lesson 2.1 Ideas and Unity 21
Lesson 2.2 Elaborating with Supporting Details 23
Lesson 2.3 Organization and Coherence 26
Lesson 2.4 Types of Paragraphs 29
Lesson 2.5 Writing Essays 32

CHAPTER 3 **Writing Effective Sentences** **35**
Lesson 3.1 Varying Sentence Beginnings 36
***Lesson 3.2** Combining Sentences: Compound Subjects and
Compound Verbs 38
***Lesson 3.3** Combining Sentences: Using Coordinating
Conjunctions 40
***Lesson 3.4** Combining Sentences: Inserting Phrases 42
***Lesson 3.5** Combining Sentences: Using Subordinate Clauses 44
***Lesson 3.6** Eliminating Short, Choppy Sentences 46
***Lesson 3.7** Eliminating Wordiness 48
Revising and Editing Worksheet 50

CHAPTER 4 **Writing Workshops** **51**
Lesson 4.1 Narrative Writing: Autobiographical Incident 52
Lesson 4.2 Persuasive Writing 57
Lesson 4.3 Expository Writing: Compare and Contrast Essay 62
Lesson 4.4 Writing About Literature: Analyzing Fiction 68
Lesson 4.5 Expository Writing: Research Paper 74
***Lesson 4.6** Writing a Timed Essay 83

* Denotes lessons with skills most commonly assessed on standardized tests.

GRAMMAR

CHAPTER 5 Parts of Speech **87**
  Lesson 5.1 Nouns 89
  Lesson 5.2 Pronouns 91
  Lesson 5.3 Verbs 93
 * **Lesson 5.4** Adjectives 95
 * **Lesson 5.5** Adverbs 97
  Lesson 5.6 Prepositions 99
  Lesson 5.7 Conjunctions and Interjections 101
  Lesson 5.8 Determining a Word's Part of Speech 103
  Revising and Editing Worksheet 104
  Chapter Review 105

CHAPTER 6 Parts of a Sentence **107**
 * **Lesson 6.1** Using Complete Sentences 109
  Lesson 6.2 Subject and Predicate 111
 * **Lesson 6.3** Correcting Sentence Fragments 113
  Lesson 6.4 Finding the Subject 115
 * **Lesson 6.5** Run-on Sentences 117
  Lesson 6.6 Direct and Indirect Objects 119
  Lesson 6.7 Predicate Nominatives and Predicate Adjectives 121
  Revising and Editing Worksheets 123
  Chapter Review 125

CHAPTER 7 Phrases **127**
  Lesson 7.1 Prepositional Phrases: Adjective and Adverb Phrases . . 129
  Lesson 7.2 Participles and Participial Phrases 131
  Lesson 7.3 Effective Paragraphs: Varying Sentence Beginnings . . . 133
  Lesson 7.4 Gerunds and Gerund Phrases 135
  Lesson 7.5 Infinitives and Infinitive Phrases 137
  Lesson 7.6 Appositives and Appositive Phrases 139
  Revising and Editing Worksheet 140
  Chapter Review 141

CHAPTER 8 Clauses **143**
  Lesson 8.1 Independent Clauses and Subordinate Clauses 145
  Lesson 8.2 Adjective Clauses 147
  Lesson 8.3 Adverb Clauses 149
  Lesson 8.4 Noun Clauses 151
  Lesson 8.5 Four Types of Sentence Structures 153
  Revising and Editing Worksheets 155
  Chapter Review 157
  Cumulative Review, Chapters 5–8 159

(* Denotes lessons with skills most commonly assessed on standardized tests.

USAGE

CHAPTER 9 Using Verbs **161**
  Lesson 9.1 Regular Verbs 163
  Lesson 9.2 Irregular Verbs 1 165
  Lesson 9.3 Irregular Verbs 2 167
* **Lesson 9.4** Verb Tense 169
* **Lesson 9.5** Parallel Structure 171
  Lesson 9.6 Using the Active Voice 173
  Revising and Editing Worksheet 174
  Chapter Review 175

CHAPTER 10 Subject-Verb Agreement **177**
***Lesson 10.1** Agreement in Person and Number 179
***Lesson 10.2** Indefinite Pronouns, Inverted Subjects 181
***Lesson 10.3** Agreement with Compound Subjects 183
***Lesson 10.4** Agreement with Special Nouns 185
  Revising and Editing Worksheets 187
  Chapter Review 189

CHAPTER 11 Using Pronouns **191**
  Lesson 11.1 Using Subject Pronouns 193
  Lesson 11.2 Using Object Pronouns 195
***Lesson 11.3** *Who* or *Whom?* 197
  Lesson 11.4 Appositives and Incomplete Constructions 199
***Lesson 11.5** Agreement with Antecedent 201
  Revising and Editing Worksheet 202
  Chapter Review 203

CHAPTER 12 Using Modifiers **205**
  Lesson 12.1 Degrees of Comparison 207
***Lesson 12.2** Using the Degrees of Comparison 209
***Lesson 12.3** Double Negatives 211
***Lesson 12.4** Misplaced and Dangling Modifiers 213
  Revising and Editing Worksheets 215
  Chapter Review 217
  Cumulative Review, Chapters 9–12 219

MECHANICS

CHAPTER 13 Punctuation: End Marks and Commas **221**
  Lesson 13.1 End Marks and Abbreviations 223
  Lesson 13.2 Commas in a Series 225
  Lesson 13.3 Compound Sentences and Phrases 227

* Denotes lessons with skills most commonly assessed on standardized tests.

*Lesson 13.4 Sentence Interrupters and Nonessential Elements . . . 229
Lesson 13.5 Other Comma Uses 231
*Lesson 13.6 Correcting Run-on Sentences and Sentence Fragments . . 233
Editing and Proofreading Worksheets 235
Chapter Review 237

CHAPTER 14 **Punctuation: All the Other Marks** **239**
Lesson 14.1 Colons 241
Lesson 14.2 Semicolons 243
Lesson 14.3 Underlining (Italics) 245
Lesson 14.4 Quotation Marks 247
Lesson 14.5 Punctuating Dialogue 249
Lesson 14.6 Apostrophes 251
Editing and Proofreading Worksheets 253
Chapter Review 255

CHAPTER 15 **Capitalization** **257**
Lesson 15.1 Proper Nouns and Proper Adjectives 259
Lesson 15.2 Titles 261
Lesson 15.3 First Words, Organizations, Religions, School Subjects . . 263
Lesson 15.4 *I* and *O*; Historical Events, Documents, and Periods;
             Calendar Items; Brand Names 265
Editing and Proofreading Worksheets 267
Chapter Review 269

CHAPTER 16 **Spelling** **271**
Lesson 16.1 Using a Dictionary 273
Lesson 16.2 Spelling Rules 275
Lesson 16.3 Prefixes and Suffixes 277
Lesson 16.4 Noun Plurals 279
Editing and Proofreading Worksheets 281
Chapter Review 283
Cumulative Review, Chapters 13–16 285

STANDARDIZED TEST PRACTICE

SAT Practice: Identifying Sentence Errors 288
SAT Practice: Improving Sentences 293
SAT Practice: Improving Paragraphs 299
ACT Practice 302
Practice Test 308
Commonly Confused Words 324
Index 328

* Denotes lessons with skills most commonly assessed on standardized tests.

The Writing Process

Prewriting: Gathering Ideas

▐▐▐▶ **Prewriting** is all the thinking, planning, and organizing you do before you actually start writing.

"What shall I write about?" Every writer wrestles with this question. As you start to think about writing, choose a topic (a) that interests you, (b) that's important to you, or (c) that you know a lot about.

Narrow your topic to one that is limited, thus allowing you to cover it adequately in the number of words or pages you're expected to write.

TOO BROAD	new cars
LIMITED	How new cars are named
	Who evaluates new cars, and how?
	Shopping for a car on the Internet

It may take you several tries to get a topic that fits your assignment. Use the five prewriting strategies below, both to discover topics and main ideas to write about, and to help you gather supporting details that elaborate on the topics.

PREWRITING STRATEGIES

1. Writer's Notebook Keep a separate notebook or folder in which you jot down experiences and thoughts about anything that interests you.

Later you can convert these jottings into effective paragraphs, essays, stories, and so on. You might put such things in your notebook as quotations, cartoons, and poems that "speak" to you; then explain why you like them. Think of your notebook entries as memory joggers.

Writing Model

Tues. 4/7. Arch Creek office for driver's license test. My appointment was for 8 A.M., waited til almost 10. So nervous I felt sick. Examiner—a woman, never smiled. Do this, do that; left turn, right turn; parallel park. Heavy rains and wind. What did she write on the forms?? I have to wait—results come in the mail.

2. Brainstorming Focus on a single word, and list everything that pops into your head.

Don't *think* about what you've written; just get every idea down on paper. If you brainstorm with a partner or group, have one person do the writing. When you run out of thoughts, go back over your list, and check or circle the ones that seem most usable.

Writing Model

TOPIC: Driving

BRAINSTORMING NOTES:

red convertible	huge trucks, accidents	ticket for speeding
changing flat tire	Jeff's collision with stop	rolling stop
time we went camping	sign; safety belts	insurance cost?

---

3. Freewriting This strategy is similar to brainstorming, but it involves nonstop writing.

Focus on a word or topic, and write continuously for three to five minutes. Don't worry about complete sentences, grammar, or spelling. If you can't think of anything new to write, write the same word over and over until a new thought develops. In other words, keep moving forward; do not back up and reread.

Writing Model

TOPIC: Car safety
What kinds of things do they look for during car inspections? Do they check tires? How? How often do you need to take a car in for an inspection? I'd better keep up regular maintenance. Maintenance. Of what? Of seat belts? What's to maintain? Doesn't matter. Point is to wear seat belts? Why? Dumb question. . .

---

4. Clustering (also called **Mapping** or **Webbing**) Create a cluster diagram to explore a topic, to break a large topic into smaller parts, or to gather details.

First, write your topic (or any word or phrase) in the middle of a piece of paper, and then circle it. Around the circled topic, write subtopics—related words and phrases. Circle each new word or phrase, and connect it to your original topic by drawing a line. Each new word or phrase may have subtopics, too. Keep going until you run out of thoughts.

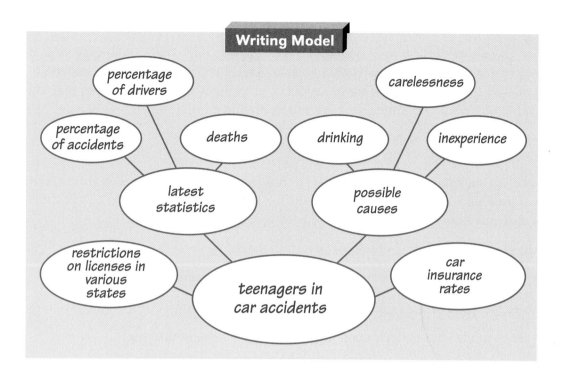

5. 5-W and How? Questions Asking the questions *Who? What? When? Where? Why?* and *How?* about any topic will help you narrow, or limit, your essay.

For some topics, not every question will apply; for other topics, you may think of several questions beginning with the same word. Here are one writer's questions about the Model T, one of the early automobiles.

EXERCISE 1 Starting a Writer's Notebook

If you haven't started a writer's notebook yet, begin one now. Use a small notebook, a folder, or a section of your loose-leaf notebook. Create two entries—one for yesterday and one for today. Write notes about experiences, thoughts, and observations for both days that you would be willing to share with a writing group. Encourage students to make a dedicated writer's notebook to keep throughout the school year.

EXERCISE 2 Thinking of Topic Ideas

For each of the following numbered items, think of three or four topics to write about. Use at least three different prewriting strategies—the technique suggested in parentheses or a different one—to help you generate writing topics. Students' lists will vary.

1. A description of a place, object, or person (freewriting)

2. A story about something that really happened (brainstorming)

3. An explanation of how something works (*5-W and How?* questions)

4. A letter to the editor about a community or school issue (clustering)

EXERCISE 3 Narrowing a Topic

Choose two of the five broad, general topics below. For each topic, suggest three limited topics that you could cover in a three-page paper. Students' topics will vary.

EXAMPLE	TOO BROAD	LIMITED
	Rock Music	*A visit to the Rock 'n' Roll Hall of Fame in Cleveland, Ohio*
		The earliest recordings by Elvis Presley
		Disc jockey Alan Freed's influence on rock music

1. Horses   4. Earthquakes

2. Television   5. Baseball

3. Art

EXERCISE 4 Gathering Supporting Details

For one of the limited topics you identified in Exercise 3, use brainstorming, clustering, and/or the *5-W and How?* questions to gather details about that topic.
Students' details will vary.

Organizing the Ideas and Drafting

▬▶ Now that you've gathered your ideas, think about the order in which you want to present them. Decide whether the best way to sequence your ideas would be, for example, chronological order, order of importance, or cause and effect.

▬▶ You may want to use your prewriting notes to create an **outline**. An outline is a writing plan consisting of the most important points. An outline forces you to make two important decisions about your prewriting notes: (1) which main ideas and details to include in support of your topic and (2) what order to present them in.

Outlines work well for writing that explains, persuades, or describes. A model of a brief outline is at the right.

▬▶ Before you begin writing, decide on your writing style. **Style** is the manner in which you express your ideas. Your writing style is determined by your audience and your purpose. Your **audience** is the person or persons who will read what you write. Your **purpose** may be to describe, to inform, to tell a story, to persuade, to entertain, or a combination of these.

Thinking about your audience helps you to decide how much background information and which supporting details you should include. Ask yourself questions such as, "Does my audience need definitions of the technical terms or proper nouns that I'm going to use?" Thinking about your purpose also helps you to sift through the supporting details and to choose the most appropriate ones.

▬▶ **Drafting** is the step in the writing process when you start putting your thoughts into sentences and paragraphs.

DRAFTING STRATEGIES

1. **Write the Big Idea** Remember your writing purpose and audience, and draft a sentence that expresses the main idea of your paragraph or essay. Some writers begin their draft with this sentence, and some simply keep this sentence in mind as they write.

2. **Grab Your Reader** Start out with a "hook," or a statement or question that will catch your reader's attention.

Writing Model

A Rough Outline:
Chinese Immigration

I. Early Chinese immigration to US (late 1800s)

  A. California gold rush (1849)

  B. Transcontinental railroad

  C. Exclusion of Chinese laborers

   1. Chinese Exclusion Act (1882)

II. Wave of immigration after San Francisco fire (1906)

  A. Angel Island immigration station, 1910–40

WRITING HINT

Write in your own voice —that is, sound like yourself. Don't try to sound "intelligent" by using words you don't know or by writing complicated sentences. Express your ideas clearly and simply.

As you compose your draft, make sure to write complete sentences, and vary their structures and lengths. See Lessons 3.1 and 7.3 for suggestions on how to do this.

3. **Stay Flexible** Follow the general direction of your organizational plan, but feel free to make appropriate changes and add or drop details if necessary. Don't worry about mistakes when you draft. Just get your ideas down on paper.

4. **Create an Ending** Conclude your writing in the final paragraph by including one or more sentences that restate your main idea. A good conclusion wraps up your writing logically and gracefully and can contain a quote, a call to action, or a final thought on the subject.

Below is a first draft based on the brief outline on page 13. The writer's purpose was to inform history classmates about Chinese immigration. Remember, when you're drafting, don't stop your flow of ideas to fix mistakes. You'll have time for that during the next two steps in the writing process: revising and editing. Students will see a revised version of this draft in Lesson 1.3.

Does the writer use a hook to grab your attention?

What information appears in the draft that wasn't in the outline?

Does the writer include an ending?

Remember, drafting is just one part of the writing process.

Writing Model

The first big bunch of Chinese immigrants came to "Gold Mountain" (which is what they called the United States) after the California gold rush, which happened in 1849. They worked as cooks and household workers. They also worked as storekeepers and trying to find gold. There was a great push to finish building the transcontinental railroad across the American continent after the gold rush. Nine tenths of the railroad workers who were working on the western leg of the transcontinental railroad were Chinese. They worked for about 12 cents an hour. Racial discrimination against the Chinese and violence against the Chinese led to the Chinese Exclusion Act of 1882. No Chinese person could enter the US for ten years and it was extended another ten years and no Chinese could become a citizen until various restrictive laws ended in 1943.

EXERCISE 5 Writing Your First Draft

Draft two or more paragraphs using the prewriting notes you made for a limited topic in Exercise 4 on page 12. First decide on an audience and purpose. Then make an outline. When you're ready to start drafting, follow the drafting strategies suggested in this lesson.

Students' drafts will vary. Students will be asked to revise this draft on page 17 in Lesson 1.3, Exercise 7.

Revising

||||➡ When you **revise**, you shape your draft into its almost-final form.

At this stage in the writing process, you try to make your written thoughts clearer. You may need to add new information, cut words or sentences, change the order of sentences and paragraphs, and replace weak words with stronger ones.

REVISING STRATEGIES

When you revise, you look for ways to eliminate problems with ideas and unity, organization and coherence, sentence variety, and word choice. To begin revising, try this four-step strategy. Reread your first draft four separate times, concentrating on only one of the issues below with each reading.

1. **Ideas and Unity** Can you summarize your main idea(s)? (In a narrative, you need to ask yourself whether you can summarize the event or events rather than the main idea or ideas.) Do you have enough supporting details or too many? Will adding or cutting details improve your draft? Do you need more background information? Is everything relevant, or related, to your main idea(s), or have you wandered off track?

2. **Organization and Coherence** Does the opening sentence grab the reader's attention? Can you improve your draft by moving paragraphs? by moving sentences? Is information presented in a logical order, an order that makes sense to the reader? Would adding transition words help? Does the last sentence bring closure to the writing?

3. **Sentence Variety** Have you varied the beginnings, lengths, and structure of your sentences? Would some sentences sound better combined?

4. **Word Choice** Is your vocabulary too formal or informal for your audience? Do technical terms need to be defined or explained? Can you delete unnecessary words or phrases? Look for general, vague words, and replace them with precise ones. If you've used a cliché or an overworked word, such as *very* or *great*, think of a fresh way to express the same idea.

> **Enriching Your Vocabulary**
>
> *Narrare*, Latin for "to make known or to tell," gives us the noun *narrative* (story or narration). A writer may win critical praise for her exciting *narratives*.

Below is the first draft on Chinese immigration from Lesson 1.2. Notice the revisions the writer has made to it.

Does the writer use a hook to capture your attention?

Do you see any new ideas in this piece of writing?

What do you notice that's different between the first draft and this revision?

How did the writer's changes in word choice and sentence variety affect the quality of the writing?

Does the writer create an ending?

Writing Model

Did you know that in the late 1800s Chinese people were the largest immigrant group on the West Coast? The first big ~~bunch~~ *wave* of Chinese immigrants came to "Gold Mountain" (~~which is what they called~~ the United States) after the California gold rush~~, which happened~~ in 1849. They worked as cooks and household workers. ~~They also worked as~~ storekeepers and ~~trying to find gold.~~ *miners.*

After the gold rush,
¶ There was a great push to finish building the transcontinental railroad ~~across the American continent after the gold rush.~~ Nine tenths of the railroad workers ~~who were working~~ on the western leg of the transcontinental railroad were Chinese. ~~They~~ *who* worked for about 12 cents an hour. Racial discrimination ~~against the Chinese~~ *along with a fear of cheap labor* and violence against the Chinese led to the *passage of the* Chinese Exclusion Act of 1882. *This law banned all Chinese immigration* ~~No Chinese person could enter the US~~ for ten years and ~~it~~ *later* was extended another ten years ~~and~~ no Chinese could become a cit- *Congress repealed* izen until various restrictive laws ~~ended~~ in 1943. Since that time, Chinese Americans have overcome many of the social and economic inequalities that confronted the earlier immigrants.

▐▶ **Working With a Writing Partner** involves using revising strategies to give feedback to your classmates and getting help from them on your works in progress.

EXERCISE 6 Revising a Draft

The writer's purpose of the following draft was to inform history classmates about the Dust Bowl. Revise it, focusing separately on ideas and unity, organization and coherence, sentence variety, and word choice. Write your revised version on a separate piece of paper, and talk about your revisions with a writing partner. Refer to the revising strategies in this lesson to focus your discussion.
Revised drafts will vary. Sample revisions shown.

¹In studying United States history, you probably heard of the Dust Bowl,

the ~~biggest and~~ greatest drought the country has ever seen. ² ^It^ ~~The drought~~ lasted for

^almost^ ~~nigh onto~~ ten years. ³ ~~The drought~~ ^and^ began in the midwestern and southern Great Plains in

~~the year~~ 1931. ⁴ ~~Because of~~ the drought ~~there was no rain so~~ crops, and grass, and trees ^killed^ ~~died.~~

⁵ ~~Then~~ when the land was bare, the winds blew the topsoil away in huge "black blizzards."

⁶The five dust bowl states that were hit ~~most~~ hardest were Kansas, and Oklahoma, ~~and~~ Texas,

~~and~~ New Mexico, and Colorado. ⁷Although the drought affected the whole country. ^When^ ⁸The

drought ended in the fall of 1939. ⁹ ^G^overnment agencies taught farmers new techniques to

control soil erosion, ~~then,~~ such as crop rotation. ¹⁰The Dust Bowl changed the American

landscape forever.

EXERCISE 7 Working with a Writing Partner

1. Revise the paragraphs that you drafted in Lesson 1.2, Exercise 5. Use the revising strategies in this lesson to improve your draft.

2. Now, work with a partner to revise your draft. Allow your partner to read your draft without your input. Your partner should respond to your writing using the revising strategies on page 15 as a guide. Encourage your writing partner to make comments directly on your pages.

3. Review your writing partner's comments on your draft and incorporate those that you feel will improve your writing. Don't be discouraged if you have to rewrite some passages.
Caution writing partners to be positive about the drafts they read. Encourage them to suggest possible solutions to problems they find.

Editing and Proofreading

▐▐▐▶ When you **edit** or **proofread** (these terms refer to the same task), you search for mistakes in spelling, punctuation, capitalization, and usage.

Don't let these errors slip by. Part of the quality of your writing depends on your ability to use the conventions of standard written English. Use the following list as you edit your work. If you are in doubt, use the index to find rules about specific conventions.

EDITING QUESTIONS

See, **Mechanics**, Chapters 13–16 for more on the rules for many of the errors you are looking for as you proofread your work.

1. **Spelling** Are words spelled correctly? (Use a college dictionary or a spell checker on a computer.) Have you used a correctly spelled word that doesn't fit the sentence (*you're* instead of *your*, for example, or *hear* instead of *here*—mix-ups that a computer's spell checker won't catch)? Chapter 16: Spelling

2. **Capitalization** Do proper nouns and proper adjectives begin with capital letters? Have you capitalized a word that's supposed to start with a lowercase letter? Chapter 15: Capitalization

3. **Punctuation** Are commas and other punctuation marks used correctly? Is dialogue correctly punctuated? Chapters 13 and 14: Punctuation

4. **Sentence Correctness** Are there any fragments, run-ons, or misplaced modifiers? Chapter 6: Parts of a Sentence; Chapter 12: Using Modifiers

5. **Verbs** Do all present tense verbs agree with their subjects? Are verb tenses consistent and correct? Chapter 9: Using Verbs; Chapter 10: Subject-Verb Agreement

6. **Pronouns** Do all the pronouns agree with their antecedents? Are pronoun references clear? Chapter 11: Using Pronouns

7. **Usage** Are adjectives modifying nouns and pronouns? Are adverbs modifying verbs, adjectives, and other adverbs? Are comparisons clear and complete? Do comparisons use *-er/more* and *-est/most* forms correctly? Chapter 12: Using Modifiers; Lesson 5.4 Adjectives; Lesson 5.5 Adverbs

Enriching Your Vocabulary

The verb *transpose* comes from the Latin *transponere*, which means "to change the position of." *Transpose* can also be used in the sense of "to change in nature or form." The director *transposed* the setting of *Romeo and Juliet* from Verona to Civil War America.

Proofreading Symbols		
CORRECTION	**SYMBOL**	**EXAMPLE**
Delete (remove).	ℰ	He grated the the onions.
Insert.	∧	We planed the party.
Transpose (switch).	⌐⌐	I only spent a dollar.
Capitalize.	≡	did you visit Walden Pond?
Make lowercase.	/	The irises bloom each Spring.
Start a new paragraph.	¶	¶"No," she said.
Add space.	#	Allegra lives in SanJuan.
Close up space.	⌣	Pat is a child hood friend.

EXERCISE 8 Editing a Paragraph

Find and correct every error in the following paragraph.

¹People who make maps are called cartographers. ²They <s>carefuly</s> *carefully* draw each country's borders. ³During the 1930s cartographers began to draw <s>there</s> *their* maps from photographs taken from airplanes. ⁴Now they use <s>satelite</s> *satellite* photographs to create more accurate maps.

⁵If you look at a map, <s>youll</s> *you'll* find New zealand, two large islands and several smaller islands southeast of australia. ⁶According to *The columbia Encyclopedia*, New Zealand contains 103,377 square miles. ⁷How can geographers figure out the number of square miles New Zealand contains. *They* ⁸It can't possibly multiply <s>it's</s> *its* length by <s>it's</s> *its* width. ⁹Modern map makers and geographers use computers to draw maps. ¹⁰They also use computers to measure a country's square <s>miles</s> *mileage* .

EXERCISE 9 Creating Editing and Proofreading Exercises

 Working Together

Create an editing/proofreading practice for your classmates. Write one or two paragraphs that have at least ten mistakes (or more if you want) in spelling, punctuation, capitalization, and usage. Exchange paragraphs with your classmates, and see if you can correct all the errors. Answers will vary.

CHAPTER 2

Writing Effective Paragraphs and Essays

Ideas and Unity

||||▶ A paragraph has **unity** (it is unified) when all of its sentences focus on a single main **idea**.

||||▶ A **topic sentence** directly states the paragraph's main idea.

When a topic sentence is the first or second sentence in a paragraph, it announces what's coming in the rest of the paragraph. When a topic sentence is at the end of a paragraph, it summarizes the main idea that has not been directly stated in the preceding sentences.

Not all paragraphs have directly stated topic sentences. The main idea may be **implied** rather than stated directly. But even without a topic sentence, the main idea should be clear to the reader.

||||▶ A paragraph that starts with a topic sentence may end with a **clincher sentence** which restates or summarizes the main idea.

Clincher sentences can be especially effective in persuasive paragraphs, but you should use them sparingly in an essay.

The following annotated model illustrates the principle of unity.

> See Lesson 2.4 for more techniques on writing different types of paragraphs.

WRITING HINT

In an essay, a topic sentence does double duty: It states the paragraph's main idea, *and* it ties the paragraph to the rest of the essay.

Writing Model

¹Ashe leaves us with a good lesson: There is a place in sports for smart people. ²Intelligence—used well in analysis, study, practice— helps you in anything you try to do, whether it's a backhand lob at a surprising moment or a moral stand on a complex issue. ³He was a very talented tennis player, blessed with extraordinary reach and power and touch, but his victories were victories of the wits. ⁴When he faced Connors on Centre Court in 1975, it certainly seemed like old smarts and old bones against the brashly cruel, indefatigable force and speed of youth. ⁵So it was. ⁶Force and speed never had a chance. ⁷Ashe showed that if you are better at thinking, you can then work hard physically to keep the advantage when you move into the field of action. ⁸Arthur the Man blew Jimbo the Boy away. ⁹Nine years later, Connors gave us the opportunity to see that Ashe's shrewdness was

Topic sentence about intelligence

Background information

Incident that supports main idea

Second incident
that supports
main idea

not just an advantage conferred by age and experience. [10]In the 1984 final, Jimbo—still playing in full force as The Boy, despite his seniority —was utterly destroyed by the much smarter John McEnroe. [11]Like Ashe, McEnroe demonstrated a strategic control (is *that* what manliness is?) that made Jimmy's reckless force and willful cuteness (and is *that* boyishness?) look ridiculous.

—Bruce Brooks, "Arthur Ashe"

SKILLS FOR MAINTAINING UNITY

1. Topic Sentence Keep in mind that there's more than one way a writer can word a topic sentence. Here's another option Brooks could've used.

Ashe proved that the best athletes are smart athletes.

But the following sentences would have been too weak to be topic sentences for Brooks's paragraph.

Everyone thinks all the time. [too broad]

Ashe had a high IQ. [too narrow]

2. Single Main Idea All the sentences in the model paragraph stick to the main idea. Brooks avoids cluttering his paragraph with unnecessary sentences such as the following two:

Ashe's intelligence was nurtured by the schools of Richmond, Virginia.

Wit, after all, is what separates humans from animals.

3. Clincher Sentence Brooks could have summed up his paragraph with a clincher sentence such as the following:

So we see in these two incidents that brains can dominate muscles.

EXERCISE 1 Choosing a Topic Sentence

1. Which of the following sentences would work in place of the topic sentence that Brooks wrote? Give reasons for your choice on a separate piece of paper.
   a. We will remember Ashe for what he taught us about smarts in sports.
   b. Ashe made a positive impression on lots of people. Students' reasons will vary.

2. Which of the following sentences could more easily be added to Brooks's paragraph without detracting from its unity? Explain your choice on a separate piece of paper.
   a. Ashe spoke intelligently and movingly about AIDS. Choice **a** is too specific for the information in the paragraph.
   b. We need more athletes with Ashe's intelligence. Choice **b** adequately relates to the main idea of the paragraph.

Elaborating with Supporting Details

▯▯▯▶ **Elaboration** is the process of adding details to support a main idea.

Develop, or support, the paragraph's main idea with the following kinds of details: **facts**, **statistics**, **quotations**, **definitions**, **anecdotes** or **incidents**, **examples**, **reasons**, and **comparisons**. It's fine to use more than one kind of supporting detail in a single paragraph. Just make sure that each sentence adds something new.

The writer of the following paragraph realized that the first draft did not contain enough specific details to support the topic sentence. Notice the details she added during revision.

Review **Composition** Lessons 3.4 and 3.5 for more about combining sentences by inserting phrases and clauses.

Writing Model

¹Every spring and summer, the Coast Salish of the

Pacific Northwest moved from their winter villages to

temporary camps near the coast and beside the rivers with

the goal of gathering food for the winter. ²The men ~~brought~~ *used spears and nets to catch salmon, cod, trout, and halibut.* ~~in fish.~~ ³They smoked and dried the surplus fish for winter

food for the whole village. ⁴The women and children *shellfish from the beaches and edible wild plants and roots.* collected ~~food too.~~

Enriching Your Vocabulary

The origin of the noun *debris*, as used in Exercise 3, can be traced to the French verb *debriser*, which means "to break to pieces." The objects in a mound of *debris* are broken and battered. Archaeologists can learn many things from the *debris* of an ancient civilization.

EXERCISE 2 Improving Unity and Adding Details

Work with a partner or small group to revise the paragraph at the top of the following page. Cross out any words or sentences that damage the paragraph's unity because they move away from the main idea. Then from the list below the paragraph, select the details that you think would improve the paragraph. (Some of the details can be inserted as phrases and clauses.) Write the letter of the detail where you think it belongs in the paragraph. Then write your revised paragraph on a separate piece of paper.

[1]Blue jeans as we know them go back to 1853. [2]In that year in San Francisco, Levi

Strauss, a Bavarian immigrant, made the first pair of jeans. [3]~~Bavaria was a state in the~~

~~southeastern part of Germany.~~ [4]Strauss used a tough, brown canvas_∧. [5]He sold his durable
                                                    Detail A

work pants, called Levi's, to gold miners. [6]~~Gold was discovered at Sutter's Mill in 1848.~~
                           Details C and D
[7]Soon Strauss switched to denim_∧ ~~(the word *denim* comes from the French *de Nimes*).~~

Details

A. ~~The rough, brown canvas was~~ originally meant for the tops of covered wagons.
B. Thousands of miners rushed to California to hunt for gold.
C. Denim originally was a heavy cotton cloth imported from Nimes, France.
D. Strauss dyed the denim indigo blue.

EXERCISE 3 Improving Unity and Adding Details

Work with a partner or small group to revise the following paragraph. Cross out any
words or sentences that damage the paragraph's unity because they move away from
the main idea. Then from the list at the top of page 25, select the details that you think
would improve the paragraph. (Some of the details can be inserted as phrases and
clauses.) Write the letter of the detail where you think it belongs in the paragraph. Then
write your revised paragraph on a separate piece of paper.

[1]Several theories have been advanced to explain the disappearance of dinosaurs from

Earth. [2]The current favorite theory is that a gigantic asteroid struck Earth approximately

65 million years ago. [3]The impact created billions of tons of smoke, dust, and debris in
                    Detail A
Earth's atmosphere. _∧[4]Plants died, then plant-eating dinosaurs, then the dinosaurs that fed

on the plant-eating dinosaurs. [5]~~By examining the anatomy of dinosaur fossils, scientists~~

~~can decide whether dinosaurs ate plants or animals or both.~~ [6]~~Tyrannosaurus rex, a~~

~~a widely-studied dinosaur, was a flesh-eating dinosaur.~~ [7]There are other theories, too.
                                                          Detail C
[8]Some speculate that dinosaurs became extinct because of climate changes. _∧[9]Other

scientists think they may have been wiped out by a dinosaur disease; still others believe

that mammals might have wiped out all dinosaurs by eating their eggs.

Details

A. The pollution in the atmosphere may have kept sunlight from reaching Earth for six months to a year.

B. Tyrannosaurus rex is also the most easily recognized dinosaur.

C. The climate changes, with extremes of heat and cold, would have been more than the dinosaurs could handle.

EXERCISE 4 Writing a Paragraph from Notes

On a separate piece of paper, write a unified, well-developed paragraph based on the information in the note card below. You do not need to use all of the information. Begin your paragraph with a topic sentence. Students' paragraphs will vary.

American Sign Language (known as ASL)

Used by deaf and hearing-impaired people

Based on gestures (hand movements), facial expressions, and body movements to represent ideas (concepts)

Examples of ASL signs:

"not"—move thumb forward under chin

"school"—hands held horizontally in front of body; clap hands twice, left palm up

"happy"—with one hand, pat chest several times, using upward motion

"know"—with right hand, tap upper right forehead with four fingers (not thumb) held flat

ASL also uses finger spelling: manual alphabet with different finger/hand positions or gestures for each letter

---

EXERCISE 5 Elaborating on a Topic Sentence

Write a paragraph using one of the topic sentences below or one of your own. Support the topic sentence you choose with quotations, anecdotes, examples, or any other details. Reread your paragraph to eliminate any details that do not support the topic sentence.
Students' paragraphs will vary. Use the assessment rubrics in the teacher pages to evaluate student writing.

A. Being a good shopper means watching out for good bargains.

B. The best way to learn about music is to listen to it often.

C. The real heroes in life are those people for whom simple things are difficult.

Organization and Coherence

▏▏▶ Each of your paragraphs should be **coherent**; that is, its sentences should be sensibly **organized** so that your reader can follow your thoughts easily.

STRATEGIES FOR WRITING COHERENTLY

1. **Be Clear** Express your thoughts simply and directly.

2. **Guide the Reader** Use signposts that show the reader what lies ahead and how thoughts relate to one another. Some signposts are transitional expressions like those on page 27. Others are pronouns and synonyms (words that mean almost the same thing), which refer to terms you have already used. Repeating key words or terms also improves coherence.

3. **Put Your Thoughts in Order** Arrange information so that "first things come first."

The following list includes four common ways of organizing paragraphs and essays. Unless you have a good reason not to do so, choose one of these orders as a framework.

- **Chronological Order** Organizing your writing chronologically means telling about events in the order in which they occurred. Use chronological order for narrative paragraphs, which may tell a true story or a fictional one; for writing about a historical event; and for describing steps in a process.

- **Spatial Order** Organize your paragraph spatially when you want to describe a person, an animal, a place, or an object. Include details in an orderly way; move from left to right, top to bottom, near to far, or inside to outside.

- **Order of Importance** Organize your writing by degree of importance when trying to persuade your audience. State the least important reasons and other details first, and end with the most important ones—or the reverse.

- **Logical Order** Organize your paragraph logically to give information in the order a reader needs to know it. Usually, logic determines which details you group together or where you provide background information or definitions of terms.

The revisions in the following model show how one writer improved organization and coherence in response to a writing partner's notes in the margin.

Writing Model

[1]Here's how to throw a boomerang so that it returns to you.

First,

Add transition. [2]Hold the boomerang vertically, not horizontally. ~~The boomerang's~~ *Because*

Move and make into a complex sentence. ~~wings are unequal.~~ *Then it* Throw ~~the boomerang into the air~~ with a quick

snap of the wrist. [5]A right-handed boomerang will lean a little ~~bit of~~

Add transition. ~~the way~~ to the left. *and* [6]~~It will~~ start to fly in ~~the shape of~~ a big circle.

[7]A boomerang keeps leaning to one side more and more as it flies ~~in~~

until gradually it becomes

Eliminate wordiness. ~~the air.~~ [8]~~It will change its position relative to the earth.~~ [9]~~It will~~

rotors

Use precise noun. ~~become~~ horizontal like the blades on ~~the top of~~ a helicopter. [10]If you

correctly,

Eliminate wordiness. have thrown the boomerang ~~in just the right kind of way,~~ it will

return ~~and come back~~ to you.

Some Common Transitional Words and Expressions

To show **time**		To show **examples**		To show **order of importance**		To **compare**	
after	first	for example	namely	above all	second	also	as
afterward	immediately	for instance	that is	finally	then	and	similarly
at last	later	in addition		first	lastly	like	too
before	soon	in other words		most importantly		likewise	
during	then						
finally	when	To **summarize**		To show **cause and effect**		To **contrast**	
		all in all	finally			although	but
To show **position**		as a result	therefore	as a result	since	however	still
above	inside	in conclusion		because	so	in contrast (to)	yet
across	into	in summary		consequently	so that	nevertheless	
among	off			if . . . then	therefore	on the other hand	
behind	outside	To **emphasize**		for that reason			
below	there	for this reason	again				
between	through	moreover	in fact				
in front of	under	most important					

Exercise 6 Revising a Paragraph for Organization and Coherence

Work with a partner or small group to improve the organization and coherence of the following paragraph. Try adding transitional words and expressions, reordering information, and combining sentences. Make any other changes you think will improve the paragraph. Write your revised paragraph on a separate piece of paper.

¹In 1810 Mary Ann Anning was eleven years old. ²She and her brother collected fossil seashells. ³They sold the seashells to make money. ⁴Their mother was a widow. ⁵They needed the money they made from selling seashell fossils to support themselves. ⁶Mary Ann uncovered huge bones in the chalk of a cliff *in Lyme Regis in southwestern England.* ⁷The bones were four flippers, tail, head, backbone, ribs, and teeth *of an extinct dinosaur.* ⁸Have you heard the tongue twister "She sells seashells down by the seashore?" ⁹It is supposed to be about Mary Ann Anning. ¹⁰Paleontologists came to see Mary Ann's discovery. ¹¹Mary Ann discovered the fossilized bones of an extinct dinosaur. ¹²*They* The paleontologists named the extinct dinosaur *whose bones she* discovered Ichthyosaurus *, which means "fish lizard."* ¹³Mary Ann found it on the beach in Lyme Regis in southwestern England. ¹⁴Ichthyosaurus means "fish lizard."

Exercise 7 Writing a Paragraph from Notes

Write an organized, unified paragraph based on the following note card. Include a topic sentence. Students' paragraphs will vary. Use the assessment rubrics in the teacher pages to evaluate students' writing.

> *Langston Hughes (1902–1967)—African American poet. Called Poet Laureate of Harlem.*
>
> *How Hughes was "discovered": working as busboy in Washington, D.C., hotel. Vachel Lindsay, a white poet, staying there. Hughes put 3 poems beside Lindsay's plate.*
>
> *"The next morning on my way to work, as usual I bought a paper—and there I read that Vachel Lindsay had discovered a Negro busboy poet! At the hotel the reporters were already waiting for me." (autobiography The Big Sea, 1940)*
>
> *1st book of poems, The Weary Blues (1926)*

Types of Paragraphs

Your writing varies not only because of its content but also because of its purpose. In this lesson, you will study four different purposes for writing paragraphs and essays.

DESCRIPTIVE

When your purpose is to describe a person, a place, an object, or an animal, use the following suggestions.

- Use **sensory details** to appeal to the reader's five senses (sight, hearing, smell, touch, and taste) and to create a **main impression,** or **mood**.

- Use **spatial order** to present the sensory details from left to right, top to bottom, or closest to farthest.

Writing Model

¹From a safe distance, I measured the crocodile with my eye. ²It was longer than three average basketball players laid out head to foot in a straight line. ³It lay flat on its belly in the dusty pen, open mouthed. ⁴Dozens of pointed teeth edged the huge jaws. ⁵I could see two nostrils toward the base of its narrow snout and two glittering eyes set in bumps on its flat head. ⁶Large scales of varying size covered its whole body except for what looked like sharp, black claws on the powerful, short legs. ⁷Like armor, rows of spikes lined its back down to the end of its powerful tail. ⁸Even at rest, the crocodile seemed dangerous and armed.

Context—writer's position and setting

Spatial order: head first

Sight detail

Touch details
Spatial order: tail last
Main impression

NARRATIVE

When your purpose is to tell a story—either a fictional story or a true narrative—or to explain the steps in a process, use the following suggestions. See Lesson 4.1: Narrative Writing: Autobiographical Incident.

- Break the story or process into its most critical events or steps.

- Use **chronological order** (time order) to relate events in the order they occurred. This is also a useful order for explaining a step-by-step process.

WRITING HINT

Writers sometimes use a one-sentence paragraph for emphasis. When the surrounding paragraphs are longer, a single-sentence paragraph packs a punch.

Writing Model

Event A — ¹Through the night, emergency workers piled sandbags along the river banks, and behind them other workers built emergency dikes. ²But nothing could stop the Red River at Grand Forks, North

Event B — Dakota. ³On April 18, the river crested, rushing over sandbags and dikes. ⁴As the waters flooded downtown and residential

Event C — neighborhoods, residents fled, some in motorboats. ⁵The next day, Saturday, all of Grand Forks's 50,000 residents were ordered to leave.

Event D — ⁶As they left, a second disaster struck: an electrical fire downtown. ⁷With waist-deep water everywhere and fire hydrants underwater, the firefighters couldn't control the blaze.

EXPOSITORY See Lesson 4.3: Expository Writing: Compare and Contrast Essay. There are several ways to explain and to inform: You can compare and contrast; you can discuss cause and effect; you can define, classify, or analyze. When writing exposition, use the following suggestions.

- State your **main idea** as early and as clearly as possible.

- Use facts, examples, quotations, statistics, and definitions as supporting details to develop the main idea.

- Present the details in a **logical order**—in a way that makes sense to the reader. Transitions help your reader follow your thinking.

Writing Model

Main idea
Facts: date, design
— ¹The Vietnam Veterans Memorial in Washington, D.C., has a simple, powerful design. ²But in 1981 when judges chose Maya Lin's V-shaped design from 1,421 entries, controversy erupted. ³For instance, some people complained that the two black intersecting walls were too plain. ⁴There was nothing to see, they said, nothing

Transition
Statistic: number of names
heroic. ⁵Yet in the years since, visitors have often praised two features. ⁶First, on the monument's walls, the names of the 58,156 dead or missing Americans are engraved in chronological order of their death or disappearance; people find this order more emotional than alphabetical order. ⁷Second, they comment positively on Lin's choice of a highly polished black granite for the two long walls. ⁸She

Quotation
wanted, she said, to have visitors, especially veterans, "see their own reflection" in the names.

PERSUASIVE See Lesson 4.2: Persuasive Writing.

When your purpose is either to convince someone that your opinion is right or to persuade someone to take action, use the following suggestions:

- Begin with a sentence that is an **attention grabber**.

- Include an **opinion statement** that clearly expresses your point of view.

- Supply **reasons** and other **evidence** (facts, examples, statistics, anecdotes, quotations) to support your opinion.

- Arrange the supporting details in the **order of importance**—from most to least important, or the reverse.

- Include a **call to action** that tells the reader what to do.

Writing Model

Attention grabber

Statistic

Drastic solutions to make a point

Opinion statement
Call to action

¹Something drastic must be done. ²Fewer than half of the eligible voters actually go to the polls to elect a president, and in local elections, the turnout is abysmal. ³Perhaps the government should issue a tax credit to voters, or perhaps nonvoters should pay a fine. ⁴Maybe nonvoters shouldn't be allowed to get or renew their driver's licenses. ⁵Voting isn't just a privilege that half the citizens can ignore; it's a serious responsibility. ⁶Have you registered to vote yet? ⁷Do it now. ⁸If you are registered, go to the polls every chance you get.

EXERCISE 8 Writing for Different Purposes

Write at least two different types of paragraphs. You may use the suggested topics below or choose a topic of your own. Students' paragraphs will vary. Use the assessment rubrics in the teacher pages to evaluate students' writing.

1. A persuasive paragraph for or against wearing school uniforms or imposing a curfew on teenagers

2. A descriptive paragraph about a favorite place, a piece of clothing, an animal, or a person

3. A narrative paragraph about an accident, a surprise, or an adventure

4. An expository paragraph giving information about your school, your community, an invention, or a sports figure

Writing Essays

▷ All **essays** (pieces of writing on a limited topic) have three things in common: an introduction, a body, and a conclusion.

INTRODUCTION

The beginning paragraph of an essay accomplishes two things: It makes the reader think, "I'd like to continue reading this," and it presents the overall idea of the essay.

The **thesis statement** of an essay is its overall idea. It can also be called a **claim** or a **controlling idea**.

The thesis statement is for the whole essay what the topic sentence is for the paragraph. Each paragraph in the body of your essay should support your thesis statement. For example, the paragraph about blue jeans on page 24 could be part of an essay with the following thesis statement.

> The wardrobe of most Americans consists of three garments with remarkable histories: jeans, T-shirts, and sneakers.

The side column at the left lists some ways to begin an essay. Here's what not to write:

> In this paper, I am going to write about . . .
> This paper is about . . .

BODY

The body of the essay can be several paragraphs long. Here is where you say everything you have to say about your thesis. The following three suggestions will help you draft the body of an essay.

1. **Ideas and Unity** Think of the body as a series of main ideas, each one expressed in the topic sentence of a paragraph and each one supported by relevant details.

2. **Organization and Coherence** Arrange your main ideas logically, in the way that's easiest to follow. Begin with background information, and then move through your main ideas in the way your reader needs to know them. When you outline an essay before you write, you are organizing the ideas for the body.

3. **Word Choice** Avoid repetition, and eliminate wordiness. First ask yourself, "What am I trying to say?" Then say it as clearly as you can.

Some Ways to Begin an Essay

anecdote
vivid image
example
quotation
question
bit of dialogue
interesting statement
or fact

Enriching Your Vocabulary

The English adjective *nocturnal*, as used in Exercise 11, comes from the Latin adjective, *nocturnus*, which means "of, at, or by night." Many animals are *nocturnal* hunters.

For more on outlining see **Composition** Lesson 1.2.

CONCLUSION

When you've said everything that is important about your topic, stop writing. The concluding paragraph has only one job to do: It provides a definite ending. It doesn't have to be long; sometimes even only one or two sentences are sufficient. See the box at the right for some ways to end an essay.

Here's what not to write:

I'm sorry I can't tell you more about ...
That is all I know about ...

Some Ways to End an Essay

- summary of main ideas
- comment on importance of topic
- thought-provoking question
- quotation
- prediction about the future
- call to action

EXERCISE 9 Drafting an Introduction

Assume you have to write a narrative essay based on an autobiographical incident, and you choose to tell about the time you were called to the stage to receive an award. Going up the steps in full view of every student and teacher, you tripped and landed on your face. Draft an introduction that will make your classmates want to read your whole essay. Make up any details that you need.
Encourage students to be creative and to begin with an exciting attention grabber. Students' paragraphs will vary.

EXERCISE 10 Drafting a Conclusion

Draft a concluding paragraph for a persuasive essay about a proposed curfew law for teenagers in your community. (See page 31 for some suggestions on writing persuasively.) In your conclusion, state your opinion and the main reasons for your opinion.
Students' paragraphs will vary.

EXERCISE 11 Writing Body Paragraphs Based on Notes

Use the following notes to write one or more paragraphs for the body of a research paper about bats. Give each paragraph a topic sentence, and support the topic sentence with facts. Your audience should be your high school science class. Students' paragraphs will vary.

Characteristics of bats (background info)

Only mammal that flies **Nocturnal** *(awake at night; sleep by day)*

Use echolocation (a kind of sonar) to navigate in dark and locate food

More than 1,000 species; many endangered

impt: all those species can be classified into only 2 kinds of bats:

(1) larger megabats (called "flying foxes") eat fruit, nectar, pollen; pollinate trees and plants in rain forests

(2) smaller microbats mostly eat insects; live in caves

EXERCISE 12 Revising an Essay

Revise the following brief essay to strengthen the introduction, body, and conclusion. Eliminate sentences that damage the unity of the essay, and reorganize the paragraphs so that information is presented in the most logical order. Make any other changes to improve the essay. Students' revisions will vary. Sample revisions suggested.

[1]~~The main point of this paper is to tell you that~~ stargazing can be ~~pretty~~ easy to start even if you live in a city where there is a lot of light. [2]At no cost to yourself, you can learn about the natural universe from your backyard or rooftop. [3]You'll enjoy fitting the pieces of the night sky together using a simple star map. [4]Even if you live in a place where lights stay on all night, you may have the most access to learning about the stars. [5]~~I learned about the stars from my brother who has a night guard job.~~ [6]~~He watches stars a lot.~~

[7]Look for constellations that are particularly bright such as Orion the Hunter, Cassiopeia's Chair, and The Big Dipper. [8]Next, start identifying the constellations of the zodiac. [9]You'll find that some of them look like their name, such as Taurus the Bull. [10]Others bear no relation to their name, such as Aires the Ram. [11]One of the most rewarding ways to start learning about the stars is to get a copy of a star map from an encyclopedia, from a newspaper, or from a star atlas in your library. [12]A star map will help you locate the most well-known constellations. [13]~~When you go out on a cold night, take warm clothes and a dim light so you can see your map.~~

[14]People who live in cities often feel that only people in the country can get a clear view of the stars. [15]Not true! [16]Cities often have several amateur organizations for observing stars. [17]These groups are filled with people, young and old, who are fascinated by the beauty and mystery of the stars. [18]In addition, cities often have excellent planetariums with weekend and evening programs on the universe, stars, or even the seasons. [19]~~Visiting a planetarium is more interesting than visiting an art museum.~~ [20]On a clear night, the brightest constellations are visible even in the most light-polluted areas in the country. [21]Furthermore, unlike rural areas, most large cities are fantastic centers of sky observing.

[22]That's about all I can tell you about looking at stars. [23]I know that if you start going out on clear nights in a city, or if you ever visit the desert where the air is dry and clear, you will be able to pick out dozens of constellations with very little practice.

Students should rewrite conclusion.

Writing Effective Sentences

Varying Sentence Beginnings

▌▶ For variety, begin some of your sentences with a subordinate clause.

Lesson 7.3 provides practice in beginning sentences with different phrases. Subordinate clauses give you another tool for varying sentence beginnings. Here is the same idea expressed in a number of ways.

ORIGINAL	Giacomo Puccini died in 1924 before he finished the last act of his opera *Turandot*.
PREPOSITIONAL PHRASE	**In 1924,** Giacomo Puccini died before he finished the last act of his opera *Turandot*.
PARTICIPIAL PHRASE	**Not yet finished with the last act of his opera *Turandot*,** Giacomo Puccini died in 1924.
ADVERB CLAUSE	**Before he finished the last act of his opera *Turandot*,** Giacomo Puccini died in 1924.
NOUN CLAUSE	**That Giacomo Puccini died in 1924,** before finishing the last act of his opera *Turandot*, meant that another composer had to finish it.

Too much of anything becomes monotonous, so don't make your sentences all simple or all compound or all complex. An experienced writer, which is what you are becoming, is able to express ideas by using a variety of sentence structures.

EXERCISE 1 Revising Sentence Beginnings

On a separate piece of paper, rewrite each sentence to change the way it begins. You may reword the sentences if necessary.   Answers will vary. Sample revisions given.

1. When Hank Aaron hit 755 home runs during his major league career, he broke Babe Ruth's home-run record.

2. In 1961, Cuban exiles tried to invade Cuba during the Bay of Pigs invasion, but their attempt failed.

3. In 1948, Harry S. Truman won the election despite the fact that newspapers and commentators predicted his defeat.

4. In 1890 at Wounded Knee Creek in South Dakota, army troops killed two hundred Sioux men, women, and children.

5. In 1893, more than twenty years before American women could vote, New Zealand gave women the right to vote.

1. Hank Aaron broke Babe Ruth's home-run record when Aaron hit 755 home runs during his major league career.

2. Cuban exiles tried to invade Cuba during the Bay of Pigs invasion in 1961, but their attempt failed.

3. Harry S. Truman won the election in 1948 despite the fact that newspapers and commentators predicted his defeat.

4. Two hundred Sioux men, women, and children were killed by army troops in 1890 at Wounded Knee Creek in South Dakota.

5. New Zealand gave women the right to vote in 1893, more than twenty years before American women could vote.

EXERCISE 2 Revising a Press Release

Work with a partner or small group to revise the following press release. Your audience is the readers of your local newspaper. In your revision, try to vary some sentence beginnings and structures. Combine sentences, and find other ways to eliminate unnecessary repetition. See teacher pages for revising and editing suggestions.

¹Tarquin is the Shaw High School drama club. ²Tarquin will present *Kiss Me, Kate*. ³*Kiss Me, Kate* will be presented November 6, 7, and 8. ⁴Performances are in the Shaw High School auditorium. ⁵Performances begin at eight o'clock. ⁶Tickets are $8.00. ⁷Jim Austin and Nancy Magnusson play the leading roles. ⁸Jim Austin plays Petruchio, and Nancy Magnusson plays Kate.

⁹*Kiss Me, Kate* is a musical by Cole Porter. ¹⁰It opened in 1948. ¹¹Some popular songs from *Kiss Me, Kate* are "So in Love" and "We Open in Venice." ¹²Cole Porter based *Kiss Me, Kate* on *The Taming of the Shrew*. ¹³*The Taming of the Shrew* is a play by William Shakespeare.

EXERCISE 3 Writing a Paragraph

Use the notes below to write a paragraph on a separate piece of paper. Try to vary your sentence beginnings and structures. See teacher pages for writing assessment suggestions.

> U.S. flag—also called Stars and Stripes, Old Glory
>
> Betsy Ross (seamstress in Philadelphia) sewed & designed first American flag—no proof of this story; a legend?
>
> Congress adopted official flag, June 14, 1777: 13 red/white stripes (1 for ea. colony); 13 stars on blue field—representing a "new constellation"
>
> Flag Day celebrated June 14, anniversary of date
>
> Flag changed many times—new stars added for new states; stripes remain @ 13

See Lesson 2.4 for more on writing an expository paragraph.

Students may wish to extend the exercise by writing a brief report on the American flag. Remind students to save their paragraphs in their writer's notebooks.

Combining Sentences: Compound Subjects and Compound Verbs

The repetition in the following sentences not only wastes space but also sounds boring.

ORIGINAL   Emma is on the All-Star soccer team. Liz is on the All-Star soccer team. Jody is on the All-Star soccer team.

A writer can say the same thing more efficiently and gracefully in a single sentence with a compound subject.

REVISED   Emma, Liz, and Jody are on the All-Star soccer team.

The word *compound* means "two or more of something." Any sentence part can be compound.

▶ A sentence with a **compound subject** has two or more subjects sharing the same verb. Use a conjunction to join the separate subjects.

SEPARATE SUBJECTS   Coal is a fossil fuel. Natural gas is a fossil fuel. Petroleum is a fossil fuel.

COMPOUND SUBJECT   **Coal**, **natural gas**, and **petroleum** are fossil fuels.

SEPARATE SUBJECT   Alaska has large deposits of oil. Texas has large deposits of oil.

COMPOUND SUBJECT   Both **Alaska** and **Texas** have large deposits of oil.

▶ A sentence with a **compound verb** has two or more verbs sharing the same subject. Use a conjunction to join the separate verbs.

SEPARATE VERBS   People can heat their homes with fossil fuels. People can drive their cars with fossil fuels.

COMPOUND VERB   People can not only **heat** their homes but also **drive** their cars with fossil fuels.

SEPARATE VERBS   Many people waste fuel. Many people complain about the high cost of fuel.

COMPOUND VERB   Many people **waste** fuel yet **complain** about the high cost of fuel.

P.S. If you've spoken English all your life, you already know how to combine sentences when you talk. Think of sentence combining as a useful tool to help you vary sentence lengths and create smoother-sounding sentences when you write.

TEST-TAKING TIP

On a standardized test you may see an item in which compound subjects are connected by the correlative conjunctions *neither . . . nor* or *either . . . or*. In such cases, make sure the verb agrees with the subject nearer the verb. See item 1 on page 293 for an example.

Refer to Lessons 13.2 through 13.5 for rules about using commas.

WRITING HINT

Use these conjunctions to create a compound subject or a compound verb.

COORDINATING CONJUNCTIONS
and or but nor yet

CORRELATIVE CONJUNCTIONS
either . . . or
neither . . . nor
not only . . . but also
both . . . and

EXERCISE 4 Combining Sentences

On a separate piece of paper, combine the sentences in each numbered item into a single sentence with a compound subject or a compound verb. In your revised sentences, underline the subject(s) once and the verb(s) twice. Do not underline the conjunction as part of the compound. **Hint:** You may have to drop or change some words as you combine sentences. See Answer Key at www.grammarforwriting.com.

1. Photography developed in the 1820s. Photography became a new art form.

2. The scenes in photographs can be both moving and powerful. The faces in photographs can be both moving and powerful.

3. During the Civil War, Mathew Brady photographed soldiers and battle scenes. Mathew Brady's assistants also photographed soldiers and battle scenes during the Civil War.

4. In 1888, George Eastman's box camera made photography easy for everyone. That year George Eastman's roll film made photography easy for everyone.

5. Margaret Bourke-White photographed Americans during the Great Depression of the 1930s. Walker Evans photographed Americans during the Great Depression of the 1930s. Dorothea Lange photographed Americans during the Great Depression of the 1930s.

EXERCISE 5 Revising a Report

With a partner or small group, improve the following passage from a report. Look for ways to combine sentences, using compound subjects and compound verbs. Compare your revised passage with those of other pairs or groups.

¹In 1955, Edward Steichen created a special photography exhibit. ²Steichen called it *The Family of Man*. ³Photographs from sixty-eight countries appeared in the exhibit. ⁴Quotations from all over the world appeared in the exhibit. ⁵Steichen grouped the photos according to themes. ⁶Steichen hung the photos in the Museum of Modern Art in New York City. ⁷He was curator of photography there. ⁸Children are the subjects in the photos. ⁹Families are the subjects in the photos. ¹⁰Workers are the subjects in the photos. ¹¹The photographs show activities common to all people. ¹²The photographs convey a simple message: We are all part of one family—the human family.

Answers will vary but should show correct use of compound subjects and verbs.

HINT

Not every sentence in the passage needs to be changed.

Combining Sentences: Using Coordinating Conjunctions

▶ You can combine a series of short, related sentences by using the coordinating conjunctions *and, but,* and *or.*

ORIGINAL   Kerri is looking for a summer job. Jeff is looking for a summer job. I am looking for a summer job.

COMBINED   Kerri, Jeff, **and** I are looking for summer jobs.

When you combine related sentences, some words will drop out, and some may change. For example, in the combined sentence above, the verb has changed from the singular (*is looking* and *am looking*) to the plural form (*are looking*). Notice also that commas come after the names *Kerri* and *Jeff* because they are part of a series. (For more about commas in a series, see Lesson 13.2.) Here are some more examples:

ORIGINAL   Summer jobs give students the chance to earn money. A summer job also gives them the opportunity to gain work experience.

COMBINED   Summer jobs give students the opportunity to earn money **and** gain work experience.

ORIGINAL   Money from a paycheck can be saved for a long-term goal. The long-term goal might be college. The long-term goal might be a car.

COMBINED   Money from a paycheck can be saved for a long-term goal, such as college **or** a car.

EXERCISE 6 Using Coordinating Conjunctions

Combine the sentences in each numbered item by using a coordinating conjunction (*and, but,* or *or*). Combined sentences should eliminate repetition.

1. Most high school students want summer jobs. Most high school students have trouble finding them.

2. Job applicants should be on time for an interview. Job applicants should dress neatly. Job applicants should answer questions truthfully.

3. Teens want to work to help their families. They want to work to buy clothes. They want to work to buy cars.

4. When the summer ends, many teenagers continue to work weekends. Many teenagers continue to work after school.

5. Some nonprofit agencies help students fill out applications. Some nonprofit agencies help students look for jobs.

Eliminating wordiness is part of the revising process. See Lesson 3.7.

EXERCISE 7 Revising a Paragraph

With a partner or small group, make any changes you think will improve Wilma's flyer, below, which she will hang in her local grocery store. Look for opportunities to combine sentences. Compare your revision with those of other pairs or groups.

Babysitting Jobs Wanted

[1]Do you need a babysitter during the week? [2]Do you need a babysitter on the weekend? [3]I will take your child to the library. [4]I will take your child to the playground. [5]I will take your child to the park. [6]If it rains, we will read books. [7]We will paint. [8]We will draw. [9]We will sing songs. [10]I am very experienced. [11]I am very reliable. [12]I have many satisfied customers. [13]You can ask the parents. [14]You can ask the children. [15]Please call me during the day. [16]You can call me in the evening. [17]My number is 555-7809. [18]You can also reach me at 555-7728. [19]My e-mail address is wilmaj@cosmic.com.

Wilma Jeffers

Check that coordinating conjunctions are used correctly. Students may wish to use this as a model to write their own flyers.

EXERCISE 8 Writing a Paragraph

Using the notes below write a paragraph describing the summer jobs of Dino and his friends. You don't have to use all of the information. You can add new details and change wording. Write in complete sentences. As you write, see if you can combine related ideas by using coordinating conjunctions.

> *Dino—dog-walking business; $3 a day per dog; walk three times a day*
>
> *Maria, Shira—pet vacation care (walking & feeding): dogs, cats, birds, other creatures*
>
> *Sam, Harriet, Adam—gardening: planting, weeding, cutting grass*
>
> *Annie—swimming lessons to adults; swimming lessons to children; Red Cross certification as lifesaver & swimming instructor; 2 years' experience at day camp*

HiNT

You will have to drop repeated words, and you may also have to add commas for a series of three or more.

Paragraphs will vary. Extend this exercise by asking students to write a paragraph describing their summer or year-round jobs.

Combining Sentences: Inserting Phrases

Besides combining sentences using compound subjects and verbs and compound sentences (see Lessons 3.2 and 8.5), writers combine sentences with phrases.

▶ Combine related sentences by inserting a phrase from one sentence into another sentence. Sometimes the phrase you move from one sentence to another requires a slight change. Sometimes you can just pick up a phrase from one sentence and drop it into another. Usually there is more than one way to combine two sentences.

ORIGINAL   Danny was practicing his trumpet. He hit a wrong note.

COMBINED   **Practicing his trumpet,** Danny hit a wrong note.
    [participial phrase]

ORIGINAL   John set up his tent. He set up his tent near a pile of rocks. The rocks were on the beach.

COMBINED   John set up his tent **near a pile of rocks on the beach.**
    [prepositional phrases]

ORIGINAL   Mia has a goal tonight. She wants to finish her first draft.

COMBINED   **Finishing her first draft** is Mia's goal tonight.
    [gerund phrase]

COMBINED   **To finish her first draft** is Mia's goal tonight.
    [infinitive phrase]

EXERCISE 9 Combining Sentences

On a separate piece of paper use phrases to combine the sentences in each numbered item. Don't forget to add commas where they belong.

EXAMPLE   Many college students receive letters. The letters urge them to apply for credit cards. The credit cards are already approved.
    Many college students receive letters urging them to apply for already approved credit cards.
    Answers will vary. Sample answers given.

1. Credit-card companies charge very high interest. The interest is charged on all unpaid balances. Credit-card companies charge very high interest on all unpaid balances.

2. Every month the finance charge increases the debt. The debt increases even with no new purchases. Every month the finance charge increases the debt even with no new purchases.

3. A thirty-year-old woman is struggling. She is named Carol. She struggles to pay her $16,000 credit-card bill.
A thirty-year-old woman named Carol is struggling to pay her $16,000 credit-card bill.

4. Carol wishes she had never used a credit card. Carol works two jobs. She works hard to pay off her debt. [**Hint:** Use an introductory participial phrase.]
Wishing she had never used a credit card, Carol works hard at two jobs to pay off her debt.

5. It will take her five years. By then, she will pay off her debt. The debt is overwhelming. It will take her five years to pay off her overwhelming debt.

6. The average debt for young people is $2,400. The young people are in their twenties. The average debt for young people in their twenties is $2,400.

7. They pay $75 a month. At that rate, it will take three and a half years to pay off the debt. At the rate of $75 a month, it will take three and a half years to pay off the debt.

8. Experts advise these young people. They say young people should not incur more debt. They should destroy their credit cards. Experts advise these young people not to incur more debt and to destroy their credit cards.

HiNT There is more than one way to combine most of these sentences.

EXERCISE 10 Writing Paragraphs — Working Together

Use the information in the charts and graph below to write one or more paragraphs about credit-card debt. Exchange papers with a partner, and make suggestions for improving each other's paragraphs. Try combining related sentences by inserting phrases. See teacher pages for assessment rubrics.

Consumer Credit Counseling Services

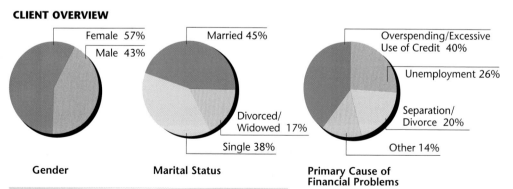

AVERAGE DEBT ON MAJOR CREDIT CARDS

Legend: 1990, 1996

Age group	1990	1996
All ages	$1,236	$2,512
20–29	$885	$2,399
30–39	$1,383	$2,855
40–49	$1,444	$2,968
50–59	$1,479	$2,718
60+	$880	$1,546

CLIENT OVERVIEW

Gender: Female 57%, Male 43%

Marital Status: Married 45%, Divorced/Widowed 17%, Single 38%

Primary Cause of Financial Problems: Overspending/Excessive Use of Credit 40%, Unemployment 26%, Separation/Divorce 20%, Other 14%

Typical Client Age: 34 Monthly gross income: $2,600
Average debt: $15,100 Average number of creditors: 8.4

Source: Claritas, Inc.

Combining Sentences: Using Subordinate Clauses

||||▶ You can combine two sentences by turning one sentence into an adjective clause.

Begin the adjective clause with *who, which, that,* or another word from the list on page 147. Then insert the adjective clause to modify a noun or pronoun in the remaining sentence. Don't forget the commas to set off nonessential adjective clauses.

ORIGINAL   Jack won first prize in the art contest. Jack is Peggy's brother.

COMBINED   Jack, **who is Peggy's brother**, won first prize in the art contest.

COMBINED   Jack, **who won first prize in the art contest**, is Peggy's brother.

ORIGINAL   He won it for an oil self-portrait. He painted his self-portrait in art class.

COMBINED   He won it for an oil self-portrait, **which he painted in art class**.

||||▶ You can combine two sentences by turning one sentence into an adverb clause.

Use a subordinating conjunction to create an adverb clause out of one sentence. Then attach the adverb clause to the remaining sentence. Choose a subordinating conjunction that shows how the ideas in the two sentences are related. For example, *because* and *since* show a cause-effect relationship; *while, when, whenever, before, after,* and *until* show a time relationship; and *although, however,* and *but* show contrast.

ORIGINAL   The blizzard dumped thirty inches of snow on the city. Schools will be closed tomorrow.

COMBINED   Schools will be closed tomorrow **because the blizzard dumped thirty inches of snow on the city**.

ORIGINAL   A few main streets are plowed. Schools and businesses will remain closed.

COMBINED   **Although a few main streets are plowed**, schools and businesses will remain closed.

> Transition words are critical for essays written in chronological or step-by-step order.
> See **Composition** Lesson 4.3 for more on using transition words.

EXERCISE 11 Sentences with Adjective Clauses

Work with a partner to combine each pair of sentences into a single sentence by changing the second sentence into an adjective clause. An introductory word is suggested in parentheses. Write your responses on a separate piece of paper and underline the adjective clause. **Remember:** Set off nonessential adjective clauses with commas. See Answer Key at www.grammarforwriting.com.

EXAMPLE   The Zuni are known for their jewelry. The Zuni are a Pueblo people. (who)
The Zuni, who are a Pueblo people, are known for their jewelry.

1. Blood plasma is a colorless liquid. Blood plasma contains red blood cells, white blood cells, and blood platelets. (which)

2. George Washington Carver developed hundreds of uses for the peanut. He was a chemist and a botanist. (who)

3. Mary Cassatt is an American Impressionist painter. Mary Cassatt's paintings often portray mothers with children. (whose)

4. In 1947 an observer coined the term flying saucer. The observer saw strange objects in the sky near Mt. Rainier. (who)

5. Nitrogen is a chemical element. Nitrogen makes up almost 80 percent of Earth's atmosphere. (which)

EXERCISE 12 SENTENCES WITH ADVERB CLAUSES

Combine each pair of sentences into a single sentence with an adverb clause. Use the subordinating conjunction suggested in parentheses—or one of your choice. Write your responses on a separate piece of paper, and underline the adverb clause. See Answer Key at www.grammarforwriting.com.

EXAMPLE   Germans rejoiced. The Berlin Wall came down in 1989. (when)
Germans rejoiced when the Berlin Wall came down in 1989.

1. The Beast turns into a handsome prince. Beauty agrees to marry him. (when)

2. Don Quixote attacks a windmill. He thinks it is a giant. (because)

3. Dorothy clicks her ruby-red shoes together. She finds herself back in Kansas. (as soon as)

4. According to Aesop's fable, the ever-plodding tortoise won the race. The sleeping hare could run much faster. (even though)

5. The giant chased Jack down the beanstalk. Jack stole the goose that laid golden eggs. (after)

Eliminating Short, Choppy Sentences

Effective writers can come up with alternatives to a long series of short, choppy sentences. They combine sentences by inserting key words from one sentence into another sentence.

ORIGINAL   The trees swayed in the wind. The trees were palms. The trees swayed wildly. The wind was fierce.

COMBINED   The **palm** trees swayed **wildly** in the **fierce** wind.

The combined sentence sounds smoother because it avoids unnecessary repetition. Notice that the single words inserted into the sentence work as modifiers—adjectives and adverbs.

ORIGINAL   A museum opened in Rapid City, South Dakota. The museum is new. It opened recently.

COMBINED   A **new** museum opened **recently** in Rapid City, South Dakota.

Sometimes the key words change form when you combine sentences (in the first example above, *palms* becomes *palm*).

ORIGINAL   The museum combines stories about the Black Hills with exhibits. The exhibits are by geologists. The stories belong to the Lakota Indians.

COMBINED   The museum combines **Lakota Indian** stories about the Black Hills with **geological** exhibits.

ORIGINAL   Mt. Rushmore is part of the Black Hills. The Black Hills are mountains.

COMBINED   Mt. Rushmore is part of the **mountainous** Black Hills.

STEP BY STEP

Combining Sentences

To combine a series of short sentences:

1. Find the sentence that gives the most information.

2. In the other sentences, look for single words that can be picked up and inserted into the sentence you picked in Step 1.

3. Insert the single words where they make sense. You may need to change the word forms.

4. Re-read the combined sentence to see if it sounds natural.

EXERCISE 13 Combining Sentences

With a partner, on a separate piece of paper combine the following groups of sentences into single sentences. You may have to drop some words and change the form of others. For the last two numbered items, follow the hints in parentheses. Compare your combined sentences with those of other pairs.

EXAMPLE Frank Lloyd Wright was an architect. He was famous. He was born in America.
Frank Lloyd Wright was a famous American architect.

> Combined sentences should not omit any information from the given sentences.

1. Mercury is an element used in dental fillings. The element is metallic.

2. The novelist Mary Renault wrote about Greece. The Greece she wrote about is ancient. Mary Renault was English.

3. Pierre-Auguste Renoir was a painter known for his style. Renoir was French. His style was colorful.

4. James Naismith invented basketball in 1891 as a sport. The sport was played indoors. (Change *indoors* to an adjective form.)

5. Romans founded London in A.D. 43 as a city. The Romans were ancient. The city had walls. (Change *walls* to an adjective form with an *-ed* ending.)

EXERCISE 14 Revising a Paragraph

With a partner, improve the following paragraph. Look for opportunities to combine sentences. Compare your revised paragraph with those of other pairs.

[1]"Share a Smile Becky" is a friend of Barbie's. [2]Like all Barbie dolls, Becky has outfits. [3]Her outfits are many and different. [4]She is an 11½-inch blond. [5]Her blond hair is a strawberry color. [6]What's important about Becky is her wheelchair. [7]That's really important. [8]Becky's wheelchair is hot pink. [9]Becky's legs have joints so she can sit. [10]The joints are bendable. [11]The company that produces the toys tries to acknowledge children with disabilities. [12]Other companies produce toy buses and schoolhouses with ramps. [13]The ramps are for wheelchairs. [14]Kids play with the toys. [15]Kids learn about disabilities. [16]Some kids have their own physical disabilities. [17]Some kids do not have physical disabilities. [18]Kids who play with Becky might understand disabilities better. [19]The company hopes that Becky will help.

Paragraphs will vary. Look for sentence variety and correct grammar.

Eliminating Wordiness

Here are techniques for writing what you mean as clearly as possible.

▶ **Get Rid of Padding and Unnecessary Repetition**. Don't say the same thing twice, using different words, in the same sentence. When you revise, look for unnecessary words and get rid of them.

ORIGINAL   In my opinion, I think that having all students who are in ninth grade take a class in debate should be a requirement.

REVISED   I think debate class should be required for all ninth-graders.

REVISED   Debate class should be required for all ninth-graders.

▶ **Write in Your Own Voice**. Don't try to impress your reader with difficult vocabulary words and complicated sentences. Say what you mean simply and directly.

ORIGINAL   The practice of acquiring skills in how to debate and in presenting arguments aids and encourages students in their development of logical skills in thinking.

REVISED   Debating helps develop logical thinking.

<table>
<tr><td>

WRITING HINT

When you write an essay, you may sometimes restate your main idea or main points in a concluding paragraph. Repetition there is fine. In general, though, avoid repeating or restating the same idea in sentences that follow each other. That's padding.

</td></tr>
</table>

EXERCISE 15 Revising Sentences

On a separate piece of paper, revise the following wordy sentences.
Answers will vary. Sample answers given.

1. Those who are debaters embark on a learning experience in supporting their opinions and what they think about the issues.
   Debaters learn to express their opinions clearly.

2. They mention and cite factual evidence with facts and examples to back up and support their ideas and main points. They support their ideas by citing facts and examples.

3. In addition, debaters also acquire the development of the skill and the ability to argue both sides and positions of any issue that they debate.
   Debaters also develop the ability to argue both sides of an issue.

4. Frequently, debaters often discover and come to see that there are no easy, simple solutions to complex problems that are complicated.
   Debaters often discover that there are no simple solutions to complex problems.

5. By reading recent newspapers and magazines, debaters gather evidence about the issues being debated and discussed through their reading of current periodicals, including magazine articles and newspaper articles.
   By reading newspapers and magazines, debaters gather evidence about current issues.

6. It is good form for people who are participants in a debate, any debate, to listen intently, carefully, and respectfully to the arguments presented by all of their opponents, whether they agree with the points made or not.

7. It is an effective strategy for debaters to begin their turn at the podium with a clear, easy-to-understand, simple-to-grasp and forceful presentation of the meat, the marrow, of their argument.

8. Many, perhaps most, or perhaps even all debaters believe that a strong and effective way to conclude their argument is with an aggravating or disturbing remark or two.

9. Although what I believe should win a debate, I think, is the strength and soundness of one's argument, it is nonetheless true, unfortunately, that often times a loud, clear voice, effective and persuasive mannerisms, or a winning smile or personality can strongly influence the responses and reactions of listeners or judges.

10. At one time in our history debates were a popular and well-attended form of entertainment; people of all ages flocked to listen to talented debaters craft thoughtful arguments much as we today fill stadiums and arenas for rock concerts, operas, music festivals, and sporting events, such as baseball, basketball, and football games.

EXERCISE 16 Revising a Paragraph to Eliminate Wordiness

On a separate piece of paper, revise the paragraph below to trim wordy expressions and make the writing as clear as possible. Revised paragraphs will vary.

[1]Do you know any person, such as a friend, colleague, teacher, or anyone else, who tells the same jokes and stories over and over again? [2]Well, I do. [3]My friend Alex here is in the habit of telling the same tired, overused, old joke or boring, tedious, tiresome story whenever he meets someone whom he thinks hasn't heard it. [4]And it seems as if he always waits until I'm standing there to do this, so that I'm right there. [5]"Alex," I want to say, "I've heard that one again and again and again, and it wasn't all that hilarious and funny the other times that you told it before." [6]Wouldn't I just love to pull out a list of his one-liners, witticisms, quips, or wisecracks, and point to the joke that he just told on the list, and bring it to his attention so that he sees in writing that he's told it before! [7]But I'm afraid that I never would do that to my friend Alex. [8]After all, what I want to say is that I think that occasionally some of his jokes are actually quite funny and, once in a while, he does come up with a new one or two or three. [9]By the way, have you heard the one about the duck who . . .

6. It is good form for participants in a debate, no matter what their viewpoints are, to listen intently and respectfully to the arguments presented by their opponents.

7. It is an effective strategy for debaters to begin their turn at the podium with a clear and forceful presentation of the essence of their argument.

8. Many debaters believe that an effective way to conclude their argument is with a provocative remark or two.

9. Although the strength and soundness of one's argument is what should win a debate, it is true that often times a loud, clear voice, effective mannerisms, or a winning personality can strongly influence the outcome.

10. At one time in our history debates were a popular form of entertainment; people flocked to listen to talented debaters craft thoughtful arguments much as we today fill stadiums and arenas for music and sporting events.

Revising and Editing Worksheet

Improve the following draft by revising for ideas, organization, word choice, and sentence variety. After revising, edit the draft for errors in spelling, capitalization, punctuation, and usage. Write your revised and edited version on a separate piece of paper. Compare your changes with those of a writing partner.

Revisions will vary.

[1]How many times have you been asked whether you wanted your sandwich bread toasted? [2]How often have you been asked whether you wanted toast with your eggs? [3]Today, when we think of toast, we think of its delicious taste. [4]Sometimes we think of its crunchy texture. [5]We most likely order it for those reasons. [6]But this way to think of toast is a relatively modern one. [7]The Egyptians began baking bread nearly 5,000 years ago. [8]They toasted it not to make it taste better. [9]They toasted it to preserve it. [10]They preserved it by removing the moisture.

[11]Egyptians parched their bread by skewering it on a prong. [12]They suspended the prong over a fire. [13]That was the standard toasting practice for centuries. [14]Even in colonial America a few hundred years ago, what people called a "toaster" was really nothing new. [15]It was simply a pair of linked long-handled forks used to hold bread over a fire. [16]Then, in the nineteenth century, a revolution in toasting occurred, in the form of the toaster oven. [17]It was a wire and tin cage. [18]It was designed to sit on the opening of a coal stove. [19]It held four slices of bread. [20]The bread had to be watched diligently. [21]One side was darkened by the fire. [22]Then the bread had to be turned over.

[23]Electricity arrived at the end of the century. [24]The days of flipping bread ended forever. [25]By the early 1900s, skeletal wire structures made their appearance. [26]But people still had to pay attention to the toasting process. [27]That is because the bread placed within the apparatus did not pop up to announce itself toasted. [28]But people no longer needed to fire up the whole stove in order to simply enjoy a slice of buttered toast.

[29]By the 1920s, pop-up toasters with timers came onto the scene. [30]Toasters were the rage and they were here to stay. [31]People wanted them not only in their kitchens. [32]People also wanted them in every room of the house.

Writing Workshops

Narrative Writing: Autobiographical Incident

Everyone has stories to tell. When you write about an autobiographical incident, you tell a true story about something that happened to you.

In his memoir *Days of Grace*, tennis great Arthur Ashe recalls two incidents and what they meant to him. As you read, think about how each incident relates to what Ashe says about character.

Character
from *Days of Grace* by Arthur Ashe

Ashe comments on the incidents he will present.

[1]What others think of me is important, and what I think of others is important. [2]What else do I have to go by? [3]Of course, I cannot make decisions based solely on what other people would think. [4]There are moments when the individual must stand alone. [5]Nevertheless, it is crucial to me that people think of me as honest and principled. [6]In turn, to ensure that they do, I must always act in an honest and principled fashion, no matter the cost.

Presents first incident and its setting

[7]One day, in Dallas, Texas, in 1973, I was playing in the singles final of a World Championship Tennis (WCT) tournament. [8]My opponent was Stan Smith, a brilliant tennis player but an even more impressive human being in his integrity. [9]On one crucial point, I watched Smith storm forward, racing to intercept a ball about to bounce a second time on his side of the net.

Introduces conflict

[10]When the point was over, I was sure the ball had bounced twice before he hit it and that the point was mine. [11]Smith said he had reached the ball in time. [12]The umpire was baffled. [13]The crowd was buzzing.

[14]I called Smith up to the net.

Quotes dialogue

[15]"Stan, did you get to that ball?"

[16]"I did. I got it."

[17]I conceded the point. [18]Later, after the match—which I lost—a reporter approached me. [19]Was I so naive? [20]How could I have taken Smith's word on such an important point?

[21]"Believe me," I assured him, "I am not a fool. [22]I wouldn't take just anybody's word for it. [23]But if Stan Smith says he got to the ball, he got to it. [24]I trust his character."

Presents second incident and its setting

[25]When I was not quite eighteen years old, I played a tournament in Wheeling, West Virginia, the Middle Atlantic Junior Championships. [26]As happened much of the time when I was growing up, I was the only black kid in the tournament, at least in the under-eighteen age section. [27]One night, some of the other kids trashed a cabin; they absolutely destroyed it.

Introduces
conflict

[28And then they decided to say that I was responsible, although I had nothing to do with it. 29The incident even got into the papers. 30As much as I denied and protested, those white boys would not change their story.

States feeling

31I rode to Washington from West Virginia with the parents of Dickie Dell, another one of the players. 32They tried to reassure me, but it was an uncomfortable ride because I was silently worrying about what my father would do and say to me. 33When I reached Washington where I was to play in another tournament, I telephoned him in Richmond. 34As I was aware, he already knew about the incident. 35When he spoke, he was grim. 36But he had one question only.

Quotes more
dialogue

[37"Arthur Junior, all I want to know is, were you mixed up in that mess?"

38"No, Daddy, I wasn't."

39He never asked about it again. 40He trusted me. 41With my father, my reputation was solid.

Comments
after
presenting
incidents

42I have tried to live so that people would trust my character, as I had trusted Stan Smith's. 43Sometimes I think it is almost a weakness in me, but I want to be seen as fair and honest, trustworthy, kind, calm, and polite. 44I want no stain on my character, no blemish on my reputation.

Critical Thinking   After you read the autobiographical incident, answer the questions below. Use the following questions to lead a class discussion.

1. Suppose you had a chance to talk with Ashe about his views on character. What would you say to him?

2. How does each incident relate to Ashe's comments on character? Which incident do you think has more impact on the reader? Which do you like better? Why?

3. Imagine that both incidents were reported without dialogue. What does the dialogue add?

4. Choose one of the two incidents that Ashe narrates, and pay close attention to *how* he describes it. Analyze (a) the order and (b) the amount of space given to each of the following: background information, setting, dialogue, and report of what happened. What kinds of details does Ashe omit?

5. With a partner, read aloud one of the accounts of the incidents. Then analyze the sentences for variety in length, structure, and beginnings.

6. Build your vocabulary. Underline the words in the selection that you do not know. Use a dictionary to find their meaning and write a brief definition in the margin or in your notebook. The following list may help: *principled* (sentence 5), *integrity* (sentence 8), *intercept* (sentence 9), *naive* (sentence 19), *blemish* (sentence 44).

Writing Strategies   The purpose of writing an autobiographical incident is to narrate the series of events that made the incident come about. The audience can be any that you choose. For example, you might write for children, for your peers, or for a far-away friend. Use the following strategies to help.

1. **Select an incident.** An incident is a mini-story. It has a plot (what happens), characters, and a setting (when and where the events occur). You are the "I," the narrator, who is telling your story from the first-person point of view.

2. **Watch time order.** An incident doesn't stretch over a long period of time; it happens all at once or in a few hours or (at most) days. Usually, you can break an incident into several, individual events that happen in chronological order, beginning at the beginning and marching straight through to the end.

3. **Ask questions.** Your readers will want to know *Who? What (happened)? Where? When? Why?* and *How?* (These are the *5-W and How?* questions that newspaper reporters answer at the beginning of a news story. For more about these questions, see page 11.) *Why?* and *How?* are complicated, but make sure you answer as many of the other questions as you can, and provide enough background information for the reader to understand the incident.

4. **Answer, "What's the point?"** You remember an incident for a particular reason. Why? Is it an example of something? What does it show or prove? Once you have determined the whole point of the incident, you will be able to comment on what it means to you. Look back at Arthur Ashe's comments. How well do his comments fit the two incidents?

5. **Include your thoughts and feelings.** Try to remember what you thought and felt at the time the incident happened. Then see if you can figure out what you feel and think about the incident now. Include your thoughts and feelings as you write.

6. **Sprinkle with sensory details.** A few sensory details (sights, sounds, smells, tastes, sensations of touch) will help the reader imagine clearly what you remember. Watch out, however, because too much description dulls and delays the story.

7. **Add some dialogue.** No one remembers exactly what was said long ago, but you probably have a general idea. Take a guess at who said what, and add some dialogue. Look back at the narrative "Character" to see how and where Ashe uses dialogue.

EXERCISE 1 Get Started

Use one or two of the prewriting techniques (clustering, writer's notebook, etc.)
discussed on pages 9–11 to jot down some incidents you might write about. You might,
like Ashe, write about "a moment when you stood alone." Or you might try to think of
a "first," for example, a first day on a job, a first date, or a first time driving a car. As
you brainstorm, be sure to include notes on your feelings about the incident.

Remember: (1) The incident must be in some way important to you. (2) You must
remember the incident vividly. (3) It must have taken place in a short time period.
You might want to refer to the teacher pages "Purposes of Writing" for additional information.

EXERCISE 2 Plan Your Autobiographical Incident

Use a **story map** to plan your essay. A story map is a graphic device that you can use
as you gather details when you write a story or when you report an autobiographical
incident. Fill in the right column of the story map below.

Story Map

a. What is the **setting**?	
b. Identify the main **characters**, and describe them briefly.	
c. Identify the **conflict**, and briefly summarize the **plot**.	
d. What are your **feelings** about the incident?	

EXERCISE 3 Draft the Autobiographical Incident

Draft your paper in whatever way feels comfortable to you. Your audience for the incident should be your classmates. Your purpose can be to let them know you better. Like Ashe, you might make a personal comment both before and after the incident(s). Or you might choose to comment only once—either at the beginning or the end. Here are some strategies for drafting the incident.

- **Zero in on what's important**. Ashe probably could have written much more about each incident, but he gets right to the point. His incidents are not bogged down by too much description and detail.

- **Be clear about what the incident means to you**. Ashe says it twice—at the beginning and the end. Summarize your feelings about the incident at least once in your essay.

EXERCISE 4 Revise Your Autobiographical Incident

Try reading your paper aloud to yourself. Work on getting the sentences to read smoothly. Then—or maybe at the same time—focus on your word choice. See if you can find the right words to replace any vague, general nouns and verbs. Go back over your comment(s) and incident(s) to eliminate padding and unnecessary words. When you are satisfied with your paper, share it with a partner and ask for comments, questions, and suggestions.
See "Step-by-Step Revising and Editing" in the teacher pages for more information.

EXERCISE 5 Proofread and Publish

Proofread your revised paper for errors in spelling, punctuation, capitalization, and usage. You might increase its chances of being error-free by exchanging papers with a partner—or several—to see if you've missed anything.

Share your autobiographical incident with friends and family, especially with anyone who was present when the incident happened. If you have enjoyed this assignment, you might write several more incidents and bind them together as a memoir. You might give the bound book to a relative as a gift, or keep it and add to it as the years go by.
Refer to Chapters 13–16 for punctuation, capitalization, and spelling rules. See teacher pages for "Proofreading Checklist."

Persuasive Writing

When you write to **persuade**, you try to make your reader agree with your opinion. You build an argument based on the **logical appeals** of reasons and evidence. You may also add **emotional appeals** to persuade your reader. The persuasive essay below was written by former Senate Majority Leader Bob Dole and former Senator George McGovern. As you read the essay, think about *how* the authors try to persuade you.

Ending Child Hunger
by Bob Dole and George McGovern

[1]When he delivered his Nobel Lecture in 1964, Dr. Martin Luther King Jr. asked, "Why should there be hunger and privation in any land, in any city, at any table when man has the resources and the scientific know-how to provide all mankind with the basic necessities of life?" [2]More than 40 years later, we are still asking the same question in our own country.

> Grabs reader's attention

[3]As we honor Dr. King, it is an important time to think about the hopes and dreams we share for our children. [4]Too many live in poverty and start each school day hungry, which lessens the odds that they will be able to rise above the challenges they face.

> States position

[5]In our nation's public schools, 29 million children participate in the school lunch program each day—17 million from low-income households—while only nine million receive breakfast. [6]Some of these children get breakfast at home, but many do not. [7]They go to school hungry and unable to concentrate, which puts them at a disadvantage to succeed before the day even starts. [8]It's a rarely discussed problem with wide-ranging implications for all Americans, not just our children. [9]Their future is our future.

> Statistic supports position

> States reasons for position

[10]That is why we have joined the new "got breakfast?" campaign as national spokesmen. [11]"Got breakfast?" was launched last month by leaders in the Federal government, nonprofit and private sectors to raise awareness about the problem of child hunger and to promote the adoption of healthy breakfast programs in our nation's school systems.

> Supports position with a proposed solution

[12]The issues of child hunger and school nutrition have occupied a spot at the top of our agendas for all of our public lives. [13]As members of the United States Senate we worked together to write and enact legislation designed to improve nutrition in our nation's schools. [14]We have continued to work together to address these issues since leaving the Senate. [15]The fight is a constant and ongoing battle.

> Restates position

Cites reason for opposition to position

[16]The challenge of feeding millions of children may seem enormous, but there are more solutions available today than ever before to help us eliminate child hunger. [17]Unfortunately, one answer that is sitting right in front of us is not being used to its fullest potential.

Counters opposition with statistic

[18]A brand new report by the Food Research Action Center estimates that states have failed to access more than $382 million in federal funds that could have been used to provide breakfast at school to children in need.

[19]While we have all seen the success of the National School Lunch Program, its companion, the School Breakfast Program has been significantly underutilized. [20]FRAC notes that for every 100 low-income children who eat school lunch every day, only 44 eat a school breakfast. [21]Through the "got breakfast?" campaign, we are seeking to remind school administrators, teachers and parents that the School Breakfast Program is a viable, easily implemented solution to an unnecessary problem.

[22]Developed by Share Our Strength, the Alliance to End Hunger, the School Nutrition Association, the National Dairy Council and Breakfast Breaks, "got breakfast?" demonstrates how the nonprofit and private sectors can join

Call to action

together to achieve a common goal. [23]By working together, we can ensure that our children get the nutritious breakfast they need in order to have a productive, successful day at school—and a productive, successful life ahead.

Restates opinion in conclusion

[24]With greater concern over how to remain competitive in a global marketplace, it is vital that we provide the best possible education and learning environment for the next generation of Americans. [25]Nutrition is a critical building block for realizing this goal. [26]Hungry children cannot learn and an uneducated workforce cannot compete. [27]For these reasons, it is critical that we work together to encourage participation in the School Breakfast Program so that every child can reap the benefits of a healthy breakfast.

Critical Thinking   After you read the persuasive essay, answer the questions below.
Use the following questions to lead a class discussion.

1. Briefly outline how Dole and McGovern try to persuade you that their opinion is right.

2. Who do you think the audience is for this essay?

3. In sentence 16, the authors write "The challenge of feeding millions of children may seem enormous. . . ." Do you think that they address this concern effectively? Why or why not?

4. Reread sentence 23. Explain how the essay supports the authors' argument that "working together" will result in fewer hungry children.

5. What do you think about the following statement from sentence 26: "Hungry children cannot learn and an uneducated workforce cannot compete"?

Writing Strategies   A letter to the editor is brief—perhaps two or three paragraphs long. A persuasive essay, such as the one written by Dole and McGovern, gives you more room to argue your point. For both types of persuasive writing, however, the same strategies apply.

1. **Present a clear opinion, or position statement**. No one should come away from your letter or essay wondering what you think. State your opinion as clearly as you can in a single sentence or two. In a letter to the editor, the opinion statement usually comes at the beginning. In a persuasive essay, the opinion statement (also called a **thesis statement**) often comes in the essay's introduction—but not always. Dole and McGovern's opinion is stated in the first two paragraphs of the essay.

STEP BY STEP

Building Your Argument
Opinion statement
• Reason 1 supported by evidence
• Reason 2 supported by evidence
• Reason 3 supported by evidence

Conclusion or Restatement of Opinion

Call to Action

(You may add emotional appeals, but you should not rely solely on such appeals.)

---

2. **State reasons for your opinion**. A **reason** is a statement that tells why you hold your opinion. Usually, you will need two or three strong and distinctly different reasons to support your opinion.

3. **Support reasons with evidence**. To support your reasons, use a variety of evidence, such as facts or expert opinions.

   • A **fact** is a statement that can be proven. Make sure that you get your facts from reliable reference sources.

   • Use **expert** opinions or quotations. Choose someone who knows a great deal about your topic. Be sure to identify the expert and, if quoting, use that person's exact words.

   • A **definition** is a statement of the meaning of a word or phrase. Definitions are often used for emphasis.

   • **Statistics** are facts expressed in numbers: ". . . 29 million children participate in the school lunch program each day—17 million from low-income households— while only nine million receive breakfast."

   • You know what an **example** is—a particular type or instance used as an illustration. Use examples to support your position.

   • An **anecdote** is an incident that actually happened, one that is often based on the writer's personal experiences or observations.

For more on punctuating quotations, see **Mechanics**, Lesson 14.5.

4. **Support reasons with emotional appeals**. Persuasive writers sometimes appeal to a reader's fears, hopes, wishes, or sense of fairness. **Loaded words**—words carrying either positive or negative connotations—can sway the reader's emotions.

5. **Present and, if possible, demolish counterarguments**. A persuasive writer may acknowledge the opposing point of view and then give reasons and evidence to prove that view wrong.

6. **End with a call to action**. Some persuasive writing ends with a call to action. The writer urges the reader to do something such as write a letter, donate money, vote for a candidate, or buy a product.

EXERCISE 6 Choose a Topic

Work with a small group to brainstorm at least three topics for a persuasive essay or letter to the editor. Use these hints. Students' topics will vary. You may wish to propose one of the topic ideas found in the teacher pages.

• The topics must be arguable, not just a matter of personal taste. They should be something that people disagree about.

• The topics must be something you have a strong opinion about. Be careful! Not every topic is appropriate for school assignments. Check with your teacher if you are unsure about the appropriateness of your topics.

EXERCISE 7 State Your Opinion

1. Discuss these three opinion statements with your writing group. Decide which is the strongest and tell why.

   (a) In my opinion, I think that school breakfast programs are probably a good idea.

   (b) School breakfast programs are a good idea.

   (c) In order to receive federal funding, all schools should provide breakfast programs to children from low-income households.

2. Choose one of the topics you brainstormed in Exercise 6. Try to state your opinion clearly, precisely, and forcefully in one or two sentences. You might draft several different versions of your opinion statement; then choose the best one.

EXERCISE 8 Support Your Opinion

Support the opinion statement that you drafted in Exercise 7. Before you do this, think about your audience so that you can choose the reasons, evidence, and emotional appeals that are suited to your readers. You also should give them the background information that they will need to understand your subject. Use the following hints:

• **Be specific**. Provide specific examples, facts, and numbers from reliable sources. Avoid general expressions, such as "most states" or "many people . . . ." Mention your sources; your audience will be impressed that you've done your research.

• **Stay focused**. Keep your argument tight. Don't waste words or wander.

EXERCISE 9 Draft Your Letter or Essay

Write your first draft. Remember these three elements of effective writing:

• **Provide support**. The more support you give for your opinion, the more persuasive you'll be. Just make sure that everything you say is relevant—to the point.

• **Give cues**. As you follow a brief outline like the one on page 59 called "Building Your Argument," let your readers know where your argument is headed. For example, you might mention the number of reasons you'll give: "I oppose the proposed curfew for three reasons. . . ." Then, as you mention each reason, alert your reader with transitions, such as *First, Second, Third,* and *Finally*.

• **Aim for clarity**. Concentrate on expressing every thought as clearly as you can.

EXERCISE 10 Revise, Edit, and Publish

Revise your essay by adding, deleting, or moving content. Eliminate unnecessary words and sentences, and tighten your argument by dropping anything that doesn't directly support your main point. Edit for errors in spelling, capitalization, punctuation, and usage. Share your paper with a writing group, or use the following publishing suggestions.

• If you've written a letter to the editor, send it to your local paper. Begin it with "To the Editor:" and end it with your name, address, and phone number.

• If you've written a persuasive essay, send it to a government representative or an official who might act on the issue you've discussed.

• Send any kind of persuasive writing to a local radio or TV station.

Refer to "Step-by-Step Revising and Editing" in the teacher pages for more information. You might want to have the rest of the class be reviewers of students' essays before the essays are submitted to publishers.

Expository Writing: Compare and Contrast Essay

When you **compare**, you identify the way two or more subjects, or topics, are alike. When you **contrast**, you identify differences between subjects. Here are parts of an essay about two Civil War generals.

Grant and Lee: A Study in Contrasts
an excerpt by Bruce Catton

[1]When Ulysses S. Grant and Robert E. Lee met in the parlor of a modest house at Appomattox Court House in Virginia, on April 9, 1865, to work out the terms for the surrender of Lee's Army of Northern Virginia, a great chapter in American life came to a close, and a great new chapter began. . . .

[*Most of Catton's essay analyzes how the two generals differ. Catton discusses Lee first. Lee had an aristocratic Virginia background, he believed in a society ruled by landowners, and he was intensely loyal to the South. Then Catton contrasts the same three features in Grant. Grant had a working-class Western background, he believed in a democratic society where anyone can achieve wealth and power through hard work, and he was fiercely loyal to the Union. Then Catton continues as follows.*]

[2]Yet it was not all contrast, after all. [3]Different as they were—in background, in personality, in underlying aspiration—these two great soldiers had much in common.

[4]Each man had, to begin with, the great virtue of utter tenacity and fidelity. [5]Grant fought his way down the Mississippi Valley in spite of acute personal discouragement and profound military handicaps. [6]Lee hung on in the trenches at Petersburg after hope itself had died. [7]In each man there was an indomitable quality . . . the born fighter's refusal to give up as long as he can still remain on his feet and lift his two fists.

[8]Daring and resourcefulness they had, too, the ability to think faster and move faster than the enemy. [9]These were the qualities which gave Lee the dazzling campaigns of Second Manassas and Chancellorsville and won Vicksburg for Grant.

[10]Lastly, and perhaps greatest of all, there was the ability at the end to turn quickly from war to peace once the fighting was over. [11]Out of the way these two men behaved at Appomattox came the possibility of a peace of reconciliation. [12]It was a possibility which was not wholly realized in the years to come but which did, in the end, help the two sections to become one nation again . . . after a war whose bitterness might have seemed to make such a reunion wholly impossible. [13]No part of either man's life became

Conclusion: restatement of thesis statement

him more than the part he played in their brief meeting in the McLean house at Appomattox. [14]Their behavior there put all succeeding generations of Americans in their debt. [15]Two great Americans, Grant and Lee were very different, yet under everything very much alike. [16]Their encounter at Appomattox was one of the great moments of American history.

Critical Thinking   After you read the compare and contrast essay, answer the questions below. Use the following questions to lead a class discussion.

1. Reread the introduction and the conclusion of the essay. What do you think the author's purpose is?

2. Name the ways Catton says the two generals are alike. What proof, or support, does he give?

3. The word *yet* at the beginning of the second paragraph is a **transition**; it indicates that an opposite idea will follow. List some other transitions Catton uses to help the reader follow his thinking.

4. Build your vocabulary. Look at the following three words in context, and discuss what each word means: *aspiration* (sentence 3), *tenacity* (sentence 4), and *reconciliation* (sentence 11). If you can't define or aren't sure of a word, check a dictionary, and add the word to your vocabulary notebook. Encourage students to use these words when they speak and write.

Writing Strategies   The purpose of writing a compare and contrast essay is to inform your readers about a subject or to explain a subject. It is critical, therefore, that you plan your essay carefully and that you organize your thoughts clearly. Use the following suggestions.

1. **Choose your subjects**. If your topic is not assigned, choose one that allows you to compare and contrast two subjects that you know something about—and about which you want to think even more. For example, choose two persons, two places, two events, or two objects. Refer to "Writing Ideas" in the teacher pages for additional topics.

2. **List their features**. Think about your subjects in terms of as many features, or categories, as possible. Start with the following categories.

appearances   histories or backgrounds

advantages or disadvantages   costs and benefits

actions or behaviors   effects on you or other people

most special qualities or traits

3. **Use a Venn diagram**. A Venn diagram is a useful prewriting tool for identifying differences and similarities. In the overlapping part of two circles, list features that your two subjects share. In the parts of the circles that do not overlap, list their differences. Use the following model as a guide.

GENERAL LEE

1. Background: aristocratic Virginian

2. Believed in government by landowners

3. Loyal to the South

SIMILARITIES

1. Tenacious and loyal

2. Resourceful

3. Ready for peace

GENERAL GRANT

1. Background: working-class, Westerner

2. Believed in government by everyone

3. Loyal to the Union

4. **Organize**. Use one of the two basic formats for organizing a compare and contrast essay listed on the chart on page 65. Choose the one that best makes your points.

In the **block method**, discuss one subject at a time. First, discuss all the features about one subject. Then move on to the second subject, discussing the same features in the same order.

In the **point-by-point method**, first deal with one feature in subject 1 and subject 2. Then present a second feature in subject 1 and subject 2, and continue the same way for the remaining features.

In general, the block method works better for shorter papers; the point-by-point method is better for longer ones.

5. **Use clear transitions**. Transitional expressions help the reader follow your thinking. *Like, also, similarly, both,* and *in the same way* signal similarities. *Yet, but, on the other hand, in contrast,* and *nevertheless* signal differences. Transitions can also highlight each new feature: *first, second, finally, more important,* and *most significant.*

Two Methods for Organizing a Compare and Contrast Essay

Block Method:
One subject at a time

All about Lee

Feature 1: background
Feature 2: government
Feature 3: loyalty to region

All about Grant

Feature 1: background
Feature 2: government
Feature 3: loyalty to nation

Point-by-Point Method:
Contrast one feature at a time

Feature 1: Background

Lee: Southerner
Grant: Westerner

Feature 2: Government

Lee: Government by the few
Grant: Government by the many

Feature 3: Loyalty

Lee: Loyal to the South
Grant: Loyal to the Union

EXERCISE 11 Choose Subjects

Use one or all of the following suggestions to come up with two things to compare or contrast.

Apples and oranges The subjects you choose may be very different or quite similar, but they *must* have at least one feature in common—as apples and oranges do. The easiest subjects to write about are specific, limited ones which you can observe directly. Try comparing or contrasting two of the following items

people	paintings	movies	singers	food
places	TV shows	animals	sports (teams, players)	events

Then/Now You might compare a single subject in the past with the same subject in the present. For example, what was your community like a hundred years ago? How is it different today? Suggest that students research what their community was like a hundred years ago.

An imaginative comparison Use your imagination to find similarities between two situations or actions that seem, at first, to have nothing in common. For example, how is pumping up a bicycle tire like listening to a complaining friend?
Encourage students to look for the humor in this comparison.

EXERCISE 12 Gather Information

Decide which features of your two subjects you will examine as you compare and contrast. As you begin prewriting, use one or more of the following techniques.

- **Observe your subjects**. Take notes as you actually look at and/or listen to your subjects.

- **Do some research**. If you're writing about subjects you don't know a lot about (such as Grant and Lee), use encyclopedias or other reference books to gather facts, examples, and other information. You will need specific details to back up your general statements.

- **Know the difference between fact and opinion**. Don't confuse them. A **fact** is a statement everyone agrees is true; it is something that you can measure or prove. An **opinion** is a person's idea or belief. It cannot be proven true, but it can be supported with reasons and other evidence.

After you have gathered information, choose the features of comparison that you will use in your essay. A Venn diagram may help you sort out your notes (see page 64).

EXERCISE 13 Organize Your Essay

1. Limit the number of features. From the notes you've made about the features of your subjects, choose only two or three to focus on. List the features you've chosen on the organizer below.

2. Choose the organization that suits your subjects and features better—the block or point-by-point method. Decide which subject you will put first and why, or decide which feature you will mention first and why.

3. On a separate piece of paper, make a rough outline. Your rough outline should look like one of the two methods for organizing an essay shown on page 65.

Organize Your Essay

Feature 1 _____

_____

Feature 2 _____

_____

Feature 3 _____

_____

EXERCISE 14 Draft Your Essay

Remember the three elements that need to be included in your essay.

1. **Introduction** Your first paragraph should (1) identify your subjects, (2) let your reader know whether you will discuss their similarities or differences or both, and (3) catch your reader's attention. Be sure to draft a **thesis statement** that summarizes the essay's main (or controlling) idea. Refer to Lesson 2.5 to help you draft a thesis statement.

Make sure all your comparisons are complete. If you write, "Killer whales are larger," will your reader know that you mean "larger than dolphins"?

2. **Body** Following the order of your rough outline, begin explaining your information to your readers. Insert transition words to help your reader follow your explanation.

3. **Conclusion** Summarize your findings at the end of your essay. You might point out how the subjects are more alike or more different or how one feature of comparison is more important than all the rest.

EXERCISE 15 Revise

Revise your essay using the four-step revising strategy that was suggested on page 15. Be sure you have given enough support for each general statement. Eliminate wordiness, and add transitions to help the reader follow your thoughts.
Usage, Chapters 9–12 will help students revise their essays.

Refer to "Step-by-Step Revising and Editing" in the teacher pages for more information.

EXERCISE 16 Proofread and Publish Your Essay

Reread your paper and ask a partner to check it, too. Once you have corrected every error in spelling, capitalization, punctuation, and usage, find a way to share your paper with an audience. Refer to Chapters 13–16 for punctuation, capitalization, and spelling rules.

Read your paper aloud to classmates. Ask them to take notes as they listen. Can they summarize the controlling idea of your comparison or contrast essay?

Compile separate anthologies of compare and contrast essays on individual topics such as history, biology, or literature. Donate these anthologies to other classes or to the school library for other students to use.

Writing About Literature: Analyzing Fiction

When you write about a story or novel, you usually create one of three kinds of essays. The three serve very different purposes.

1. In a **personal response** essay, you write about how you felt and what you thought as you read, about the passages that seemed particularly meaningful, and about the other works that the story reminded you of.

2. In an **evaluation**, you write about how good or bad the work is. Your evaluation is based on objective **criteria**, or standards, that are used to measure the excellence of a literary form. For example, here are two criteria for measuring a short story:

• The characters are believable.

• The plot engages the reader's interest.

3. In a **literary analysis**, you discuss one or more of the **elements of fiction**: characters, plot, setting, point of view, and theme.

The following excerpt is from a long literary analysis of Ernest Hemingway's novel *The Old Man and the Sea*. Here, Carlos Baker discusses the feelings that the main character, Santiago, has for birds and fish while he is battling a marlin.

Hemingway's Ancient Mariner
an excerpt from an essay by Carlos Baker

Reference to the poem "The Rime of the Ancient Mariner" by Coleridge

[1]According to the ancient mariner of Coleridge, "[h]e prayeth best who loveth best all things both great and small." [2]Along with humility, pride, and piety, Hemingway's ancient mariner [Santiago] is richly endowed with the quality of compassion. [3]Of course, he is not so foolish as to love all creatures equally. [4]He dislikes, for example, the Portuguese men-of-war, whose beautiful "purple, formalized, iridescent, gelatinous" bubbles serve to buoy up the "long deadly purple filaments" which trail a yard behind them in the water and contain a poison which will paralyze the unwary passersby. . . . [5]He has another set of enemies in the water of the tropic sea. [6]For he genuinely hates, and gladly destroys, the voracious sharks which attack and disfigure the marlin he has fought so long to win.

Thesis statement

Example

Another example

General statement

Many examples

[7]But his hatred is more than overbalanced by his simple love and compassion for all those creatures which swim or blindly soar. [8]His principal friends on the ocean are the flying fish. [9]He loves the green turtles and the hawksbills "with their elegance and speed." . . . [10]Porpoises delight him. [11]"They are good," he says. [12]"They play and make jokes and love one another.

[13]They are our brothers like the flying fish." [14]Several times in the course of his struggle he feels pity for the great marlin he has hooked—so "wonderful and strange" in his power to pull the skiff for so many hours, without sustenance, without respite, and with the pain of the hook in his flesh.

General statement

[15]For the lesser birds his compassion is greatest, "especially the small delicate dark terns that were always flying and looking and almost never finding." [16]The birds, he reflects, "have a harder life than we do except for the robber birds and the heavy strong ones. [17]Why did they make birds so delicate and fine as those sea swallows when the ocean can be so cruel? [18]She is kind and very beautiful. [19]But she can be so cruel and it comes so suddenly and such birds that fly, dipping and hunting, with their small sad voices are made too delicate for the sea."

Quotations

General statement

[20]His grateful sense of brotherhood with the creatures of the water and the air is, though full of love, essentially realistic and unsentimental. [21]His implied or overt comparisons between subhuman and human brothers often open out, therefore, in as many directions as our imaginations wish to follow. [22]A memorable example of this tendency appears in the incident of the land-bird, a warbler, which comes to rest on Santiago's skiff far out at sea. . . .

[23]This gently humorous monologue with its serious undertone of implied commentary on the human condition encourages the old man at this stage of his struggle. [24]"Stay at my house if you like, bird," he said. [25]"I am sorry I cannot hoist the sail and take you in with the small breeze that is rising. [26]But I am with a friend." [27]It is just at this point that the marlin gives a sudden lurch, the tautened line jerks, and the warbler flies away—towards whatever it is that awaits him on the long voyage home. [28]Hawks or sharks, the predators wait, whether for tired young birds or tired old men. . . .

[29]To their hazard or their sorrow, Hemingway's heroes sometimes lose touch with nature. . . . [30]But Santiago is never out of touch. [31]The line which ties him to the fish is like a charged wire which guarantees that the circuit will

Comparison with St. Francis

remain unbroken. [32]Saint Francis with his animals and birds is not more closely allied to God's creation than this Santiago with his birds and his fish.

Quotation

[33]These are his brothers, in all their sizes. [34]"I am with a friend," he cheerfully tells the warbler. [35]When the bird has departed, he is momentarily smitten by

Reference to incident

a sense of his aloneness on the vast waters. [36]Then he looks ahead of his skiff to see "a flight of wild ducks etching themselves against the sky over the water, then blurring, then etching again." [37]Once more he is convinced of what he has only momentarily forgotten: No man is ever alone on the sea.

Conclusion

[38]This sense of solidarity with the visible universe and the natural creation is another of the factors which help to sustain him through his long ordeal.

Critical Thinking   After you read the analysis above, answer the following questions.

Use the following questions to lead a class discussion.

1. From what you have read of Baker's essay, would you enjoy reading *The Old Man and the Sea*? Explain why or why not.

2. Find two or three general statements that Baker makes. Then find the support Baker gives for each of these general statements.

3. In your own words, summarize the essay's controlling idea.

4. With a partner or small group, focus on the last paragraph of the essay. Read it aloud. How does Baker make his sentences flow smoothly? What connecting words or phrases does he use?

5. Build your vocabulary. Underline the words in the selection that you do not know. Use a dictionary to find their meaning and write a brief definition in the margin or in your notebook. The following list may help: *compassion* (sentence 2), *voracious* (sentence 6), *respite* (sentence 14), *monologue* (sentence 23), *smitten* (sentence 35), and *solidarity* (sentence 38).

Writing Strategies   The purpose of an essay about a literary work is to explain your interpretation of it. Use the following strategies as you write.

Encourage students to use these words when they speak and write.

1. **Identify title and author**. In the first paragraph, identify the work you are writing about.

2. **Present a thesis statement**. A **thesis statement** at the end of your introduction clearly summarizes your controlling idea in a sentence or two.

3. **Give a very, very, very brief plot summary**. Here is where many students make a big mistake: Don't get bogged down in details. Spend no more than *a few sentences* summarizing a short story and no more than a *paragraph* summarizing a novel.

4. **Make clear, general statements**. Your main points about your thesis statement form the backbone of your essay.

5. **Use present tense**. When you refer to characters or events in the work, their actions should be stated in the present tense.

> EXAMPLE   Santiago **struggles** with the marlin and **battles** the sharks.

> See
> **Composition**
> Lesson 2.5 for more about writing a thesis statement.

6. Support your statements. The stronger your support, the better your reader will understand each of your general statements. Use the following hints.

- **Quote from the text**. Enclose a direct quotation in quotation marks that show direct examples of your point. Sentence 34 is a good example of this.

- **Refer to details in the text**. You can refer to an incident or character without quoting from the text. Find at least one example of such a reference in Baker's essay.

- **Make comparisons**. Baker refers to a poem by Coleridge when he quotes, "He prayeth best. . . ." A comparison or contrast with a different text may clarify the point you are making.

- **Summarize an expert**. Do research to discover literary criticism about the work or the writer. If you quote or summarize another critic's ideas, give full credit to that writer.

7. Watch your tone. The tone of your essay should be formal and serious. Avoid contractions, sentence fragments, and slang.

> **WRITING HINT**
>
> When you are quoting from a text:
> - check to see that you have quoted exactly.
> - enclose single words, phrases, and short sentences in quotation marks.
> - make sure that quotations larger than three lines are indented as a block; do not enclose the indented block in quotation marks.
> - use ellipsis points (. . .) to indicate omissions in a quoted text. At the end of a sentence, indicate an omission with (. . . .), a period followed by three ellipses points.

Questions for a Literary Analysis

The following questions will help you come up with an idea for writing. Also try clustering or brainstorming. See page 10.

> See
> **Mechanics**
> Lesson 14.5
> for help with punctuation of quotations.

Characters What does the character want or need at the beginning of the story? How does the main character change by the end? What does the main character learn or discover? What is the character's relationship with other characters? How does the writer reveal what the main character is like?

Plot What is the conflict or conflicts? Is the conflict external or internal? How is it resolved? What does the outcome reveal about the theme? Does the writer use foreshadowing or suspense?

Setting Could the story take place in a different setting? How does the setting influence the characters, action, or outcome?

Point of View Who tells the story? Is the narrator a character in the story? How would the story change if the story were told from a different point of view?

Theme Does the work convey a message about life or people? Is this message universal? Which passages most clearly convey the theme? If the theme isn't expressed directly, how can the reader figure it out? (The title, changes in the main character, and the outcome of the conflict often provide clues to the theme.)

EXERCISE 17 Prewriting: Choose and Limit a Topic

Choose a story you have already read and want to write about. Use the questions above to help you choose one literary element to write about. Of all the elements, character, plot, and theme are the ones that are the most likely to yield suitable topics. After choosing your literary element, narrow your focus further. In his essay Baker focuses by analyzing *one* aspect of Santiago's character: his compassion for animals.

EXERCISE 18 Prewriting: Major Points and Supporting Details

1. Reread the literary work carefully. Take notes on everything you notice that is relevant to your limited topic.

2. Write your two or three main points—your general statements on the organizer below.

3. From the main points, draft a thesis statement, a single sentence that expresses what you will cover in your essay. Don't agonize about it; you can change it later.

4. List specific details (quotations, incidents, examples) that "prove" each main point, and mark the strongest details with a check. (If you put notes—especially quotations—on a computer, you can add them to your essay when you draft it.)

Organize Your Analysis

General
Statement 1 _____

_____

General
Statement 2 _____

_____

General
Statement 3 _____

_____

EXERCISE 19 Organize and Draft Your Essay

Before you start writing, review your notes. Choose two or three of your most important points. Then sit down and start writing—anywhere in the essay. Do not worry about perfect sentences. Just get your ideas down in sentences and paragraphs so that you will have something to revise.

- **Introduction, body, conclusion** Make sure you have included everything that belongs in each of the three basic parts.

- **Title** Think of a possible title; try out several. Your title should suggest both the work and your essay's focus.

> **A Literary Analysis**
> **INTRODUCTION**
> • Author and title
>   of work
> • Brief plot summary
> • Thesis statement
> **BODY**
> • Major point 1
>   Support, support
> • Major point 2
>   Support, support
> **CONCLUSION**

EXERCISE 20 Revise Your Essay

Let the draft sit awhile. Then use the four revising strategies suggested in Lesson 1.3. Think about your audience, and read for ideas and unity, organization and coherence, and sentence variety. As you and your writing partners revise, ask these questions:

Usage, Chapters 9–12 will help students revise their essays.

- Is the essay coherent, or well-organized?

- Are the general statements clearly expressed but not wordy?

- Have you elaborated enough to support or "prove" each main point?

- Is everything unified, or directly related to, the main point?

EXERCISE 21 Proofread and Publish Your Essay

Double-check each quotation for accuracy and for punctuation. When you are satisfied that you have corrected all errors in spelling, capitalization, punctuation, and usage, exchange papers with a partner to check for any you may have missed.

Refer to Chapters 13–16 for punctuation, capitalization, and spelling rules.

You might form two reading-and-discussion groups: one for short stories and one for novels. Take turns reading aloud papers to the appropriate group. If others in the group have read the work you have written about, see if they agree with your analysis and if they have comments or ideas to add. Your group might also name other stories or novels that members might enjoy.

You might also compile a "lit crit" anthology of everyone's essays analyzing literature. Then share the anthology with other English classes.

Refer to "Step-by-Step Revising and Editing" in the teacher pages for more information.

Expository Writing: Research Paper

You may be asked to write a research paper in all of your classes, not just in English class. A **research paper** is based on a thorough investigation of a limited topic. There are four types:

1. The most common type of research paper **summarizes** or **explains information** you have gathered from several different sources. You **synthesize** (put together to form a new whole) what other writers have reported.

2. Another type of research paper adds your **evaluation**, or opinion. For example, in a **problem–solution** research report, you might discuss a community problem and evaluate the effectiveness of several proposed solutions.

3. A third type of paper summarizes your **original research**. In social studies, you might draw conclusions and present findings based on surveys, questionnaires, or interviews you have conducted. A science research paper might report a long series of your observations and experiments. Your paper details the hypothesis, or theory, that you began with and the carefully controlled experiments you conducted to test that theory. You also include a survey of the literature, which includes scientific articles related to your investigation.

4. An **I-Search paper** narrates the story of how you wrote your research paper. It not only presents information you discovered about a limited topic but also explains why you chose that topic, how you conducted your research, and what you experienced along the way.

Science research papers follow a format and style of documentation that is different from the Modern Language Association (MLA) style described in this workshop.

On the following pages are excerpts from a high school student's research report that explains and synthesizes what other writers said about a world event that occurred in 1962. The research paper also evaluates the effects of the event. The paper includes parenthetical references to its sources and ends with a Works Cited list, both of which are discussed later in this workshop.

4-line heading:
Name/Teacher/
Class/Due Date

Leslie Porter
Mr. Charles Fass
U.S. History
September 3, 2006

Title and subtitle

**The Cuban Missile Crisis:
Immediate Responses and Lasting Effects**

Attention-
grabber about
Chinese
character

Reference to
book on Works
Cited list

Thesis statement
ends introduction

The Chinese character for the word "crisis" has two very different meanings. The first is the meaning we usually associate with the word in English: "a dangerous event or period." But the same character can also mean "opportunity." The fact that a crisis can actually have beneficial effects or can be the means for reaching a new understanding is often overlooked in international politics (Craig and George 129). Yet by reviewing the press coverage of the Cuban Missile Crisis at the time it was happening and by considering the crisis from our later perspective, we can see that the crisis had important, positive effects in both national and world politics.

A brief summary of the events from October 16 through October 28, 1962, is helpful in order to understand the importance of the crisis. On Tuesday morning, October 16, President John F. Kennedy received word that aerial photographs proved conclusively that the Soviets were building offensive—not defensive—nuclear weapons bases in Cuba. Kennedy and his advisors spent six days deliberating what the best course of action would be. They discarded the notion of an invasion of Cuba and settled on a blockade, which they decided to call a quarantine.

News of the crisis first reached the American public on the evening of October 22, when Kennedy addressed the nation on radio and television. The President detailed the discovery of Cuban missile bases, announced the U.S. quarantine of Cuba, and promised that the U.S. would take further action if necessary. For the next several days, the world breathlessly awaited a direct confrontation that, luckily, never happened. Soviet Premier Nikita Khrushchev ordered Russian ships to turn around or avoid the American blockade. However, work on the missile bases continued. Finally, on October 26, Khrushchev sent Kennedy a letter ordering to withdraw the missiles in return for a U.S. pledge not to invade Cuba. The next day a second letter arrived from Khrushchev, demanding U.S. withdrawal of missiles from Turkey. The U.S. ignored the second letter but responded affirmatively to the first, warning that withdrawal must take place by October 28 or the U.S. would conduct an air strike on Cuba. On October 28 Khrushchev announced the withdrawal of the missiles from Cuba. . . .

Some
background
information has
been omitted from
these excerpts.

Result 1

One result of the Cuban Missile Crisis was a change in the way people and nations viewed President Kennedy. Joseph Grunwald, who lived in Miami at the time, remembers that before the Cuban Missile Crisis, people thought of

Porter 2

Eyewitness
interview

Kennedy as "immature, young, and inexperienced" and especially weak on foreign policy (Grunwald). . . . After the crisis, Kennedy's popularity and power increased greatly. . . . *Newsweek* summed it up: "Mr. Kennedy's behavior during the past two weeks has given Americans a sense of deep confidence in the temper of their president" ("Lessons").

Result 2

The crisis was almost uniformly seen as a tremendous victory for the United States in the Cold War. A November 2 editorial in *Life* proudly announced, "The Cuban blockade is a major turning point in the 17-year Cold War. The U.S. has dramatically seized the initiative." ("New"). We had taken a stand, made our position quite clear, and in the game of military chicken, the Russians jumped first. Not only was American public opinion overwhelmingly behind the President, but the U.S. got the support of its allies, including a 19-0 vote of confidence from the OAS (Reston). On the other hand, "the Soviet setback in Cuba clearly diminished Khrushchev's prestige in the Communist world," and Khrushchev was seen as discredited and handicapped ("What"). . . .

The Cuban Missile Crisis made the ever-present fear of nuclear war dramatically apparent. This was nowhere more evident than in South Florida, only 90 miles from Cuba. The Miami airport closed, and the military arrived by planeloads and truckloads. Fearing nuclear attack, people descended on supermarkets for canned foods, water, candles, and batteries (Grunwald). . . .

The crisis showed the necessity of communication and direct negotiations between the superpowers. The whole concept of escalation suggested that events could very easily spiral out of the policymakers' control. In a letter to JFK, Khrushchev wrote that it would be dangerously simple for "matters to slide into the disaster of war" (Kennedy 126). Two weeks after the crisis had ended, a letter writer in *Newsweek* made this hopeful forecast: "The success of the Cuban blockade will truly prove a victory for all mankind if Russia and the U.S. will now sit down to serious and fruitful disarmament talks" (Walker). . . .

Result 3

The Cuban Missile Crisis had acted like a bucket of cold water thrown over the heads of world leaders, who were so frightened by the nuclear danger that they decided that negotiation and communication were of the utmost importance. As a result of the crisis, the following year the United States and the Soviet Union hammered out the Limited Nuclear Test Ban Treaty. Also, a special "hotline" was established for instant communication between the White House and the Kremlin. During the crisis, it had become clear that "seven-hour delays for messages to reach Washington and the reliance on bicycle-riding Western Union messengers were unacceptable means of communication in a nuclear age" (Finklestein 109). These were perhaps the two biggest dividends of the Cuban Missile Crisis.

Porter 3

Concluding
paragraph—
importance of
crisis

Observers at the time recognized that the Cuban Missile Crisis held tremendous significance for the nation and the world. "The ships of the U.S. Navy were steering a course that would be marked boldly on the charts of history," *Life* proclaimed, and "the steel perimeter clamped around Cuba by the U.S. could be the tripwire for World War III" ("Blockade"). *Newsweek* predicted that the crisis "may turn out to have consequences of incalculable importance for this century" ("Showdown"). Things could have turned out very differently

Recalls Chinese
character for
"crisis"

than they did, but the prudence and caution of both Kennedy and Khrushchev altered this crisis into an opportunity for peace.

Porter 4

Works Cited

unsigned article

"The Blockade: The U.S. Puts It on the Line." *Life* 2 Nov. 1962: 35.

essay found on
Internet

Chang, Laurence, and Peter Kornbluh. "The Cuban Missile Crisis, 1962: An Introduction." *The Cuban Missile Crisis, 1962: A National Security Archive Documents Reader.* New York: New Press, 1992. Online. Internet. 18 Sept. 1995 Available www.seas.gwu.edu/nsarchive/nsa/cuba_mis_cri/cmcintro.html/.

book by two
authors

Craig, Gordon A., and Alexander L. George. *Force and Statecraft.* New York: Oxford UP, 1990.

book by one
author

Finklestein, Norman H. *Thirteen Days/Ninety Miles: The Cuban Missile Crisis.* New York: Julian Messner, 1994.

original interview
by student

Grunwald, Joseph. Personal interview. 2 Dec. 1995.

Kennedy, Robert F. *Thirteen Days: A Memoir of the Cuban Missile Crisis.* New York: Norton, 1969.

"The Lessons Learned." *Newsweek* 12 Nov. 1962: 25.

"A New Resolve to Save the Old Freedoms." *Life.* 2 Nov. 1962: 4.

Reston, James. "Khrushchev's Misjudgment on Cuba." *New York Times* 24 Oct. 1962, sec. 1: 38.

"Showdown-Backdown." *Newsweek* 5 Nov. 1962: 28.

Walker, William. Letter. *Newsweek* 12 Nov. 1962: 4.

"What Happened in the Kremlin?" *Newsweek* 12 Nov. 1962: 26.

Writing Strategies   The following specific strategies apply to all four types of research papers. You must also use the writing strategies in Chapter 1 and the general advice for writing essays in Lesson 2.5.

1. Budget your time. Don't wait until the last minute. The chart on page 78 suggests a time budget for each step.

2. **Find multiple sources**. Your assignment may require you to use both primary and secondary sources.

A **primary source** is an original text or document, such as a literary work, a diary, letters, a speech, an interview, or a historical document.

A **secondary source** presents the writer's comments on a primary source. Reference books, biographies, literary criticism, and history and science textbooks are secondary sources.

By using a computer, you can find a wealth of primary and secondary information. In many libraries, electronic databases have replaced card catalogues, the *Readers' Guide to Periodical Literature*, and newspaper indexes. For example, when you enter key words to search Infotrac's General Reference Center, you access not only the titles of relevant magazine articles but also the text of the articles. A writer doing a research paper today could enter the key term "Cuban Missile Crisis" in Infotrac and get a listing of encyclopedia excerpts, reference book excerpts, newspaper articles, and periodical articles. By selecting the titles that are listed, the researcher could read and print the articles that seem most useful. In addition, a contemporary researcher can use various Internet search engines to explore the World Wide Web for new information about the Cuban Missile Crisis.

Research Schedule		
STEP	TOTAL TIME	
	6 weeks	8 weeks
Choose and limit topic.	2 days	3 days
Find and evaluate sources; make bibliography cards.	2 days	3 days
Take notes.	1 week	1 ½ weeks
Draft thesis statement and title.	1 day	2 days
Draft outline.	2 days	1 week
Write first draft.	1 week	1 week
Document sources.	1 day	2 days
Revise.	1 ½ weeks	1 ½ weeks
Proofread.	2 days	2 days
Prepare final manuscript.	3 days	3 days

3. **Evaluate possible sources**. All sources are not equal. The secondary sources you consult should be up-to-date, accurate, and relevant.

- **Up-to-date** Which is a better source for information about space stations: a twenty-year-old book or last month's article in *Scientific American*?

- **Accurate** Don't believe everything you read. Reliable sources are both accurate and unbiased. You can trust a *New York Times* article more than the headline in a sensational tabloid. Be careful about Internet sources, too. A government database is a reliable source; someone's personal home page might not be.

- **Relevant** Finally, the information you spend time with must directly relate to your limited topic. Do not start straying into information that is fascinating but unrelated.

4. **Keep track of your sources**. For every source you use, make a **source card** (sometimes called a bibliography source card) containing all essential publishing information. Give each source a number, and write the number in the upper

SAMPLE SOURCE CARD

Chang, Laurence, and Peter Kornbluh.   1
"The Cuban Missile Crisis, 1962: An Introduction."

The Cuban Missile Crisis, 1962: A National
Security Archive Documents Reader. New York:
New Press, 1992.

Accessed online via Microsoft Internet Explorer.
18 Sept. 1995
www.seas.gwu.edu/nsarchive/nsa/cuba_mis_cri/
cmcintro.html/.

Number of source

Some Sources to Explore

- Periodicals (newspapers, magazines, journals)
- Books about your topic
- Reference books (encyclopedias, specialized books such as atlases)
- Publications by government agencies
- Publications by nonprofit organizations
- Internet
- Electronic databases
- Other media (movies, television, radio, CD-ROMs)
- Museums, zoos, and other institutions
- Published interviews and surveys
- Original interviews you conduct

right-hand corner of the source card. Then, when you take notes, instead of rewriting all this information on each note card, you can place the source's number in the upper right-hand corner of your note card.

5. **Take notes**. After you have read a source, you may quote it exactly (use quotation marks!), or you may put the information into your own words. Do your best to use your own words when you can.

- You can **summarize** the information by giving only the most important ideas in your own words.

- Or you can **paraphrase** the information, restating every idea in the same order as in the original—but in your own words.

At the top of each note card, write the main idea, and underline it.

SAMPLE NOTE CARD

National Security Archive worked to get documents   1
about Cuban Missile Crisis declassified.

In 1980s, filed Freedom of Information Act requests
and lawsuit to make State Dept. release files from the
crisis of 1962.   (page 23)

By mid-1989: 2,000 docs. were totally or partially
declassified   (page 24)

Main idea

Summary in researcher's own words

6. **Make an outline**. Look for three or four main ideas in your note cards, and follow the outline format at the right. Also, learn the two-point rule. You need at least two points under every heading; you can't have just one point.

7. **Draft a thesis statement**. It's a toss-up whether you write an outline or draft a thesis statement first. Either way is acceptable. Your **thesis statement**, or statement of your controlling idea, can come at the beginning or end of your introduction. The thesis statement tells your readers what you are going to tell them in the rest of your paper.

8. **Give credit**. A research paper shows where your information comes from. You will need to acknowledge a source whenever you (1) quote a phrase, sentence, or passage directly; or (2) summarize or paraphrase another person's ideas in your own words. The Modern Language Association (MLA) has created a system for giving credit to sources. The research paper model on pages 75–77 demonstrates the system:

- The student uses **parenthetical documentation** at the point of citing each source.

- The student gives complete information about each source at the end of the paper in the **Works Cited** list.

Sample Outline

Draft of thesis statement:
The crisis led to positive developments.

I. First result: better opinions of President Kennedy
  A. Bad views of JFK
    1. Bay of Pigs fiasco
    2. Cold War in general
  B. Improved views
    1. Support from media
    2. Still, ongoing criticism
      a. from Republicans
      b. from conservative citizens

II. Second result: victory for U.S.

For more information about MLA style, consult the *MLA Handbook for Writers of Research Papers*, 6th edition, by Joseph Gibaldi, or go to www.mla.org. Be aware that some instructors prefer that students cite each source in a footnote or endnote rather than in parentheses in the paper itself.

Social studies and science research papers usually follow the APA (American Psychologial Association) style, which differs from the Modern Language Association (MLA) format used in this workshop. If you are writing a social studies or science paper, find out which style your teacher prefers. Then use an Internet search engine to find out details about the APA style.

9. **Don't plagiarize**. Using someone else's words or ideas without giving credit is **plagiarism**, which is a serious offense. High-ranking officials have lost their jobs because of plagiarism, and writers have been sued. Do not attempt to borrow or buy someone else's research paper either. Teachers and other readers can detect writing that is not your own.

Use the rules listed in **Mechanics** Lessons 14.4 and 14.5 for punctuating quotations and dialogue.

Exercise 22 Prewriting: Choose a Limited Topic

"What can I write about?" Your teacher may specify a general subject (animals and the environment, for instance), or you may have the whole world to choose from. Use the suggestions below to choose a topic and limit it to a manageable size.
Refer to "Writing Ideas" in the teacher pages.

Inquiry-based The best research topic answers your own questions. Brainstorm a list of statements that begin, "I wonder . . . ." Or jot down a list of questions you are curious about. Try freewriting or looking back at your writer's notebook for topic ideas.

Not too big, not too little—just right Your topic should be limited enough for you to be able to cover it sufficiently in the number of pages you are supposed to write. (See Lesson 1.1 for strategies on how to limit topics.)

Exercise 23 Prewriting: Gather Information

Write a **direction statement** about what you are planning to research—for example, "I am going to write about the good effects of the missile crisis."

Use Strategies 2–5 on pages 78–79 to begin your research. As you locate sources and examine them, keep the following ideas in mind:

- **Purpose** Your purpose is to give information. You may need to provide background information and define technical terms. But also look for new and interesting information; don't give only facts that your readers already know.

- **Audience** Your audience is likely to be your teacher and classmates, but keep in mind that you may publish your research paper more widely.

Exercise 24 Prewriting: Write an Outline

After you have prepared notes from a number of sources, make piles of note cards that relate to the same main idea. Here are three common problems and some advice:

- **Too few main ideas** You will need at least three or four. Can some of your main ideas be divided? If you have too few main ideas, you need to do more research.

- **Not enough supporting information**. Are you sure you need more? If the answer is yes, do more research. Explore new sources.

- **Too much information**. Arrange your note cards with the strongest cards at the top, the weakest at the bottom. You may discard the weakest note cards later.

Once you have fixed any problems, you are ready to create your outline (Strategy 6 on page 80). Your outline will set up a working structure to get you started.

EXERCISE **25** Write a First Draft with Documentation

Start drafting long before your paper is due so that you will have plenty of time to revise. Apply Skills 7–9 from page 80. Keep the following advice in mind, too.

- **Title** As you draft, think about what you might title your research paper.

- **Quotations** Quotations show that you have done your research, but don't overload your paper. It should be mostly your own words.

- **Documentation** Work in your parenthetical citations and complete citations as you draft.

- **Introduction and conclusion** Many writers write these parts last, after they see what they have written.

EXERCISE **26** Revise Your Draft

Note that the timetables on page 78 allow more than a week for revising. Read through your draft many times, focusing on something different each time: ideas and unity, organization and coherence, sentence variety, and word choice. Check to see that you've arranged your ideas in the most logical order. Look for places to add transitions within a paragraph as well as at the beginning of a paragraph. Do the best revising job you can, and then ask for input from writing partners.
Usage, Chapters 9–12 will help students revise their essays.

EXERCISE **27** Proofread Your Paper

Now is the time to check the accuracy and punctuation of all the quotations that you have included. Check the style of the parenthetical citations and of Works Cited list, too. Make sure you have provided publishing information in the right order and punctuated exactly as required. Be sure to also proofread the entire paper for spelling, capitalization, punctuation, and usage.
Refer to Chapters 13–16 for punctuation, capitalization, and punctuation rules.

EXERCISE **28** Prepare the Final Copy and Publish

Congratulations! Your final paper is an enormous accomplishment, so prepare it carefully. Double-space your entire paper, including the Works Cited page. Read the final paper again before you turn it in. If you find any last-minute mistakes, correct them neatly in ink. Ideally, your paper should be error-free.
See "Step-by-Step Revising and Editing" in the teacher pages for more information.

Writing a Timed Essay

Essay questions on standardized tests measure your ability to generate ideas relevant to a specific topic and to present those ideas clearly and logically in an appealing style, while applying the conventions of standard written English. You are asked to do all of this within a limited amount of time.

On a standardized test, you will find essay topics, also called "prompts," usually presented in one of these two ways:

Agree or Disagree. This type of prompt provides you with one or two quotations or a brief paragraph. You are directed to write an essay explaining whether you agree or disagree with the prompt. You are asked to develop and support your position with examples, facts, statistics, observations, or personal experience.

Solve a Problem. This type of prompt provides you with an issue or problem that needs solving. You are asked to propose a possible solution in an essay in which you develop and support your point of view with examples, facts, statistics, observations, or personal experience.

The writing prompt below is similar to one you might find on a standardized test. After the prompt, you will find one writer's essay in response to it.

> Consider the following issue. Then write an essay as directed.
>
> A former Secretary of Education remarked that if his son had approached him and said, "You promised to pay for my tuition at [a prestigious university]; how about giving me $50,000 instead to start a little business?" he might have thought it a good idea.
>
> **Assignment:** Do you agree or disagree? Write an essay in response to this issue. Develop and support your position with ideas, facts, and examples gained from your reading, observations, or personal experience.

TEST-TAKING TIP

Most standardized test essays are scored from 6 (highest) to 1 (lowest).

Although the idea of starting a business rather than continuing your education through college may sound appealing, I believe that the plan is short-sighted. Furthering your education is not only important, it is essential for ourselves, our families, and communities. Studying at a university provides an excellent opportunity to learn more about who we are as we explore the world of ideas around us. We encounter new views in classes and in clubs and student organizations. We have opportunities to see plays, films, and art exhibits. In such a rich learning atmosphere, we are exposed to ideas that

Expresses position on the topic in thesis statement

inspire us to lead fuller, more productive lives and help us to become better informed citizens and wiser voters.

However, there is a case to be made for skipping college and leaping right into the world to make one's mark. Examples from American history support this view. Many successful Americans had little or no formal education. Would Abraham Lincoln's achievements and contributions been greater had he spent more than a few precious months in school? Henry Ford made his mark on the world but had no education to speak of. Where is Babe Ruth's diploma or Mohammed Ali's? Where is Paul Revere's?

Cites examples from history that oppose position

As history shows, it is possible to lead a rewarding life and earn a living without higher education, just as it is possible to do so without reading, traveling, or going to plays, concerts, or poetry readings. But the accomplished people I have mentioned above are the exceptions. College provides the tools most of us need for success.

Counters opposition with observations

By going to college, we open avenues to growth in ways that diving straight into the working world will not do. My uncle Jake went into his family's wedding dress business as soon as he finished high school. He makes a substantial income and is respected in his community. In running the business, he has acquired many skills. He has learned to trust his instincts and to work with and listen to others. He has learned to take on responsibility and to tackle and solve problems. Uncle Jake says he is content with his life. But he also says that he wishes he had gone to college to broaden his exposure to new opportunities. He insists that the advantages of higher education are too important to pass up and that his children will be lost without them in this demanding and changing world.

Cites example from personal experience

I believe strongly that my college years will introduce me to new ways of seeing the world and myself and that they will open up exciting opportunities for me. They will help me to become a better learner and better thinker and, therefore, a valuable participant in the world community. Also, the college experience can enrich me financially. Studies show a positive correlation between years of education and income. Therefore, by going to college, we not only enrich ourselves, we enrich our bank accounts as well.

Concluding paragraph—restates main idea

Critical Thinking   After you read the essay on pages 83–84, answer the following questions.

1. Where in the essay does the writer make clear her position on the issue stated in the writing prompt?

2. What support does the writer give for her opinion? Briefly outline the reasons, examples, and facts in the essay.

3. Using the scoring suggestion on page 83, how would you score this essay? Why?

Writing Strategies   Use the following strategies as you write a timed essay.

1. **Read the prompt carefully.** Make sure you understand exactly what you are asked to do. For example, is the purpose to inform or persuade? Then identify (underline or circle) key ideas as you read the prompt again.

2. **Prewrite: Narrow your focus.** Remember that you will have only a limited amount of time and space in which to write your essay. Know what your word and time limit will be, and plan accordingly. You will not be able to write all you know about a topic, so limit your response to a clear and manageable focus. Use your best ideas.

3. **Prewrite: Gather and organize ideas.** You might use an outline or a cluster diagram to generate ideas. Spend no more than two or three minutes jotting down ideas, key words, and supporting details. Order the ideas in the sequence you plan to use them.

4. **Write the main idea in a thesis statement.** Remember that this sentence usually appears at or near the beginning of your essay and communicates your position on the topic.

5. **Start writing and stick to the point.** Begin with an introductory paragraph that includes your thesis statement and grabs the reader's attention. Use details that support your ideas in the clearest, most logical way possible. Use topic sentences and transitions to organize your writing. End with a brief concluding paragraph.

6. **Consider word choice and sentence variety.** Clarity is your goal, so avoid vague words and confusing sentences. Strive for vocabulary and sentence variety that fit your writing purpose.

7. **Proofread your essay.** Save two or three minutes to reread your essay and *neatly* correct any errors in spelling, capitalization, punctuation, or usage.

EXERCISE 29 Read the Prompt Carefully

Choose one of the prompts provided, and refer to that prompt as you complete Exercises 30–33. (You might want to set a time limit for yourself of 25–30 minutes to simulate testing conditions.)

A former president of the National Geographic Society once said, "If you don't know where you are, you're nowhere."

Assignment: Do you agree or disagree? Write an essay in response to this issue. Develop and support your position with ideas, facts, and details gained from your reading, observations, or personal experience.

Imagine that your school district officials are trying to come up with ways to increase the amount of time students spend working on core subjects in school so that they score higher on standardized tests. They have considered lengthening the school day, eliminating electives and a few after school activities, shortening spring or fall vacations, lengthening the school year, and so on.

Assignment: Write an essay in which you propose a way to address the concerns of the school district about how to increase time spent on core subjects. Support your ideas with examples and details.

EXERCISE 30 Prewrite: Focus, Gather, and Organize Ideas

Decide on your position, and list the ideas you will use as support (facts, statistics, details, personal experience or observations, examples from literature, history, and/or current events). You might use a graphic organizer or an outline. Number your ideas in the sequence you plan to use them.

EXERCISE 31 Prewrite: Thesis Statement

Write your main idea in a thesis statement. Decide where you will place this sentence in your introduction.

EXERCISE 32 Write Your Essay

Begin with an introductory paragraph that grabs the reader's attention and includes your thesis statement. Say everything as clearly and logically as you can, and develop your essay with relevant examples that support your main idea. Use topic sentences and transitions to organize your ideas. Remember to choose only words and sentences that execute your writing purpose. End with a brief concluding paragraph that restates your main idea, poses a new question, or provides a final thought.

EXERCISE 33 Revise and Proofread Your Essay

Save two or three minutes to reread your writing. Make sure the sentences flow smoothly and are clear and succinct. Neatly cross out anything that strays from or takes away from your main idea. Correct any errors in spelling, capitalization, punctuation, and usage.

Parts of Speech

Direct students to
www.grammarforwriting.com
for chapter-specific
portfolio projects.

STUDENT WRITING
Narrative Essay

One Meal Made a Big Difference
by Sarah Swenson

high school student, The Woodlands, Texas

I fixed the big, rubber glove on my hand as I nervously grabbed the tray I was handed from my right. I took the spoon in my other hand and put a big spoonful of food, if you can even call it that, on the tray. I couldn't even bear to look up as I passed the tray over the counter. I feared that I would totally break down if I looked into their eyes.

After a while, I switched spots with someone and started handing out trays. All of a sudden, this lady walked out of the line and over to the piano. She played for a minute before she scurried back into line. As she moved toward me, I looked up into her eyes. They were a gentle brown.

I quickly swallowed the lump in my throat and pushed the tears from my eyes as I tried to put on my brightest smile.

"That was beautiful," I managed to get out.

"Thank you," she said as the line moved forward. "How has your day been?" she asked me as we were now standing almost face-to-face.

"Good," I replied, "and yours?"

"Mine has been pretty good," she responded as she reached to take her tray. "I'm alive, so it's good."

I don't know her name and it doesn't matter. That day, that one person changed my whole life. After that, I couldn't resist watching the smiles on people's faces as we gave them food.

When I first looked at what we were told to serve, I was disgusted. I never would have touched it. But then, I'm not really sure what happened. Everything just changed. I realized that for once in my adolescent life, I was making a difference. It may not seem like a big deal, but it was to me.

I was feeding people who needed to be fed—not because they had had a small breakfast, but because this was the only meal that they would have all day.

In fact, that one meal which I helped serve would have to tide them over for two days.

Ever since Sunday, I have tried so hard to go back to my peaceful, simple teen-aged life, but my mind keeps wandering back to those people.

I wonder, 'Why are they out there? How do they manage to live on the street?' I just can't get those people out of my mind.

And now, instead of being afraid of going and serving them food, I find that I can't wait until I get to go again.

Allow time for
students to
discuss the
student writing.
Suggest that
they identify its
strengths and
propose
possible
improvements.
Use the model
to introduce the
concepts in the
chapter.

> The events in Sarah's autobiographical essay take place in a short period of time. She also includes dialogue to make the events seem more real. Most important, in the last two paragraphs, she explains why the incident is important to her.
>
> As you complete the writing exercises in this chapter and then write your own autobiographical incident, you will become aware of the parts of speech of each word you write.

Nouns

Everything that you can see and touch and many things that are invisible are named by a noun.

▶ **Nouns** are words that name persons, places, things, or ideas.

PERSONS	grandfather, Serena, player, friend, Tiger Woods
PLACES	home, bridge, Chicago, Washington Monument
THINGS	computer, Internet, parade, refrigerator, mailbox
IDEAS	love, democracy, justice, fear, happiness

▶ Nouns that name ideas, such as the ones listed above, are called **abstract nouns**. You use abstract nouns when writing or speaking about feelings, characteristics, or qualities. In contrast, **concrete nouns** name things that you can see, hear, smell, taste, or touch.

ABSTRACT	courage, intelligence, **vitality**, theme, cost
CONCRETE	lemon, snow, sand, telephone, puppy

Enriching Your Vocabulary

Vitality stems from the Latin *vita*, which means "life." The word *vitality* may be used to mean not only physical but intellectual energy as well. The English philosopher Alfred North Whitehead, for example, observed that "the vitality of thought is in adventure."

▶ **Proper nouns** name particular persons, places, things, or ideas. Always capitalize proper nouns. Some proper nouns contain two or more words. Because **common nouns** are general, not particular, they are not capitalized.

PROPER	Texas, Empire State Building, Mexico, President Adams
COMMON	state, building, country, judge

▶ **Collective nouns** name a group of people or things. How many groups named by collective nouns are you part of?

> family, team, group, troop, committee, herd

▶ **Compound nouns** consist of two or more words. Use a dictionary to find out if a compound noun is hyphenated or written as one word or two words.

> great-uncle, one-third, paperweight, firefighter, high school, New Mexico

WRITING HINT

Use nouns that are as specific as possible.

terrier
The ~~dog~~ barked at the *letter carrier* ~~man~~.

bride
The ~~woman getting married~~ *roses and baby's breath* wore ~~flowers~~ in her hair.

P.S. Don't feel overwhelmed by the names for these different types of nouns. The whole point of learning the names and functions of the eight parts of speech is so that you can use them effectively—and correctly—when you write and speak.

EXERCISE 1 Identifying Nouns

Underline all the nouns in the following passage. Look for common nouns, proper nouns, abstract nouns, concrete nouns, compound nouns, and collective nouns.

[1]At the start of the twentieth century, students usually carried their own chalkboards or pads to school. [2]As the twenty-first century gets under way, many students still use paper in class and for homework. [3]Some of them prefer loose-leaf notebooks, and others favor spiral-bound ones. [4]At the same time, a small but growing percentage of students come to classrooms, studios, labs, and libraries without paper notebooks but with computerized notebooks, also known as laptops.

[5]Why do young people use laptops (which weigh less than some textbooks)? [6]Here are three reasons to start with. First, they use the machines to take notes, to copy down assignments, to write stories and essays, and to create art. [7]Second, they load a CD-ROM or similar collection of data onto their machines and find huge amounts of organized information at their fingertips. [8]Third, they use the laptops to communicate and to tap into up-to-the-minute text, sound, and pictures.   Do not penalize students who identify leaf and spiral in sentence 3 as nouns. Explain that these function as adjectives.

EXERCISE 2 Revising a Paragraph

The paragraph below is weak because it contains so many vague words. With a partner, improve it by replacing the italicized words with specific, concrete nouns or proper nouns. Also, add details, drop or add words, and combine sentences. Compare your revisions with those made by other pairs.

[1]One *day* at *a certain time, a person* was picking *fruit*. [2]She was in *a place* that was owned by *a relative*. [3]She listened to the *sounds* around her. [4]She enjoyed the *smells*. [5]She especially liked the *sights*. [6]After *time* had passed, she could see and feel the coming *weather*. [7]She dropped her *container* half filled with *fruit* and hurried toward a *building*. [8]*The person's pet* ran beside her. [9]When they reached *the building, the person* and *her pet* waited *a long time* for the *weather* to stop.
Paragraphs will vary. Caution students to avoid singsongy descriptions.

Pronouns

▶ **Pronouns** are words that take the place of a noun or other pronouns.

Most—but not all—pronouns clearly refer to another word in the sentence or in a preceding sentence. The word the pronoun replaces is called its **antecedent**. In the following sentences, arrows point to the antecedents of the pronouns.

Terra and **her** sister are disc jockeys. **They** have a radio program on

Saturday morning. **It** is on WZZZ.

The list at the right shows different types of pronouns.

▶ The pronouns you use the most are the **personal pronouns** and their **possessive forms**.

PERSONAL   **I** went with **him** to the movies.

POSSESSIVE   **My** cat licks **her** chops at **their** parakeet.

▶ **Indefinite pronouns** express an amount or refer to an unspecified person or thing.

Most of us studied.   **Somebody** sneezed.

Anything you can do, I can do better.

▶ **Demonstrative pronouns** point to specific people or things.

That is Ivan's cousin.   **Those** are mine.

This will go down in history.

▶ **Interrogative pronouns** begin a question.

Who has the key?   **What** is the problem?

▶ **Reflexive pronouns** end in *-self* or *-selves* and refer to an earlier noun or pronoun in the sentence. **Intensive pronouns** add emphasis.

Tricia cut **herself** slicing a bagel.

I **myself** don't believe the story.

For information about **relative pronouns** and **adjective clauses**, see Lesson 8.2.

EDITING TIP

Possessive pronouns never take an apostrophe.

its
The dog wagged ~~it's~~ tail.

hers
That backpack is ~~her's~~.

Personal Pronouns

I	me	we	us
you	he	him	she

Possessive Pronouns

my	her
mine	hers
your	his
yours	their
our	theirs
ours	its

Some Indefinite Pronouns

all	another
any	anybody
anyone	anything
both	each
either	everybody
everyone	everything
few	most
many	neither
nobody	none
no one	one
several	some
somebody	someone

Demonstrative Pronouns

this	these
that	those

Some Interrogative Pronouns

Who?	Whom?
Whose?	What?
Which?	

Reflexive and Intensive Pronouns

myself	yourself
himself	herself
itself	ourselves
yourselves	themselves

EXERCISE 3 Identifying Pronouns

Underline all the pronouns in this paragraph, including possessive pronouns that come before nouns. **Hint:** You'll find 21 pronouns.

[1]A while ago Wynton Marsalis played some of his music on television. [2]Then he talked to students in the audience. [3]They hoped to become musicians themselves. [4]This is part of his advice to them: [5]Write out a practice schedule, and set goals to chart your development. [6]Concentrate when you practice. [7]Relax and practice slowly; invest yourself. [8]Play everything as if you were singing. [9]Don't be too hard on yourself when you make a mistake. [10]Remember, it is not the end of the world. [11]Just make sure you learn from your mistakes. [12]Think for yourself and be optimistic. [13]How you feel about living in the world determines your success.

EXERCISE 4 Writing with Pronouns

Write ten interesting, complete sentences about yourself—about your family, friends, hobbies, hopes, and memories. Try to use each kind of pronoun from the preceding page at least once. Underline all of the pronouns in your sentences. Look for sentence variety and accurate use of pronouns.

Write What You Think

The principal of your school has asked you to write a letter to a student named Anja. She has always lived in Finland, but her family is moving, and Anja will attend your school next year. She is worried that she won't fit in at your school. On a separate piece of paper, write her a letter in which you give her advice on how to be a successful ninth-grader in your school. You might cover such topics as friends, clothing, classes, studying, tests, sports, clubs, and so on. After you have revised and edited your writing, underline all of the pronouns that you've used. See teacher pages for assessment rubrics.

Verbs

For many reasons, verbs are the heart of a sentence. You can't make a statement about a noun or pronoun unless you use a verb, too.

▐▌▐▶ **Verbs** are words that express an action or a state of being. Every sentence has at least one action verb or one linking verb.

Some action verbs express an action you can observe: *slide, giggle, carry*. Other action verbs express an action you usually can't see: *worry, dislike, love, appreciate*.

> George Lucas **wrote** and **directed** Star Wars. His ideas for the plot **came** from Hollywood Westerns and the myths of many cultures.

Verbs change form to indicate time. (For more about verb tenses, see Lesson 9.4.)

> The bear **roared**. The bear **roars**. The bear **has been roaring**.

Some action verbs (V) take direct objects (DO). (For more about direct objects, see Lesson 6.6.)

>   V   DO
> The boys **ate sushi** for dinner.

▐▌▐▶ **Linking verbs** join—or link—the subject of a sentence with a word that identifies or describes it. (For more about subjects and predicates, see Lesson 6.2.)

> For 123 years Mt. St. Helens **remained** dormant.

Some verbs can be both linking and action verbs—but not at the same time. They are linking verbs only when they are followed by a word that identifies or describes the subject.

LINKING VERB	The milk **tastes** sour. He **grew** quiet.
ACTION VERB	Jill **tasted** the milk. The farmer **grew** corn.

▐▌▐▶ A **verb phrase** contains a main verb plus one or more **helping verbs** (HV).

>   HV   V
> They **may have gone** home.
> HV   V
> **Does**n't anyone here **speak** Spanish?

Not (*n't* in a contraction) is never part of a verb phrase.

Linking Verbs: Some Forms of Be

am	are	is
was	were	being
can be	have been	
will be	should be	
would have been		

Some Other Linking Verbs

appear	become
feel	grow
look	remain
seem	smell
sound	taste

Some Helping Verbs

be (is, am, are, was, were, be, been, being)
have (has, have, had)
do (does, do, did)

can	could	may
might	must	shall
should	will	would

Using forms of the verb *to be* makes a sentence passive. Refer to Lesson 9.6 on the active voice.

WRITING HINT

Use vivid action verbs to help readers imagine an action clearly.

>   *roared*
> "Aha!" she ~~said~~.
> *gripped*
> She ~~held~~ the doorknob.

EXERCISE 5 Identifying Verbs

Underline every verb and verb phrase in the following sentences. **Hint:** Two sentences have more than one verb.

1. The Anasazi Indians built a community on steep cliffs.

2. Their stone dwellings contain hundreds of rooms.

3. When Spanish explorers found these cliff dwellings, they called the area Mesa Verde, which means "green table."

4. The Anasazi grew corn, squash, beans, and cotton.

5. They made cloth, turquoise jewelry, pottery, and baskets.

6. Sometime around 1300 the Anasazi abandoned Mesa Verde.

7. Archaeologists guess that they left because of a drought, an epidemic, or enemy raids.

8. For hundreds of years, Mesa Verde remained empty.

9. Ranchers rediscovered the dwellings in the 1800s.

10. In 1906, the federal government declared Mesa Verde a national park.

EXERCISE 6 Revising a Paragraph

The following paragraph is weak because it contains imprecise verbs and nouns. With a partner, strengthen the paragraph by adding vivid verbs and precise nouns. You can make up details and add, drop, or combine sentences. Compare your revision with that of other pairs.

¹One summer a boy wanted a job. ²He went to places and talked to people and asked people for a job, but no one gave him one. ³The boy thought about what he could do. ⁴He was good at sports. ⁵He played a musical instrument, and he could fix things that broke. ⁶Sometimes he took care of his young relatives. ⁷The boy went to a place that took care of children. ⁸He talked to a person there. ⁹She gave him a job. ¹⁰He helped with children. ¹¹He showed them how to play sports. ¹²He liked his summer job.

Paragraphs should correctly use a variety of verbs. Suggest that students read the paragraph aloud to hear the awkward, choppy sound.

Adjectives

Whenever you describe a thing, a person, or a place, you use adjectives.

▶ **Adjectives** are modifiers. They give information about the nouns and pronouns they modify.

WHAT KIND?	**gray** clouds, **irreverent** humor, **crisp** apple, **quiet** pond
HOW MANY?	**three** weeks, **several** mistakes
HOW MUCH?	**less** noise, **more** dessert
WHICH ONE?	**first** answer, **this** jacket, **next** year, **best** poster

Give students a hint for when to use a comma with two or more adjectives. If you can reverse the last two adjectives before a noun, use a comma. If you can't, then the last adjective is part of the noun.

the white, fluffy cloud
the fat mother hen

Two or more adjectives may modify the same noun.
Five funny, clumsy ducklings waddled after their mother.
Picasso's ceramics are **colorful** and **humorous**.

▶ The adjectives *a* and *an* are called **indefinite articles**. They refer to any one member of a group and so are indefinite. The adjective *the* is called a **definite article**. It points out a particular noun and so is definite.

indefinite   **A** puppy makes a good pet.
definite   **The** puppy chewed her shoe.

▶ **Proper adjectives**, which come from proper nouns, always begin with a capital letter.

Shakespearean sonnet	**Mexican** fiesta
African mask	**Democratic** candidate

▶ Many adjectives come right before the noun they modify, but **predicate adjectives** follow a linking verb to modify the subject of a sentence. (For more about subjects, see Lesson 6.2.)
The tulips are **purple**.
The ocean looks **blue** and **clear**.

When a noun modifies another noun, it functions as an adjective.

kitchen table	**church** music
Romeo's sword	**porch** swing

Enriching Your Vocabulary

The prefix *ir-*, like *in-*, usually serves to form a word opposite in meaning to the root word to which it is joined. *Irreverent*, for example, means lacking reverence or respect. Other examples of such *ir-* words are *irregular*, *irrational*, and *irreversible*.

WRITING HINT

Replace general, all-purpose adjectives with adjectives that make your writing sharper.

The candidate gave a *concise but persuasive* ~~good~~ speech.

EXERCISE 7 Identifying Adjectives

Underline the adjectives and proper adjectives in the following paragraph. Do not underline definite and indefinite articles.

¹<u>Regional</u> and <u>ethnic</u> music in America has <u>many</u> roots. ²<u>Traditional</u> <u>American</u> <u>Indian</u> music uses <u>male</u> voices and sometimes drums and rattles. ³During the 1890s, jazz developed from <u>two</u> <u>African</u> <u>American</u> traditions: ragtime and blues. ⁴<u>Gospel</u> music dates back to the 1930s. ⁵Thomas A. Dorsey wrote the <u>first</u> <u>gospel</u> songs, based on <u>African</u> <u>American</u> spirituals and <u>jazz</u> rhythms. ⁶<u>One</u> source of <u>Appalachian</u> music is <u>Irish</u> <u>folk</u> tunes. ⁷<u>Tex-Mex</u> music blends the sounds of <u>Mexican</u> bands with the <u>polka</u> rhythms of <u>German</u>, <u>Polish</u>, and <u>Czech</u> immigrants. ⁸<u>Cajun</u> music in Louisiana, led by the accordion and fiddle, has <u>French</u> and <u>Creole</u> roots. ⁹<u>Jewish</u> <u>klezmer</u> bands, traditionally made up of violins and clarinets, first played in <u>eastern</u> <u>European</u> cities and towns. ¹⁰Hawaiians developed a <u>unique</u> sound with the <u>steel</u> guitar.

EXERCISE 8 Revising Sentences to Add Information

Revise the sentences below to give the reader more information and to create more interesting sentences. You may add or change words and make up details. Underline all of the adjectives in your revised sentences. Do not underline definite and indefinite articles.

EXAMPLE   A man served the food.
          The <u>elderly</u> owner of the <u>Polish</u> restaurant served us a
          <u>delicious</u> casserole with potatoes and kielbasa.

1. Clouds filled the sky.

2. The woman lives in a house on a street.

3. The dog wore a sweater.

4. The girl chose a toy.

5. Students are doing projects in class.

6. Boats crowded the harbor.

7. The child played with a ball.

8. A car was parked in the lot.

9. A man stood on the beach.

10. Friends ate pizza.

Encourage students to use several types of adjectives and to be creative with their sentences. Students may wish to read their favorite sentences aloud to the class.

See **Composition** Lesson 2.4 for more about details in descriptive paragraphs.

Adverbs

▶ **Adverbs** modify—or tell more about—verbs, adjectives, and other adverbs. They tell *when, where, how,* and *to what extent.*

MODIFIES VERB	We **happily** visited Adam.
MODIFIES ADJECTIVE	The **extremely** graceful swan swims.
MODIFIES ADVERB	Jackie ran **very** quickly.

Many adverbs can come either before or after the verbs they modify.

Suddenly the light went out.

The light went out **suddenly**.

The light **suddenly** went out.

Many adverbs end with the suffix *-ly* (*quickly, easily, carefully,* for example). However, many frequently used adverbs do not end in *-ly* (*soon, never, quite,* for example).

▶ **Intensifiers** are adverbs that answer the question *to what extent?*

I feel **rather** tired today.

The movie was **too** long.

Mozart was an **extraordinarily** gifted child.

No one was **more** surprised than I!

It's a **really** good book.

Some Common Adverbs That Do Not End in *-ly*

almost	already	also
always	fast	here
just	late	more
much	not (n't)	never
seldom	still	then
there	today	too
well	tomorrow	
yet	yesterday	

Some Common Intensifiers

exceptionally		less
extraordinarily		least
more	most	nearly
only	quite	rather
really	so	very
truly	too	
somewhat		

Exercise 9 Identifying Adverbs

Underline the adverbs in each sentence below.
Hint: One sentence contains more than one adverb.

1. Jeff did <u>not</u> spear the line drive to right field.

2. Tanisha <u>easily</u> won the girls' triple jump with her 39-foot jump.

3. <u>Yesterday</u> our team squandered a 3-run lead and lost in the final inning.

4. Kim <u>also</u> ran the 400-meter hurdles in 52.97 seconds.

5. Richard bowled <u>well</u> though he missed five spares in the final game.

6. The tournament was delayed <u>again</u> by <u>exceptionally</u> heavy rains.

7. Benji lost control of his model plane and wrecked it <u>completely</u>.

8. Marie has <u>just</u> won her fifth track-and-field trophy.

STEP BY STEP

Adjective or Adverb?

To decide whether you need to use an adjective or an adverb, decide which word you need to modify.

1. If you need to modify a noun or pronoun, use an adjective.

   The drill was **quick**.

2. If you need to modify a verb, adjective, or another adverb, use an adverb.

   The towel dried **quickly**.

EXERCISE 10 Choosing the Correct Modifier

When you write and speak in school and in business, you need to use the modifier—adjective or adverb—that correctly fits the sentence. Underline the correct modifier in the sentences below.

1. Tai-chi movements are (real, <u>really</u>) (<u>graceful</u>, gracefully).

2. A tornado can touch down (quick, <u>quickly</u>) and then move on.

3. Residents of Quebec, Canada, speak French (regular, <u>regularly</u>).

4. Harry Houdini could escape (easy, <u>easily</u>) from locks and chains.

5. Being overweight makes a health problem more (<u>serious</u>, seriously).

6. Pizza tastes quite (different, <u>differently</u>) with pineapple.

7. Mangoes and papayas can't survive in a (real, <u>really</u>) cold climate.

8. Hiawatha was (extreme, <u>extremely</u>) successful in ending feuds.

9. The beetle has an (unbelievable, <u>unbelievably</u>) large number of species—350,000.

10. In a parallelogram, opposite sides are parallel and (<u>equal</u>, equally).

EXERCISE 11 Adding Adjectives and Adverbs

Give the reader a clearer picture by adding adjectives and adverbs to the following sentences. Replace general nouns and verbs, and add details.

EXAMPLE   The child picked up the toy.
Jimmy, a wiry toddler, quickly grabbed the dump truck.

1. The animal moved.

2. A box lay on the table.

Answers will vary. Students may wish to read their revised sentences aloud to the class.

3. The girl heard a series of sounds.

4. The wind damaged the car.

5. A line of people waited outside the building.

6. His pet was frightened.

7. The woman jogged around the lake.

8. The man served dessert to his guests.

9. The bird dove into the water for a fish.

10. The girl knit a sweater.

Prepositions

▮▶ Prepositions connect another word in a sentence to a noun or pronoun (and its modifiers, if any) to form a prepositional phrase. A preposition never stands alone. (For more about prepositional phrases, see Lesson 7.1.)

Will we travel **beyond** the Milky Way?
What do you see **over** the rainbow?

Some prepositions are **compound** (made up of more than one word).

His health improved **on account of** new research.
Who will attend **in addition to** us?

Words that are prepositions in one sentence may be adverbs in another sentence. Look to see if the word is part of a prepositional phrase. If it is not part of a prepositional phrase, it is an adverb.

ADVERBS   Please put the package **down** carefully.
                  We had seen her **before** at the football game.

PREPOSITIONS   Alice fell **down** a rabbit hole.
                  She stood **before** the Red Queen.

EXERCISE 12 Expanding Sentences

On a separate sheet of paper, expand the sentences below by adding prepositional phrases. Avoid adding more than four to each sentence. (More than four can make a sentence sing-songy.) Make up all the details you need in order to create interesting sentences. Underline all of the prepositions you add to the sentences.

EXAMPLE   Carla found her notes.

           Yesterday <u>after</u> dinner Carla found her missing notes <u>for</u> her research paper <u>under</u> the front seat <u>in</u> her older brother's car.

1. Jenna slipped and fell.
2. Cary threw the ball.
3. The cat leaped.
4. We heard a sound.
5. No one noticed.
6. We go.
7. Can you tell?
8. Nobody was home.
9. It's dark.
10. We were alone.

Sentences will vary. Students may wish to read their favorite sentences aloud to the class.

Some Commonly Used Prepositions

about	above	across
against	along	around
at	before	below
beside	between	beyond
but (meaning "except")		
by	during	except
for	from	inside
into	like	near
of	off	on
out	outside	over
since	through	to
toward	under	until
up	upon	
with	without	

Some Common Compound Prepositions

according to	along with
apart from	aside from
as to	due to
instead of	in front of
in place of	in spite of
because of	out of
in addition to	

WRITING HiNT

In the past, students were taught never to end a sentence with a preposition. British Prime Minister Winston Churchill is said to have challenged this rule by saying: "This is the sort of [English] up with which I will not put." Today, ending a sentence with a preposition is usually acceptable.

What are you looking **for**? Here's the pen I spoke **about**.

EXERCISE 13 Choosing Prepositions

Some prepositions help pinpoint location and time. In the parentheses in each sentence below, underline every preposition that makes sense in the sentence. Notice how the meaning changes, depending on which preposition you use.

1. (Before, Until, After, During, In spite of) dinner Lisa noticed a dark blob (in, on, under, in front of, between, above) the front door.

2. A giant spider was crawling (up, down, around, through) the front door.

3. When she saw the spider, Lisa ran (toward, out, in front of, over, on, under, near) the door.

4. Her brother hid (under, behind, inside, above, beneath, next to, near, with, between) the couch.

5. "Boy, these kids are scary!" the spider thought (within, inside, toward, to, upon, before) himself.

EXERCISE 14 Distinguishing Prepositions from Adverbs

Fill in the blank with *PREP* if the underlined word is functioning as a preposition or with *ADV* if the underlined word is functioning as an adverb.

__PREP__ 1. In this state, you can turn right on a red light.

__ADV__ 2. Turn the light on, please.

__ADV__ 3. "Look up!" shouted the child watching the fireworks.

__PREP__ 4. Go up the stairs quietly so that you don't wake anyone.

__ADV__ 5. Are you going out tonight?

__PREP__ 6. Look out the window to see when the taxi arrives.

__PREP__ 7. The spilled milk soaked through the tablecloth.

__ADV__ 8. I want to be the first student through with the test.

__PREP__ 9. The mouse ran down the clock.

__ADV__ 10. When the battery ran down, the clock stopped.

Conjunctions and Interjections

▐▶ **Conjunctions** join words or groups of words.

▐▶ **Coordinating conjunctions** join words or groups of words that are equal in importance.

> Darren **and** *she* have finished their science projects.
> They are done, **but** *I am not.*

▐▶ **Correlative conjunctions** are always used in pairs.

> **Either** *Elisha* **or** *I* will call you. **Both** *Karen* **and** *Jules* are nurses.

It is important to place the correlative conjuction correctly. The words or phrases joined by a correlative conjuction should play the same role in a sentence. For example, a correlative conjunction might join two subjects or two clauses.

> INCORRECT   Either the girls like or dislike the movie.
> CORRECT   The girls either like or dislike the movie.
> CORRECT   Either the girls like the movie, or they dislike it.

▐▶ **Subordinating conjunctions** connect adverb clauses to main clauses. (For more about adverb clauses and a list of subordinating conjunctions, see Lesson 8.3.)

> Kabuo bought a fishing rod **because** *he had always wanted one.*
> **When** *an underwater earthquake takes place,* tidal waves form.

▐▶ **Interjections** express mild or strong emotion.

Interjections have no grammatical connection to the rest of the sentence. They are set off by a comma or by an exclamation point.

> **Hey**! Watch where you're going!   **Well**, I certainly am surprised!

EXERCISE 15 Adding Interjections to a Dialogue

Insert interjections where they seem natural in the following dialogue.

1. LEAH: David, what do you say?

2. DAVID: I was just thinking about you.

3. LEAH: What were you thinking?

4. DAVID: I was wondering if maybe you'd like to go to a movie.

5. LEAH: What's playing?

6. DAVID: Have you seen *E.T.*?

Coordinating Conjunctions

| and | but | or |
| nor | so | yet |

Some Correlative Conjunctions

both . . . and
either . . . or
neither . . . nor
not only . . . but also
whether . . . or

Some Common Interjections

aha	cool	oh
yo	hooray	ouch
well	wow	ugh
hey		

Enriching Your Vocabulary

Mediators, used in Exercise 16, comes from the Latin *mediare,* which means "to be in the middle." The verb form stems from the Latin *medius,* or "middle," which is the root of many other English words (for example, *media, median, mediocre,* and *medieval*).

Have pairs of students read the dialogue aloud to help them find the interjections that sound most natural to their ears.

7. LEAH: I hate that movie.

8. DAVID: What about *Return of the Jedi*?

9. LEAH: I'd love to.

10. DAVID: I'll see you Saturday.

Exercise 16 Identifying Conjunctions

Underline all of the conjunctions in the paragraph below. **Hint:** Not every sentence contains a conjunction.

¹Peer-mediation centers are spreading to elementary, middle, and high schools throughout the country. ²As peer mediators, student volunteers receive special training. ³They practice how to get students in conflict to sit down and listen to each other. ⁴In one middle school in Cleveland, mediators most often deal with disputes caused by name-calling, rumors, teasing, or gossip. ⁵Each student presents his or her side of the dispute, and the other student must listen without interrupting. ⁶Conflicts are defused either with an apology and a handshake or a promise to stay away from each other. ⁷In a dispute, students say they are more likely to listen to their peers than to a teacher or guidance counselor. ⁸Both students and school officials praise peer-mediation programs.

Write What You Think

Here are the steps in peer mediation:

- Any student involved in a conflict can ask for a mediation hearing.
- Peer mediators track down the other student or students involved in the dispute and bring the parties together.
- Each student must listen to the other side without interrupting.
- Peer mediators help students find ways of ending the dispute.

What kinds of disputes do you see among students in your school? Do you think that all—or most—of these arguments can be settled with peer mediation? On a separate piece of paper, write a paragraph on this topic. Support your opinions with facts and examples. Be sure to revise and edit your writing.
See teacher pages for assessment rubrics.

Determining a Word's Part of Speech

Some words can function as more than one part of speech. For example, if you look up the word *light* in a dictionary, you will find that it can be a noun, a verb, an adjective, or an adverb.

▐▶ A word's part of speech is determined by how the word is used in the sentence.

NOUN	A prism separates **light** into a rainbow of colors.
VERB	Two paper lanterns **light** the path to the party.
ADJECTIVE	They played two innings in a **light** rain.
ADVERB	To mix a **light** pink color, add a bit of red to white.

EXERCISE 17 Identifying Parts of Speech

Fill in the blank to identify the part of speech of each underlined word as it is used in the sentence. You can use these abbreviations:

N=noun   ADV=adverb
PRON=pronoun   PREP=preposition
V=verb   CONJ=conjunction
ADJ=adjective   INTER=interjection

_____N_____ 1. Word histories, or <u>etymologies</u>, show how meanings change.

_____V_____ 2. Sometimes a word's meaning <u>changes</u> gradually.

____ADV____ 3. *Nice* <u>originally</u> meant "frivolous" or "ignorant."

_____N_____ 4. In the thirteenth century *nice* meant "foolish."

____ADJ____ 5. Later, a <u>shy</u> person was called nice.

____PREP____ 6. <u>During</u> the 1700s, the word *nice* started to mean "agreeable."

____ADJ____ 7. "<u>Nice</u> guys finish last," claimed baseball manager Leo Durocher.

____PRON____ 8. Would you be pleased or insulted if <u>someone</u> called you nice?

_____N_____ 9. *Nice, wonderful,* and *great* are used so often that they are tired <u>words</u>.

_____V_____ 10. You <u>should try</u> to avoid tired words when you write.

Enriching Your Vocabulary

Frivolous here means "lacking in seriousness" or "silly." It can also mean "of little importance" or "without basis" as, for example, in describing a lawsuit or claim.

Revising and Editing Worksheet

Improve the following draft by revising for ideas, organization, word choice, and sentence variety. After revising, edit the draft for errors in spelling, capitalization, punctuation, and usage. Write your revised and edited version on a separate piece of paper. Compare your changes with those of a writing partner.

[1]Elephants are the largest land mammals. [2]There are two species of elephants. [3]There are african elephants. [4]There are Indian elephants. [5]The african elephant is bigger. [6]The african elephant has larger ears. [7]The african elephant has a longer trunk. [8]A male african elephant may be 13 feet tall. [9]A male african elephant may be as much as 6 to 8 tons heavy on a scale. [10]A male Indian elephant may be 9 feet tall. [11]It may measure 3.5 tons on a scale.

[12]An elephant's nose and upper lip form a trunk. [13]An elephant uses it's trunk to gather food. [14]They use their trunks for picking up objects. [15]They use their trunks for sucking up water. [16]They also suck up dust. [17]They spray the water into they're mouths. [18]They spray the dust on their bodies.

[19]Elephants in the wild have no homes. [20]They travel in a herd. [21]They travel to find food. [22]The herd is large—100 elephants. [23]They travel at about 4 miles an hour. [24]They can run faster. [25]They run quick at 30 miles an hour. [26]They do this when they are angry, threatened.

[27]Elephants can live for 60–70 years. [28]They are an animal in danger from extinction. [29]Hunters kill elephants for the ivory in their long tusks. [30]Ivery is carved into nice art objects. [31]To protect elephants, many countries have banned trade in ivory.

Revised and edited report should use parts of speech correctly. Students may wish to use this report as a model for writing a short report on their favorite animals.

Chapter Review

EXERCISE A Identifying Parts of Speech

In the space provided, identify the part of speech of the underlined word in each quotation. Use these abbreviations:

N=noun   ADV=adverb
PRON=pronoun   PREP=preposition
V=verb   CONJ=conjunction
ADJ=adjective   INTER=interjection

___ADJ___ 1. If a man does not keep pace with his companions, perhaps it is because he hears a <u>different</u> drummer.—*Henry David Thoreau, Walden*

___ADV___ 2. <u>Always</u> do right. This will gratify some people and astonish the rest.—*Mark Twain, from a speech*

___V___ 3. If I read a book and it makes my whole body so cold no fire can ever <u>warm</u> me, I know that is poetry.—*Emily Dickinson, Letters*

___PRON___ 4. <u>We</u> all live with the object of being happy; our lives are different and yet the same.—*Anne Frank, The Diary of a Young Girl*

___PRON___ 5. Everything happens to <u>everybody</u> sooner or later if there is only time enough.—*George Bernard Shaw, As Far As Thought Can Reach*

___PREP___ 6. No one can make you feel inferior <u>without</u> your consent. —*Anna Eleanor Roosevelt, This Is My Story*

___INTER___ 7. <u>Oh</u>, beat the drum slowly, and play the fife lowly. . . . —*The Cowboy's Lament*

___CONJ___ 8. History knows no resting places <u>and</u> no plateaus. —*Henry Kissinger, White House Years*

___N___ 9. We must build a new world, a far better world—one in which the eternal <u>dignity</u> of man is respected.—*Harry S. Truman, from a speech*

___ADJ___ 10. The ballot is <u>stronger</u> than the bullet.—*Abraham Lincoln, from a speech*

EXERCISE B Choose the Correct Modifier

Underline the correct modifier in the sentences below.

1. It was (unbearable, <u>unbearably</u>) hot during the opening rounds of the tennis tournament.

2. The artist Winslow Homer was (full, <u>fully</u>) committed to the theme of struggle with the sea.

3. On a (<u>remote</u>, remotely) Alaskan archipelago, scientists seek the causes of a worrisome decline in fur seal population.

4. The crowd watched in horror; all hoped the cyclist was not hurt (bad, <u>badly</u>) in the spill.

5. Now, more than a century after his death, science fiction writer Jules Verne appears more (<u>prophetic</u>, prophetically) than ever.

6. The newly elected politician spoke (frank, <u>frankly</u>) to his staff about the challenges ahead.

7. Nowhere is Ireland's new prosperity more (conspicuous, <u>conspicuously</u>) on display than in Dublin.

8. All the nominees tried to look as (<u>calm</u>, calmly) as they could as the host opened the envelope that contained the winner's name.

9. After crawling through the brush in the (near, <u>nearly</u>) total darkness, the surprised young soldier found himself (<u>close</u>, closely) enough to the camp to hear singing.

10. Orcas are not only intelligent, but very playful; they are (extraordinary, <u>extraordinarily</u>) social animals.

Write What You Think

Think of an issue in your community or school. Write a persuasive speech about how the issue might be settled. Remember to state your opinion clearly and support it with facts and statistics. Be sure to answer the following questions in your speech.

> What is the issue?
> How is the issue affecting the listener?
> What should the listener do to help settle the issue?

Be sure to revise and edit your writing.

Answers will vary. Give students full credit if they have stated an opinion on an issue and attempted to support the opinion. They should also have written grammatically complete sentences that begin with a capital letter and end with an appropriate end punctuation mark.

Parts of a Sentence

Direct students to
www.grammarforwriting.com
for chapter-specific
portfolio projects.

STUDENT WRITING

Book Review

Atlas Shrugged by Ayn Rand
Review by Peter Tanpitukpong
high school student, Wilmington, Delaware

Ayn Rand's most notable, as well as most controversial novel, is spellbinding excitement. From the beginning, *Atlas Shrugged* includes suspense, deceit, and a pedagogical analysis of her philosophy, Objectivism. What distinguishes this novel from other classic best-sellers is that Ayn Rand "writes for all ages."

Ayn Rand lived in Soviet Russia under the flag of Communism. Her philosophy, Objectivism, portrays the antithesis of this ideology. Her dealings and life experiences behind the harsh "Iron Curtain," where bread for the poor was a rarity but caviar for the leaders was abundant, tremendously influenced her book.

The novel follows the mind of the main character, Dagny Taggart, who is the epitome of the industrialist: ambitious, knowledgeable, greedy. But the negative connotation of "greedy" is suddenly reversed in a purely ironic fashion. To [Taggart], money is not just a stamp collection [in which] the accumulation of more stamps for the sake of impressing others is the goal; rather, it would be solely for the enjoyment and pleasure of the philatelist. Monetary gain is a form of enjoyment for Dagny Taggart because it reflects what matters most to her: her work.

The suspense of this book stems from the unending subplots. There are no dull moments; in the beginning, Dagny tells of her preoccupation with her biggest project; she later suffers mercilessly at the hands of a stifling directive; later, she goes on a futile search for John Galt, [a media mystery figure].

The most impressive feature of this book to me is its intellectual content. *Atlas Shrugged* has different outlooks and the way it was written impresses me. I recommend this book as a timeless classic of literature even if you don't agree with Rand's philosophy.

This book review contains a brief opinion statement, a short plot synopsis, and a concluding paragraph. The writer also includes some background on the author of the book, a sketch of the main character, and a description of the most impressive feature of the book.

The sentences have a good tempo because the writer has seamlessly combined short sentences into long ones. The lessons in this chapter will help you become more aware of the parts of sentences as you write.

Allow time for students to discuss the student writing. Suggest that they identify its strengths and propose possible improvements. Use the model to introduce the concepts in the chapter.

Using Complete Sentences

▐▶ A **sentence** is a grammatically complete group of words that expresses a thought.

A sentence must tell you two things: (1) the person, animal, or thing that the sentence is about and (2) what that person, animal, or thing does or is.

Every sentence begins with a capital letter and ends with an end punctuation mark—a period, a question mark, or an exclamation point.

▐▶ A **sentence fragment** is a group of words that is not grammatically complete. Avoid sentence fragments when you write.

Fragments may look like sentences because they start with a capital letter and end with an end punctuation mark, but don't let that fool you.

FRAGMENT	Sketched the lions. [Who sketched the lions?]
FRAGMENT	Jerri and I. [This doesn't tell what Jerri and I do.]
SENTENCE	Jerri and I sketched the lions.
FRAGMENT	While Jerri and I sketched the lions. [The word *while* turns the words into an incomplete thought.]
SENTENCE	While Jerri and I sketched the lions, they slept.

▐▶ A sentence always has one of four purposes:

1. **Declarative sentences** make a statement. They end with a period.

   The parade starts at three o'clock.

2. **Imperative sentences** make a command or a request. They end with either a period or (if the command shows strong feeling) an exclamation point.

   Come to the parade with us. Hurry up, you guys!

3. **Interrogative sentences** ask a question. They end with a question mark.

   Isn't that elephant heading straight toward us?

4. **Exclamatory sentences** express strong feeling. They end with an exclamation point.

   Run for your life! Oh, the elephant's loose!

> **WRITING HINT**
>
> Even though sentence fragments are not acceptable in standard written English, you often use them when you talk and when you write dialogue.
>
> If you say so. Right. OK.

EXERCISE 1 Identifying Sentences and Sentence Fragments

For each numbered item, circle the letter before the words that form a complete sentence.

1. a. Ellis Island in New York harbor, where millions of immigrants entered United States from 1892 to 1943.
   b. Millions of immigrants entered the United States from 1892 to 1943 at Ellis Island in New York harbor.

2. a. In the United States, women won the right to vote in 1920.
   b. In the United States, the right to vote in 1920.

3. a. Although glaciers cover Greenland and Antarctica.
   b. Glaciers cover Greenland and Antarctica.

4. a. Almost half of the 206 bones in the human skeleton are in the hands and feet.
   b. Almost half of the 206 bones in the human skeleton.

5. a. Because the greenhouse effect raises temperatures on Earth.
   b. The greenhouse effect raises temperatures on Earth.

EXERCISE 2 Writing Complete Sentences

On a separate piece of paper rewrite the following notes (which are fragments) as complete sentences. Work with a partner or small group. Be sure to begin each sentence with a capital letter and to add the appropriate end punctuation mark. Compare your sentences with those of other pairs or groups.

> Helicopter = type of aircraft.
> Vertical (straight up and down) take-off and landing. Can hover (stay in one place without moving).
> Lifts by means of horizontal rotor (like airplane's propeller).
> Rotor powered by engine.
> Leonardo da Vinci (16th-century Italian inventor & artist) = first to imagine helicopter but no engines then.
> 1st successful helicopter flight: 1907.
> Igor Sikorsky, U.S. engineer—1939: designed 1st practical single-rotor helicopter; 1941: designed 1st commercial helicopter.
> Helicopter from Greek: helico = "spiral"; ptero = "wing."

Sentences will vary. Check that none are fragments. You may wish to have students combine the sentences into a paragraph.

Subject and Predicate

Every sentence has two essential parts: a subject and a predicate. The subject is the part of the sentence that names the person, thing, or idea that the sentence is about. The predicate is the part of the sentence that tells what the subject does, what it is, or what happens to it.

SUBJECT	PREDICATE
The eagle on the Great Seal	holds a motto in its beak.

A subject and a predicate may be a single word or a group of words.

▒▶ The **simple subject** is the key word or words in the subject. When a proper noun is the simple subject, it may be more than one word. The complete subject is made up of the simple subject and all of its modifiers such as adjectives and prepositional phrases.

▒▶ The **simple predicate** is always a verb or verb phrase that tells something about the subject. The complete predicate contains the verb and all its modifiers, objects, and complements.

You'll review objects and complements in Lessons 6.6 and 6.7.

Throughout the rest of this book, the term *subject* refers to the simple subject, and the term *verb* refers to the simple predicate. The verb may be a single verb or a verb phrase. In the examples below, the highlighted words are the simple subject and the simple predicate.

COMPLETE SUBJECT	COMPLETE PREDICATE
The **eagle** on the Great Seal	**holds** a motto in its beak.
E Pluribus Unum	**has been** the motto of the United States for a long time.
The **motto**	**means** "out of many, one."
Many other **symbols**	**are** also **included** on the Great Seal.

P.S. No one outside the world of school will ever ask you to identify subjects and predicates when you write or speak. You're learning how to identify subjects so that you will know how to choose verbs that agree with their subjects. You'll learn more about subject-verb agreement in Chapter 10.

Enriching Your Vocabulary

From the Latin adjective *unus* (*una*, *unum*), which means "one," comes the stem for many English words. *Unison*, for example, means "agreement" or "a sounding together as one." Other common words formed from *unus* are *unity*, *union*, *unit*, *unite*, *universe*, and *uniform*.

EXERCISE 3 Identifying Subjects and Verbs

In each sentence, underline the subject (the simple subject) once and
the verb (the simple predicate) twice. **Remember:** When the subject is
a proper noun, underline the entire proper noun.

EXAMPLE   Alfred Nobel <u>was</u> a nineteenth-century Swedish chemist and inventor.

1. He made a great deal of money as the inventor of dynamite.

2. Nobel created a fund for prizes for outstanding achievement.

3. Since 1917, committees of Swedish experts have been awarding annual
   prizes in chemistry, physics, medicine, literature, and peace.

4. Each prize carries a cash award, a medal, and worldwide recognition.

5. Nobel Prize winners are called Nobel laureates.

6. Sometimes two or more persons share an award.

7. In some years, no award is given in a field.

8. Winners in literature have included Wole Soyinka from Nigeria and Octavio
   Paz from Mexico.

9. Dr. Martin Luther King, Jr., won the Nobel Peace Prize in 1964.

10. The Dalai Lama has also won the Peace Prize.

EXERCISE 4 Writing Complete Sentences

On a separate piece of paper, rewrite the following notes (which are fragments)
as complete sentences. Work with a partner or small group. Be sure to begin
each sentence with a capital letter and to add the appropriate end punctuation
mark. Compare your sentences with those of other pairs or groups.

Nitrogen cycle—essential to all living things.
Nitrogen = colorless gas; makes up 78% of Earth's
atmosphere.
Nitrogen from soil to plants, which manufacture necessary
proteins (nitrogen compounds) for the plants.
Waste products from plants & animals. Plants/animals: die,
decay.
Bacteria in soil: they act on decaying matter (to release
nitrogen compounds).
Resulting nitrogen gas goes back to atmosphere and soil.
Nitrogen cycle: on and on and on.

Sentences will vary. Students may wish to combine the sentences into a paragraph and store it
in their Writing Notebook.

Correcting Sentence Fragments

Use these three strategies to correct sentence fragments.

1. **Attach it**. Join the fragment to a complete sentence before or after it.

FRAGMENT   When you were in elementary school. Did you ever know a bully?

REVISED   When you were in elementary school, did you ever know a bully?

2. **Add some words**. Add the missing subject or verb or whatever other words are necessary to make the group of words grammatically complete.

FRAGMENT   Two major problems. How to change a bully's behavior and to protect a bully's victims.

REVISED   Two major problems are how to change a bully's behavior and how to protect the bully's victims.

3. **Drop some words**. Drop the subordinating conjunction that creates a fragment.

FRAGMENT   Because children need to learn strategies for coping with a bully.

REVISED   Children need to learn strategies for coping with a bully.

You may be asked to identify a fragment on a standardized test. Remember: A sentence must express a complete thought. See item 8 on page 289 for an example.

TEST-TAKING TIP

STEP BY STEP

The Sentence Test

To determine whether a group of words is a sentence, ask these three questions:

1. Does it have a subject?

2. Does it have a verb?

3. Does it express a complete thought?

If you can't answer yes to all three questions, you have a fragment. Fix it.

EXERCISE 5 Editing Sentence Fragments

On a separate piece of paper, edit each numbered item to correct all sentence fragments. Use the three strategies just presented.

1. Bullies are usually older and bigger. Than their victims.
   Bullies are usually older and bigger than their victims.
2. Because a typical victim blames himself or herself for being

   pushed around.   A typical victim blames himself or herself for being pushed around.
3. When a child can become a bully.   A child can become a bully.

4. Schools coping with the problem of dealing with bullies.
   Schools cope with the problem of dealing with bullies.
5. One strategy that may work for young children. Ignoring a
   One strategy that may work for young children is to ignore a bully's threats.
   bully's threats.

EXERCISE 6 Editing Sentence Fragments

Read the paragraph below carefully. If the numbered group is not a sentence, add words or omit words to make it a sentence.

¹Have you ever read Black Boy? ²Richard Wright's autobiography first published in 1937. ³One episode called "The Streets of Memphis." ⁴Often appears in literature anthologies. ⁵In this episode, Wright, who is very young, and his brother and mother are living in Memphis, Tennessee. ⁶One day Wright's mother sends him to the grocery store. ⁷With a basket, some money, and a shopping list. ⁸Before he gets to the store. ⁹A gang of boys attack him. ¹⁰They knock him down. ¹¹And take his money and basket. ¹²That same evening when his mother sends him to the store again. ¹³The boys take his money and hit him. ¹⁴When Wright comes home crying a second time. ¹⁵His mother gives him more money and a heavy stick. ¹⁶Tells him that she will beat him. ¹⁷If he comes home without the groceries. ¹⁸Terrified and furious. ¹⁹Wright goes back to the street and fights the whole gang. ²⁰When they try to steal his money a third time. ²¹He uses the stick and chases them. ²²"That night," the author writes, "I won the right to the streets of Memphis." Paragraphs will vary. Students should use complete sentences with correct end punctuation.

CONNECTING
Writing & Grammar

Additional tips for writing a persuasive paragraph are in **Composition** Lesson 2.4.

Write What You Think

On a separate piece of paper, write what you think about one of the questions below. When you've finished revising your writing, edit it to make sure that each sentence has a subject, a verb, and expresses a complete thought.

1. What do you think causes someone to become a bully?

2. What do you think schools and students can do to prevent bullies from threatening and hurting other students?

3. What do you think parents should teach their children about how to deal with bullies?

Answers will vary. Give students full credit if they have stated an opinion on one of the issues and attempted to support the opinion. They should also have written grammatically complete sentences that begin with a capital letter and end with an appropriate end punctuation mark.

Finding the Subject

In every sentence you write, you need to be able to identify the subject so that you can choose the right verb to go with it. In some cases, however, finding the subject in a sentence takes a careful read.

▶ In an **inverted sentence**, the verb (v) comes before the subject (s).

v   s   s
At the end of the tunnel are a green **door** and a red **one**.

v   s
Behind one of the doors is a mysterious **prize**.

▶ The words *here* and *there* are never the subject of a sentence. In a sentence beginning with *here* or *there*, look for the subject after the verb.

v   s
Here are the missing golden **apples**.

v   s
There can be only one **reason** for their disappearance.

▶ The subject of a sentence is never part of a prepositional phrase.

s   v
Different **areas** on the tongue register sweet, salty, sour, and bitter tastes. [The subject is not *tongue* because *on the tongue* is a prepositional phrase modifying *areas*, the subject.]

s   v
The two **functions** of the human ear are balance and hearing.

▶ To find the subject of a question, turn the question into a statement.

v   s
How long is your Works Cited **list**? [Your Works Cited list is _____ long.]

▶ In a command or request (an imperative sentence), the subject is always *you* (the person being spoken to).

The word *you* is called the **understood subject** because it does not appear in the sentence.

s   v   v
[You] Please turn off the lights, and lock the door.

Even when the name of the person being spoken to is mentioned, the subject is still understood to be *you*.

s   v   v
Tony, **[you]** please turn off the lights and lock the door. [*You* is the understood subject of the verbs *turn* and *lock*.]

STEP BY STEP

Finding the Subject

1. Find the verb or verb phrase.
2. Ask "Who?" or "What?" before the verb.
   The girl in the red sweater plays second base.
   VERB plays
   WHO PLAYS? girl
3. **Remember**: *There* and *here* are never subjects, and prepositional phrases never contain the subject.

Exercise 7 Identifying Subjects and Verbs

In each sentence, underline the simple subject once and the verb twice.
If the subject is understood to be *you*, write the word *you* after the sentence.
Remember: When the subject is a proper noun, underline the entire
proper noun.

1. During the Middle Ages, there were many popular stories about King Arthur and his knights of the Round Table.

2. The legendary King Arthur may have been based on a Celtic war chief of the fifth and sixth centuries.

3. At first, there was only the oral tradition of the storytellers, bards, and minstrels.

4. Among the earliest written stories about King Arthur were those by the twelfth-century writer Wace.

5. Toward the end of the Middle Ages, Sir Thomas Malory wrote *Morte d'Arthur*.

6. Did Malory write *Morte d'Arthur* during his last twenty years in prison?

7. Can you name any of the knights of the Round Table?

8. There were Sir Gawain, Sir Launcelot, Sir Galahad, and many others.

9. Here is a copy of *Sir Gawain and the Green Knight*.

10. Carey, please tell us about Tennyson's *The Idylls of the King*. you

11. Have you read T. H. White's *The Once and Future King*?

12. Don't miss this exciting, easy-to-read retelling. you

13. In White's retelling of the Arthur story, Merlin changes young Arthur into different animals.

14. From each experience as an animal, Arthur gains some wisdom.

15. The young Arthur in Malory's version pulls a sword from a marble block.

16. All of the English nobles had tried but failed.

17. After pulling out the sword, Arthur is crowned king of all Britain.

18. There have been several movies about Arthur and a successful musical.

19. In the starring roles on Broadway were Richard Burton as Arthur and Julie Andrews as Guinevere.

20. Have you seen the movie version of Lerner and Lowe's *Camelot*?

Run-on Sentences

▐▶ A **run-on** sentence is made up of two or more sentences that are incorrectly run together as a single sentence.

Use these five strategies for correcting a run-on sentence.

1. **Separate them**. Add end punctuation and a capital letter to separate the sentences.

   RUN-ON   In 1921, Franklin Delano Roosevelt was stricken by polio, seven years later, he was elected governor of New York.

   CORRECTED   In 1921, Franklin Delano Roosevelt was stricken by polio**. S**even years later, he was elected governor of New York.

2. **Use a conjunction**. Use a word like *and, but, or, yet,* or *so* preceded by a comma.

   RUN-ON   "Life was meant to be lived curiosity must be kept alive."

   CORRECTED   "Life was meant to be lived**, and** curiosity must be kept alive." —*Eleanor Roosevelt*

3. **Try a semicolon**. Use a semicolon to separate the two sentences.

   RUN-ON   "Speak softly and carry a big stick, you will go far."

   CORRECTED   "Speak softly and carry a big stick**;** you will go far." —*Theodore Roosevelt*

4. **Add a conjunctive adverb**. Use a semicolon together with a conjunctive adverb (*however, therefore, nevertheless, still, also, instead,* etc.). Be sure to put a comma after the conjunctive adverb.

   RUN-ON   On November 19, 1863, Edward Everett spoke for two hours, President Lincoln's speech, The Gettysburg Address, lasted only three minutes.

   CORRECTED   On November 19, 1863, Edward Everett spoke for two hours**; however,** President Lincoln's speech, The Gettysburg Address, lasted only three minutes.

5. **Create a clause**. Turn one of the sentences into a subordinate clause. (See Chapter 8 for more on subordinate clauses.)

   RUN-ON   Lincoln's speech lasted only three minutes it is one of the most famous speeches in American history.

   CORRECTED   **Although Lincoln's speech lasted only three minutes**, it is one of the most famous speeches in American history.

EDITING TIP

A run-on with only a comma separating its sentences is called a **comma splice**.

COMMA SPLICE
John Adams was the second president, his oldest son was the sixth president.

CORRECTION
John Adams was the second president, and his oldest son was the sixth president.

TEST-TAKING TIP

If you are asked on a standardized test to correct a run-on sentence, consider using a semicolon, providing that the two independent clauses are clearly and closely related. See item 4 on page 294 for an example.

EXERCISE 8 Editing Run-on Sentences

On a separate piece of paper, correct and rewrite the run-on sentences by adding words and punctuation marks. Use a variety of strategies.
See Answer Key at www.grammarforwriting.com.

1. Freedom Riders rode buses in the South their goal was to end racial segregation on public buses.

2. Alaska became the forty-ninth state in 1959, Hawaii became the fiftieth state in that same year.

3. Anthropology is the scientific study of human beings archaeology is the scientific study of ancient societies.

4. Lewis Carroll wrote *Alice in Wonderland*, in real life he was Charles Lutwidge Dodgson, a mathematics lecturer at Oxford.

5. Butterflies, cockroaches, and fleas are insects scientists have identified more than a million species of insects.

EXERCISE 9 Editing a Report

Work with a partner or small group to correct all of the run-on sentences and fragments in this report. Use a variety of strategies. Compare your edited report with those of other pairs or groups.

[1]George Orwell is the pseudonym, or pen name, of Eric Blair he was a twentieth-century English essayist and novelist, Orwell's best-known works are the novels *Animal Farm* (1945) and *Nineteen Eighty-Four* (1948).

Find a list of strategies for writing your own report about literature in **Composition** Lesson 4.4.

[2]*Animal Farm* is a political satire it is also a fable, complete with talking animals. [3]In this novel, the animals of Manor Farm rebel against the cruelty of Farmer Jones, at first the animals in Orwell's novel work fairly well together soon the pigs usurp power over all the other animals. [4]"All animals are equal but some animals are more equal than others" the pigs post this proclamation on the barn, it's the most famous quotation from *Animal Farm*.

[5]Orwell's *Nineteen Eighty-Four* presents a frightening picture of a future society. [6]With no individual freedom. [7]Its citizens are controlled by government from birth to death "Big Brother is watching you." Is the slogan on posters all over the society.

Answers will vary. You may wish to extend this exercise by having students use this as a model for writing a brief report on their favorite books.

Direct and Indirect Objects

In this lesson, you'll review two kinds of objects: direct objects and indirect objects.

▶ A **direct object** (DO) is a noun or pronoun that receives the action of an action verb. A direct object answers the question *whom* or *what* following the verb.

> **DO**
> Jenny takes advanced **algebra**. [Takes—*what?*—algebra. *Algebra* is the direct object.]
>
> **DO**
> Rob tested the **twins** in math. [Tested—*whom?*—the twins. *Twins* is the direct object.]

Do you remember the two kinds of verbs—action verbs and linking verbs? Only action verbs (see Lesson 5.3) can have objects. Not all action verbs have objects, but when they do, they're called **transitive verbs**.

▶ An **indirect object** (IO) is a noun or pronoun that answers the question *to whom* or *for whom* or *to what* or *for what* following an action verb.

Indirect objects never stand alone. You can have a direct object without an indirect object, but you can't have an indirect object without a direct object. The indirect object always comes before the direct object.

> **IO**   **DO**
> Their mother gives **them** piano **lessons**. [Gives lessons to—*whom?*—them. *Them* is the indirect object; *lessons* is the direct object.]
>
> **IO**   **DO**
> Jenny gave the calculus **problem** one more **try**. [Gave one more try to—*what?*—to the calculus problem. *Problem* is the indirect object; *try* is the direct object.]

Like subjects, direct objects and indirect objects never appear within a prepositional phrase. Even though the following two sentences mean the same thing, only the first one has an indirect object.

> **IO**   **DO**
> Please tell **Jim** the **answer**.
>
> **DO**
> Please tell the **answer** to Jim. [*To Jim* is a prepositional phrase.]

STEP BY STEP

Finding Direct and Indirect Objects

To find a direct object:

1. Find the action verb.
2. Ask the question *whom?* or *what?* after the action verb.

To find an indirect object:

1. Find the action verb.
2. Find the direct object.
3. Ask the question *to* or *for whom?* or *to* or *for what?* after the action verb.

EXERCISE 10 Identifying Direct and Indirect Objects

Underline every direct object and indirect object. Label them *DO* for direct object and *IO* for indirect oject.

EXAMPLE   Democrats gave John F. Kennedy [IO] the presidential nomination [DO] in 1960.

1. Kennedy's charm won the loyalty [DO] of many supporters.

2. However, many Democratic leaders doubted his ability [DO] to win the election.

3. Some questioned Kennedy's experience [DO] since he was just forty-three years old.

4. Others gave him [IO] high marks [DO] for the hope and energy he inspired among Americans.

5. Kennedy's calm confidence on televised debates earned him [IO] votes [DO] in a close election.

EXERCISE 11 Identifying Direct and Indirect Objects

Underline every direct object once and indirect object twice in the paragraphs below. **Hint:** Not every sentence has an object.

¹In 1960, televised debates impacted the outcome of a presidential election for the first time. ²In these debates, Democratic candidate John F. Kennedy argued his case against his opponent, Republican Richard Nixon. ³Kennedy understood the power of his television appearance. ⁴He practiced his speeches carefully. ⁵His aides gave him test questions. ⁶They anticipated the questions of the debate panel. ⁷Finally, they gave Kennedy make-up to wear that would help him look healthy and calm.

⁸Nixon did not practice his speeches. ⁹He also did not wear make-up. ¹⁰During the debate, Nixon mopped his brow. ¹¹Nixon answered questions easily, but he gave television viewers an impression of strained nervousness. ¹²Voters who watched the debate gave Kennedy their support, and in November, he won one of the closest presidential races in history.

CONNECTING Writing & Grammar

Write What You Think

On a separate piece of paper, write a paragraph in answer to the question below. Support your opinion with facts and examples. Be sure to revise and edit your paragraph.

Given the powerful impact of the media on Americans, how can you be sure you are getting a fair and accurate portrayal of national public events?

See teacher pages for writing assessment rubrics.

Predicate Nominatives and Predicate Adjectives

What's wrong with the following groups of words, punctuated as sentences?

The tall young man next to Sally is. He seems.

The verbs *is* and *seems* are linking verbs, and neither group of words expresses a complete thought.

▶ A **linking verb** needs a noun or an adjective after it in order to express a complete thought. That noun (N) or adjective is (ADJ) called a **subject complement**.

                                                 N
The tall young man next to Sally is my **cousin**.

       ADJ
He seems **happy**.

There are two kinds of subject complements: predicate nominatives and predicate adjectives.

▶ A **predicate nominative** (PN) is a noun or pronoun that follows a linking verb (LV) and renames or identifies the subject (S).

        S   LV   PN
Nina's **aunt is** a police **officer**. [*Officer* is a noun that renames the subject *aunt*.]

    S   LV PN
The **person** in charge of the investigation **is she**. [*She* is a pronoun that identifies the subject *person*.]

▶ A **predicate adjective** (PA) is an adjective that follows a linking verb and modifies, or describes, the subject.

    S   LV   PA
Justin seems angry about something. [*Angry* is an adjective that modifies the subject *Justin*.]

   LV   S   S   PA
Are Luis and **she upset**, too? [The adjective *upset* modifies the subjects *Luis* and *she*.]

Linking Verbs

All the forms of *be* are linking verbs. These other verbs can also be linking verbs:

appear	remain
become	seem
feel	smell
grow	sound
look	taste

For more about linking verbs, see Lesson 5.3.

EDITING TIP

In formal usage, a pronoun used as a predicate nominative must be in the subject form. (See Lessons 11.1 and 11.2.) The correct answer to the question "Is Rosa there?" is: "This is *she*."

EXERCISE 12 Identifying Predicate Nominatives and Predicate Adjectives

Underline every predicate nominative and predicate adjective in the sentences below. In the space provided, write *PN* for predicate nominative or *PA* for predicate adjective.

__PN__ 1. For Todd, the most difficult test questions are word <u>analogies</u>.

__PA__ 2. Those little green peppers on the pizza certainly taste <u>fiery</u>.

__PN__ 3. Rachel became the youngest <u>member</u> of the jazz band.

__PA__ 4. Jed feels extremely <u>uncomfortable</u> in airplanes, so he doesn't fly.

__PA__ 5. Does this quart of milk smell <u>sour</u> to you?

EXERCISE 13 Writing a Description

A movie director is looking for a place to film her new movie. Work with a partner to write a letter describing your community or neighborhood as the possible location for the movie. When you've finished writing, underline and label every predicate adjective and predicate nominative in your sentences. Use the worksheet below to help you start.

Additional tips for writing a descriptive paragraph are in **Composition** Lesson 2.4.

A Great Place to Make a Movie

Type of community (city, small town, farm, suburb)

Type of land (hilly, desert, seashore, etc.)

What my community looks like

What the main street looks like

What the building I live in looks like

What my street looks like

What my school looks like

Community descriptions will vary. Students may wish to store this community description in their Writing Notebooks.

Revising and Editing Worksheet 1

Improve the following draft by revising for ideas, organization, word choice, and sentence variety. After revising, edit the draft for errors in spelling, capitalization, punctuation, and usage. Write your revised and edited version on a separate piece of paper. Compare your changes with those of a writing partner. Revised and edited report should be free of fragments and run-on sentences.

[1]Every September in Coos Bay, Oregon, a race called the Prefontaine Memorial Run occurs the race is held in honor of a track athlete from Coos Bay named Steve Prefontaine. [2]Steve Prefontaine did not win any Olympic gold medals, but Steve Prefontaine is considered to be one of the greatest distance runners who ever lived. [3]In his senior year of high school, Steve Prefontaine, nicknamed Pre, broke the U.S. high school record for running two miles by nearly seven seconds. [4]He ran two miles in eight minutes, forty-one and a half seconds. [5]Pre was not tall and lanky like some great runners. [6]But Pre had determination. [7]And confidence that he could run faster and longer than anyone else. [8]His high school track coach Walt McClure said, "His talent was his ability to control his fatigue and his pain. [9]His threshold for pain was higher than that of most people."

[10]Steve Prefontaine held every American outdoor track record from the 2000 meters through the 10,000 meters. [11]In all, he set fourteen American records and broke the four-minute-mile barrier nine times. [12]A remarkable feat among distance runners.

[13]At age 21, Pre competed in the 5,000 meter race at the 1972 Olympic Games. [14]A dramatic race. [15]Pre finished fourth against the fastest runners of his day? [16]He trained for two years after that year, and many thought that Pre would win the 1976 Olympic race.

[17]Pre never competed in the 1976 Olympic Games on May 30, 1975, Pre died in a car accident. [18]The world would never know if Pre had the stamina to be the fastest man in the world.

Revising and Editing Worksheet 2

Improve the following draft by revising for ideas, organization, word choice, and sentence variety. After revising, edit the draft for errors in spelling, capitalization, punctuation, and usage. Write your revised and edited version on a separate piece of paper. Compare your changes with those of a writing partner.
Revised and edited drafts should be free of fragments and run-ons.

¹Today, bathing is, like, common practice, but was it always so. ²The answer is no. ³In fact, bathing practices and views on bathing which have undergone much change over the centuries. ⁴Now let me explain.

⁵In approximately 2500 B.C., Mohenjo-Daro, a city in the Indus valley, was one of the world's earliest urban spots. ⁶At its summit atop a large mound was something known as the "Great Bath" archaeologists are uncertain as to whether the Great Bath were built for ceremonial, therapeutic, or practical things. ⁷But its discovery made one thing clear: washing will be part of daily life 4,500 years ago.

⁸Actual bath tubs began to appear in Mesopotamia about a thousand years later. ⁹Many great civilizations took bathing to a more sophisticated level than just using tubs. ¹⁰Egyptians were keen on personal hygiene. ¹¹In a number of Egyptian people's homes, bathing rooms were found adjacent to bedrooms, in addition to these private bathing rooms, the Egyptians built ornate bathhouses. ¹²Bathing in this was a ceremonial event and a time for socializing, too.

¹³Like the Egyptians: the Greeks prized it. ¹⁴When guests arrived at a Greek home, the host would often prepare a hot, cented bath for him.

¹⁵It was the Romans, though, which took the practice to the ultimate heights of sophistication and luxury. ¹⁶By the end of the fourth century, there were nearly 900 public baths in Rome? ¹⁷Then, the Roman Empire collapsed and a thousand years of Grime and Filth followed. ¹⁸Although the tradition of public baths was carried on by societies in the East for most Europeans, bathing was seen as leud. ¹⁹And immoral.

²⁰By the time of the French Revolution, the thinking had changed. ²¹People believed that dirt spread disease. ²²Bathing again has become respectable. ²³Public and private baths began to appear again. ²⁴Having a bathroom in their house was a symbol of status. ²⁵Bathing was back. ²⁶The question now is: Is it here to stay?

Chapter Review

EXERCISE A Identifying Subjects and Verbs

In each sentence, underline the simple subject once and the verb twice. If the subject is understood to be *you*, write *you* following the sentence.

1. During the famine of the 1840s, many Irish <u>people</u> <u>emigrated</u> to America.

2. <u>Have</u> <u>you</u> <u>seen</u> photos of the 1500-mile-long Great Wall of China?

3. Please <u>explain</u> this reference to the Trojan horse.   you

4. High in the Himalayas, north of India, <u>is</u> <u>Nepal</u>.

5. According to the Boy Scout Law, <u>scouts</u> <u>should be</u> trustworthy and kind.

6. <u>Ben Franklin</u> <u>wrote</u> *Poor Richard's Almanack* and a famous autobiography.

7. In an eclipse of the sun, the sun's <u>light</u> <u>is blocked</u> by the moon.

8. <u>Romeo</u> and <u>Juliet</u> <u>fall</u> in love and <u>marry</u> but <u>do</u> not <u>live</u> happily after.

9. In what year did the <u>Berlin Wall</u> <u>come</u> down?

10. <u>Cesar Chávez</u> <u>organized</u> the United Farm Workers union.

EXERCISE B Identifying Complements

In each sentence, identify the italicized word(s). Above each word, write *DO* (direct object), *IO* (indirect object), *PA* (predicate adjective), or *PN* (predicate nominative).

1. "The Secret Life of Walter Mitty" is a popular *story* [PN] by James Thurber.

2. Harriet Tubman led *hundreds* [DO] of former slaves to freedom via the Underground Railroad.

3. Carbon dioxide is a *compound* [PN] with one atom of carbon and two of oxygen.

4. Utah's Great Salt Lake is *large* [PA], *shallow* [PA], and *salty* [PA].

5. The government gives *applicants* [IO] for citizenship a written *test* [DO].

6. Margaret Mead became a leading *anthropologist* [PN].

7. Thousands of meteorites strike the *earth* [DO] each year with great force.

8. Before the storm, the sky became *yellow-green* [PA].

9. Old Mother Hubbard did not give her *dog* [IO] a bone.

10. Clara Barton founded the *American Red Cross* [DO] in 1881.

EXERCISE C Fix Sentence Fragments and Run-ons

On a separate piece of paper, use a variety of strategies to correct the following fragments and run-on sentences. See Answer Key at www.grammarforwriting.com.

1. The paintings that were here. Have been moved to a new location.

2. Pluto, discovered by scientists at the Lowell Observatory in Flagstaff, Arizona.

3. The island boasts a bounty of beautiful beaches it also has an abundance of steep volcanic peaks and lush green valleys.

4. In our nation's capital, the National Museum of the American Indian recently opened on the Mall it is the last building site there.

5. After we took a private tour of Taliesin West, the architecture school Frank Lloyd Wright built out of desert materials.

6. Antarctica is far from being a wasteland of snow and ice, it is alive with color and life.

7. Fifty-six delegates convened for the first Continental Congress in Philadelphia to protest British trade restrictions, it was September, 1774.

8. A huge volcanic eruption. Burying Pompeii, Italy, nearly 2,000 years ago.

9. Like many remakes, this one fares poorly when compared with the original, it was filmed more then seventy years ago.

10. Although the parade created traffic jams throughout the city. The mayor declared the event a huge success.

Write What You Think

On a separate piece of paper, write two paragraphs stating what you think about both of these questions.

1. Should everyone be required to take three years of a foreign language in high school? Why or why not?

2. Which language would you most like to learn? Explain why.

After revising your paragraphs, edit them to make sure that every group of words marked as a sentence is indeed a complete sentence.

Answers will vary. Give students full credit if they have stated an opinion on an issue and attempted to support the opinion. They should also have written grammatically complete sentences that begin with a capital letter and end with an appropriate end punctuation mark.

Phrases

STUDENT WRITING

Expository Essay

Help the Environment by Recycling
by Dorothy Schardt
high school student, Darien, Illinois

The students of Hinsdale South are committed to many organizations and ideals. Sports, academics, service, drug-free life styles—these and many others are an integral part of our everyday lives. However, there is one important area in which our school is lacking, and that is in our commitment to the planet.

One hundred and sixty million tons of garbage per year enters our country's landfills. On an individual level, that is approximately three and a half pounds of trash per person every day. Our cafeteria certainly produces a share of that waste.

Communities both large and small, in this country and others, have been swept up in the wave of recycling. In many European countries, for example, fines are given for throwing out recyclables, which include a variety of things such as multicolored glass or cork. Numerous school communities, from around the country and this area, have followed these models and started up school recycling programs. . . .

While we already recycle white office paper and aluminum cans, it is possible to implement a far more extensive program to encompass all parts of our lives. At a nominal charge, one that would appear to balance the cost of renewable waste disposal, [a private collector] would pick up our recyclable waste on a weekly basis. On our part, we would be required to collect recyclables in sorted bins. Styrofoam, plastics, glass, paper, and aluminum, generated at lunch time, could all be collected. The Environmental Concerns Club would be willing to help pay for the bins, and it has been suggested that the community-based students in the deaf and hard-of-hearing program would be interested in clearing the containers. If the school does not want to start such an extensive program, certainly it would be a good idea to start with just some of the materials previously mentioned. As a last resort, we could even simply switch from styrofoam to recycled paper plates.

While people can certainly think of many excuses as to why any recycling program would be impractical, expensive, and time-consuming, we must look at these reasons for what they are—excuses.

The future of our planet rests on how we care for it today, and no excuse can be good enough to justify our continued and blatant destruction of the earth that sustains us. We cannot keep taking from the earth. While recycling does not constitute giving anything new to the earth, it does allow us to give back what we have taken. While some people may be against this plan because it necessitates more time and energy than does merely throwing all waste into one place, recycling is the right thing to do, not only for us, but for the people of the future.

Dorothy's expository essay identifies a problem and offers a solution. She lists statistics that give evidence of the problem and a detailed explanation of a solution. Her essay ends with an emotional appeal for support.

As you study phrases in this chapter, you will recognize the many types that Dorothy uses in her essay. Phrases add variety to the sentences in an essay and help a writer combine short sentences into longer, more interesting ones.

Prepositional Phrases: Adjective and Adverb Phrases

▐▐▐➤ A **prepositional phrase** always begins with a preposition and ends with an object (a noun or pronoun). A prepositional phrase may have a compound object. All modifiers of the object(s) are part of the prepositional phrase.

PREP	ADJ	OBJ	PREP	OBJ	OBJ	PREP	ADJ	OBJ
under	the green	couch	to	her and	me	in	three	hours

▐▐▐➤ A prepositional phrase adds information to a sentence by modifying another word in the sentence.

The gorilla ran. [Which gorilla? Where did it run?]

The gorilla **near the fence** ran **to the zookeeper** **with food**.

Sometimes, as in the sentence above, a prepositional phrase modifies the object in a preceding prepositional phrase. Also, more than one prepositional phrase may modify the same word.

For several minutes the gorilla stared **at me**. [Both phrases modify the verb *stared*.]

▐▐▐➤ An **adjective phrase** is a prepositional phrase that modifies a noun or pronoun in the sentence. Adjective phrases (like adjectives) answer the questions "Which one?" or "What kind?"

The gorilla **in the tree** is named Sam. [The adjective phrase modifies the noun *gorilla*.]

Sam is one **of the gorillas** born last spring. [The adjective phrase modifies the pronoun *one*.]

▐▐▐➤ An **adverb phrase** is a prepositional phrase that modifies a verb, an adjective, or another adverb.

The gorilla laughed **at me**. [The adverb phrase modifies the verb *laughed*.]

He was the largest **of all the gorillas**. [The adverb phrase modifies the adjective *largest*.]

Remember: Some words function as either an adverb or a preposition, depending on the sentence. Prepositions never stand alone. They are always part of a prepositional phrase. If the word is alone, it's an adverb for sure.

ADV	PREP
Lee Ann fell **down**.	Lee Ann fell **down** the steps.

WRITING HINT

Help readers visualize objects, people, and actions by using prepositional phrases to add specific details.

NO DETAILS
The man beckoned.

DETAILS
The man in **the black hat** beckoned **to me**.

EXERCISE 1 Identifying Adjective and Adverb Phrases

Underline every prepositional phrase in the sentences below, and draw an arrow to the word each phrase modifies. Label the phrase *ADJ* for an adjective phrase or *ADV* for an adverb phrase.

EXAMPLE   Mumps is caused **by a virus**. [ADV]

1. Mumps is common during childhood but may also strike adults. [ADV]

2. Infants are given shots for measles, mumps, and rubella. [ADJ]

3. Distant objects look blurry to people with myopia. [ADV] [ADJ]

4. Nearsighted people can see distant objects with eyeglasses or contact lenses. [ADV]

5. Iron is a mineral for red blood cells. [ADJ]

6. Foods rich in iron include spinach, liver, lima beans, and green peas. [ADV]

7. Calcium for bones and teeth is found in all dairy products. [ADJ] [ADV]

8. Most vegetarians eat all types of vegetables, fruits, and beans. [ADJ]

9. A diet without any meat can still provide plenty of protein. [ADJ] [ADJ]

10. What do you eat on a typical day for breakfast, lunch, and dinner? [ADV] [ADV]

EXERCISE 2 Revising and Editing a Paragraph

Work with a partner or small group to revise the following draft of a newspaper story for your local paper. Newspaper stories are supposed to answer the questions "Who?" "What?" "When?" "Where?" "Why?" and "How?" Make up details for the story; and on a separate piece of paper, see how many prepositional phrases you can add. Be on the lookout for sentence fragments and run-on sentences. Correct them. When you have finished improving the paragraph, underline every prepositional phrase. Compare your improved news story with those of your classmates. See teacher pages for assessment rubrics.

> [1]There was a car accident. [2]One driver was driving a van. [3]The second driver was driving a car. [4]Both cars were damaged. [5]A passenger was injured. [6]A police car arrived. [7]Then an ambulance, then two tow trucks. [8]The police officer ticketed the driver. [9]Traffic stopped. [10]The street was blocked.

HiNT

Some sentences have more than one prepositional phrase.

See **Composition** Lesson 1.1 for more on the 5 W and H strategy.

Participles and Participial Phrases

A **verbal** is a verb form that functions as a different part of speech. Three kinds of verbals that you will learn are participles, gerunds, and infinitives. (See Lessons 7.4 and 7.5.)

▶ A **participle** is a verb form that acts as an adjective, modifying a noun or a pronoun. There are two kinds of participles: present and past. **Present participles** always have an *-ing* ending; **past participles** usually end in *-d* or *-ed*. The past participles of irregular verbs have different endings. (See Lessons 9.2 and 9.3.)

When you put a helping verb before a participle, you have a verb phrase. When you use a participle alone, you have a modifier that functions as an adjective.

VERB PHRASE	Laurie **is winning** the race.
PARTICIPLE	Who has the **winning** ticket?
VERB PHRASE	**Have** you ever **broken** a bone?
PARTICIPLE	The X-ray showed a **broken** bone.

▶ A **participial phrase** is made up of a participle and all of its modifiers. A participial phrase may contain objects, modifiers, and prepositional phrases. The whole phrase acts as an adjective.

Looking intently at the map, Jerry found New Hope.

Larry made the crown **worn by Queen Esther.**

See Lesson 13.4 for a discussion of punctuating phrases.

WRITING HINT

Place a participial phrase close to the word it modifies. Otherwise, you may say something you do not mean.

I watched a TV show about a wild elephant ⊙ sitting in my living room.

Lesson 12.4 covers misplaced and dangling modifiers more thoroughly.

EXERCISE 3 Identifying Participles

Underline every participle or participial phrase in each sentence. Draw an arrow to the word each participle or participial phrase modifies.

EXAMPLE   The doctor showed Jim the X-ray of his leg broken in two places.

1. Have you ever had an X-ray taken by a doctor or a dentist?

2. X-rays made in hospital emergency rooms reveal broken bones.

3. Reading X-rays of internal organs, doctors can diagnose diseases.

4. Dental X-rays show cavities and teeth growing below the gum line.

5. Superman, famed for his X-ray vision, can see through buildings.

6. A German physicist named Wilhelm Roentgen discovered X-rays in 1895.

7. Patients <u>admitted to a hospital</u> often have a routine chest X-ray.

8. <u>Penetrating</u> light rays travel through solid bodies and register images on a photographic plate.

9. X-rays can destroy living tissue in patients <u>exposed for too long.</u>

10. Earth's atmosphere protects us from X-rays <u>emanating from the sun.</u>

EXERCISE 4 Writing Sentences with Participial Phrases

For each of the following participial phrases, write a complete sentence on a separate piece of paper. Place the participial phrase close to the word it modifies.

EXAMPLE   taken at the beach

This photograph, taken at the beach, shows Grandma as a girl.

1. written on a tiny scrap of paper

2. celebrated on July 4th

3. floating just offshore

4. run by volunteers

5. quoting from a famous speech

6. visiting from Mars

7. surprised by the news

8. warning of danger

9. seen up close

10. sliding into first

Answers will vary. Check that phrases are not used as verbs.

EXERCISE 5 Identifying Participles

Underline any participles and participial phrases in the following paragraph.

¹The workers <u>struggling to build the Panama Canal</u> were at grave risk of getting yellow fever. ²The disease, <u>carried by mosquitoes</u>, killed thousands of canal workers. ³<u>Charged with improving the sanitary conditions of the canal zone</u>, Colonel William C. Gorgas borrowed techniques from <u>respected</u> Cuban and American scientists. ⁴Gorgas drained swamps, cleared the land <u>infested with mosquitoes</u>, and killed rats <u>carrying the plague.</u>
⁵The canal, <u>completed in 1914</u>, took ten years to build. ⁶<u>Dedicated</u> workers dug through mountains and swamps to make an <u>easily navigated</u> passageway for ships. ⁷It continues to be a <u>frequently used</u> shipping lane between the Atlantic and the Pacific oceans.

Write What You Think

On a separate piece of paper, write five sentences on any topic that contain participles and participial phrases. Exchange papers with a partner to revise and edit your work. Student sentences will vary.

Effective Paragraphs: Varying Sentence Beginnings

When every sentence in a paragraph starts with its subject, the rhythm of the sentences becomes quite monotonous.

▐▶ For variety, begin some of your sentences with a phrase.

ORIGINAL   Katie threw a Frisbee to her dog for fifteen minutes.

REVISED   **For fifteen minutes**, Katie threw a Frisbee to her dog. [prepositional phrase placed first]

ORIGINAL   Jed swam through the underwater tunnel, holding his breath.

REVISED   **Holding his breath**, Jed swam through the underwater tunnel. [participial phrase placed first]

ORIGINAL   The old house, battered by gale-force winds, remained undamaged.

REVISED   **Battered by gale-force winds**, the old house remained undamaged. [participial phrase placed first]

Watch your punctuation. Insert a comma following a participial phrase at the beginning of a sentence.

> See **Composition** Lesson 1.3 for more on revising your writing for content and style.

EXERCISE 6 Rewording Sentences

Underline every prepositional and participial phrase in each sentence, and write *PREP* for a prepositional phrase or *PART* for a participial phrase. On a separate piece of paper, rewrite the sentence so that it begins with one or more phrases.

EXAMPLE   Jiro paused <u>for a moment</u> <u>at the top</u> <u>of the stairs</u>.
　　　　　　　PREP　　　　　PREP　　　　PREP
　　　　　　　At the top of the stairs, Jiro paused for a moment.

1. Mike changed his mind <u>at the last minute</u>.
   　　　　　　　　　　　　PREP

2. Cinderella lost one <u>of her glass slippers</u> <u>rushing down the steps</u>.
   　　　　　　　　　　PREP　　　　　　　　PART

3. Bev's mom, <u>standing at the top of the ladder</u>, still couldn't
   　　　　　　PART
   reach the kitten.

4. Grandpa Max recalled his childhood, <u>speaking into the tape</u>
   　　　　　　　　　　　　　　　　　　PART
   <u>recorder</u>.

5. The winding road, <u>covered by a heavy fog</u>, was impassable.
   　　　　　　　　　PART

> ### EDITING TIP
>
> It's never wrong to use a comma after one or a series of introductory prepositional phrases, but it's not always necessary to do so.
>
> **COMMA OR NO COMMA OK**
> To me you look great.
> To me, you look great.
>
> **COMMA NECESSARY TO PREVENT MISREADING**
> After dinner, time flies.
> In German, nouns are capitalized.

6. He received news of the art contest winners <u>after more than a month</u>.
_{PREP}

7. Lobster Shack has been serving its famous clam chowder <u>in this same spot</u>
_{PREP}
<u>since 1935</u>.
_{PREP}

8. Sean, <u>exploring the World Wide Web</u>, found many sites <u>about Ireland</u>.
_{PART} _{PREP}

9. Lionfish, <u>protected by a deadly poison on their fins</u>, aren't bothered <u>by</u>
_{PART}
<u>predators</u>.
_{PREP}

10. The Greek goddess Athena, <u>known for her wisdom</u>, has an owl <u>as her</u>
_{PART}
<u>symbol</u>. Reworded sentences should begin with a phrase.
_{PREP}

EXERCISE 7 Writing a Paragraph

Use the following notes to write a paragraph on a separate piece of paper. Vary your sentence beginnings. Start at least one sentence with a prepositional phrase or phrases and begin at least one sentence with a participial phrase. Work with a partner or small group and compare your finished paragraphs.

> ### Antigone
>
> Ancient Greek mythology: Antigone (daughter of Oedipus), a heroine
>
> <u>Antigone</u>, tragedy by Sophocles, ancient Greek dramatist— written about 411 B.C.
>
> Theme of play: conflict between society's law vs. higher moral law (individual's conscience)
>
> Creon, king of Thebes, orders people not to bury Antigone's brother's body (his enemy)
>
> Antigone refuses to obey uncle's order ; she twice performs burial ritual for her brother
>
> Conflict mounts: Antigone discovered as the one disobeying Creon's order; Creon refuses to change his mind.
>
> End of play, Antigone & Haimon (Creon's son)—both dead

See teacher pages for assessment rubrics.
You may wish to extend this exercise by having students read *Antigone* and write a brief report on the play.

Gerunds and Gerund Phrases

The present participle of a verb (the *-ing* form) sometimes functions as an adjective (see Lesson 7.2). This lesson shows what else *-ing* words can do.

▐▶ A **gerund**, ending in *-ing*, is a verb form that acts as a noun. Gerunds in a sentence can do anything that nouns can do.

> **Skiing** is her favorite sport. [subject]
> Her favorite sport is **skiing.** [predicate nominative]
> Have you ever tried **skiing?** [direct object]
> Give **skiing** a chance. [indirect object]
> Sue borrowed a book about **skiing.** [object of the preposition]

▐▶ A **gerund phrase** is a phrase made up of a gerund and all of its modifiers and complements. The entire phrase functions as a noun. A gerund's modifiers include adjectives, adverbs, and prepositional phrases.

> **Waiting a long time in a restaurant** annoys him. [subject]
> His pet peeve is **waiting in a restaurant.** [predicate nominative]
> Anna tried **taking tennis lessons.** [direct object]
> Jason left for school without **taking his backpack.** [object of the preposition]

EDITING TIP

Nouns and pronouns that modify a gerund should be in the possessive form.

The **baby**'s crying didn't stop.

We admired ~~him~~ his dancing.

EXERCISE 8 Identifying Gerunds and Gerund Phrases

Underline every gerund and gerund phrase in the sentences below. A gerund phrase may contain one or more prepositional phrases. Count these as part of the gerund phrase.

1. Karla's ambition is <u>hitting two home runs in one game.</u>

2. Laughing, Jeff says he would be happy with <u>scoring a run or two.</u>

3. Lenny admits his <u>pitching</u> is sometimes erratic.

4. The home team's fans went wild at Ken's <u>stealing third base.</u>

5. Patrick left the dugout without <u>telling anyone.</u>

6. The umpire stopped play because of fans' <u>throwing things onto the field.</u>

7. The manager protested the umpire's <u>ruling</u> on a close play at second.

8. The pitcher's batting average is .074, so the cheering fans were astonished at his <u>hitting a double.</u>

Enriching Your Vocabulary

The adjective *erratic*, like its verb and noun relations *err* and *error*, stems from the Latin *errare*, "to wander." *Erratic* has come to mean "lacking consistency." Its close relative *errant* has among other meanings that of "straying from a proper path." From an *erratic* pitcher, therefore, you might see thrown an *errant* pitch.

9. In the bottom of the eighth, Kirk's team tied the game by <u>scoring two runs</u>.

10. The game ended at 7–6 with Marla's <u>hitting a home run</u>.

EXERCISE 9 Writing Sentences with Gerunds and Gerund Phrases

This exercise is a good addition to the Writer's Notebook described in **Composition** Lesson 1.1.

On a separate piece of paper, answer each question below in a complete sentence that contains one or more gerunds or gerund phrases. In brackets following each question, you'll find a suggested sentence starter or sentence ending for your answer. Underline each gerund or gerund phrase in your sentences. Exchange papers with a partner or small group to compare your answers. A sample response is given.

Questionnaire

1. What are your hobbies? [. . . are my hobbies.] <u>Painting, reading, and watching TV are my hobbies.</u>

HINT

Not every *-ing* word is a gerund. A gerund functions as a noun in sentences.

2. If there were one extra day in the week, how would you spend it?

   [I would spend it . . .]

3. Do you have chores or responsibilities at home? If so, what are they?

   [Some of my jobs are . . .]

4. What jobs or careers are you considering? [I am considering . . .]

5. Name at least two skills that are important in the careers you are

   considering. [. . . are important skills in the careers I am considering.]

6. What would you consider a perfect vacation? [. . . are my ideas of a

   perfect vacation.]

7. What do you do when you have a cold and fever? [I treat a cold and

   fever by . . .]

8. If you could choose six courses you really wanted to study, what would

   you take next semester? [I would spend next semester . . .]

9. What do you think are the most important responsibilities of a parent?

   [A parent's most important responsibilities are . . .]

10. How do you think a good friend behaves? [A good friend shows his or

    her friendship by . . .]

Infinitives and Infinitive Phrases

▐▐▐▶ An **infinitive** is a verb form that is almost always preceded by the word *to*. In a sentence, an infinitive can act as a noun, an adjective, or an adverb.

> Anne-Marie likes **to paint.** [infinitive as noun]
> We were among the first people **to leave.** [infinitive as adjective]
> He is quick **to anger.** [infinitive as adverb]

The word *to* is called the sign, or marker, of the infinitive. But remember that *to* can also be a preposition. *To* is part of an infinitive if it is followed by a verb; *to* is a preposition if it's the start of a prepositional phrase.

INFINITIVE	PREPOSITIONAL PHRASE
The toddler likes **to sing.**	The toddler hands the doll **to her father.**

▐▐▐▶ An **infinitive phrase** is a phrase made up of an infinitive and all of its modifiers and complements. It may contain one or more prepositional phrases.

> **To become an electrical engineer** is David's ambition.
> It is easy **to paint a room with a roller.**

Sometimes the *to* of an infinitive or an infinitive phrase is left out; it is understood.

> Hal helped **[to] wash the car.**
> Please let me **[to] finish this mystery.**

P.S. Knowing about infinitives and infinitive phrases gives you another tool for expressing your ideas. When you write and speak, you don't have to know whether the infinitives you use are functioning as nouns, adjectives, or adverbs as long as you use them correctly.

TEST-TAKING TIP

In checking test items for words and phrases that should be parallel in form, remember that in a series of infinitive phrases, the word *to* does not have to be repeated. See item 14 on page 290 for an example.

EXERCISE 10 Identifying Infinitives and Infinitive Phrases

Perhaps the most famous infinitives are Hamlet's in Act III:

> "To be, or not to be, that is the question. . . ."

Underline every infinitive and infinitive phrase in the following quotations from William Shakespeare's works. Remember to include in an infinitive phrase all its modifiers (including prepositional phrases) and complements.

1. "If you have tears, prepare to shed them now." —*Julius Caesar*

2. "To weep is to make less the depth of grief." —*Henry VI, Part III*

WRITING HINT

When a modifier comes between *to* and the *verb*, the infinitive is said to be **split.** Avoid split infinitives unless by doing so the result is awkward or sounds unnatural.

to boldly go where no one has ever gone before

3. "I had rather have a fool <u>to make me merry</u> than experience <u>to make me sad</u>." —*As You Like It*

4. "Conscience is but a word that cowards use, / Devised at first <u>to keep the strong in awe</u>." —*Richard III*

5. "These words are razors to my wounded heart." —*Titus Andronicus* no infinitive

6. "Who buys a minute's mirth <u>to wail a week</u>? / Or sells eternity to get a <u>toy</u>?" —*The Rape of Lucrece*

7. "He was not born to shame; / Upon his brow shame is ashamed <u>to sit</u>." —*Romeo and Juliet*

8. "See what a scourge is laid upon your hate, / That heaven finds means <u>to kill your joys with love</u>." —*Romeo and Juliet*

9. "Things sweet <u>to taste</u> prove in digestion sour." —*Richard II*

10. "He was wont [inclined] <u>to speak plain</u> and to the purpose." —*Much Ado About Nothing*

Working Together

EXERCISE 11 Revising and Editing a Biography

Underline the infinitives and infinitive phrases in this draft of a brief biography of Shakespeare. Then work with a partner to correct sentence fragments and to make any other changes you think will improve the biography. (Review in Lesson 6.3 the strategies for correcting sentence fragments.) Revised biographies will vary.

¹William Shakespeare is generally acknowledged. ²<u>To be the greatest playwright of all time</u>. ³Born in Stratford-upon-Avon in 1564. ⁴He attended Stratford Grammar School for seven years. ⁵Learning Latin, English composition, and the Bible. ⁶At the age of eighteen Shakespeare married Anne Hathaway, who was eight years older than he. ⁷The couple had a daughter and then twins, a boy and a girl. ⁸About 1587 or 1588, Shakespeare left his family and went to London. ⁹<u>To become an actor and a playwright</u>. ¹⁰By 1592, he had written several plays. ¹¹He soon achieved great fame and prospered. ¹²He managed. ¹³<u>To write more than 36 plays and 150 poems</u>. ¹⁴Shakespeare left London in 1612 or 1613. ¹⁵<u>To retire to his home in Stratford, where he lived quite comfortably</u>. ¹⁶Continued <u>to manage his London acting company and their two theaters</u>. ¹⁷<u>To write plays until his death in 1616</u>.

Appositives and Appositive Phrases

▐▐▐▶ An **appositive** is a noun or pronoun that identifies or explains the noun or pronoun that precedes it. An **appositive phrase** is a phrase made up of an appositive and all of its modifiers.

Using appositives and appositive phrases helps you to combine sentences and avoid unnecessary repetition. In the following examples, the appositive phrases are set off from the rest of the sentence with commas.

ORIGINAL   Bryan is moving to Colorado. He is our next-door neighbor.

COMBINED   Bryan, **our next-door neighbor**, is moving to Colorado.

Do not use commas if an appositive is essential to understand the sentence.

NO COMMAS   Then explorers **Lewis and Clark** traveled through the Northwest Territory. [Since there were many explorers the appositive is essential. Do not use commas.]

COMMAS   The capital of Colorado, **Denver**, is one mile above sea level. [The appositive adds extra information but is not essential since there is only one capital.]

TEST-TAKING TIP

You might be asked to repair a rambling or run-on sentence on a standardized test by converting explanatory information into an appositive phrase and place it alongside the noun it identifies. For an example, see item 13 on page 297.

EXERCISE 12 Combining Sentences with Appositives

On a separate piece of paper, combine the sentences in each numbered item with an appositive or appositive phrase. **Hint:** Clues tell you if the appositive is essential. See Answer Key at www.grammarforwriting.com.

1. Geronimo attended Teddy Roosevelt's inauguration. Geronimo is an Apache leader.

2. The reformer worked to obtain the vote for women. The reformer is Susan B. Anthony.

3. This ancient Greek statue is famous for its beauty. *Venus de Milo* is famous.

4. Portuguese is spoken in Brazil. The largest South American country is Brazil.

5. World War II ended in Europe on V-E Day. May 8, 1945 is V-E Day.

6. Sean's dog is named Sniffles. Sniffles disappeared three days ago. [Sean has three other dogs.]

7. I play my favorite CD loudly. Vivaldi's *The Four Seasons* is my favorite.

8. Diana got an *A* on Friday's test. Friday's test was her algebra final.

9. This postcard is from my friend in London. Jerrie sent me this postcard. [I have four friends in London.]

10. Ben's job starts today after school. His job is working in a bookstore.

Revising and Editing Worksheet

Improve the following draft by revising for ideas, organization, word choice, and sentence variety. After revising, edit the draft for errors in spelling, capitalization, punctuation, and usage. Write your revised and edited version on a separate piece of paper. Compare your changes with those of a writing partner.
See teacher pages for assessment rubrics.

[1]Hercules is the greatest figure in ancient Greek mythology. [2]Known for his great strength. [3]The Greeks called him Heracles. [4]Hercules is his Roman name. [5]Hercules was the son of Zeus and a mortal woman. [6]His mother was named Alcmena. [7]She was princess of ancient Thebes. [8]Zeus was the chief god.

[9]Hercules is legendary for performing twelve labors. [10]As punishment for a terrible deed. [11]Hercules had to serve the king of Mycenae for twelve years. [12]He had to do what the king commanded. [13]His labor the first year. [14]To kill the Nemean lion a ferocious lion no weapon could wound. [15]The second labor was. [16]To kill a monster called Hydra. [17]Hydra was a water snake. [18]Her nine heads grew back every time Hercules cut them off.

[19]Hercules's fifth labor is his most famous. [20]Cleaning the Augean stables in a single day. [21]For many years, no one had ever cleaned the stables, where thousands of cattle lived. [22]Hercules accomplished the deed by doing something. [23]He diverted two rivers. [24]He made them flow through the stable.

[25]The eleventh and twelfth labors were the most difficult. [26]In the eleventh year, Hercules had to find the Golden Apples of the Hesperides. [27]And in the twelfth, he journeyed to the Underworld. [28]To bring the three-headed dog Cerberus up from the Underworld. [29]The twelfth labor was Hercules's last.

[30]In the northern skies, you can see a large constellation. [31]It is named after this Greek hero. [32]Hercules's name is also remembered. [33]The name appears in two English expressions. [34]A *herculean task* is one that requires enormous effort. [35]To accomplish. [36]A *herculean effort* is what it takes. [37]To complete a herculean task.

Chapter Review

EXERCISE A Matching Definitions

Match the term in Column 1 with its definition in Column 2. Write the letter of the definition in the space provided.

COLUMN 1		COLUMN 2
_e_	1. gerund	a. The *-ing* verb form that functions as an adjective
_c_	2. preposition	b. A verb form that is almost always preceded by the word *to*
_b_	3. infinitive	c. A word used to show the relationship between two words in a sentence, such as *in*, *with*, or *over*.
_a_	4. participle	d. A noun or pronoun that identifies or explains the noun or pronoun preceding it
_d_	5. appositive	e. The *-ing* verb form that functions as a noun

EXERCISE B Identifying Phrases

Identify each underlined phrase by writing one of these abbreviations above the phrase:

PREP = prepositional phrase INF = infinitive phrase
PART = participial phrase APP = appositive phrase
GER = gerund phrase

Remember: When a prepositional phrase is part of another kind of phrase, you don't have to label the prepositional phrase separately. For example, the sentence below shows *published in 1884* labeled as a participial phrase but does not identify *in 1884* as a prepositional phrase.

                      PART
EXAMPLE *The Adventures of Huckleberry Finn* by Mark Twain, <u>published in 1884</u>, has been called "the first American novel."

                PART
1. The novel is a masterpiece of realism, <u>portraying life on and around the Mississippi River about 1845.</u>

         PREP
2. Twain drew <u>from his boyhood memories</u> of Hannibal, Missouri.

               PART
3. Huck is the novel's narrator, <u>observing the events around him.</u>

         GER
4. Twain excelled at <u>writing dialect</u>, the way people talk in a certain region.

   PREP
5. <u>At the beginning of the novel</u>, Huck lives with Widow Douglas.

6. Huck's brutal father appears one night and forces him <u>to leave the widow's home.</u> ^{INF}

7. <u>Locked in a cabin by his father,</u> Huck escapes and runs away. ^{PART}

8. After a few days alone, he finds Jim, <u>a runaway slave from his hometown.</u> ^{APP}

9. The two drift <u>down the beautiful Mississippi River</u> on a raft. ^{PREP}

10. By the novel's end, Huck has learned a great deal <u>about life and loyalty.</u> ^{PREP}

EXERCISE C Vary Sentence Beginnings

Read each sentence. Then revise it by changing the way it starts. You may reword the sentence if necessary.   See Answer Key at www.grammarforwriting.com.

1. It is surprising that many people remain unconcerned about global warming.

2. Aid workers in helicopters arrived at the mountain camps, bringing much needed food and medicine.

3. Soldiers carefully lifted the ill and injured onto the trucks.

4. The scrambling and hustling home team came from four runs down to win the game in extra innings.

5. After the flood, several terrified survivors and their pets were found stranded on rooftops.

6. The restaurant owner generously prepared meals for the hungry.

7. Scientists who are studying the harmful effects of loud music on both musicians and their audiences are finding interesting results.

8. The guide's knowledge of first aid came in handy more than once during our hazardous trek through the rugged wilderness.

9. The young designer proudly showed her bold, new clothing line at this year's fashion show.

10. The captain of the debate team, who had a strong background in the subject matter, led her squad to an unexpected victory in the debate with Douglass School.

Clauses

STUDENT WRITING

Research Paper

Biedermeier Vienna and the Music of Franz Schubert
by Emma Sheanshang
high school student, New York, New York

At the close of the eighteenth century, the only true capital in the German–speaking countries was Vienna. Vienna had—and still retains—the reputation of being the most enchanting city in Europe, famous for coffee houses, a beautiful historic district, and above all, music. In the past, many people have based their impressions of the city exclusively on these pleasant elements. This romanticized image of Vienna does not encompass other equally important aspects of its rich culture and history. At the beginning of the nineteenth century, during the time Beethoven and Schubert lived and worked in Vienna, Europe was beginning to emerge from a period of almost constant warfare. In 1815, the year in which many believe the modern world began, war ended and the populace grew excited at the promise of peace. But while the resulting period of stability benefited the empire, it came at the expense of the people and, in particular, the new middle class that was emerging in Vienna. In the early nineteenth century, the Viennese found themselves occupying a city that simultaneously illuminated and endangered their lives. Various conflicts and paradoxes complicated every aspect of daily life, causing profound confusion throughout the populace. An understanding of these paradoxes is essential [if one is] to penetrate the seductive facade of tranquillity and gain a real sense of the spirit and culture of the city.

> The first paragraph of a research paper should carefully set up the rest of the paper. Here, the writer begins with general statements that grab a reader's attention. Next, she provides some background information to give a context for her thesis. She ends with a three-sentence thesis statement.
>
> The writer has used clauses to improve sentence variety and to help achieve a lively writing style. In this chapter you will practice using clauses in your own writing.

Allow time for students to discuss the student writing. Suggest that they identify its strengths and propose possible improvements. Use the model to introduce the concepts in the chapter.

Independent Clauses and Subordinate Clauses

Every clause is either independent or subordinate.

▶ **An independent** (or **main**) **clause** has a subject and a verb and expresses a complete thought.

Does this definition sound familiar? It should. It's also the definition for a sentence. An independent clause can stand alone as a sentence; that's why it's called independent.

$$\overset{\text{S}}{\text{}} \qquad \overset{\text{S}}{\text{}} \ \overset{\text{V}}{\text{}}$$
INDEPENDENT CLAUSE   Karen and Jon are late as usual.

A **compound sentence** is made up of two or more independent clauses joined by a conjunction.

CONJ
We finished the jigsaw puzzle, but two pieces were missing.

▶ A **subordinate** (or **dependent**) **clause** has a subject and a verb but doesn't express a complete thought.

S V   S V
that I told you about   because she is trying to save money

A subordinate clause can't stand alone. It must be attached to or inserted into an independent clause, or the word that makes it a subordinate clause must drop out.

SUBORDINATE CLAUSE   INDEPENDENT CLAUSE
S   V   S   V
Because she is trying to save money, Sheila has been packing her lunch. [The subordinate clause has been attached to an independent clause.]

SUBORDINATE CLAUSE
S   S   V   V
The house **that I told you about** sold this morning. [The subordinate clause has been inserted into the independent clause.]

> **EDITING TIP**
>
> Remember that a subordinate clause can't stand alone. When it does, it's a **clause fragment** and needs to be corrected.
> ~~Because~~ helium is lighter than air.
> OR
> Because helium is lighter than air, it is used in balloons.

> **TEST-TAKING TIP**
>
> On a standardized test you might see an item in which a subordinate clause is placed between the subject and verb of an independent clause. Don't let the subordinate clause distract you. Make sure the subject and verb of the independent clause agree. For an example, see item 9 on page 289.

EXERCISE 1 Identifying Clauses

On the blank for each numbered item, write *I* for an independent clause or *S* for a subordinate clause. On a separate sheet of paper, revise every subordinate clause to make it a complete sentence.

_____I_____ 1. Responsibly written articles and research papers are factual and well documented.

_____S_____ 2. Because you can't always tell whether the articles and stories you read are true.

_____I_____ 3. Statistics interpreted carelessly weaken a paper.

_____S_____ 4. Avoiding the risk of angry readers and objections.

_____S_____ 5. When you write a research paper, carefully documented sources.

_____S_____ 6. That your documentation is important to prove that you did not make up your facts.

_____I_____ 7. Reliable sources are academic journals, reference books, and articles or books written by experts in a field.

_____S_____ 8. Being proud of your accuracy.
Revised sentences will vary.

EXERCISE 2 Editing a Paragraph

Review the following paragraph, correcting all fragments. Then, edit the paragraph for spelling and punctuation mistakes.
See teacher pages for revising and editing suggestions.

¹Establishing political rights for, citizens in the American colonies was sometimes a rocky process. ²In 1735, John Peter Zenger helped establish the right of freedom of the press. ³Zenger was a German immigrant. ⁴Who went to work for newspaper called; *The New York Weekly Journal*. ⁵Zenger and the newspaper attacked corrupt officials in New York. ⁶Printing articles that told the truth about the actions of the officials. ⁷Zenger's articles printed in the newspaper. ⁸Soldiers were ordered to burn the newspaper in the public square. ⁹John Peter Zenger was arrested and charged with libel. ¹⁰Or making a false, statement in writing to injure a person's reputation! ¹¹Zenger's trial forced the jury to answer this question: Should the press be permitted to criticize the acts of public officials? ¹²After only ten minutes of deliberation. ¹³The jury found Zenger not guilty. ¹⁴A decision that helped paved the way for freedom of the press.

Write What You Think

Write a paragraph in response to the following statement, and give reasons to support your opinions.

> Among the many political rights of American citizens, the right to freedom of the press has the most impact on our lives.

After you finish revising, edit your work to make sure you have written complete sentences. At least two of your sentences should include subordinate clauses. Answers will vary. Students should use independent and subordinate clauses correctly.

Adjective Clauses

You will learn about three kinds of subordinate clauses: adjective clauses, adverb clauses, and noun clauses.

▐▐▐▶ An **adjective clause** is a subordinate clause that functions as an adjective. It modifies a noun or pronoun.

An adjective clause follows the word it modifies.

> Dave, **who is six feet tall**, is Elaine's boyfriend.
> He is the person **whom I told you about in my letter**.
> San Diego is the city **where he grew up.**

Look for the introductory words listed on the right. Often (but not always), they signal the beginning of an adjective clause. These words are generally called **relative pronouns** and **relative adverbs**. Most of these words also function as other parts of speech.

An introductory relative pronoun may be omitted from the sentence. Read aloud the sentences below. You'll see that they make sense without the bracketed words.

> Where is the CD [**that**] **I lent you**?
> Sara is the person [**whom**] **you should see**.

When an adjective clause is **essential** to the meaning of a sentence, it should not be set off from the rest of the sentence with commas. But when an adjective clause is **nonessential**, it is set off with commas. An essential clause adds information that is necessary to understand the sentence. A nonessential clause adds information that is not necessary.

Some Words that Introduce Adjective Clauses

Relative Pronouns

that	whom
which	whose
who	

Relative Adverbs

than	where
when	

EDITING TIP

WHO OR WHOM?
Who serves as the subject of a clause, and *whom* serves as the object of a clause. If *he* or *she* would make sense in the sentence, use *who*; if *him* or *her* would make sense in the sentence, use *whom*.

[**Who** or **He**] wants to eat dinner.

The dinner is served to [**him.** or **whom**?]

ESSENTIAL (no commas)	NONESSENTIAL (set off with commas)
Every player **who hits a home run** receives a trophy.	The players, **who vary in age from eight to twelve**, wear blue uniforms.
Jeff is looking for the dog **that bit his sister yesterday**.	The dog, **which no one recognized**, is a black poodle.

P.S. You learned about essential and nonessential clauses when you studied appositives in Lesson 7.6. The same rules about commas apply to adjective clauses. In other textbooks, you may see the term *nonrestrictive* used for *nonessential* and *restrictive* used for *essential*. These terms are synonyms.

EXERCISE 3 Identifying Adjective Clauses

Underline the adjective clauses in the sentences below. **Hint:** Not every sentence has an adjective clause. Write *None* if the sentence does not have an adjective clause.

1. Tai chi is an exercise <u>that is more than five thousand years old</u>.

2. Tai chi, <u>which is one of the martial arts</u>, developed in ancient China.

3. In China, you can visit parks <u>where hundreds of people do tai chi</u>.

4. Tai chi is a low-impact exercise <u>that a person can do alone</u>.

5. Do you know anyone <u>who practices tai chi</u>?

6. Tai chi, <u>which is a continuous series of gentle movements</u>, is said to relieve stress.

7. According to tai chi teachers, tai chi improves balance, strengthens leg muscles, and creates energy. None.

8. An exerciser balances his or her chi, or internal energy, during a tai chi workout. None

9. Each series of tai chi movements has a name <u>that sounds like poetry</u>.

10. "The White Crane Spreads Its Wings" is a series of moves <u>that involves the entire body</u>.

EXERCISE 4 Writing Sentences with Adjective Clauses

Your class is planning a yearbook with a photograph and brief biographical information for every student. Underline the adjective clauses in the biography below. Then, on a separate piece of paper, write a paragraph about yourself that you would feel comfortable including in the yearbook. In your paragraph, use at least three adjective clauses and underline them.

See **Composition** Lesson 4.1 for strategies for writing an autobiographical essay.

[1]Last year my family moved here from Chicago, <u>where I was born and grew up</u>. [2]We lived in Hyde Park on the South Side, and I knew everyone <u>who lived in my neighborhood</u>. [3]It was really hard for me to move. [4]When I first came to this school, everyone seemed so unfriendly. [5]But after a couple of weeks, I became friends with some students <u>who are in my classes</u>, and now I like it here. [6]I'm a long-distance runner on the track team, <u>which I really like a lot</u>. [7]One of my friends taught me to play chess, and I joined the chess club. [8]Mrs. Caleb, <u>who is the adviser</u>, wants me to join the chess team. [9]The class <u>that I enjoy most</u> is debate. [10]I've learned debating techniques <u>that I use on my older brother</u>.

See teacher pages for writing rubrics. Students should use adjective clauses correctly in their paragraphs.

Adverb Clauses

▷ **An adverb clause** is a subordinate clause that functions as an adverb. It modifies a verb, an adjective, or another adverb.

Because the school bus broke down, Jeff missed first period.
[modifies the verb *missed*]
I am three years older **than she is**.
[modifies the adjective *older*]
Tamiko left for work ten minutes earlier **than she usually does**.
[modifies the adverb *earlier*]

Look for the introductory words listed at the right. Often (but not always), they signal the beginning of an adverb clause and at such times they are called **subordinating conjunctions**.

In an **elliptical adverb clause,** some words are omitted. In the following examples, the bracketed words are understood.

Julio is older **than Sheila [is]**.
I'm more worried about the math test than you are **[worried about the math test]**.
Have you ever met anyone as confident as **Andrew [is]**?

EXERCISE 5 Identifying Adverb Clauses

Underline each adverb clause in the following sentences.
Hint: Not every sentence contains an adverb clause, and some have more than one.

1. Whenever lightning strikes, it is always accompanied by thunder.

2. Thunder occurs when lightning heats the air and causes it to expand rapidly.

3. Even though thunder sounds scary, it poses no danger.

4. A person who is struck by lightning receives a severe electric shock.

5. Because light travels much faster than sound, you can see lightning before you hear the thunder.

6. If you count the seconds in the interim between the lightning and thunder, you can judge the distance of the source of the lightning.

7. When you see lightning and hear thunder at the same time, watch out because the lightning is very close.

Subordinating Conjunctions

after	so that
although	than
as	though
as long as	unless
as soon as	when
as though	whenever
because	where
before	wherever
even though	whether
if	while
since	

WRITING HINT

When you use an adverb clause at the beginning of a sentence, follow it with a comma. If you use an adverb clause at the end of a sentence, you do not need to use a comma before it.

If you're outdoors in a thunderstorm, find shelter right away.

Find shelter right away **if you're outdoors in a thunderstorm**.

Enriching Your Vocabulary

Interim comes to us unchanged in form from the Latin adverb meaning "meanwhile." In English the noun means "the time between." The word is also an adjective meaning "temporary" or "coming between two points in time."

8. If you are caught outside in an electrical storm, stay away from water because water is a good conductor of electricity.

9. Don't stand under a tree during an electrical storm because lightning hits the tallest objects.

10. Talking on a telephone is dangerous, too, since lightning can travel through the wires.

EXERCISE 6 Writing Sentences with Adverb Clauses

Work with a partner or small group to write (and perhaps illustrate) a small pamphlet about lightning safety. Your audience is children in the third and fourth grades, so make your sentences easy to read. Use the following notes as an outline for topics to cover in your pamphlet. When you have finished writing a first draft of your pamphlet, underline all of the adverb clauses you have used. You may wish to extend this exercise by having students write pamphlets for a school event or on a subject of their choice.

What to Do During an Electrical Storm

Stay off the phone. [Explain why.]

Stay out of water. [Explain why.]

Don't stand under a tall tree. [Explain why.]

Stay indoors, and stay away from open windows. [Explain why.]

EXERCISE 7 Revising a Story Beginning

Look for revising strategies in **Composition** Lesson 1.3.

On a separate piece of paper, rewrite this story beginning to make it more interesting. Work with a partner or small group to add specific details and information about how and where and why the events happened. Make any other changes that you think will improve the paragraph. When you're finished revising, underline any adverb clauses you may have added.

[1]The power went out. [2]The streets were totally dark. [3]The traffic signals didn't work. [4]Volunteers controlled traffic in each intersection. [5]People were stuck for hours in elevators. [6]People were stuck in crowded subways. [7]A spirit of patience and cooperation prevailed. [8]No one was hurt. [9]There was no TV. [10]People talked to each other.

See teacher pages for revising suggestions. Students may wish to complete the story for extra credit.

Noun Clauses

▶ A **noun clause** is a subordinate clause that functions as a noun.

A noun clause can do any job a noun can do. It can function as a subject, predicate nominative, direct object, indirect object, or object of a preposition. In the following examples, notice that noun clauses can have modifiers and complements. They can come at the beginning, middle, or end of a sentence.

> **Which of the twins is older** is not important. [subject]
> The big question is **whether she will finish the marathon**.
> [predicate nominative]
> I could see **that you were annoyed**. [direct object]
> Please give **whoever calls** this message. [indirect object]
> Neeley is ready for **whatever she encounters**.
> [object of preposition]

See at the right a list of words that can introduce a noun clause. Sometimes a noun clause's introductory word is not stated but understood.

> We hope [that] **the rain delay ends soon**.
> All of the fans know [that] **this game is crucial**.

Some Words That Introduce Noun Clauses

how	which
if	who
that	whoever
what	whom
whatever	whomever
when	whose
where	why
whether	

TEST-TAKING TIP

Remember: A noun clause that stands alone is a fragment. You might be asked to correct such a fragment on a standardized test by incorporating it into an independent clause, usually without additional punctuation. See the Example on page 293.

EXERCISE 8 Writing Sentences with Noun Clauses

On a separate piece of paper, write a sentence using each group of words as a noun clause. Check your work to be sure that you have written a noun clause, not an adjective or adverb clause.
See sample answers.

1. that many children are afraid of the dark

2. how to change a flat tire

3. whether it will rain tomorrow

4. whoever attends the concert

5. why birds fly south in fall

6. that you're my best friend

7. what we need most

8. whoever crosses the finish line first

9. what you have learned

10. that the worst of the storm is over

1. Everyone knows that many children are afraid of the dark.
2. Our driving instructor showed us how to change a flat tire.
3. Whether it will rain tomorrow is anybody's guess.
4. Whoever attends the concert will receive a free ticket to next week's concert.
5. Can you tell me why birds fly south in fall?
6. Have I ever told you that you're my best friend?
7. She asked us to think about what we need most.
8. Whoever crosses the finish line first will win the gold medal.
9. Please tell me what you have learned so far.
10. I suspect that the worst of the storm is over.

EXERCISE 9 Create Your Own Exercise

With a partner, make up ten sentences that have noun clauses.
Your sentences can be about any topic. Exchange sentences with
another team, and see if you can identify all of the noun clauses.
Students' sentences will vary.

EXERCISE 10 Revising a Biology Report

When Jeff wrote the biology report below, he tried to make his writing sound
very intelligent. Jeff's teacher returned the report to him with this note: "Please
say what you mean more clearly." First, underline all of the noun clauses in
Jeff's report. Then work with a partner or small group to revise the report,
expressing the ideas as clearly and as directly as possible. Eliminate wordiness
and repetition, and make any other changes you think will improve the report.

[1]That all green plants require air to manufacture food has been known by
scientists for a long period of time. [2]Who first determined this fact is Jan
Ingenhousz, an eighteenth-century Dutch scientist. [3]Biology textbooks tell
whoever studies biology that the process by which plants manufacture food is
called *photosynthesis*. [4]"Putting together by light" is what the word *photosynthesis*
means. [5]No one doubts that the essential ingredients for a plant to manufacture
glucose are sunlight, water, and carbon dioxide. [6]What has been determined
is that the cells of green leaves contain chlorophyll and that the chlorophyll in
the cells of green leaves collects energy from sunlight. [7]Furthermore, scientists
know that the energy from sunlight provides the power for a chemical reaction
within the green leaves. [8]Carbon dioxide from the air and water from the soil
react chemically to produce glucose and oxygen. [9]Whoever studies biology
should recognize this formula:

$$6CO_2 + 6H_2O \rightarrow C_6H_{12}O_6 + 6O_2.$$

[10]What this formula is is the chemical formula for the process of photosynthesis.
Look for clarity in students' revisions. Students should eliminate wordiness and repetition.

Four Types of Sentence Structures

All sentences can be classified according to their structure. You need to be able to think about the variety of sentence structures so that you can vary your sentences when you write a paragraph or a longer paper.

IIII➤ A **simple sentence** has one independent clause and no subordinate clauses.

You may be surprised to find that simple sentences can be quite long and complicated. A simple sentence may have a compound subject, a compound verb, and many different kinds of phrases.

> S   V
> Unlike many other languages, the English alphabet has twenty-six letters to represent the sounds of its words.

IIII➤ A **compound sentence** has two or more independent clauses and no subordinate clauses.

> S   V   S   V
> *Alphabet* comes from *alpha* and *bet*; these are the names of the first two letters in the Greek alphabet.

IIII➤ A **complex sentence** has one independent clause and at least one subordinate clause.

> S   S   V   V
> The Cyrillic alphabet, which is the writing system for Russian, has thirty-one characters. [subordinate clause within independent clause]

IIII➤ A **compound-complex** sentence has two or more independent clauses and at least one subordinate clause.

> S   S   V   V
> Sequoyah, who lived from 1766 to 1843, created a writing system,
>
> S   V
> and he taught it to other Cherokee.

EXERCISE 11 Identifying Sentence Structure

Identify the sentence structure of each sentence in the paragraph below. On the blank before each numbered sentence, write *S* for simple; *CD* for compound; *CX* for complex; and *CD-CX* for compound-complex.

¹ _CD_ Every language has different rules, and there are many different writing systems. ² _S_ For example, Hebrew is written from right to left on horizontal lines. ³ _CX_ A Hebrew book begins at what English

speakers would consider the back of the book. [4] _S_ The traditional Chinese writing system doesn't use letters. [5] _CD-CX_ Instead, the Chinese writing system, which dates back to the fourteenth century B.C., uses ideograms, and each ideogram stands for a syllable or a whole word. [6] _CX_ Although the languages differ, the Japanese borrowed Chinese ideograms for their writing system. [7] _CX_ Both Chinese and Japanese are traditionally written in vertical columns, which are read from top to bottom and right to left. [8] _S_ Learning to read and write Japanese requires knowing several thousand ideograms. [9] _CX_ Modern Chinese and Japanese governments have tried to simplify the writing system so that more people can read and write.

EXERCISE 12 Revising Sentences

Expand each of the following simple sentences by making up interesting details. On a separate piece of paper, identify the type of sentence you have written. Write at least one example for each type of sentence structure. Compare your expanded sentences with a partner or small group.

EXAMPLE Andie is in first grade.
Although Andie is in first grade, she is learning to speak French, English, and Korean.
COMPLEX

1. Andie likes to read.

2. She is only six.

3. She is learning to write.

Expanded sentences will vary. Students should identify the sentence structures correctly.

4. Spelling is a problem.

5. Andie uses her imagination.

6. Mrs. Warner tells the class.

7. Everyone writes books.

8. Kyle and Andie draw pictures.

9. They listen to each other's stories.

10. Their families enjoy the books.

Revising and Editing Worksheet 1

Improve the following draft by revising for ideas, organization, word choice, and sentence variety. After revising, edit the draft for errors in spelling, capitalization, punctuation, and usage. Write your revised and edited version on a separate piece of paper. Compare your changes with those of a writing partner.
See teacher pages for revising and editing suggestions.

[1]As soon as the lights went out. [2]Sally heard a tiny sound. [3]The sound came from the closet. [4]The closet was next to her bed. [5]It was a faint sound. [6]She lay there hardly breatheing. [7]So that she could hear the faint sound. [8]Listening.

[9]What could the faint sound be? [10]She had never heard the noise before. [11]What on Earth could it be? [12]Sally decided something. [13]Something alive was in her closet.

[14]Sally knew something. [15]She was alone in the house. [16]Her parents were out. [17]Her parents wouldnt be back for hours.

[18]Sam wasn't home. [19]Sam was Sally's brother. [20]Sam was eight years older than Sally. [21]Sam was spending the weekend with Jerry. [22]Jerry was Sam's best freind. [23]Jerry, Sam, and Jerry's father were camping at Lake Nelly.

[24]Even Maggie was away. [25]Maggie was the family dog. [26]She was staying overnight in the kennel. [27]Maggie had had majory surgery. [28]The vet wanted to keep her overnight. [29]He would let her come home. [30]He knew that she was all right.

[31]Sally listened. [32]She was intent. [33]All her being was focused on the sound. [34]The sound happened several times a minute. [35]Seemed to be getting louder. [36]And maybe faster. [37]What could she do?

Suggest that students complete the story in their own way.

Revising and Editing Worksheet 2

Improve the following draft by revising for ideas, organization, word choice, and sentence variety. After revising, edit the draft for errors in spelling, capitalization, punctuation, and usage. Write your revised and edited version on a separate piece of paper. Compare your changes with those of a writing partner.

See teacher pages for revising and editing suggestions.

[1]Recycling is important. [2]Because it reduces solid wastes. [3]Landfills are filling up. [4]Landfills are where governments dump solid wastes. [5]Recycling reduces pollution. [6]And saves natural resources, too.

[7]Many American cities started recycling during the 1970s. [8]During the 1970s the ecology movement became populer. [9]In some states, charged nickel or dime deposits to customers. [10]These were the customers who bought food or drinks in glass and plastic containers. [11]Container deposits also helped reduce litter. [12]Many cities have recycling programs today. [13]They recycle glass. [14]They recycle paper. [15]They recycle plastics. [16]They recycle metals.

[17]Recycled glass is used in makeing new glass. [18]First, the recycled glass is sorted into colors. [19]Then it is crushed. [20]Crushed glass is called *cullet*. [21]Because cullet melts at a lower temperature then the raw materials used in making glass. [22]When cullet is used to make glass. [23]Less energy is needed.

[24]Aluminum companies pay people by the pound. [25]For recycled aluminum. [26]Because aluminum is very light. [27]It takes many soft drink cans to weigh a pound. [28]About 65,000 soft drink cans are recycled every minute in the United States. [29]Recycled aluminum is used to make ships, planes, aluminum foil, and more soft drink cans.

[30]California and Connecticut were the first states with recycleing laws. [31]Now many other states require. [32]That manufacturers use recycled materials. [33]For example, by the year 2005, 65 percent of glass containers in California will be made of recycled glass. [34]Some states require that phonebooks and newsprint be made of 50 percent recycled material. [35]Recycling paper and cardboard saves trees. [36]And helps reduce pollution, to.

Chapter Review

EXERCISE A Identifying Independent and Subordinate Clauses

On the blank before each numbered item, write *I* for an independent clause or *S* for a subordinate clause.

EXAMPLE _____*S*_____ Who was an important American painter.

_____I_____ 1. Henry O. Tanner decided to be a painter.

_____S_____ 2. When he was thirteen years old.

_____I_____ 3. His father was a bishop in the African Methodist Episcopal Church in Pittsburgh.

_____S_____ 4. Before Tanner was a student at Philadelphia's Academy of Fine Arts.

_____I_____ 5. He studied with the American painter Thomas Eakins.

_____I_____ 6. Tanner left the United States to study art in Paris.

_____I_____ 7. His greatest successes were paintings of biblical scenes.

_____S_____ 8. Which are naturalistic and at the same time filled with emotion.

_____I_____ 9. For the rest of his life, Tanner remained in Paris.

_____S_____ 10. When the French government made him a Chevalier of the Legion of Honor.

EXERCISE B Identifying Types of Clauses

On the blank before each numbered item, identify the underlined clause in each sentence by writing *ADJ*, for an adjective clause, *ADV* for an adverb clause, or *N* for a noun clause.

EXAMPLE _____*N*_____ If you have to ask <u>what jazz is</u>, you'll never know.
— *Louis Armstrong*

_____ADJ_____ 1. These are the times <u>that try men's souls.</u> —*Thomas Paine*

_____ADJ_____ 2. No one will ever get at my verses <u>who insists on viewing them as a literary performance.</u> —*Walt Whitman*

_____ADV_____ 3. <u>When I think of our condition</u>, my heart is heavy.
—*Chief Joseph of the Nez Percé*

_____N_____ 4. I know <u>why the caged bird sings!</u>—*Paul Laurence Dunbar*

_____ADJ_____ 5. "Music is the thing of the world <u>that I love most.</u>"
—*Samuel Pepys*

_____ADV_____ 6. No question is ever settled / <u>Until it is settled right</u>.
—*Ella Wheeler Wilcox*

_____ADJ_____ 7. A truth <u>that's told with bad intent</u> / Beats all the lies you can invent.
—*William Blake*

_____N_____ 8. <u>What's virtue in man</u> can't be vice in a cat. —*Mary Abigail Dodge*

_____ADV_____ 9. The game isn't over <u>till it's over</u>. —*Yogi Berra*

_____ADV_____ 10. There are only two or three human stories, and they go on repeating themselves as fiercely <u>as if they had never happened</u> before.
—*Willa Cather*

EXERCISE C Identifying Sentence Structure

Underline every subordinate clause in the sentences below. Then on the blank before each numbered item, identify the sentence structure by writing *S* for simple, *CD* for compound, *CX* for complex, and *CD-CX* for compound-complex.

_____S_____ 1. In 1927, Charles Lindbergh flew nonstop and alone across the Atlantic.

_____CD-CX_____ 2. The Nile River, <u>which is more than four thousand miles long</u>, flows north from central Africa through Egypt; it is the world's longest river.

_____S_____ 3. Two stars in the bowl of the Big Dipper point to Polaris, the North Star.

_____CX_____ 4. The pull of gravity is so great in a black hole <u>that not even light can pass through it</u>.

_____CX_____ 5. Veterans Day is observed on November 11, <u>which is the day the fighting stopped in World War I</u>.

_____CX_____ 6. DNA molecules contain information <u>that controls hereditary features</u>.

_____CX_____ 7. <u>After Johan Gutenberg printed the first Bible in 1455</u>, books became available to ordinary people.

_____CD_____ 8. The Mercalli scale measures an earthquake's intensity; the Richter scale measures its magnitude.

_____CX_____ 9. Did you know <u>that a judo expert wears a black belt</u>?

_____CX_____ 10. Dr. Seuss is the pen name of Theodor Geisel, <u>who wrote *The Cat in the Hat*</u>.

Cumulative Review

EXERCISE A Identifying Parts of Speech

In the space above each numbered item, identify the part of speech of each underlined word in the sentences below. Use these abbreviations:

N = noun	ADJ = adjective	CONJ = conjunction
PRON = pronoun	ADV = adverb	INTER = interjection
V = verb	PREP = preposition	

>   *INTER*
> EXAMPLE   <u>Alas</u>, this is the last day of vacation.

        ADJ   PREP
1. She found an <u>old</u> letter <u>between</u> the pages of the photo album.

  INTER   N
2. <u>Look</u>, here is the list of e-mail <u>addresses</u> you asked for.

     PRON
3. Has <u>anyone</u> been looking for me?

         ADV   PREP
4. The restaurants <u>usually</u> close <u>for</u> the summer.

           CONJ   V
5. Neither Scott <u>nor</u> Tomás <u>wants</u> the job.

EXERCISE B Writing Complete Sentences

Revise and edit the following paragraph to correct sentence fragments and run-on sentences and to eliminate wordiness. Revised paragraphs will vary.

    [1]Old Faithful is a geyser in Yosemite National Park in Wyoming, it erupts regularly. [2]Usually about every sixty-five minutes. [3]Like other geysers, Old Faithful is a hot spring. [4]A geyser is a fissure, or crack, in the earth's surface. [5]Connected to a water supply far below the surface. [6]Geysers shoot steam and boiling water high into the air. [7]Old Faithful, about 150 feet into the air. [8]And about eleven thousand gallons of water each time. [9]The word *geyser* comes from the name of a specific geyser in Iceland, it means "gusher." [10]Geysers are found in Iceland, New Zealand, and the western United States.

EXERCISE C Identifying Phrases

On the blank before each numbered item, identify each underlined phrase by writing one of these abbreviations in the space provided:

PREP = prepositional phrase	INF = infinitive phrase
PART = participial phrase	APP = appositive phrase
GER = gerund phrase	

> EXAMPLE   <u>*APP*</u> Mr. Haas, <u>the band teacher</u>, plays the cello and bass.

   <u>PREP</u>   1. You'll find the hammer <u>in the bottom drawer</u> of the desk.

_____INF_____ 2. Jonas is ready <u>to leave for school</u> by 7 A.M.

_____GER_____ 3. The twins enjoy <u>playing table tennis</u> and are really good at it.

_____PREP_____ 4. Amanda sent a thank-you note <u>to her grandmother</u>.

_____INF_____ 5. <u>To raise money</u>, Key Club members are collecting aluminum.

_____APP_____ 6. Elliot cooked French toast, <u>his favorite breakfast</u>.

_____GER_____ 7. Whose responsibility is <u>washing the car</u>?

_____PART_____ 8. Tree branches <u>broken during the ice storm</u> lay across the road.

_____PREP_____ 9. This year classes begin the week <u>before Labor Day</u>.

_____PART_____ 10. Anya was able to grab the kitten <u>hiding under the bed</u>.

EXERCISE D Identifying Clauses

Underline every subordinate clause in the sentences below. Then identify each clause by writing _ADJ_ for an adjective clause, _ADV_ for an adverb clause, or _N_ for a noun clause in the space before each sentence.

__ADJ__ [1]The word _volcano_ comes from Vulcan, <u>who was the Roman god of fire and destruction</u>. __ADV__ [2]<u>When most people think of volcanoes</u>, they visualize cone-shaped mountains with fire and lava exploding from the top. __ADJ__ [3]Volcanoes are actually vents—or cracks—in the earth's surface <u>that connect directly to the molten rock deep below the surface</u>. __ADV__ [4]<u>When a volcano is active</u>, it belches forth molten lava, hot gases, and ash. __ADV__ [5]Some volcanoes are called dormant (sleeping) <u>because they have been inactive for a very long time</u>. __N__ [6]Scientists know <u>that a dormant volcano can become active without any warning</u>. __ADJ__ [7]In 1980, Mount St. Helens, <u>which had been dormant for more than 120 years</u>, erupted violently. __N__ [8]Scientists expect <u>that an extinct volcano will never erupt again</u>. __ADV__ [9]There are volcanoes underwater too, and <u>when they erupt</u>, they can form islands. __ADJ__ [10]Hawaii, <u>which is made up of twenty volcanic islands</u>, has an active volcano, Mauna Loa, and a dormant one, Mauna Kea.

Using Verbs

STUDENT WRITING
Narrative Essay

Direct students to www.grammarforwriting.com for chapter-specific portfolio projects.

Dancing
by Joshua Vinitz

high school student, Queens, New York

I go to parties and dances a lot. The problem is that until recently, I hated to dance. I disliked the music, and I still do. I used to go to the dances because all of my friends did. Now I go to them for the "right" reason—to dance.

For many years, I would just sit in the back and talk with my friends as our girlfriends danced the night away. None of us really liked to dance, and it would usually take an act of Congress to get us on the floor. The girls would constantly try to get us to dance while we tried to get them to sit down with us and talk. Both sides' attempts were futile. We weren't about to lose our seats and they weren't about to stop partying.

Not too long ago, however, all of this changed for me. I don't know what came over me, but one of the girls just connected. She just plucked me out of my chair; I had no choice in the matter. I started dancing, and I liked it!

I won't say that I'm good at it or anything. As one of my friends commented, "You dance worse than you parallel park." But I have discovered something. Dancing is a lot more fun than sitting on the side and complaining to my friends about how bad the music is. Time goes so much faster when you're out there dancing.

Joshua wrote the narrative above to explain how he changed his mind about dancing. He starts his narrative essay using present-tense verbs. He tells the anecdote in the past tense; then he summarizes his new opinion of dancing in the present tense again. Joshua uses verbs to lead his reader through his experience. The lessons in this chapter will help you notice the verb tenses you use in your own writing.

Allow time for students to discuss the student writing. Suggest that they identify its strengths and propose possible improvements. Use the model to introduce the concepts in the chapter.

Regular Verbs

▐▌▐▌➡ All verbs have four basic forms, or **principal parts**. They are the present, the present participle, the past, and the past participle.

Verbs are classified as either regular or irregular, depending on the way they form their past and past participle.

▐▌▐▌➡ Regular verbs add *-d* or *-ed* to the present to form the past tense and past participle.

Principal Parts of Regular Verbs			
PRESENT	PRESENT PARTICIPLE (Use with *am, is, are, was, were.*)	PAST	PAST PARTICIPLE (Use with *has, had, have.*)
join	(is) joining	joined	(had) joined
carry	(is) carrying	carried	(had) carried
hike	(is) hiking	hiked	(had) hiked

The **present participle** of regular verbs ends in *-ing*. It works with the verb *be* (*am, is, are, was,* or *were*), to make a verb phrase.

> I **am waiting** for a bus.   Joey **was waiting** at home.

The **past participle** of regular verbs ends in *-d* or *-ed*. It works with the helping verb *have* (*has, have,* or *had*), to make a verb phrase.

> I **have asked** for help.   Joey **had** also **asked** for help.

When you add *-ing* and *-ed* to the present form of a verb, you have to apply spelling rules about dropping the final *-e*, changing *-y* to *i*, and doubling consonants: *hope, hoping, hoped; carry, carried; shop, shopping, shopped.* (For more about spelling rules, see Lesson 16.2.)

P.S. Don't get too worried about the labels for all the verb forms. It's the correct *use* of verb forms that is important in writing.

Enriching Your Vocabulary

The noun *migration* comes from the Latin verb *migrare*, which means "to change one's home." It is one of many English words used in connection with the movement of people or animals from place to place. A related word, *migrant*, is used in Exercise 1. The discovery of gold in California triggered a great westward *migration*.

EDITING TIP

Both present and past participles work alone as adjectives (see Lesson 7.2), but they always need a helping verb to function as a verb.

PARTICIPLE
Lee is wearing **hiking** shoes.

INCOMPLETE VERB
She hiking on the Appalachian Trail.

VERB PHRASE
She **is hiking** on the Appalachian Trail.

EXERCISE 1 Using the Principal Parts of Regular Verbs

Complete each sentence by writing the correct past form or past participle form of the verb in parentheses. Some sentences have more than one verb in parentheses.

> EXAMPLE   All but the grin of the Cheshire cat (fade) __*faded*__ .

1. During the Great Depression, many banks (fail) __failed__ .

2. In 1955, Rosa Parks (refuse) __refused__ to give up her seat on a bus.

3. The Texans who (defend) __defended__ the Alamo (die) __died__ in the massacre of 1836.

4. The nineteenth-century writer Ralph Waldo Emerson (advise) __advised__ his readers, "Hitch your wagon to a star."

5. Before she (marry) __married__, Charlotte Brontë had (live) __lived__ at the parsonage with her father.

6. By l962, César Chávez had (organize) __organized__ migrant farmers into a union.

7. William the Conqueror (defeat) __defeated__ the English in 1066.

8. More than seventy-five thousand people (listen) __listened__ to Marian Anderson sing at the Lincoln Memorial.

9. John James Audubon (travel) __traveled__ *(or* travelled*)* across America and (paint) __painted__ birds.

10. A wall built by the Roman emperor Hadrian (stretch) __stretched__ across Britain.

Exercise 2 Revising a Story Beginning

Revise the story beginning so that it describes an event that happened in the past. Use the past form or past participle form of the italicized verbs. Compare the original version and your version. Does the story sound better to you in the present tense or in the past tense? Work with a partner or small group to finish the story.

¹A mysterious figure *approaches* [approached] the old house. ²The person *walks* [walked] carefully up the broken steps and *knocks* [knocked] on the cracked door. ³From inside the old house, the knock *echoes* [echoed] through the empty rooms. ⁴No one *lives* [lived] there anymore. ⁵Outside the house, the dark trees and grasses *look* [looked] wild and overgrown. ⁶The garden *disappears* [had disappeared *or* disappeared] under a tangle of weeds. ⁷Patiently, the stranger *waits* [waited] before the door. ⁸In an instant, clouds *appear* [appeared], *darken* [darkened] the sky, and *spatter* [spattered] the visitor with huge drops of rain. ⁹Who *answers* [answered] the door when it *creaks* [creaked] open on rusty hinges? ¹⁰And what *happens* [happened] next? Challenge students to use words that connote a humorous, frightful, or surprising ending.

For more information about writing a narrative, see **Composition**, Lesson 2.4.

Irregular Verbs 1

All languages have irregular verbs, and English has a lot of them. **Irregular verbs** do not form their past or past participle in a predictable pattern. That is, they don't add *-ed* to the present form the way regular verbs do. In fact, because they form their principal parts in various ways, there's no single rule to help you learn them.

▐▐▐▶ Use the principal parts of these common irregular verbs correctly when you write and speak. The verb *to be* is used to form the present and past participles. The forms are listed at the right.

Forms of *to be*

Present

I am	we are
you are	you are
he is	they are

Past

I was	we were
you were	you were
he was	they were

Principal Parts of Common Irregular Verbs			
PRESENT	**PRESENT PARTICIPLE** (Use with *am, is, are, was, were.*)	**PAST**	**PAST PARTICIPLE** (Use with *has, had, have.*)
[be] is, are	(is) being	was, were	(had) been
begin	(is) beginning	began	(had) begun
blow	(is) blowing	blew	(had) blown
break	(is) breaking	broke	(had) broken
bring	(is) bringing	brought	(had) brought
burst	(is) bursting	burst	(had) burst
catch	(is) catching	caught	(had) caught
choose	(is) choosing	chose	(had) chosen
come	(is) coming	came	(had) come
do	(is) doing	did	(had) done
drink	(is) drinking	drank	(had) drunk
drive	(is) driving	drove	(had) driven
eat	(is) eating	ate	(had) eaten
fall	(is) falling	fell	(had) fallen
find	(is) finding	found	(had) found
freeze	(is) freezing	froze	(had) frozen
give	(is) giving	gave	(had) given
go	(is) going	went	(had) gone
grow	(is) growing	grew	(had) grown
know	(is) knowing	knew	(had) known
lead	(is) leading	led	(had) led
lie [to fib]	(is) lying	lied	(had) lied
lose	(is) losing	lost	(had) lost
make	(is) making	made	(had) made
put	(is) putting	put	(had) put

EDITING TIP

The verb *lie* (to fib) is different from the verbs *lay* (to place or put) and *lie* (to rest or recline). Watch out! Their principal parts are similar and they are easy to confuse.

P.S. When you aren't sure about a verb form, check a dictionary. All dictionaries list the principal parts of irregular verbs. The entry word is the present form. The past, past participle, and present participle forms are listed after the pronunciation:

break (brāk) **broke, broken, breaking**

If no verb forms are listed following the entry word, you can be sure that the verb is regular.

EXERCISE 3 Using Irregular Verbs

Rewrite each sentence on a separate piece of paper. Use the past form or past participle form of the verb in parentheses. **Remember:** With a form of the helping verb *have,* use the past participle.

EXAMPLE   Owen and his bride have (choose) their new dishes.
Owen and his bride have chosen their new dishes.

1. Have you (bring) your binoculars with you?   brought

2. Has anyone (be) in touch with Vanessa lately?   been

3. When the temperature was below zero last week, the water pipes (freeze) and (burst).   froze   burst

4. Takeo has (lose) ten pounds by exercising.   lost

5. During the game, players (drink) a lot of water.   drank

6. Ilene (catch) the high pop fly at last week's game.   caught

7. Trees (fall) when winds (blow) sixty miles an hour.   fell   blew

8. When I (go) to the video store last night, I (choose) an Alfred Hitchcock movie.   went   chose

9. Last year, Sam (drive) from Maine to Oregon.   drove

10. Have you ever (eat) one of Guillermo's burritos?   eaten

11. The pencil marks on the door show how Benjy has (grow) since he (be) six.   grown   was

12. Amelia has (put) her name on all her books.   put

13. When he (lead) the hike, Mike (break) a trail through the sawgrass.   led   broke

14. Have you (come) to any conclusion in your research?   come

15. Ed and Gene have (be) in a workshop all day.   been

16. The contest (begin) last week, but Madeline has not yet (begin) her entry.   began   begun

17. Oscar was upset when he (lose) the watch his grandfather had (give) him.   lost   given

18. Jeanetta and her sister (make) the dresses they (be) wearing.   made   were

19. I had (do) the best I could but did not finish.   done

20. Kathy and Marion have (know) each other and have (be) friends since they (be) six.   known   been   were

Irregular Verbs 2

The verbs in this lesson and the previous lesson are not the only irregular verbs, but they are ones that you use most often.

▐▐▐➡ Use the principal parts of these common irregular verbs correctly when you write and speak.

Principal Parts of Common Irregular Verbs			
PRESENT	PRESENT PARTICIPLE (Use with *am, is, are, was, were.*)	PAST	PAST PARTICIPLE (Use with *has, had, have.*)
ride	(is) riding	rode	(had) ridden
ring	(is) ringing	rang	(had) rung
rise	(is) rising	rose	(had) risen
run	(is) running	ran	(had) run
see	(is) seeing	saw	(had) seen
shake	(is) shaking	shook	(had) shaken
shrink	(is) shrinking	shrank	(had) shrunk
sing	(is) singing	sang	(had) sung
sink	(is) sinking	sank	(had) sunk
sit	(is) sitting	sat	(had) sat
speak	(is) speaking	spoke	(had) spoken
spend	(is) spending	spent	(had) spent
steal	(is) stealing	stole	(had) stolen
sting	(is) stinging	stung	(had) stung
strike	(is) striking	struck	(had) struck
swear	(is) swearing	swore	(had) sworn
swim	(is) swimming	swam	(had) swum
take	(is) taking	took	(had) taken
teach	(is) teaching	taught	(had) taught
throw	(is) throwing	threw	(had) thrown
wear	(is) wearing	wore	(had) worn
write	(is) writing	wrote	(had) written

Ring meaning "to surround" takes the past form *ringed.*

Enriching Your Vocabulary

Both the adjective *requisite* and the past participle *required* as used in Exercise 5, come from the Latin verb *requirere*, which means "to need." A course that is *requisite* or *required* for graduation is one that you need to take.

EXERCISE 4 Using Irregular Verbs

Rewrite each sentence on a separate piece of paper. Use the past form or past participle form of the verb in parentheses.

1. Paul Revere (ride) a horse to warn the colonists. rode

2. The jack of hearts had (steal) the tarts. stolen

3. As the *Titanic* (sink), passengers (sing) hymns. sank   sang

4. The Liberty Bell cracked when it (ring) in 1835. rang

5. In 1954, Roger Bannister (run) a sub-four-minute mile. ran

6. Native Americans (teach) the Pilgrims how to grow corn. taught

WRITING HINT

American English has many different **dialects**, or ways of speaking, in certain regions or among certain groups. When you write in school and at work, use standard English verb endings for the irregular verbs.

7. Have you (take) a close look at M. C. Escher's drawings? taken

8. Alex Haley (write) a family history, called *Roots,* that became a best seller. wrote

9. Miss Havisham had (wear) her wedding dress for years. worn

10. Mark Antony (speak) the words "Brutus is an honorable man." spoke

11. Who was frightened when a spider (sit) down beside her? sat

12. When two bees (sting) Lynn, she had an allergic reaction. stung

13. Lightning (strike) the kite that Benjamin Franklin flew. struck

14. Every president has (swear) to uphold the Constitution. sworn

15. Robinson Crusoe had (swim) to the shipwreck to get supplies. swum

EXERCISE 5 Editing a Paragraph

Cross out each incorrect verb, and write the correct verb above it. Make any other changes you think will improve the letter.

To the Editor:

¹This is the first time I have ~~wrote~~ written a letter to the editor. ²Our community has ~~saw~~ seen too many people who have drowned. ³A friend of mine ~~swum~~ swam way out. ⁴When she got caught in a riptide, a lifeguard ~~swimmed~~ swam out and ~~bringed~~ brought her back to shore. ⁵No one has ~~teached~~ taught us students swimming safety. ⁶Not all parents have ~~teached~~ taught their youngsters to swim. ⁷Young people have ~~took~~ taken too many chances. ⁸I think the people who ~~have ran~~ run the schools are making a mistake. ⁹They have ~~shrinked~~ shrunk from making swimming required. ¹⁰Too many swimming disasters have already ~~striked~~ struck this community.

CONNECTING
Writing & Grammar

For more information about writing persuasive essays, see **Composition,** Lesson 4.2.

Write What You Think

On a separate piece of paper, write a paragraph giving your opinion about the statement below. Do you agree or disagree with it? Support your opinion with reasons and examples. After you finish revising, edit your work to make sure your verb forms are correct.

Before students can graduate from high school, they should be required to pass swimming and lifesaving tests.

Answers will vary. Give students full credit if they have stated an opinion and attempted to support their opinions. Look for grammatically complete sentences that begin with a capital letter and end with an appropriate end punctuation mark.

Verb Tense

||||▶ A **verb tense** expresses the time an action was performed.

Every English verb has three **simple tenses** (present, past, and future) and three **perfect tenses** (present perfect, past perfect, and future perfect).

The Six Verb Tenses		
TENSE	**WHAT IT SHOWS**	**EXAMPLE**
present	action happening in the present; action that happens repeatedly	I **finish**. The sun **rises** and **sets**.
past	action completed in the past	I **finished**.
future	action that will happen in the future	You and he **will finish**.
present perfect	action completed recently or in indefinite past	I **have finished**. He **has finished**.
past perfect	action that happened before another action	I **had** already **finished** when the rain started.
future perfect	action that will happen before a future action or time	By tomorrow, he **will have finished**.

Each tense also has a **progressive form**, which is made up of a helping verb and the present participle (the -*ing* form). The progressive forms show ongoing action.

The Progressive Forms for the Six Tenses	
PROGRESSIVE FORM	**EXAMPLE**
present progressive	(am, is, are) finishing
past progressive	(was, were) finishing
future progressive	(will, shall) be finishing
present perfect progressive	(has, have) been finishing
past perfect progressive	had been finishing
future perfect progressive	will have been finishing

||||▶ Don't switch verb tenses needlessly. Keep tenses consistent whenever possible.

ORIGINAL   Scott **gets** out of the car and **looked** around him. He **had** no idea where he **is**.

CONSISTENT   Scott **got** out of the car and **looked** around him. He **had** no idea where he **was**.

A shift in verb tense is sometimes necessary because the meaning requires it. Use verb tenses that make sense in the sentence.

Scott **left** home yesterday; he **is taking** an overnight bus. He **will arrive** here tomorrow.

Everyone **wants** to meet Sara, whom no one **has seen** yet.

EDITING TIP

When you write about literature, use the **literary present tense** (see page 70). Talk about the writer and the characters as if they exist in the present. In "The Most Dangerous Game," Connell **writes** about a strange kind of hunting. As the story **begins**, Rainsford **falls** off a yacht and **swims** to an island.

TEST-TAKING TIP

When checking a verb in a standardized-test item, make sure that its tense is consistent with the frame of reference established by the sentence. See item 23 on page 292 for an example.

EXERCISE 6 Using Verb Tenses

Replace the italicized verbs in sentences 1–6 to show actions completed in the past.

¹In 1947, India and Pakistan ~~become~~ [became] independent nations. ²Great Britain's control of India ~~dates~~ [dated] back to 1857. ³The Empress of India ~~is~~ [was] none other than Britain's Queen Victoria. ⁴Mohandas K. Gandhi ~~has led~~ [led] India's struggle for independence. ⁵Followers ~~call~~ [called] him "Mahatma" Gandhi, which means "great soul." ⁶Gandhi ~~believe~~ [believed] in nonviolent resistance.

Replace the italicized verbs in sentences 7–10 with a progressive form to show ongoing action.

⁷Gandhi's nonviolent strategies ~~continued~~ [are continuing] to influence us today. (present progressive) ⁸When Dr. Martin Luther King, Jr., organized civil-rights protests in the 1960s, he ~~thought~~ [was thinking] of Gandhi. (past progressive) ⁹He also ~~modeled~~ [was modeling] his protests on Thoreau's essay called "On Civil Disobedience." (past progressive) ¹⁰We ~~honor~~ [will be honoring] Gandhi, Thoreau, and King long into the future. (future progressive)

EXERCISE 7 Making Verb Tenses Consistent

On a separate piece of paper, revise any of the following sentences in which you find unnecessary shifts in verb tense. If a sentence doesn't need revising, write *No change.* Students may make sentences consistent by changing either verb. Sample answers given.

1. Larry sings whenever he ~~arrived~~ [arrives] home from work.

2. Everyone cheered when the last bell of the school year ~~sounds~~ [sounded].

3. Tomorrow will be Dan's picnic; ~~we've~~ [we will] certainly ~~enjoyed~~ [enjoy] it.

4. Karim tripped on a tree root and ~~breaks~~ [broke] his toe.

5. The heat was awful, so no one left their air-conditioned rooms. No change

6. More registered voters ~~stayed~~ [stay] home than come to vote.

7. Joy scalded two fingers when she ~~pours~~ [poured] water for tea.

8. We announce the winners only when the results ~~had been~~ [are] official.

9. Gary ~~is glancing~~ [glanced] at his watch every few minutes as he waited.

10. A dog ~~arrives~~ [arrived] at our back gate, but no one knew whose it was.

HINT

Most of the sentences that need revising can be fixed in more than one way.

Parallel Structure

||||▶ To write sentences that have parallel structure, use the same grammatical form for two or more similar ideas. Using parallel structure makes it easier for readers to understand your writing.

NOT PARALLEL   In the summertime, I love **swimming**, **hiking**, or **to relax** with a good book. [*Swimming* and *hiking* are gerunds, but *to relax* is an infinitive.]

PARALLEL   In the summertime, I love **swimming**, **hiking**, or **relaxing** with a good book. [All the verb forms are gerunds.]

or

PARALLEL   In the summertime, I love **to swim**, **hike**, or **relax** with a good book. [All the verb forms are infinitives.]

||||▶ Be sure to use parallel structure when you compare or contrast ideas.

NOT PARALLEL   **Going** to the movies is more fun than **to rent** videos at home. [An infinitive is being compared with a gerund.]

PARALLEL   **Going** to the movies is more fun than **renting** videos at home. [A gerund is being compared with a gerund.]

||||▶ When you write sentences in which articles (*the, a, an*), prepositions (*on, in, with,* etc.), or conjunctions (*and, or, but,* etc.) precede equal ideas in a series, be sure to be consistent. Either repeat the preceding word or phrase before every idea, or use it only before the first idea in the series.

NOT PARALLEL   This book is useful **for** practicing language skills, learning new vocabulary, and **for** understanding Spanish-speaking cultures. [The preposition *for* is repeated before two out of the three items in the series.]

PARALLEL   This book is useful **for** practicing language skills, learning new vocabulary, and understanding Spanish-speaking cultures. [The preposition *for* is used before only the first item in the series.]

||||▶ Use parallel structure with correlative constructions such as *both . . . and, either . . . or,* and *not only . . . but also.*

NOT PARALLEL   By spending a year in Spain, you will not only enjoy **living** among a different culture, but also **to be** able to travel easily throughout Europe. [The first verb phrase is a gerund; the second is an infinitive.]

PARALLEL   By spending a year in Spain, you will not only enjoy **living** among a different culture, but also **being** able to travel easily throughout Europe. [Both verb phrases are gerunds.]

EXERCISE 8 Editing Sentences to Create Parallel Structure

On a separate piece of paper, revise each of the following sentences so that it has parallel structure.
Revisions will vary.

1. I believe that drinking water before physical activity is more important than to drink during.

2. Fish is good for eating, for canning, and to enjoy.

3. To hike on a warm spring day is as satisfying to me as taking a dip in a swimming pool in the middle of summer.

4. My youngest brother, Matthew, started swimming at the age of three; my other brother, Andrew, started playing Little League at six; and I started to compete on the tennis circuit at seven.

5. On yesterday's hike, we stopped several times to eat, rest, and also to let the others catch up with us.

6. I was more concerned about getting to the top of the mountain before sundown than to enjoy the view along the way.

7. My goal was to catch ten fish, spot one eagle, and seeing a herd of seals.

8. It was as difficult to go up the mountain as it was going down.

9. I would like to try to compete in a triathlon or try finishing a marathon.

10. Winning is not the most rewarding part of a sport, but to play a good game is.

EXERCISE 9 Editing a Paragraph to Create Parallel Structure

On a separate piece of paper, edit the paragraph below so that the sentences have parallel structure. You may have to reword some of the sentences.
Revisions will vary. Make sure edited sentences have parallel structure.

[1]Most people will tell you that hiking is a delightful experience, but I also think that to rest after a long hike is delightful. [2]I speak from first-hand experience when I also tell you that to bound down a trail like a gazelle is much more fun than slogging up at a glacial pace. [3]However, a hard climb up can have its own rewards. [4]As my friends and I made our way up to the top of a trail yesterday, we enjoyed trading stories, chatting with other hikers, or just to nibble on our trail snacks. [5]When we reached the top, we were rewarded not only with knowing we had accomplished something challenging, but also to see a double rainbow. [6]And what awaited each of us after that grueling experience was shedding our dusty clothes, taking a hot shower, a change into clean jeans, and to pitch into what will have to rank as one of the best dinners ever.

Using the Active Voice

▐▶ When a verb is in the **active voice**, the subject of the sentence performs an action. When a verb is in the **passive voice**, the subject receives an action.

A verb in the passive voice always uses some form of the helping verb *be*.

ACTIVE   Jonah **built** the birdhouse.

PASSIVE   The birdhouse **was built** by Jonah.

ACTIVE   Emily **has seen** hummingbirds at the feeder.

PASSIVE   Hummingbirds **have been seen** by Emily.

▐▶ Use the active voice when you write because it is stronger and more direct. The passive voice is acceptable when you do not know the performer of the action or when you want to emphasize the receiver of the action, not the performer.

The car **was stolen** from the parking lot. [The performer of the action is unknown.]

Mickey Mouse **was created** by Walt Disney. [The receiver of the action, not the performer, is being emphasized.]

WRITING HINT

As you revise your writing, check your sentences for passive voice. Change to the active voice whenever possible, especially if the change saves words.

PASSIVE
The ball had been hit by Guy. (7 words)

ACTIVE
Guy hit the ball. (4 words)

The object of the preposition *by* can often be made into the subject to change a passive sentence into an active sentence.

EXERCISE 10 Using the Active Voice

Rewrite the sentences below to use the active voice whenever possible. If the passive voice is acceptable, explain why.

EXAMPLE   A ship's speed is measured in knots.

Keep the passive voice. The sentence has no "performer" of the action.
See Answer Key at www.grammarforwriting.com.

1. The Camp David agreements were signed in 1978 by Sadat and Begin.

2. The ancient city of Rome was built on seven hills.

3. Sixty-three of his sixty-six professional fights were won by Joe Louis.

4. "The Raven" was written in 1845 by Edgar Allan Poe.

5. The koala bear is found only in eastern Australia.

6. Both the Nobel Prize for chemistry and the Nobel Peace Prize were won by Linus Pauling.

7. The city of Machu Picchu was built by the Incas about 1500 A.D.

8. The border between Mexico and the United States is formed by the Rio Grande.

9. Nearly 8,500 species of birds have been identified.

10. *Gulliver's Travels*, a satire, was written by Jonathan Swift.

Revising and Editing Worksheet

Improve the following draft by revising for ideas, organization, word choice, and sentence variety. After revising, edit the draft for errors in spelling, capitalization, punctuation, and usage. Write your revised and edited version on a separate piece of paper. Compare your changes with those of a writing partner. **Hint:** The word *plankton* is plural; it takes a plural verb.

¹Plankton are tiny organisms. ²Plankton have varied in size. ³Some plankton be microscopic. ⁴You can only seen these plankton with a microscope. ⁵Other plankton are bigger and reached one to two inches long in length. ⁶Plankton can be finded in oceans and lakes all over the world. ⁷They are finded mostly in coastal waters. ⁸Especially in polar and cold waters.

⁹There are two different kinds and types of plankton: plant and animal. ¹⁰Plant plankton had only one cell. ¹¹Algae and diatoms are examples of plant plankton. ¹²Plant plankton form the basis of the food chain.

¹³Animal plankton eaten plant plankton. ¹⁴Then small marine animals eat the animal plankton. ¹⁵These small marine animals included mollusks, snails, shrimp, and mussels. ¹⁶Larger marine animals feed on these small animals. ¹⁷Including seals and porpoises. ¹⁸These animals are ate in turn by some whales and sharks.

¹⁹Plankton are of extreme importance to life on Earth. ²⁰First, plant plankton produce 70 percent of Earth's oxygen. ²¹Second, plankton played a crucial part in the world's food chain.

²²Plankton are so tiny that they cannot move on their own. ²³Instead, drifting in the ocean's currents. ²⁴Plankton float on the water's surface at night and have sank below the surface during the day. ²⁵At night they raise again to the surface.

Revisions will vary. See teacher pages for writing rubrics.

Enriching Your Vocabulary

The adjective *crucial* is based on the Latin *cruc*, or "cross." Thus, a *crucial* matter is one that requires a final decision such as the one that you need to make if you reach a crossroad.

Chapter Review

Exercise A Using Irregular Verbs

Write the form of the verb in parentheses that correctly completes each sentence. In some cases, there may be more than one correct answer.

EXAMPLE   The newspaper has been (lie) in the rain. *lying*

1. How long have you (know) Giorgio? known
2. Harriet (be) tired from working late five nights a week. is
3. No one found the diary, which (lie) right on the desk. lay
4. When she went to her son's apartment, Mrs. O'Keeffe (bring) dinner. brought
5. Has Idria (go) to the bank yet? gone
6. Who (teach) Raphael how to play the flute? taught
7. Yesterday, Shira (swim) fifty-two laps in the pool. swam
8. Justin has (write) a science fiction short story. written
9. Last night we (see) a really good movie. saw
10. I didn't finish the test because my time (run) out. ran
11. I hope you've (take) careful notes. taken
12. For dinner, Ricardo (make) roast beef and mashed potatoes. made
13. Mrs. Chan (throw) out the old magazines she had been saving. threw
14. Since the year began, Larry has (wear) cowboy boots to school. worn
15. Have you ever (ride) on a monorail? ridden

Exercise B Using the Active Voice

On a separate piece of paper, rewrite the sentences below to use the active voice when it makes sense to do so. If the passive voice is acceptable, explain why.
See Answer Key at www.grammarforwriting.com.

1. Construction of the Teatro Colón in Buenos Aires was completed in 1908.
2. Every square foot of the festival site was overtaken by trucks, trailers, and tents.
3. *Leaves of Grass* and other works of poetry were written by Walt Whitman.
4. A prolonged slave rebellion in 1831 was led by Nat Turner, a slave from Virginia.
5. The Model T car was introduced by Henry Ford in 1908.
6. In 1878, Edison Electric Light Company was founded by Thomas Edison.
7. The novel *Emma* was written by Jane Austen.
8. The 1997 movie *Titanic* was watched by millions of people world-wide.
9. The brazen robbery was committed in broad daylight.
10. The polio vaccine was developed by Jonas Salk in 1955.

EXERCISE C Using Verb Tenses

Change the italicized verbs to the verb tense specified in parentheses. You may look back at the charts on page 169. Write your answers on a separate piece of paper.

1. The twins always *wear* different outfits. (past) wore

2. Nora *make* lasagna at least once a week. (present perfect)   has made

3. Next year, everyone *sing* the school song before assemblies. (future) will sing

4. A committee *plan* the picnic. (past perfect progressive)   had been planning

5. I *hope* you would call. (past progressive)   was hoping

6. Jason *put* out the candles before he *go* to sleep. (past; past)   put; went

7. Blanca *catch* the pass. (past) caught

8. Everyone *eat*, so no one *be* hungry. (present perfect; present)   has eaten; is

9. Sondra *grow* more spinach next year. (future progressive)   will be growing

10. Leslie *worry* about her algebra final. (present perfect progressive)   has been worrying

EXERCISE D Revising and Editing a Paragraph

Edit the paragraph below for correct verb usage. Use the active voice whenever possible. Decide whether the paragraph should be past or present tense, and make verb tenses consistent. Make any other changes that you think will improve the paragraph.

¹Homes of all different shapes, materials, and kinds are built by birds. ²A shallow scrape, or nest in the dirt, is built by pressing their bodies into the earth by Arctic terns. ³Their eggs were sat on constantly by Arctic terns. ⁴Burrows were built below the ground by burrowing owls, bee-eaters, penguins, and puffins. ⁵Holes in trees have been made by woodpeckers and flickers to serve as their hidden homes. ⁶At the top of very tall poles or trees, large nests are constructed by ospreys. ⁷Tiny cup nests are created by hummingbirds. ⁸Bits of plants and moss are being woven into the cup nest by hummingbirds. ⁹Mud is shaped into nests by flamingos and cliff swallows. ¹⁰Large mud mounds on the ground are built by flamingos, but cliff swallow nests look like an apartment house under a cliff ledge.

Revisions will vary. See teacher pages for writing rubrics.

Subject-Verb Agreement

Direct students to
www.grammarforwriting.com
for chapter-specific
portfolio projects.

STUDENT WRITING
Expository Essay

A Language Plan for Success
by Hugh Field
high school student, San Diego, California

What do you call someone who speaks three languages? Trilingual. What do you call someone who speaks two languages? Bilingual. What do you call someone who speaks one language? American. This old joke has for too long been a sad reality in the schools of San Diego, a city that should be one of the most multicultural in America.

Given our proximity to Mexico, one might expect San Diego residents to have a passing knowledge of the Spanish language.

San Diego Unified School District Superintendent Alan Bersin is finally doing something to increase Spanish knowledge around San Diego. Bersin has proposed a plan in which, if passed, students will be taught both Spanish and English starting in elementary school, in a program designed to benefit both children who have been speaking English all their lives as well as those who may have grown up speaking Spanish only, or a combination of the two.

With the recent implementation of Proposition 227, Spanish speaking children are discouraged from preserving their native language skills. With [Bersin's] new measure, Spanish speaking children would learn grammar skills as well as literacy, allowing many more high school students to take AP Spanish classes. The plan would require all graduates to be academically competent in both English and Spanish.

The strong points of this initiative outweigh any downsides, making it a sensible plan for the future. However, the pilot program only covers the grades before middle school, a time when students are offered other electives that many students find more attractive than Spanish.

Such a situation arose in Miami when a similar pilot program was started. One solution is to require Spanish, in some form, in high school.

While some students may balk at the idea of not being allowed to study the foreign language of their choice, overall, teaching in Spanish and English will help schools graduate well-rounded students and ensure that these students get into college.

Last, this plan will increase the quality of life for all students who go through it. Those with special language skills are guaranteed better and higher–paying jobs, as well as better opportunities for advancement. For as the proverb goes, "He who speaks two languages is worth two."

Allow time for students to discuss the student writing. Suggest that they identify its strengths and propose possible improvements. Use the model to introduce the concepts in the chapter.

> Hugh's expository essay begins with an attention grabber. He explains the issue he plans to address; then he details the solution to the problem. Hugh even identifies opposition to the solution—and then counterattacks. His final paragraph has three convincing sentences that sum up his position.
>
> As you reread the essay, notice that Hugh uses complex sentences with clauses and phrases. Complicated sentences require a careful watch on subject-verb agreement, which you'll study in this chapter.

Agreement in Person and Number

We use the terms **person** and **number** when we discuss the subject of a sentence. The subjects *I* and *we* are **first person**. The subject *you* is **second person**. A noun subject or *he, she, it,* or *they* is **third person**.

A subject that names one thing is **singular**. A subject that names more than one thing is **plural**.

▐▶ A third-person **singular subject** takes a **singular verb**. A third-person **plural subject** takes a **plural verb**.

The chart below shows how the verbs *sweep* and *wash* change their forms when they follow a third-person singular subject.

Subject-Verb Agreement in the Present Tense		
PERSON	**SINGULAR SUBJECT**	**PLURAL SUBJECT**
First	I sweep and wash.	We sweep and wash.
Second	You sweep and wash.	You sweep and wash.
Third	He **sweeps** and **washes**. Jana **sweeps** and **washes**.	They sweep and wash. The boys sweep and wash.

The verb *be* has three forms to match person and number in the present tense. (See the side column.)

▐▶ In a verb phrase, the helping verb (HV) must agree with the subject (S).

  S   HV
Alberta **has** been running for thirty minutes.
  S   HV
She **does** not tutor on Friday.

The rules in this lesson apply not only to present tense verbs but also to present progressive and present perfect tenses.

▐▶ A prepositional phrase that comes between the subject and verb is called an **intervening phrase**.

Intervening phrases sometimes make it difficult to find the subject of a sentence. When you write, make sure the verb agrees with the subject, not with the object of a preposition in an intervening phrase.

  S   V
One of my friends **is tutoring** students in reading and math. [*Of my friends* is a prepositional phrase, so *one* is the subject, not *friends*.]
  S   V
The **students** at Martin High School **have** many different jobs. [*Have* agrees with *students*, not *school*.]

Present Tense Forms of *Be*

Singular
I **am** here.
You **are** here.
He **is** here.

Plural
We **are** here.
You **are** here.
They **are** here.

See page 165 for more forms of *be*.

Enriching Your Vocabulary

The noun *esteem* used in Exercise 2 can be traced to the French *estimer*, which comes from the Latin *aestimare*, meaning "to determine the value of something" or "to value or appraise." If you have *esteem* for someone, you have a good opinion of him or her. Your *self-esteem* is your sense of your own worth.

HiNT

One sentence is correct; some sentences have more than one subject-verb agreement error.

EXERCISE 1 Editing a Paragraph

For each mistake in subject-verb agreement in the following paragraph, cross out the incorrect verb and write the correct verb above it.

¹A volunteer ~~are~~ _is_ a person who ~~work~~ _works_ at a job without pay. ²In many schools, students in twelfth grade ~~is~~ _are_ required to complete a community-service project before they ~~graduates~~ _graduate_. ³At Martin High School, volunteers ~~works~~ _work_ at least three hours a week. ⁴Some students volunteer at day-care centers. ⁵Many seniors ~~is~~ _are_ tutoring young children in reading. ⁶Other students ~~works~~ _work_ at museums and in hospitals. ⁷Members of the football team ~~is~~ _are_ coaching at an after-school sports program. ⁸Each year the guidance counselor ~~give~~ _gives_ students a list of organizations seeking volunteers. ⁹Seniors ~~has~~ _have_ to write a proposal for their community-service project, and the counselor ~~has~~ _has_ to approve it. ¹⁰After students ~~has~~ _have_ completed their projects, they ~~writes~~ _write_ reports telling what they learned.

Students may wish to write a paragraph about their own volunteering experiences.

Working Together

EXERCISE 2 Choosing the Correct Verb

Underline the subject of each sentence and the verb in parentheses that agrees with the subject.

1. Three <u>students</u> in my biology class (volunteers, <u>volunteer</u>) at the museum.

2. <u>They</u> (helps, <u>help</u>) sixth-graders with microscopes.

3. <u>Members</u> of the Key Club (makes, <u>make</u>) sandwiches at a shelter.

4. Some <u>seniors</u> (visits, <u>visit</u>) folks in nursing homes.

5. <u>Volunteers</u> for Habitat for Humanity (builds, <u>build</u>) houses.

6. Several <u>students</u> (is, <u>are</u>) teaching about eating disorders.

7. (Is, <u>Are</u>) <u>you</u> planning to volunteer at the animal shelter?

8. Volunteer <u>work</u> (<u>increases</u>, increase) students' self-esteem.

9. Some <u>students</u> (thinks, <u>think</u>) it impresses colleges to do volunteer work.

10. <u>Others</u> (wants, <u>want</u>) to try a career that interests them.

Indefinite Pronouns, Inverted Subjects

▐▶ An **indefinite pronoun** expresses an amount or refers to an unspecified person or thing. Some indefinite pronouns are always singular and take singular verbs. Others are always plural and take plural verbs.

SINGULAR   **Everyone** in Mrs. Rivera's algebra classes **works** hard.
SINGULAR   **Neither** of the movies **is** a mystery.
PLURAL   **Both** of Kim's uncles **make** custom-designed furniture.

▐▶ The indefinite pronouns *all, any, most,* and *some* can be either singular or plural. Depending on the word they refer to, these pronouns take either a singular or plural verb.

> Lesson 11.5 explains that singular indefinite pronouns take singular possessive pronouns.

	S V
SINGULAR	**All** of your work **is** excellent.
	S V
PLURAL	**All** of the farmers **are planting** winter wheat.
	S V
SINGULAR	**Any** of the food **is** delicious.
	S V
PLURAL	**Any** of these packages **look** interesting.
	S V
SINGULAR	The report is extensive. **Most** of it **is** correct.
	S V
PLURAL	Where are those cats? **Most sleep** during the day.
	S V
SINGULAR	**Some** of the cake **is** frozen.
	S V
PLURAL	**Some** of the cookies **are** broken.

Always Singular
anybody	neither
anyone	nobody
each	no one
either	one
everybody	somebody
everyone	someone

Always Plural
both	many
few	several

EDITING TIP

The pronoun *none* is especially tricky. Use a singular verb only when you can think of the subject as "none of it." Use a plural verb when you can substitute "none of them."
None of the test **is** easy. [None of *it* is easy.]
None of your answers **are** right. [None of *them* are right.]

▐▶ A verb must agree with the subject even when the subject follows the verb.

> In a wooden box at the top of the closet **are** all our old **photographs**.
> Where **are** your **copies** of the reports?
> Here **is** a **book** I really liked.

▐▶ A verb agrees with the subject, not with the predicate nominative (PN).

Don't be confused by a predicate nominative following a linking verb. Find the subject, and then make the verb agree.

> S   V   PN
> Karin's favorite **dessert is** strawberries.

> S   V PN
> The **subject** of his report **is** solutions to combat crime.

TEST-TAKING TIP

Don't be fooled by an inverted sentence on a standardized test. Remember: Whether the verb is placed after or before the subject or subjects, it must agree in number with the subject or subjects. See item 11 on page 290 for an example.

Chapter 10 • Subject-Verb Agreement **181**

EXERCISE 3 Choosing the Correct Verb

Underline the subject of each sentence and the verb in parentheses that agrees in number with the subject. Then, with a partner write five more sentences that practice subject-verb agreement. Give a choice of two present-tense verbs in parenthesis and exchange sentences with another team. Students' additional answers will vary.

1. One of the nicknames for an American (is, are) Yankee.

2. None of our other national parks (has, have) as many geysers as Yellowstone.

3. Few (is, are) as beautiful as Yosemite in California.

4. Which part of Niagara Falls (is, are) in Canada?

5. Several of the popular sights in Washington, D.C., (is, are) the Vietnam Memorial, the Washington Monument, and the White House.

6. Anyone in Death Valley (knows, know) how dry deserts are.

7. In Denver, everybody (lives, live) a mile above sea level.

8. Some of the land in the Black Hills (is, are) sacred to the Sioux.

9. The street names in New York City (has, have) fascinating histories.

10. None of the Great Lakes (borders, border) an ocean.

EXERCISE 4 Editing Sentences

Extend Exercise 4 by asking students to write a paragraph describing a place where they would like to live and why.

Edit the sentences below. Correct any errors you find in subject-verb agreement.

1. ~~Does~~ Do you know where you would like to live someday?

2. What type of land ~~appeal~~ appeals to you most?

3. There ~~is~~ are magazines that list the ten best places to live.

4. Perhaps one of these cities ~~are~~ is already your home.

5. The best type of scenery ~~are~~ is mountainous.

6. When I ~~thinks~~ think about the place I'd most like to live, I ~~chooses~~ choose a dairy farm in northern Wisconsin.

7. Most of my friends ~~likes~~ like to watch the seasons pass.

8. Among my friends ~~is~~ are many in northern California.

9. My mother's cousins ~~has~~ have a dairy farm.

10. I ~~visits~~ visit them every summer.

Agreement with Compound Subjects

A sentence has a **compound subject** when two or more subjects share the same verb. In the present tense, use the following rules to select the correct verb form.

▐▶ When two or more singular subjects are joined by *and*, they take a plural verb.

> Jupiter, Saturn, **and** Neptune **have** many moons.
> Lién **and** Shira **know** a lot about astronomy.

▐▶ When two or more singular subjects are joined by *or* or *nor*, they take a singular verb.

> Neither Mercury **nor** Venus **has** a moon.
> Either Martin **or** Pat **takes** the dog out after school.

▐▶ When a singular subject and a plural subject are joined by *or* or *nor*, the verb agrees with the subject closer to it.

> Neither the stars **nor** the moon **is** visible tonight.
> Neither the moon **nor** the stars **are** visible tonight.
> **Is** the moon or the stars visible tonight?
> **Are** the stars or the moon visible tonight?

EDITING TIP

A compound subject that names only one thing or person takes a singular verb.
Chutes and Ladders is a board game.
Fresh berries and yogurt is Melanie's favorite snack.
My friend and adviser always offers her opinion.

EXERCISE 5 Choosing the Correct Verb

Underline the subject of each sentence and the verb in parentheses that agrees with the subject. **Hint:** Not every sentence has a compound subject.

1. The United States and Russia (has, have) cooperated in space.

2. Snack foods and her family (is, are) what Shannon Lucid missed most during her six months in space.

3. Mood and body (is, are) affected by long space missions.

4. A mother and pilot (is, are) the first woman space commander.

5. Weak muscles or bone loss (concerns, concern) scientists.

STEP BY STEP

Agreement with Compound Subjects

1. Identify the compound subjects. Watch out for prepositional phrases!

2. Find the conjunction connecting the subjects: *and*, *or*, or *nor*.

3. When *or* or *nor* connects the subjects, use a singular verb only if the subject nearer the verb is third-person singular.

6. Either a vacuum <u>treadmill</u> or another <u>piece</u> of exercise equipment (<u>helps</u>, help) to overcome these problems.

7. In space, an <u>accident</u> or <u>emergency</u> (<u>is</u>, are) always a danger.

8. <u>Mission Control</u> or <u>reporters</u> (updates, <u>update</u>) the public.

9. (<u>Is</u>, Are) a space <u>colony</u> or a temporary <u>settlement</u> likely?

10. Neither <u>Mars</u> nor the <u>Moon</u> (<u>has</u>, have) breathable air.

EXERCISE 6 Create Your Own Exercise

With a partner or group, make up five sentences like the ones in Exercise 5. You may write about any topic. Use compound subjects. Exchange sentences with another team, and see if you agree on the correct answers. Students' sentences will vary.

EXERCISE 7 Writing a Paragraph

Write a paragraph based on the following notes. Use present-tense verbs. Then get together in a small group to read your paragraphs aloud and check subject-verb agreement. Students' paragraphs will vary.

> Mercury, Venus, Mars, Jupiter & Saturn = planets known to ancient Greeks
> <u>Planet</u>, from Greek for "wanderer" (because planets move in sky)
> Mercury, Venus, Earth, Mars, Jupiter, Saturn, Uranus, Neptune, Pluto = 9 planets we know revolve around sun
> Jupiter & Saturn = 2 largest planets; Mercury, Pluto, Mars = smallest planets
> Mercury & Venus = 2 closest to sun   Neptune & Pluto = 2 most distant
> Earth = third planet from the sun

Write What You Think

On a separate piece of paper, write a paragraph about one of the following questions. Revise, then edit for complete sentences and for subject-verb agreement. Answers will vary.

1. You have been invited to spend five years in the first U.S. colony on Mars. What questions will you ask before you decide whether to go or not? What do you think you will decide? Tell why.

2. Some people say that the money spent on our space program should go instead to solving problems on Earth. Do you agree or disagree with this opinion? Give reasons.

Agreement with Special Nouns

▐▌▶ **Collective nouns**, such as the examples on the right, name a group of people or things.

Use a singular verb when you think of a collective noun as one single unit. Use a plural verb when you think of a collective noun as multiple members.

> Neely's **family is planning** a summer reunion. [*Family* refers to a single unit and takes a singular verb.]
>
> Neely's **family live** in forty different states. [*Family* refers to multiple members in the group and takes a plural verb.]

Deciding whether a collective noun is acting as a single unit or as multiple members isn't always easy. If you are not sure, use the verb form (singular or plural) that you think sounds better.

▐▌▶ Some nouns ending in *-s* function as singular subjects and take a singular verb. Some function as plural subjects and take a plural verb. A few may be either singular or plural.

The nouns that are always plural are usually a pair of something or an object made up of parts working together. See the examples on the right.

> **Measles is** a serious disease for children and adults.
>
> Your **eyeglasses are** on the bookshelf next to the dictionary.
>
> These **statistics come** from the Centers for Disease Control.
>
> **Statistics is** a required course for psychology majors.

▐▌▶ The title of a work of art (painting, literature, or music) is always a singular subject and takes a singular verb.

> Van Gogh's ***First Steps* is** a copy of a drawing by Millet.

▐▌▶ Use a singular verb with a third-person subject that names a single amount or time. Use a plural verb with a third-person subject that refers to multiple items.

> Two **dollars is** the value of that old coin. [a single amount]
>
> These two **dollars are** badly torn. [multiple dollar bills]
>
> Three **months makes** a quarter of a year. [a single time period]
>
> These three **months are** passing very slowly. [multiple items]

▐▌▶ Use a singular verb when *many a, every,* or *each* comes before a compound subject.

> **Every** ninth-grader **and** tenth-grader **takes** math and English.

Some Collective Nouns

audience	flock
class	group
club	herd
committee	(the) press
crowd	(the) public
family	team

Singular

mathematics	news
measles	physics
mumps	

Plural

binoculars	scissors
eyeglasses	slacks
pants	

Singular or Plural

acoustics	statistics
politics	

The words *media* and *data* are technically plural but are often used with singular verbs.

Enriching Your Vocabulary

Around the world, people celebrated the new *millennium*. This word, used in Exercise 8, comes from the Latin *mille*, or "thousand," and *ennium* (from *annus*), or "year." So a *millennium* is a period of a thousand years. More generally, the word means a period of happiness and freedom from life's ills.

EXERCISE 8 Choosing the Correct Verb

Underline the verb in parentheses that agrees with the subject.

1. *The Trojan Women* (is, are) a play by Euripedes, an ancient Greek dramatist.

2. A thousand years (is, are) called a millennium.

3. Every chimpanzee, ape, and gorilla (has, have) flexible hands and feet.

4. Statistics (is, are) the branch of mathematics that deals with collecting, classifying, and organizing data.

5. Many a poet and novelist (writes, write) all night.

6. The herd of goats (spends, spend) all summer in the mountains.

7. Sometimes election news (reaches, reach) the public before polls close.

8. A committee of congressional representatives (takes, take) up pressing issues.

9. Four hundred thousand dollars (was, were) destroyed in the fire at the bank.

10. Mumps (causes, cause) fever and painful swelling of the salivary glands.

EXERCISE 9 Writing Complete Sentences

On a separate piece of paper, write a complete sentence for each numbered item, using the word or phrase as the subject of the sentence. Use present-tense verbs and check your sentences for correct subject-verb agreement. Read your sentences aloud to yourself for extra practice in hearing the sound of correct agreement. Students' sentences will vary.

EXAMPLE   team
           The team has only one game left in the season.

1. committee   6. mathematics

2. audience   7. three months

3. every man and woman   8. scissors

4. ten minutes   9. team

5. *Cats!* (by Andrew Lloyd Webber)   10. *Grimm's Fairy Tales*

Challenge students to write a fun paragraph using all ten words or phrases. Allow time in class for students to read their paragraphs aloud.

Revising and Editing Worksheet 1

Improve the following draft by revising for ideas, organization, word choice, and sentence variety. After revising, edit the draft for errors in spelling, capitalization, punctuation, and usage. Write your revised and edited version on a separate piece of paper. Compare your changes with those of a writing partner.

[1]*Great Expectations* are one of Charles Dickens's most popular novels. [2]It's main character is named Pip. [3]Pip's parents is dead, and the boy lives with his bad-tempered sister and her kindly husband Joe, the village blacksmith. [4]The family live on the edge of a marsh. [5]The novel open when Pip find an escaped convict in a graveyard. [6]The convict orders Pip to bring him food and a file to remove his chains. [7]Later, there is two escaped convicts fighting, and the police arrests them both.

[8]Soon the wealthy Miss Havisham commands Pip to play with Estella. [9]A girl who live with her. [10]Pip falls in love with Estella, who treats him cruelly. [11]Many years goes by. [12]Young Pip become an apprentice blacksmith. [13]Suddenly, a lawyer announces that Pip has received a great deal of money from an anonymous benefactor. [14]Pip go to London—with great expectations—to become a gentleman.

[15]Many an adventure and misfortune befall Pip in London. [16]Pip abandons Joe, but Joe is ever faithful. [17]News of Pip's illness reach Joe. [18]Joe hurries to London to nurse the penniless Pip.

[19]*Great Expectations* were published in weekly installments from 1860 to 1861 in a magazine that Dickens edited. [20]To keep readers interested, there are a great deal of suspense and mystery in the novel. [21]When Dickens's friends complained that the novel's original ending were to unhappy. [22]Dickens rewrote the ending. [23]In the revised version. [24]Pip and Estella meets again. [25]They lives happily ever after.

> ### Enriching Your Vocabulary
>
> Charities have *benefactors* whose contributions support their good works. Such people are well named. The noun *benefactor* comes from the Latin *bene*, which means "well," and *facere*, which means "to make or do."

Students' revisions will vary. See teacher pages for assessment rubrics. Students who have read *Great Expectations* may wish to expand this worksheet into an essay for extra credit.

Revising and Editing Worksheet 2

Improve the following draft by revising for ideas, organization, word choice, and sentence variety. After revising, edit the draft for errors in spelling, capitalization, punctuation, and usage. Write your revised and edited version on a separate piece of paper. Compare your changes with those of a writing partner.

[1]In *The Odyssey*, the ancient Greek poet Homer tell a tail about Odysseus, the king of Ithaca. [2](*Ulysses* is the ancient Roman name for *Odysseus*.) [3]Odysseus with his men head home to Ithaca when the Trojan War ends. [4]They has spent ten years fighting the Trojans. [5]They are eager to return to Ithaca. [6]There journey home takes ten years. [7]Because of their many adventures. [8]In the end only Odysseus remain alive. [9]The one-eyed monster Cyclops, the Sirens, and Scylla and Charybdis is just a few of the obstacles Odysseus and his men faces on their journey home.

[10]For twenty years, Odysseus's wife and son wait for his return. [11]Telemachus, who is just a baby when his father leaves, is all ready a young man. [12]No one know if Odysseus is dead or alive. [13]Many doubts that he is alive and urges his wife, Penelope, to remarry. [14]Many a young man and old man camps out in Odysseus's castle. [15]They argues and eats a lot. [16]While waiting for Penelope to choose one of them for her new husband.

[17]But Penelope plays a clever trick. [18]She say that before she remarries, she must finish weaving a burial cloth (a shroud) for her father-in-law. [19]Penelope spends every day at her loom weaving the shroud. [20]Every night she undoes what she has woven. [21]Penelope wait loyally for her husband's return.

[22]The climax of *The Odyssey* comes when Odysseus finally returns to Ithaca. [23]He is disguised as a beggar, but his faithful dog and his old nurse recognizes him. [24]He reveals his true identity to Telemachus. [25]Together they plans revenge on the noisy, boastful suitors.

Students' revisions will vary. See teacher pages for assessment rubrics. Students who have read *The Odyssey* may wish to share their favorite episode with the class.

Chapter Review

EXERCISE A Choosing the Correct Verb

Choose the verb in parentheses that agrees with the subject.

1. The military (uses, use) camouflage to disguise and protect troops, ships, and weapons.

2. Soldiers in the jungle (wears, wear) mottled green and brown and sometimes (covers, cover) their helmets with foliage.

3. Colors and patterns (helps, help) animals hide from enemies.

4. Some moths or butterflies (looks, look) like damaged leaves.

5. The Indian leaf butterfly (becomes, become) almost invisible on a pile of leaves.

6. Every chameleon (has, have) the ability to change its color.

7. Many a snake and insect also (has, have) patterns and colors that (acts, act) as a disguise.

8. Some creatures (imitates, imitate) the color and pattern of a poisonous species.

9. Knowing that one black-and-white butterfly (tastes, taste) bad, hungry birds (avoid, avoids) the look-alike species.

10. (Is, Are) there ever times when you (wish, wishes) you had camouflage?

EXERCISE B Editing a Paragraph

For each mistake in subject-verb agreement in the following paragraph, cross out the incorrect verb, and write the correct verb above it. **Hint:** Not every sentence contains an error; some sentences have more than one error.

¹Every year, many new students from other countries ~~arrives~~ [arrive] in our school. ²Jorge and his family ~~comes~~ [come] from Cuba. ³Jorge and his father, who was a political prisoner in Cuba, both ~~works~~ [work] in the same restaurant. ⁴Jorge ~~work~~ [works] after school, and both his father and he ~~works~~ [work] on the weekends. ⁵Marta and her cousin Isabel ~~is~~ [are] from the Dominican Republic. ⁶They are looking for after-school jobs. ⁷Marta ~~live~~ [lives] with her family in an apartment across the street from the drugstore where Marta's mother works.

⁸Marta ~~study~~ [studies] hard and gets good grades. ⁹She ~~say~~ [says] that she wants to become a doctor some day, especially to help children. ¹⁰Francia ~~comes~~ [comes] from El Salvador, and

Van and his family ~~is~~ *are* from Vietnam. [11]I ~~likes~~ *like* learning about all of these countries from my new friends. [12]I especially ~~likes~~ *like* sampling the foods they ~~brings~~ *bring* for us to taste.

EXERCISE C Writing Complete Sentences

On a separate piece of paper, write a complete sentence for each numbered item. Begin your sentence with the given word or group of words. Use present-tense verbs and check your sentences for correct subject-verb agreement.

Students' sentences will vary. See sample sentence given below.

1. One of the essential ingredients in. . . *salsa is hot peppers.*
2. Pickles and ice cream. . .
3. Neither Luisa nor her little sister. . .
4. Twenty-four dollars and ninety-six cents. . .
5. Alex, Pat, and I. . .
6. Many an argument and a disagreement. . .
7. A group of students. . .
8. Where. . . ?
9. There are. . .
10. Carla or her brothers. . .
11. On top of the bookcase. . .
12. Either Jeff or his two sisters. . .
13. Everyone in all my classes. . .
14. Few of the questions. . .
15. Mathematics or statistics. . .
16. *Romeo and Juliet* by Shakespeare. . .
17. Today's bad news about the weather. . .
18. Both she and I. . .
19. Among my favorite movies. . .
20. Every man, woman, and child. . .

EXERCISE D Writing a Description

Imagine that you are standing in the doorway of a room. You might choose your favorite room in your home or a room in a museum. Using present-tense verbs, write a paragraph describing what you see for a friend who has never been in the room. Include specific details of colors and objects such as furniture, decorations, and clothing. Make some notes before you start writing, and plan your description. You might begin by considering these questions.

• What is the main impression you get from the room?
• What do you see first? What is the biggest object in the room?
• Which objects are most important to you? Why?
• Is the room brightly lit or in shadows?

Students' paragraphs will vary. Encourage students to write creatively so their descriptions will make someone want to visit their room. You may wish to have students describe their ideal room.

CHAPTER REVIEW

Using Pronouns

STUDENT WRITING

Persuasive Essay

**Security Guards' Training
Beneficial to Students**

by Damian Acosta

high school student, Coral Gables, Florida

They like to roam around campus and monitor your every move. When you're in the midst of a conversation among a herd of friends, they'll weave their way around bodies, break up the weekly gossip session, and tell you to get to class.

Those are just the smallest of tasks for the Coral Gables security guards.

You probably ask yourself: Are these guys a group of ex-convicts, terrorists, or car-jackers? [In fact, they're] not. In the long, bothersome process of becoming a security guard, they must first be approved by Miami-Dade County Public Schools and meet certain requirements before administrators even grant them a job interview.

First, the county researches the applicants' private lives and compiles background information on their pasts. If all goes well, [the applicants] advance to Round Two: the urine sample. The slightest trace of the margarita they may have drunk last month could cost them the job. Now school administrators are able to draft them.

At this point, security guards basically undergo training and attend workshops just like regular teachers do. They learn to deal with situations or emergencies that may occur in school and also how to treat students. Recognizing potential suspects or intruders who may cause a threat to campus life is also part of their training.

Violence and forms of vandalism on campus have noticeably diminished, say the guards. People scrapping, sword-fighting, or even thumb-wrestling have become unheard of.

In addition, car break-ins have declined since last year's covert operation on the notorious "strip." The plan involved a security guard who was parked on the strip in an unmarked car. [As he was] scanning the lot, [he] witnessed a break-in. He notified the police, and a car chase ensued. Unfortunately, the police never captured the suspects, but the incident decreased the frequency of car vandalism.

Instead of us nagging, whining, and complaining about the constant hassles we put up with, we should be more appreciative of their effort.

> The thesis statement of this persuasive essay is contained in the title. The writer begins with a buildup of negative impressions of his school's security guards and then demolishes those impressions with background information, details, evidence, and an example to support his thesis. He ends the essay with a call to action.
>
> In this chapter you'll learn about pronouns. As you reread the essay above, notice how the writer avoids repetition by using pronouns effectively.

Allow time for students to discuss the student writing. Suggest that they identify its strengths and propose possible improvements. Use the model to introduce the concepts in the chapter.

Using Subject Pronouns

Subject Pronouns	
SINGULAR	**PLURAL**
I, you, he, she, it	we, you, they

▶ Use one of these subject pronouns when the pronoun functions as the subject (s) of a sentence or a clause.

    S   S
Mitsuko and **I** are designing a time capsule.

  S
We will present our design to the student council.

▶ Use a subject pronoun when the pronoun functions as the predicate nominative of a sentence or clause.

Remember: A **predicate nominative** (PN) is a noun or pronoun that follows a form of *be* and renames or identifies the subject.

               PN   PN   PN
The committee members are Mitsuko, Howard, and **I**.

               PN   PN
The persons in charge of the project are Kevin and **she**.

P.S. You probably use subject pronouns correctly when the pronoun is alone. Watch out for compound subjects, as in the first example above.

WRITING HINT

If someone asks, "Who's there?" you probably answer, "It's me," not "It's I." But in speeches, in essays, and on grammar tests, be sure to use a subject pronoun when the pronoun comes after a form of *be*: "It is **I**." "It is **we**."

STEP BY STEP

To decide which pronoun to use:

Laura and (me, I) want to borrow a CD.

1. Say the sentence with just the pronoun.

    Me want to borrow a CD. [sounds wrong]

    I want to borrow a CD. [sounds right]

2. Use the pronoun that sounds right in the compound subject.

    Laura and **I** want to borrow a CD.

EXERCISE 1 Choosing the Correct Pronoun

Underline the pronoun in parentheses that correctly completes each sentence.

    EXAMPLE   The persons who thought of a time capsule are Soia and (him, <u>he</u>).

1. Julio and (her, <u>she</u>) wrote to the International Time Capsule Society (ITCS).

2. (Them, <u>They</u>) sent us information about time capsules.

3. (Him and me, <u>He and I</u>) will find a place to bury the capsule.

4. The ones who register our capsule with the ITCS are (us, <u>we</u>).

5. Noam, Helena, and (him, <u>he</u>) are in charge of publicity.

6. Terra and (them, <u>they</u>) are picking objects for the capsule.

7. Our advisors for the project are Mr. Mendez and (<u>she</u>, her).

8. (Us, <u>We</u>) will direct that the capsule be sealed until the year 3500.

9. The student who will write the sealing ceremony is (<u>he</u>, him).

10. Delores and (him, <u>he</u>) are in charge of our reunion in twenty-five years.

EXERCISE 2 Editing a Paragraph

Edit the following paragraph to correct all errors in pronoun usage.

One of the sentences contains no errors, and some sentences have more than one error.

¹Husan, Luisa, and ~~me~~ [I] presented a report about time capsules. ²~~Her~~ [She] and Husan talked about Dr. Thornwell Jacobs, the president of Oglethorpe University in Atlanta. ³The person who built the Crypt of Civilization was he. ⁴On May 28, 1940, ~~him~~ [he] and others sealed the crypt, an underground room the size of a swimming pool, at Oglethorpe University in Atlanta. ⁵The other scientists and ~~him~~ [he] left instructions not to open the crypt until May 28, 8113. ⁶In their report, Luisa and ~~him~~ [he] described some of the objects sealed in the crypt. ⁷Dr. Jacobs and ~~them~~ [they] placed newsreels, records, newspaper articles, a Donald Duck doll, a set of Lincoln logs, and many other objects in the crypt to reveal American life in the 1940s. ⁸Husan and ~~her~~ [she] said that probably ten thousand time capsules have been buried, but most have been lost. ⁹The students who talked about other time capsules were Luisa and ~~me~~ [I]. ¹⁰~~Her~~ [She] and ~~me~~ [I] described the 1947 Notre Dame capsule filled with bacteria, insects, and viruses.

Write What You Think

Get together with a small group of classmates to discuss the tasks involved with creating your own time capsule. Write a paragraph answering the questions below. Include details about who will do which jobs and what you plan to put in the capsule. After revising, edit for the correct use of subject pronouns.

Use the brainstorming techniques in **Composition** Lesson 1.1 to start this project.

1. What objects will you put in the time capsule?
2. Where will you bury the capsule?
3. When will you want it to be opened?

Paragraphs will vary. Give students full credit if they have expressed themselves clearly. They should also have written grammatically complete sentences that begin with a capital letter and end with an appropriate end punctuation mark.

Using Object Pronouns

Object Pronouns	
SINGULAR	**PLURAL**
me, you, him, her, it	us, you, them

▐▶ Use an object pronoun when the pronoun functions as the direct object (**DO**) or indirect object (**IO**) of a sentence or a clause.

       DO   **DO**
Jana told Derek and **me** about her homing pigeons.

       IO   **DO**
She showed **us** several of her favorite pigeons.

▐▶ Use an object pronoun (**OP**) when the pronoun functions as the object of a preposition in a sentence.

                                 OP
One of her pigeons delivered a message to Ana and **me**.

       OP
For Jana and **us**, the pigeons arrive faster than mail.

When an object is compound, use the Step-by-Step approach you learned on page 193. Test each pronoun alone, and say the sentence aloud to yourself. Your ear will tell you which pronoun to use.

EDITING TIP

Be sure to use an object pronoun when the pronoun functions as the object of a preposition. Avoid these common errors:

RIGHT between you and **me**

WRONG between you and I

RIGHT for Carla and **him**

WRONG for Carla and he

STEP BY STEP

To decide whether to use a subject or an object pronoun:

1. Decide what function the pronoun performs in the sentence.

2. If the pronoun is a subject or a predicate nominative, choose the subject pronoun.

3. If the pronoun is a direct object, an indirect object, or the object of a preposition, choose the object pronoun.

EXERCISE 3 Editing Sentences

Edit the following sentences for the use of subject and object pronouns. Cross out a pronoun that is used incorrectly, and write the correct one above it. If a sentence is correct, write *C*. **Hint:** First, check to see what function the pronoun performs in the sentence.

                  she   *us*
EXAMPLE   Zeeshan and ~~her~~ showed him and ~~we~~ the list of birds they've seen.

              Their very long list of birds amazed him and us. *C*

         I   her
1. Brian and ~~me~~ saw Kathy and ~~she~~ at the Audubon Christmas Count.

              her
2. Al gave Issa and ~~she~~ a copy of *Field Guide to Birds*.

                                   me
3. Elaine and he gave an Audubon field card to Jim and ~~I~~.

               her   me
4. Jenny showed ~~she~~ and ~~I~~ three different species of heron.

         him   me
5. She told ~~he~~ and ~~I~~ about the fieldfare, a bird that breeds in Greenland.

6. The fieldfare is an "accidental" sighting here, according to him and her.   C

7. Christy sent Paolo and ~~I~~ ^{me} some sketches of sandpipers.

7. Christy sent Paolo and <u>me</u> some sketches of sandpipers.

8. <u>Her</u> and her aunt drew them and other shorebirds.

[correction: 8. ~~Her~~ She and her aunt drew them and other shorebirds.]

9. I asked Myrza and ~~he~~ about their sightings of penguins.

10. "We saw two species of ~~they~~ and other Antarctic birds," she said.

11. We joined a group of amateur bird-watchers with Roger and ~~he~~.

12. The leader of our group and ~~them~~ count birds in this area every year.

13. The group will count each species of birds ~~them~~ see.

14. This year, we saw more species of birds than ~~them~~ saw.

15. Our bird count will help ~~she~~ and the Audubon Society keep track of migrations from one year to the next.

EXERCISE 4 Choosing the Correct Pronoun

Underline the pronoun in parentheses that correctly completes each sentence.

EXAMPLE   The foul ball was heading right toward Rachel and (I, <u>me</u>).

1. Neither Leah nor (<u>he</u>, him) brought a poncho to the game.

2. The coach gave (they and we, <u>them and us</u>) team T-shirts.

3. Without Brenda and (she, <u>her</u>), we wouldn't have a water polo team.

4. Ms. Juringus coached Ash and (he, <u>him</u>) every day.

5. Just between you and (I, <u>me</u>), Owen is the best discus thrower in the state.

6. Nishan and his brother beat Tom and (she, <u>her</u>) in table tennis.

7. (<u>He and I</u>, him and me) cheered Brandon and (they, <u>them</u>) after every goal.

8. Joey threw the ball toward (he and I, <u>him and me</u>), but (<u>we</u>, us) both missed it.

9. Did you watch Brett and (she, <u>her</u>) in the semifinals?

10. According to Karla and (they, <u>them</u>), Tom's backhand is weak.

11. When the match was over, the coach took (<u>them and us</u>, they and we) back to school.

12. The extra tickets are for Fiona and (I, <u>me</u>).

13. At the seventh inning, (us, <u>we</u>) stretched.

14. The stadium was crowded, so Tony and (<u>he</u>, him) had trouble finding their seats.

15. Bette and (me, <u>I</u>) have plans to go to the play-offs next week.

Who or Whom?

▸ Use the subject pronoun *who* when the pronoun functions as a subject or as a predicate nominative in a sentence or in a clause.

> **Who** was chosen as the Most Valuable Player?
> [*Who* is the subject of the sentence.]
> The player **who** was chosen as the MVP is the Bulls' forward.
> [*Who* is the subject of the adjective clause.]

You can check your choice of pronoun by replacing *who/whom* with *he/him* or *she/her*. If *he* sounds right in the sentence, use the subject pronoun *who*. If *him* sounds right, choose the object pronoun *whom*. You'll need to change a question into a statement to test for the right pronoun.

> (Who, Whom) did you call?
> [Change the question into a statement.]
> You did call (who, whom).
> [Substitute *he, him* for *who, whom*.]
> You did call (he, him).
> [When you try out each pronoun, you will hear that *him* sounds right. Therefore, the sentence requires an object pronoun.]
> **Whom** did you call? [*Whom* is the object pronoun.]

▸ Use the object pronoun *whom* when the pronoun functions as the direct object, indirect object, or object of a preposition in a sentence or in a clause.

> Please give this note to the first person **whom** you see.
> [*Whom* is the direct object of the adjective clause *you see whom*.]

When you are choosing *who* or *whom,* ignore parenthetical expressions (such as *I think* and *I hope)* that interrupt a subordinate clause.

> He is the scientist (who, whom), I think, won the Nobel Peace Prize.
> [*Who* is the subject of the clause *who won the Nobel Peace Prize*.]

P.S. Most people don't use *whom* when they talk. In formal writing and speaking, however, and on grammar tests, use *whom* whenever the pronoun functions as an object.

Subject Form
who

Object Form
whom

STEP BY STEP

When you need to choose between *who* and *whom:*

1. Decide what function the pronoun performs.

2. Use *who* if the pronoun functions as a subject or a predicate nominative.

3. Use *whom* if the pronoun functions as a direct object, an indirect object, or the object of a preposition.

Enriching Your Vocabulary

The Latin noun *artificium* gives us the English noun *artifice,* meaning "a clever skill" or "trickery." A painter uses *artifice* to create the illusion of a three-dimensional scene on a flat canvas. And, as used in Exercise 5, only an expert may be able to tell the difference between an *artificial* diamond and the real thing.

EXERCISE 5 Choosing the Correct Pronoun

Underline the pronoun in parentheses that correctly completes each sentence.

EXAMPLE   Harry Harlow was a psychologist (<u>who</u>, whom) did research on baby monkeys.

1. He and his wife, (who, <u>whom</u>) he worked with, raised monkeys for experiments.
2. Newborn monkeys (<u>who</u>, whom) were alone in cages clung to cloth diapers.
3. The Harlows, (<u>who</u>, whom) studied infant love, created artificial wire "mothers."
4. (<u>Who</u>, Whom) can guess whether the newborns clung to a cloth-covered "mother" or a bare wire one?
5. The Harlows are only two of the scientists (<u>who</u>, whom) have studied animal behavior.
6. Do you know anyone (<u>who</u>, whom) objects to using animals in experiments?
7. The Harlows, (who, <u>whom</u>) psychologists praised for their experiments, applied their findings to human babies.
8. Human newborns, (<u>who</u>, whom) are more helpless than monkeys, need warmth and contact.
9. (Who, <u>Whom</u>) would you consult for advice on raising children?
10. Would you ask a relative (who, <u>whom</u>) you trust or read a book?

EXERCISE 6 Editing a Paragraph

Edit the following paragraph to correct all errors in pronoun usage.

¹Elaine's friend Gwen objects to scientists who use animals as research subjects. ²She and her friends, ~~who~~ whom you may have met, are animal rights activists. ³They have written to government representatives ~~whom~~ who, they believe, should pass laws protecting animals. ⁴They especially oppose researchers ~~whom~~ who, for whatever reason, work with dogs and cats. ⁵They have also demonstrated against research scientists who, they say, treat monkeys cruelly. ⁶Gwen and her friends, many of ~~who~~ whom are vegetarians, oppose killing animals for fur. ⁷Doctors who test medical procedures on animals disagree. ⁸Laboratory animals benefit people who, they say, are desperately ill. ⁹Doctors apply what they learn from animal experiments to save the lives of people who need treatment. ¹⁰~~Who~~ Whom do you agree with on animal rights issues?

Extend this lesson by having motivated students write a letter to their senators explaining their views on using animals for research.

Appositives and Incomplete Constructions

Remember that an **appositive** identifies or explains the noun or pronoun that comes right before it.

▐▶ For a pronoun appositive, use a subject pronoun if the word that the appositive refers to is a subject or a predicate nominative. Use an object pronoun if the word that the appositive refers to is a direct or indirect object or the object of a preposition.

> The strongest singers, Evan and **she,** have solos.
> [The pronoun *she* refers to *singers,* the subject of the sentence.]
> The soloists are the strongest singers, Evan and **she.**
> [The pronoun *she* refers to *singers,* the predicate nominative in this sentence.]
> The director gave the solos to the strongest singers, Evan and **her**.
> [The pronoun *her* refers to *singers,* which now is the object of the preposition *to.*]
> The director gave the strongest singers, Evan and **her,** the solos.
> [The pronoun *her* refers to *singers,* which this time is the indirect object of the sentence.]

▐▶ When the pronoun *we* or *us* is followed by a noun appositive, choose the pronoun form you would use if the pronoun were alone in the sentence.

> **We** girls challenged the boys to a chess match.
> [You would say, "*We* challenged the boys. . . ."]
> The news of the strike shocked **us** baseball fans.
> [You would say, "The news . . . shocked *us.*"]
> Ms. Grunwald gave **us** students another chance.
> [You would say, "Ms. Grunwald gave *us* another chance."]

▐▶ In an incomplete construction, choose the pronoun form you would use if the sentence were completed.

An **incomplete construction** omits some words, which are understood. Usually, an incomplete construction is a comparison. It comes at the end of a sentence and starts with the word *than* or *as.* In the following incomplete constructions, the omitted words appear in brackets.

> Sara is two years older than **he** [is].
> She is not nearly as tall as **I** [am].
> Carlos likes to dance more than **she** [likes to dance].

> **EDITING** TIP
>
> Make sure that an appositive is necessary and that it identifies or explains the noun before it. Don't use a double subject.
>
> My sister ~~she~~ won the prize.

> **WRITING** HINT
>
> Some incomplete constructions have two very different meanings, depending on the pronoun you choose.
>
> Tammy likes Dave more than [she likes] **me**.
> Tammy likes Dave more than **I** [like Dave].

Exercise 7 Choosing the Correct Pronoun

Underline the pronoun in parentheses that correctly completes each sentence.

EXAMPLE   Len, an identical twin, is four minutes older than (he, him).

1. Tuoyo does not write as legibly as (she, her).

2. Aunt Bernice and (him, he) recall a time before television.

3. We petitioned our representatives, Ms. Watts and (he, him).

4. A collie waited with the crossing guards, Lenora and (he, him).

5. The crowd applauded the dancers, Fiona and (she, her).

6. Perry exercises more than either John or (I, me).

7. No one else is as funny as my friends Stacy and (he, him).

8. Awards were given to two students, (he and I, him and me).

9. Nora is a much stronger swimmer than (he, him).

10. Are you as unhappy about moving as (I, me)?

Exercise 8 Editing Sentences

Edit the following sentences for errors with pronouns. Cross out a pronoun that is incorrect, and write the correct pronoun above it. If a sentence is correct, write *C* after it.

EXAMPLE   Hilary has painted more portraits than ~~me~~. *I*

1. Please give ~~we~~ *us* students more information about the contest.

2. The two winners, ~~him~~ *he* and ~~me~~ *I*, will play in the finals.

3. Joey and Theresa have been dating longer than ~~us~~ *we*.

4. The new rules apply to all of us students. c

5. No one else plays the guitar as well as ~~him~~ *he*.

6. The last ones to leave, Theo and ~~me~~ *I*, locked the gate.

7. Our best players, Ryan and ~~him~~ *he*, each scored twenty points.

8. Melissa has always read more books than ~~me~~ *I*.

9. I wrote to my favorite cousins, Leslie and ~~she~~ *her*.

10. The first three rows are reserved for ~~we~~ *us* family members.

Agreement with Antecedent

A pronoun must agree with its **antecedent,** the word that the pronoun refers to.

▸ Use a plural pronoun to refer to two or more antecedents joined by *and.*

> Priya, Lisa, and Frank are celebrating **their** birthdays today.

▸ Use a singular pronoun to refer to two or more singular antecedents joined by *or* or *nor.*

> Either Paul or Danny has left **his** backpack under the table.

▸ Use a singular pronoun when the sentence has a compound subject but refers to only one person.

> My teacher and mentor began **her** career at Princeton University.

▸ Use a singular pronoun when the antecedent is one of the singular indefinite pronouns at right.

> Each of the girls interviewed **her** grandmother.

When a singular indefinite pronouns refers to both males and females, use *his or her.*

> Everyone must turn in **his or her** paper on Friday.
> Some texts allow the use of *their* in this case.

EXERCISE 9 Choosing the Correct Pronoun

Underline the pronoun in parentheses that agrees with its antecedent.

> EXAMPLE   Cara and Jim packed (his or her, their) lunches.

1. One of the girls will read (her, their) poem at the assembly.

2. Neither of the boys brought (his, their) flashlight.

3. Jeff's mother and father congratulated (his, their) son.

4. Either Hannah or Dot rides (her, their) bike to school.

5. Someone has left (his or her, their) keys in the door.

6. Did Alex or Dominic use (his, their) calculator on the test?

7. Each of the girls wore (her, their) new school uniform.

8. Jeannie, Bethany, and she wrote (her, their) résumés.

9. Neither Noel nor Matt has finished (his, their) research yet.

10. Bryan and Annette practiced (his or her, their) speeches.

Singular Indefinite Pronouns

anybody	anyone
each	either
everybody	everyone
neither	nobody
no one	one
somebody	someone

Refer to Lesson 10.2 for more on agreement with such indefinite pronouns as *none* and *any.*

WRITING HINT

Sometimes *his or her* sounds awkward. You can avoid this construction by making the subject plural or by rephrasing the sentence.

Students must turn in **their** papers on Friday.

Papers are due on Friday.

Enriching Your Vocabulary

The English noun *résumé* means "a summary" and comes from the past participle of the French verb *résumer,* which means "to sum up or recapitulate." When you look for a job, you need a written *résumé* of your work experience.

Revising and Editing Worksheet

Improve the following draft by revising for ideas, organization, word choice, and sentence variety. After revising, edit the draft for errors in spelling, capitalization, punctuation, and usage. Write your revised and edited version on a separate piece of paper. Compare your changes with those of a writing partner.

[1]The four youngest Brontë children, whom were destined to become famous, grew up in a gloomy parsonage. [2]It was on the windy moors. [3]The moors were in northern England. [4]Their father was a minister, their house was next to a cemetery and his church.

[5]Branwell was the only son. [6]Him and his three younger sisters, whom were Charlotte, Emily, and Anne, did not go to school. [7]They studied at home, and they entertained themselves by making up stories. [8]About soldiers and an imaginary kingdom. [9]Branwell and them wrote the stories in tiny handwriting on little pieces of paper. [10]Branwell, whom drew well, illustrated the stories.

For a list of revising strategies, look in **Composition** Lesson 1.3.

[11]When all of they grew up, Branwell, who, in the sisters' opinion, was the most talented, drank too much and lost his jobs. [12]Each of the sisters tried their hand at writing. [13]The sisters' first book, a collection of poems, was published in 1846. [14]They used the pen names of three men—Currer, Ellis, and Acton Bell. [15]Because it was hard for women to get her writings published.

[16]Charlotte wrote *Jane Eyre* in the dining room at the parsonage the novel is about a poor young governess, or teacher, whom wins the love of her wealthy employer. [17]Emily wrote only one novel, a passionate love story called *Wuthering Heights*. [18]Anne also published a novel, but her was less successful than them.

[19]Us readers are lucky that the Brontë sisters wrote their novels. [20]Charlotte and them died almost 150 years ago, but her novels are still popular among we readers today.

Students' revisions will vary. See teacher pages for revising and editing suggestions. Encourage students to investigate the Brontë novels and poems.

Chapter Review

EXERCISE A Using Subject and Object Pronouns

Fill in each blank with the correct form of a pronoun that makes sense in the sentence. Make sure that the word you add is a pronoun, not a noun.

¹Next week, Ilan, Merry, and __I__ will present our multimedia report on the Underground Railroad. ²__We__ students narrowed our topic to Harriet Tubman, __who__ was a conductor on the Underground Railroad. ³Ilan has written a script, which the three of __us__ will perform. ⁴__We__ will act out scenes from the life of Tubman, beginning when __she__ was a child. ⁵It was then that an overseer, or supervisor, struck __her__ in the forehead with a two-pound weight. ⁶Because of this injury, a sudden deep sleep sometimes overcame __her__, even when __she__ was leading slaves to freedom. ⁷Tubman escaped from slavery in 1849, but __she__ returned to the South nineteen times in ten years to lead more than three hundred slaves to freedom. ⁸__She__ and Sojourner Truth, __who__ also had been a slave, gave speeches about abolishing slavery. ⁹Merry, __who__ has made a costume, will read from Sojourner Truth's autobiography. ¹⁰Then the three of __us__ will talk about some Internet sites where Ilan and __I__ found information about Tubman.

EXERCISE B Choosing the Correct Pronoun

Underline the pronoun that correctly completes each sentence.

1. A Greek myth tells of Arachne, (<u>who</u>, whom) challenged Athena.
2. Athena, (who, <u>whom</u>) the Greeks worshipped, was the goddess of weaving.
3. Arachne, a mortal, boasted that she was a better weaver than (<u>she</u>, her).
4. The goddess warned Arachne about (she, <u>her</u>) boasting.
5. They held a contest to see (<u>who</u>, whom) could weave the more beautiful cloth.
6. Athena's tapestry showed the gods punishing mortals (<u>who</u>, whom) angered them.
7. Arachne's cloth showed mortals (who, <u>whom</u>) the gods had fallen in love with.

8. Arachne's tapestry was so perfect that jealous Athena hit (she, <u>her</u>).

9. The goddess turned Arachne into a spider, (<u>who</u>, whom) kept on weaving.

10. Scientists named spiders *arachnids* after (<u>her</u>, she).

EXERCISE C Correcting Pronoun Errors

Correct all pronoun errors in the following sentences. If a sentence is correct, write *C*. **Hint:** A sentence may have more than one mistake.

1. Ms. Li coached Justin and ~~she~~ [her] for a state math contest.

2. The sponsors, Caleb and ~~her~~ [she], presented their proposal to ~~we~~ [us] drama club members.

3. Bethany's band plays reggae music better than ~~them~~ [they].

4. Jack has more work experience than either ~~her~~ [she] or ~~me~~ [I].

5. Please tell the judges, Alexsa and me, about your project. **C**

6. Megan and ~~her~~ [she] were telling Jenna and ~~I~~ [me] about that movie.

7. The bus left without the trip leaders, Charlie and me. **C**

8. No one else in our gym class can jump as high as ~~her~~ [she].

9. ~~Us~~ [We] writers for the school paper work more hours than ~~them~~ [they].

10. Everyone ~~who~~ [whom] we students elect serves on the council for a semester.

EXERCISE D Agreement with Antecedents

Fill in each blank with a pronoun that agrees with its antecedent(s).

1. Neither Sheila nor Abby has finished __her__ weekly chores.

2. Uncle Wei and Chen have __their__ own very different opinions.

3. One of the girls lent us __her__ compass for the hike.

4. Everyone in the camera club has __his or her__ own camera.

5. Does anyone in your class have __his or her__ driver's license yet?

6. Either Mike or David needs some help fixing __his__ computer.

7. Oleg, Jessica, and Kyle spend a lot of time in __their__ garden.

8. Anyone in the group can express __his or her__ opinion.

9. Someone left __his or her__ address book in the telephone booth.

10. Alan or Marc left __his__ homework on the bus.

Using Modifiers

STUDENT WRITING

Expository Essay

Driving Home the Point
by Anna Markee
high school student, Tacoma, Washington

The glass shattered as the hammer exploded off the car's windshield. Cheers went up from the crowd. Another blow left a crater in the car's front fender, and onlookers waved their hands to be next.

After months of planning, our celebration of "World No Tobacco Day" was off the ground. Many businesses in town had rejected my request to donate a car for the event, but perseverance paid off. With a little paint and some creativity, our donated vehicle closely resembled a tobacco-branded racecar.

The best thing about this event was the attention it generated from the media and the community. It really helped drive home the message that kids were tired of being targeted by the marketing ploys of big tobacco.

As an active antitobacco advocate, I have long understood the danger of the deceptive advertising techniques used by the tobacco industry. Several years ago, I worked with the Board of Health in my town to pass a "Truth in Tobacco Advertising" resolution to restrict all forms of outdoor advertising. I talked to many local policymakers about the impact this advertising has on kids, especially [about the fact] that kids I knew decided to try a cigarette because they were impressed by slick tobacco ads showing fun, exciting times.

I think it's really important to take a stand against tobacco. That's why I joined SMOOTH (Students Mobilizing Others Out of Tobacco Habits). We've done a lot of great projects and told a lot of kids about the dangers of tobacco. Now, if we could only break the chains of tobacco addiction as easily as we broke the windshield on our donated car.

> The purpose of Anna's essay is to explain the reasons for World No Tobacco Day. The beginning of her essay is an attention grabber. She follows her opening with background information about the event; then she explains her own convictions about the tobacco industry. Her final sentence helps explain the link between smashing a car and smoking.
>
> The adjectives and modifiers Anna uses help her communicate the commitment she has to her cause. In this chapter you'll learn more about how to use modifiers correctly to emphasize your own convictions.

Allow time for students to discuss the student writing. Suggest that they identify its strengths and propose possible improvements. Use the model to introduce the concepts in the chapter.

Degrees of Comparison

Suppose you want to compare the hotness of three mustards—one on a sandwich, one on a hot dog, and one on an egg roll. To express yourself, you'll need the three **degrees of comparison**: **positive**, **comparative**, and **superlative**.

POSITIVE   The mustard on my sandwich is **hot**.

COMPARATIVE   The mustard on this hot dog is even **hotter**.

SUPERLATIVE   The **hottest** mustard I ever tasted was in a Chinese restaurant.

Here are some rules for forming the comparative and superlative degrees.

▐▐▐▶ **One-Syllable Modifiers** Add -er and -est to one-syllable modifiers. Sometimes it is necessary to double the final consonant first.

young, young**er**, young**est**   big, big**ger**, big**gest**
slow, slow**er**, slow**est**   tight, tight**er**, tight**est**

▐▐▐▶ **Two-Syllable Modifiers** Add -er and -est to most two-syllable modifiers.

yellow, yellow**er**, yellow**est**   quiet, quiet**er**, quiet**est**

Sometimes an -er or -est modifier sounds clumsy. In these cases, use *more* and *most* to form the comparative and superlative degrees.

awkward, **more** awkward, **most** awkward

▐▐▐▶ **-ly Adverbs** Use *more* and *most* for adverbs that end in *-ly.*

quickly, **more** quickly, **most** quickly

Watch out for adjectives that end in *-ly* such as *ugly* or *lively.* Add -er and -est to form their comparisons.

▐▐▐▶ **More Than Two Syllables** For modifiers of three syllables or more, use *more* and *most* to form the comparative and superlative degrees.

beautiful, **more** beautiful, **most** beautiful
responsible, **more** responsible, **most** responsible

▐▐▐▶ **Decreasing Degrees** For all modifiers, use *less* and *least* for decreasing degrees of comparison regardless of number of syllables.

sturdy, **less** sturdy, **least** sturdy

▐▐▐▶ **Irregular Modifiers** The modifiers shown at the top right form their degrees of comparison irregularly.

Irregular Degrees of Comparison

good well }	better	best
bad badly ill }	worse	worst
many much }	more	most
little	{ less *or* lesser }	least
far	farther	farthest

Enriching Your Vocabulary

Not every English word has its roots in another language. The origin of the verb *plod,* used in Exercise 1, is unknown. Some experts think the word is an example of onomatopoeia, that is, a word that imitates a sound, such as that of slow, weary footsteps. At the end of a marathon, many exhausted runners *plod* their way to the finish line.

STEP BY STEP

To form the comparative and superlative degree of modifiers:

1. Count the number of syllables.
2. Apply the appropriate rule: one syllable = -er and -est two syllables = -er and -est or *more* and *most* three syllables = *more* and *most* -ly adverbs = *more* and *most*
3. Memorize the irregular degrees of comparison.

Exercise 1 Editing a Paragraph

Cross out any incorrect modifiers and write the correct form in the space above it.

^{1}Fable writers around the world teach us lessons by telling stories. ^{2}The ~~most old~~ *oldest* fables are found in *The Panchatantra* from India. ^{3}Aesop, an ancient Greek, wrote many of our ~~familiarest~~ *most familiar* fables. ^{4}My ~~favoritest~~ *most favorite or favorite* Aesop fable tells of a race between a tortoise and a hare. ^{5}The tortoise moves so much more ~~slow~~ *slowly* than the hare that the hare takes a nap in the middle of the race. ^{6}But the tortoise plods on without stopping and finishes more speedily than the hare. ^{7}"The opinion of the ~~most strong~~ *strongest* is always the ~~most good~~ *best*" is the moral, or lesson, of a fable by Jean de La Fontaine, a seventeenth-century Frenchman. ^{8}A ~~recenter~~ *more recent* fable writer is the American James Thurber. ^{9}One of Thurber's ~~entertainingest~~ *most entertaining* fables is about a princess who must choose a husband. ^{10}She chooses neither the ~~most kind~~ *kindest* prince nor the ~~attractivest~~ *most attractive* but the one who gives her the ~~valuablest~~ *most valuable* gift.

Exercise 2 Forming the Comparative and the Superlative

On a separate piece of paper, write the comparative and superlative degrees for each modifier.

1. comfortable
more comfortable   most comfortable
2. good
better   best
3. softly
more softly   most softly
4. straight
straighter   straightest
5. dangerous
more dangerous   most dangerous

6. tensely
more tensely   most tensely
7. unusual
more unusual   most unusual
8. bad
worse   worst
9. happy
happier   happiest
10. ugly
uglier   ugliest

Exercise 3 Writing an Advertisement

Suppose you are the copywriter for an advertising agency. Make up a name for a new cereal, car, soap, toothpaste, soda, or movie. On a separate piece of paper, write an advertisement to persuade readers that this new product is better than any other of its kind. Use at least five comparative and superlative forms in your ad. Students' ads will vary. Encourage creativity. You might allow time to have students videotape their advertisements and then present them to the class.

Using the Degrees of Comparison

▮▶ Use the comparative degree to compare two things. Use the superlative degree to compare three or more things.

COMPARATIVE   Ray is three days **older** than Allyson.

SUPERLATIVE   Ray is the **oldest** of four brothers.

▮▶ **Avoid Double Comparisons** Use either *more* (or *most*) or *-er* (or *-est*), but never use the word *more* (or *most*) and the suffix together.

INCORRECT   We tried to move more closer to see more better.

CORRECT   We tried to move **closer** to see **better**.

INCORRECT   Jed is the more younger of the two brothers.

CORRECT   Jed is the **younger** of the two brothers.

▮▶ **Avoid Illogical Comparisons** Use the word *other* or *else* to compare something with others in its group.

ILLOGICAL   Tony plays chess better than anyone in his family. [Tony is a member of his family. He cannot play chess better than himself.]

LOGICAL   Tony plays chess better than anyone **else** in his family.

ILLOGICAL   Chicago is larger than any city in Illinois.

LOGICAL   Chicago is larger than any **other** city in Illinois.

▮▶ **Avoid Unclear Comparisons** Add whatever words are necessary to make a comparison clear.

UNCLEAR   Jenny is more interested in sports than Duane.

CLEAR   Jenny is more interested in sports than Duane is.

or Jenny is more interested in sports than she is in Duane.

> **WRITING HINT**
>
> In conversation, you may hear someone use the superlative form when only two things are being compared:
>
> Of the two restaurants, the one by the river is the **best**.
>
> When you write standard English, however, use the comparative:
>
> Of the two restaurants, the one by the river is **better**.

EXERCISE 4 Editing Sentences

Edit these sentences for the correct use of modifiers. If you find an error, rewrite the sentence correctly on a separate piece of paper. If a sentence is correct, write *C*. **Hint:** Some sentences have more than one error.

EXAMPLE   Teenagers have more accidents than any group of drivers.
Teenagers have more accidents than any other group of drivers.

1. The most ~~likeliest~~ likely time for teenage accidents is after 11 P.M.

2. For drivers under twenty-five, car insurance is more ~~expensiver~~ expensive than for ~~more~~ older drivers.

3. Some teenagers say that insurance costs even more than car repairs. C

4. Jason, my ~~bestest~~ ^{best} friend, is the ~~older~~ ^{oldest} of three children.

5. At sixteen, he is a safer driver than anyone _∧ in his family.
   ^{else}

6. Jason likes driving more than his brother _∧.
   ^{does}

7. Recently, some states have made their rules more difficult for their ~~most~~ youngest drivers.

8. My friend Stephanie, who is fifteen, is more ~~unhappier~~ ^{unhappy} than Jason about the state rules.

9. Stephanie, the ~~safer~~ ^{safest} driver I know, must be at swim practice by 4:30 A.M.

10. She feels ~~worser~~ ^{worse} than her mother, who gets up at 4 A.M. to drive her.

CONNECTING *Writing & Grammar*

Write What You Think

Write what you think about these two laws, and give reasons to support your opinions.

Additional tips for writing persuasively are in **Composition** Lesson 2.4.

• No one under seventeen can get a learner's permit for a driver's license. There are no exceptions.

• Drivers under eighteen cannot drive from 11 P.M. until 6 A.M. unless accompanied by a person over twenty-one years of age.

When you finish revising, edit each sentence to make sure you've used modifiers correctly. Answers will vary. Give students full credit if they have stated an opinion and attempted to support their opinion.

Exercise 5 Writing a Paragraph

Exercise 5: Students should have written gramatically complete sentences that begin with a capital letter and end with an appropriate end punctuation mark.

Write a paragraph in which you compare two or more objects, people, animals, or places. Here are some possible topics: Students' paragraphs will vary.

| two dogs or cats | three TV shows | three cars |
| two buildings | three movies | three friends |

Include at least four comparative or superlative forms in your paragraph, and underline them.

Double Negatives

English has many words that express a negative meaning.

no	not (-n't)	none	nothing	never
no one	nobody	scarcely	hardly	

▐▐▐➡ Avoid using two negative words together. Only one negative word is necessary to express a negative idea. Count the contraction *-n't* (for *not*) as a negative word.

INCORRECT	I couldn't never have finished without your help.
CORRECT	I could never have finished without your help.
CORRECT	I couldn't have finished without your help.

INCORRECT	Didn't nobody volunteer to do nothing?
CORRECT	Didn't anybody volunteer to do anything?
CORRECT	Did nobody volunteer to do anything?

INCORRECT	I haven't got no time for nothing but writing.
CORRECT	I have no time for anything but writing.
CORRECT	I haven't got time for anything but writing.
CORRECT	I have time for nothing but writing.

Note that in correcting a double negative you may need to change some words.

CHANGE	TO
nobody	anybody
never	ever
no one	anyone
nothing	anything
none	any

Note also that a double negative can usually be corrected in more than one way. Choose the way that sounds best to you.

EDITING TIP

In colloquial speech, some people say *ain't* as a contraction for *am not*, *is not*, and *are not*. In formal writing, *ain't* is widely considered inappropriate.

EXERCISE 6 Editing Misquoted Sayings

You don't have to be familiar with the original sayings to fix all of the double negatives in these misquoted sayings. Eliminate or change words as necessary. Corrected sentences will vary. Samples given.

EXAMPLE Little Bo-Peep has lost her sheep, / And cannot ~~scarcely~~ tell where to find them. . . — Nursery rhyme

1. Don't ~~never~~ sell America short. —American saying, 1920s
2. There ~~ain't never~~ no such animal. —Cartoon caption, 1907, of a farmer looking at a circus camel

   is

3. Don't ~~never~~ count ~~none of~~ your chickens before they're hatched.
   —Moral from an Aesop fable

4. The cunning seldom gain their ends; / The wise ^{are}~~aren't~~ never without friends.
   —Moral from *The Fox and the Hen*

5. Jack Sprat ^{could}~~couldn't never~~ eat no fat, / His wife ^{could}~~couldn't hardly~~ eat no lean. . . —Nursery rhyme

6. Indeed your dancing days are done / Oh, Johnny, I ~~didn't never~~ hardly knew ye. —Irish folk song

7. Old soldiers ~~don't~~ never die; / They only fade away! —British World War I song

8. Fifty million Frenchmen can't ~~hardly~~ be wrong. —American saying during World War I

9. . . . All the king's horses / And all the king's men / Couldn't ~~never~~ put Humpty Dumpty back together again. —Nursery rhyme

10. A rolling stone ~~hardly~~ gathers no moss. —Folk saying

EXERCISE 7 Editing a Paragraph

Correct all errors involving negatives in the paragraph below. Read the paragraph aloud to help you find errors.

[1]The exaggerated heros of tall tales ^{are}~~ain't~~ nothing like ordinary human beings. [2]For example, nobody ^{could}~~couldn't~~ really be as strong or as tall as Paul Bunyan. [3]Paul, the loggers' hero, didn't go ^{anywhere}~~nowhere~~ without his giant blue ox, Babe. [4]He ^{thought}~~didn't think~~ nothing of cutting down twenty-three trees with a single swing of his ax. [5]Pecos Bill, the cowboys' hero, didn't ~~scarcely~~ mind being raised by coyotes, for he learned to speak the languages of all the animals. [6]It was Pecos Bill, the cowboys say, who ^{had}~~didn't have~~ no problem lassoing a cyclone. [7]He rode the bucking cyclone to Texas, which hadn't ~~hardly~~ gotten any rain for ages. [8]People say there ^{would}~~wouldn't~~ have been no Grand Canyon without Pecos Bill, for the cyclone's rain washed out the canyon. [9]John Henry ^{was}~~wasn't~~ no ordinary steel driver, ^{either}~~neither~~. [10]He raced against a steam drill machine to see who could crush more rock. [11]He ^{had}~~hadn't~~ scarcely won the race when he keeled right over and died. Corrected paragraphs will vary but should eliminate double negatives. Accept all correct changes. Sample answers are given.

Misplaced and Dangling Modifiers

▶ A **misplaced modifier** is a word, phrase, or clause that's in the wrong place. It modifies a different word than the one it's meant to modify.

Correct a misplaced modifier by moving it as close as possible to the word it is meant to modify.

| MISPLACED | One morning I shot an elephant in my pyjamas. |
| CORRECT | In my pyjamas one morning, I shot an elephant. |

| MISPLACED | He wrote about the Loch Ness monster in his bedroom. |
| CORRECT | In his bedroom, he wrote about the Loch Ness monster. |

▶ A **dangling modifier** is a word, phrase, or clause that doesn't logically modify any word in the sentence.

Correct a dangling modifier by rewording the sentence. Add a word or words that the phrase or clause can modify.

DANGLING	Upon turning ten, my family moved to Florida.
CORRECT	When I was ten, my family moved to Florida.
DANGLING	Hot and thirsty, the lemonade was refreshing.
CORRECT	Because I was hot and thirsty, the lemonade was refreshing.

TEST-TAKING TIP

You may be asked to identify or correct a misplaced modifier in a standardized-test item. If you are unsure whether a part of a sentence is misplaced, ask yourself, "Does it modify the noun nearest to it?" See item 3 on page 294. For an example of an item with a dangling modifier, see item 17 on page 298.

EXERCISE 8 EDITING SENTENCES

On a separate piece of paper, rewrite each sentence to correct all dangling and misplaced modifiers. If a sentence is correct, write C.

EXAMPLE   Walking toward the subway, the restaurant was closed.
Walking toward the subway, I saw that the restaurant was closed.
See Answer Key at www.grammarforwriting.com.

1. We could see the mountains in the distance driving toward Colorado.

2. Scrambling wildly up the drapes, Jim tried to stop the kitten.

3. To arrive at the airport in plenty of time, the alarm was set for 6 A.M.

4. Before leaving for the movies, pictures of the wedding were shown.

5. While eating dinner, the power went off.

6. Surrounding the moon, Shelley could see a faint light during the eclipse.

7. A tern plunged into the water and came up with a fish flying just above the canal.

8. Forgetting the combination to her locker, the dream kept recurring.

Enriching Your Vocabulary

Recur comes from *recurrere*, a Latin verb that means "to return or run back." The conflict between love and duty is a theme that *recurs* in many plays and novels.

9. At the far reaches of the solar system, Reiko read about a new star.

10. Although well prepared, the algebra test was difficult.

11. The little girl held a garter snake who was wearing jeans and a red-striped T-shirt.

12. To change a flat tire, a jack is in the trunk.

13. Hoping for the best, the application was mailed.

14. Annoyed by the constant interruptions, the phone was turned off.

15. Jacques is the tall forward sitting on the bench wearing the number 27.

EXERCISE 9 Editing an Anecdote

Work with a partner to correct misplaced and dangling modifiers in this anecdote. Compare your changes with those made by other teams. Some sentences may be correct. See teacher pages for assessment rubrics. Answers will vary.

Look for additional editing strategies in **Composition** Lesson 1.3.

[1]Walking into the crowded room, the faces were unfamiliar. [2]She walked onto the terrace and stood awhile, next to a grapevine breathing in the fresh air. [3]Standing near the edge, the Brooklyn Bridge glowed in the moonlight. [4]Traffic swirled in the streets looking down from the twentieth floor. [5]At last, someone opened the door whom she had gone to school with. [6]Glad to see a familiar face, the terrace was abandoned.

[7]"It's you!" she shouted above the noise, extending her hand, made by the crowd of laughing people.

[8]"It is," the young man agreed, "but we've never met before," wearing a black T-shirt and jeans. [9]Grasping her hand, his smile was warm.

[10]She laughed and murmured, "I'm glad to meet you now," blushing and embarrassed.

EXERCISE 10 Creating Your Own Exercise

Dangling and misplaced modifiers can be funny. Work with a partner or small group to make up at least five sentences or a paragraph with dangling and misplaced modifiers. Then exchange sentences with another team or group, and correct each other's sentences. Students' sentences will vary.

Revising and Editing Worksheet 1

Improve the following draft by revising for ideas, organization, word choice, and sentence variety. After revising, edit the draft for errors in spelling, capitalization, punctuation, and usage. Write your revised and edited version on a separate piece of paper. Compare your changes with those of a writing partner.

See teacher pages for assessment rubrics.

[1]The first thing you should know about butterflies and moths is that they're insects. [2]Like all insects, they haven't got no backbone. [3]They have six legs and two antennae, their bodies are in three sections.

[4]So these are the ways butterflies and moths are alike. [5]They belong to the group of related insects called Lepidoptera. [6]They have an unusualer life cycle than any insect. [7]Because they change shapes—from a caterpillar into a chrysalis into an adult. [8]Moths and butterflies have two pairs of wings. [9]That are covered with delicate, flat scales. [10]The most small wingspan is one-eighth inch and the larger, the Atlas moth, is more than ten inches.

[11]Next, I'm going to tell you how butterflies and moths are different. [12]Butterflies' wings have more brighter colors than moths' wings. [13]Some of the most beautifulest butterflies are the monarchs, swallowtails, and peacocks. [14]Among the most strangest butterflies are the clear-winged butterflies, which have less fewer scales on there wings than any butterfly. [15]At the end of their antennae, butterflies fly during the day and have little knobs. [16]Holding them vertically over their heads at rest, butterflies close their wings.

[17]Most moths aren't hardly as colorful as butterflies. [18]Moths' wings are more dull in color. [19]Although a few are beautifuler than some butterflies. [20]When resting on leaves and bark, their dull gray and brown wings are probably for camouflage. [21]Moths have all different kinds of antennae, but none have no knobs at the end. [22]Moths hold their wings open, flat against the surface at rest.

[23]I can't tell you nothing more about butterflies and moths.

Revising and Editing Worksheet 2

Improve the following draft by revising for ideas, organization, word choice, and sentence variety. After revising, edit the draft for errors in spelling, capitalization, punctuation, and usage. Write your revised and edited version on a separate piece of paper. Compare your changes with those of a writing partner.

See teacher pages for assessment rubrics.

[1]This report is on the Battle of Gettysburg. [2]The most baddest battle in the Civil War. [3]Having decided to invade the North, the Army of Northern Virginia was led by General Robert E. Lee. [4]General George Meade led the Union troops, who had been in charge of the northern army for only five days.

[5]At dawn on July 1, 1863, a small Confederate troop in search of boots for there soldiers ran into a more large Union cavalry troop. [6]When they fought outside of Gettysburg, Pennsylvania, there wasn't no turning back. [7]Gettysburg was one of the most quietest towns, it isn't hardly more than eight miles north of the Maryland border.

[8]Both sides sent for reinforcements. [9]On that first day, the more strong Southern forces pushed back the Northern troops. [10]Union forces digged in at Cemetery Hill and Culp's Hill, south of Gettysburg. [11]The Confederates west of them at Seminary Ridge.

[12]On the second day of battle, results were lesser clear. [13]Ordered to attack Union troops, at three o'clock on the afternoon of the third day, a disastrous charge was led by Confederate General George Pickett. [14]The three-day battle at Gettysburg proved to be the most bloodiest of the war. [15]Twenty-three thousand soldiers from the North were killed, wounded, or missing. [16]The South lost twenty-eight thousand. [17]On July 4, Lee retreated homeward. [18]Prevented from crossing the Potomac, the flooded river held Lee's troops in the North. [19]Lincoln commanded General Meade to attack Lee's army. [20]General Meade didn't never pursue them.

Chapter Review

EXERCISE A Using the Degrees of Comparison

Edit the following sentences for correct use of modifiers. If you find an error, cross out the word or phrase, and rewrite it correctly on a separate piece of paper. If a sentence is correct, write *C* after the sentence. **Hint:** Some sentences have more than one error.

1. St. Augustine, Florida, is the ~~most old~~ city in the United States. [oldest]

2. Death Valley in the Mojave Desert is the ~~most~~ lowest point in North America.

3. Utah's Great Salt Lake is North America's largest saltwater lake. C

4. Which of these Great Lakes is the ~~largest~~ —Lake Erie or Lake Michigan? [larger]

5. This is one of the most ~~beautifulest~~ parts of the Appalachian Trail. [beautiful]

6. The Mississippi River, which flows more than two thousand miles, is much ~~more~~ longer than the Missouri River.

7. Bituminous coal is mined ~~most~~ frequently in West Virginia than in any other state. [more] [other]

8. Of the six New England states, Rhode Island is the ~~smaller~~. [smallest]

9. American whaling ships sailed ~~oftenest~~ from Nantucket and New Bedford. [most often]

10. Philip likes whale watching more than anyone else in his family. [else]

EXERCISE B Correcting Misplaced and Dangling Modifiers

On a separate piece of paper, rewrite each sentence to correct all misplaced and dangling modifiers. If a sentence is correct, write *C*.

See Answer Key at www.grammarforwriting.com.

1. Helen found 106 Web sites on the extinction of dinosaurs, looking for information for her research paper.

2. She printed articles from museums and scientific organizations trying to evaluate the information.

3. Reading a natural history museum's home page, new information was discovered.

4. After exploring the Internet for several days, a stack of note cards was piled high on her desk.

5. Before writing her first draft, piles of note cards were sorted.

6. Taken from Internet sources, Helen tried to evaluate the accuracy of the information.

7. She discarded articles printed from possibly unreliable Web sites.

8. Proofreading for errors, the punctuation of her Works Cited list was checked.

9. Listening to the sound of the sentences, her first draft was read aloud.

10. Congratulating herself, her paper was finished by the due date.

EXERCISE C Editing Paragraphs

Edit the following paragraphs to correct all errors in the use of modifiers.
Hint: Some sentences have more than one error. Some have no errors.

[1]Many cultures consider gold the ~~valuablest~~ [most valuable] of all metals. [2]Gold has been found on every continent, on the ~~most high~~ [highest] mountains, in deserts, and even in the frozen Arctic ground. [3]Spanish explorers [exploring the New World] looted the ~~beautifulest~~ [most beautiful] Aztec gold decorative objects ~~exploring the New World~~. [4]Searching for gold to send home, [European explorers shipped] more than four hundred tons of gold ~~were shipped~~ from the New World ~~by European explorers~~. [5]~~Visiting some of the most famousest museums in the world,~~ [You can see] exhibits of pre-Columbian gold decorative objects [in some of the most famous museums in the world.] ~~can be seen~~.

[6]In some cultures, such as ancient Egypt, gold wasn't ~~hardly~~ the most valuable of metals. [7]In ancient Egypt, silver was called white gold because it was ~~more~~ scarcer than gold. [8]In Babylonia and Sumeria, silver was also the ~~desirablest~~ [most desirable] of all the metals.

[9]~~Considered the most precious of metals, the~~ [The] search for gold [, considered the most precious of metals,] has continued. [10]~~Discovering~~ [With the discovery of] nuggets of gold at Sutter's Mill in 1848, the California gold rush brought more than forty thousand gold prospectors to California by land and sea. [11]A similar gold rush occurred three years later in Australia, which, by the way, is the ~~most small~~ [smallest] of Earth's continents. [12]The world's most ~~spectacularest~~ [spectacular] source of gold, however, is in southern Africa. [13]Huge sheets of gold ore [called reefs] have been mined there~~, called reefs~~. [14]Among the other ~~richer~~ [richest] gold-producing nations are Canada and the United States. [15]In the United States, the states where the ~~muchest~~ [most] gold is mined are South Dakota and Nevada.

Cumulative Review

EXERCISE A Using Verbs Correctly

On a separate piece of paper, correct all of the errors in verb usage in the following sentences. Look for incorrect verbs and verb forms, unnecessary shifts in verb tense, and unnecessary use of the passive voice. See Answer Key at www.grammarforwriting.com.

1. A new school record was set by Carey when the race was swum by her in fifty-eight seconds.

2. After Flora will have dived a dozen times, she becomes dizzy.

3. Flora drunk a glass of water and laid down beside the pool.

4. A towel was brung by the coach, who tells her to set awhile and rest.

5. All of the girls on the swimming team knowed that drinking plenty of water be important; the coach has speaked about it many times.

6. The coach has teached them about the dangers of dehydration.

7. Haven't you did some research and wrote a paper on heat exhaustion?

8. Once I weared heavy clothes and done hours of gardening on a very hot, dry day.

9. When I raised from my knees, I begun to feel weak, and then I faints.

10. Fluids should be gave to people with heat exhaustion, and they should lay flat or with their heads down.

EXERCISE B Subject-Verb Agreement

Underline the verb in parentheses that agrees with the subject.

1. One of the banjo's strings (is, are) broken.

2. Everyone (sings, sing) loudly, but many (sings, sing) off key.

3. None of the musical instruments (belongs, belong) to the school.

4. Neither the drummers nor the pianist (plays, play) in this piece.

5. Both Alison and Mercedes (has, have) practiced the solo part.

6. Few of the choir members (plays, play) a musical instrument.

7. The band (rehearses, rehearse) during lunch every Friday.

8. Every band member and choir member (is, are) onstage during the concert.

9. John Philip Sousa's "The Stars and Stripes Forever" (is, are) Mr. Marks's favorite march.

10. The audience (stands, stand) and (sings, sing) "The Star-Spangled Banner."

EXERCISE C Using Pronouns Correctly

Underline the pronoun in parentheses that correctly completes each sentence.

1. Maya and (I, me) are tutoring first-graders in an after-school program.
2. The coach gave Jorge and (he, him) the tennis team's schedule.
3. Just between you and (I, me), Diana really likes Vinnie.
4. Aunt Marina in Santa Fe made these mugs for Mia and (she, her).
5. Bernie is the cartoonist (who, whom) I told you about.
6. Do you know (who, whom) has a color printer?
7. Either Jeff or Scott has a radio in (his, their) desk.
8. The editorial is directed to (we, us) ninth-graders.
9. (Us, We) computer club members are writing a program for a game.
10. The essay contest winners, Lauren and (she, her), will read their essays on the school radio.

EXERCISE D Using Modifiers Correctly

Proofread the following sentences to correct all errors in the use of modifiers. **Hint:** Some sentences have more than one error. See Answer Key at www.grammarforwriting.com.

1. The expensivest car isn't always the bestest one to buy.
2. Searching for a good used car, bargains can be found.
3. The most desirablest used car has had a single owner who has taken good care of it.
4. Some cars are driven less than ten thousand miles a year.
5. Suppose you are trying to decide which of two used cars is best.
6. Experienced in fixing used cars, ask a mechanic to check both cars.
7. A skilled mechanic can hear and feel problems gooder than you.
8. Car repair and maintenance, importanter than any class, should be a required course.
9. Being sold by a friend, Lauren is buying a 1986 blue convertible.
10. The convertible is more clean and more shiny than any car she looked at, but it needs a new transmission, brakes, and four tires.

Punctuation: End Marks and Commas

STUDENT WRITING
Expository Essay

Bottled Water: Reasons Vary for Purchasing Thirst Quencher
by Leslie Harrell
high school student, Grosse Pointe Farms, Michigan

It may be free from the faucet, but slap on a label and people will pay for it.

Upon first look, bottled and tap water appear to be the same. They are both clear, refreshing, and wet. Their chemical compositions are both mainly hydrogen and oxygen. But many South students feel that one has the edge in taste that is worth the price.

"I really like bottled water," said Tracy Gehlert. "It tastes better and you can carry it around easily to class."

Bottled water, though just recently seeming to gain popularity, has been around for a long time. The first bottles were sold in 1830 in earthenware jugs, according to the home page [of a major bottled water company. Another company] has been in business for two hundred years. . . .

Bottled water is regulated by the Food and Drug Administration and has to meet all applicable federal and state standards, The Bottled Water home page reports. [One of the major water producers claims that its product] is completely natural and goes through its own filtration process underground. . . . It comes complete with minerals that filter into the water on its fifteen year journey from the French Alps.

"I like the taste of bottled water better than [that of] tap water," said Patrick Spain. "It's fresher and it's colder than water out of the tap."

Some people just don't buy all the hype about bottled water.

"I don't drink bottled water," said Ben Weaver. "There's enough of it in the faucet."

Tap-water drinkers may be happy to know that bottled water is not really any safer than tap water. Health standards for bottled water are no stricter than health standards for public water from the tap, The Bottled Water home page reports. In fact, until 1995, bottled water was not even subject to the same standards as tap water.

Facts or no facts, millions of people keep buying bottled water. The average consumer of bottled water has changed from highly educated, upscale, white-collar North Americans to all social, economic, and age groups, The Bottled Water home page reports. [One major producer] bottles and ships five to six million bottles of natural spring water around the world each day. . . .

Water is essential to the human body. Whether you drink bottled or tap water, get with the flow and join the millions of Americans [who] are switching from soft drinks to water.

> Leslie's article begins with an attention grabber that draws the reader in. She includes facts, statistics, and quotations from people she has interviewed. Her article ends with a call to action.
>
> As you reread the essay above, think about how much more difficult it would be to understand Leslie's message without punctuation! Think about how you use punctuation in the writing you do throughout this chapter.

Allow time for students to discuss the student writing. Suggest that they identify its strengths and propose possible improvements. Use the model to introduce the concepts in the chapter.

End Marks and Abbreviations

▐▐▐➡ Use a **period** at the end of a statement (declarative sentence) and at the end of a command (imperative sentence).

DECLARATIVE	No one knows who the woman in the *Mona Lisa* is.
IMPERATIVE	Please find out more about Leonardo da Vinci.

▐▐▐➡ Use a **question mark** at the end of a direct question (interrogative sentence). An indirect question ends with a period.

DIRECT	Do you know who painted the *Mona Lisa*?
DIRECT	Abby asked me, "Do you know who painted the *Mona Lisa*?"
INDIRECT	Abby just asked me who painted the *Mona Lisa*.

▐▐▐➡ Use an **exclamation point** at the end of an exclamation (exclamatory sentence).

Stop that thief! He's trying to steal the *Mona Lisa*!

▐▐▐➡ Use a period after many abbreviations.

In general, when you write a paper or report for school or work, avoid using abbreviations. Instead, spell out the word. There are some common exceptions to this rule shown in the following chart.

Periods in Abbreviations	
CATEGORY	**EXAMPLE**
Initials and Titles	Mr. A. N. O'Hara, Jr. Phyllis A. Washington, Ph.D.
Times	A.M. P.M. B.C. B.C.E. A.D.
Others	Inc. Co. Assn. etc. vs.

▐▐▐➡ Some abbreviations should not have a period.

An **acronym** is a word formed from the first letter(s) of several words, such as *NATO* (formed from *North Atlantic Treaty Organization*). Acronyms do not take periods.

The modern tendency is to omit the period following common abbreviations, such as *ft* (*foot* or *feet*) and *lb* (*pound*). Some other common abbreviations that don't take periods include *MPH (miles per hour), AM* and *FM* radio, *TV*, *FBI*, *IRS*, and postal abbreviations for states (FL, OH, TX).

P.S. If you're in doubt about whether to use a period with an abbreviation, check a college or unabridged dictionary, but be aware that even dictionaries differ in how they punctuate some abbreviations, including the abbreviations for United States (*US* or *U.S.*) and United Nations (*UN* or *U.N.*).

Beware of sentence fragments. Strategies for correcting sentence fragments appear in Lessons 6.3 and 13.6.

EDITING TIP

When an abbreviation comes at the end of a sentence, use only one period.

The movie doesn't start until 10 P.M.

Don't omit a comma, a question mark, or an exclamation point following an abbreviation.

Oh, no! The test begins at 7:30 A.M.!
How can we know what happened in 800 B.C.?

Enriching Your Vocabulary

The verb *abridge* comes from the French *abregier*, which in turn comes from the Latin *abbreviare*, "to shorten." It is usually necessary to *abridge* the text of a novel for recording on audiotape. But something that is *unabridged* has not been condensed. An *unabridged* dictionary is too big to carry in your backpack.

EXERCISE 1 Proofreading a Paragraph

Proofread the following paragraph to add end punctuation marks and periods for abbreviations as needed. If you're not sure whether an abbreviation takes a period, check a dictionary.

¹Have you ever visited Washington, DC *DC or D.C.* ? ²Last night, I watched a TV program about Washington. ³Did you see it, too? ⁴If it's on again, be sure to see it. ⁵What an interesting city Washington is! ⁶Dr. A. Rogers, the narrator, took us viewers on a tour of the White House. ⁷Did you know that the White House wasn't painted white until 1817? ⁸If I were visiting Washington, I'd like to tour the US *US or U.S.* Capitol at the foot of Pennsylvania Avenue. ⁹I'd also visit the Smithsonian's two underground museums: the Arthur M. Sackler Gallery of Asian Art and the National Museum of African Art. ¹⁰Last year, my sister visited the Holocaust Museum, but she didn't have time to see the National Air and Space Museum because her plane left at 1:30 P.M.

EXERCISE 2 Writing Sentences

Work with a partner or small group to write sentences based on the information in the graph below. Write at least one exclamatory sentence and two interrogative sentences. You don't have to use all of the information.

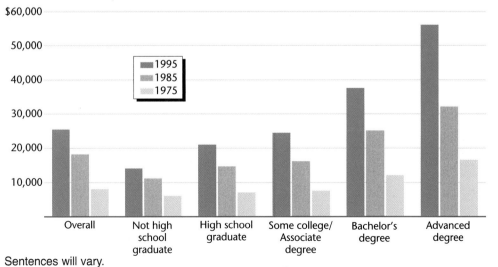

Average Annual Income of Workers 18 Years and Over by Educational Attainment (1975-1995)

Sentences will vary.

Source: Census Bureau, Current Population Survey (1995)

Commas in a Series

Commas signal a slight pause but not a complete stop. They are tricky punctuation marks that involve a lot of rules. In the next few lessons, you'll review the most important rules for using commas.

▌▌▌➡ Use commas to separate items in a series.

> Some stylebooks do not require the last comma before the conjuctions.

A **series** contains three or more similar items in a row.

> A human eye has a cornea, an iris, a lens, and a retina.
> The girls like playing golf, reading books, and riding horses.

▌▌▌➡ Use a comma to separate two or more adjectives that precede and modify the same noun.

> The human eye is a **complex, efficient** organ.

However, don't use a comma when the last adjective in a series is really part of a compound noun. You can tell if one of the adjectives belongs to the noun if you can reverse the position of the adjectives.

> Whose **red eyeglass** case is this? [*Eyeglass case* is a compound noun.]

> **Mechanics**
> See also Lesson 14.2, which explains when to use semicolons rather than commas for a series.

EDITING TiP

When a coordinating conjunction (such as *and* or *but*) connects a compound verb in a sentence, *don't* add commas. However, commas are needed between independent clauses.

Jean dropped a contact lens *and* searched for ten minutes *but* couldn't find it.

Jen dropped a lens, and she couldn't find it anywhere.

EXERCISE 3 Proofreading Sentences

The comma key is broken on her typewriter, so Abby wasn't able to put commas where she needs them. Insert all necessary commas. If a sentence is correct, write *C*. **Hint:** Not every sentence needs a comma.

1. Color blindness is an inability to distinguish one or more colors. C

2. Some birds, butterflies, and bees are to some extent color-blind.

3. Some humans cannot distinguish the colors red, blue, and green.

4. Color blindness affects twenty times more men than women. C

5. Someone with monochromatism sees only black, white, and gray.

6. Picking out socks, coordinating outfits, and choosing new clothes are problems.

STEP BY STEP

To decide whether to put a comma between two adjectives before a noun:

1. Put *and* between them. If *and* makes sense, use a comma.

   [*and*]
   I felt a sharp, stabbing pain in one eye. [use a comma]

2. If *and* doesn't make sense, don't use a comma.

   ~~*and*~~
   One tiny eyelash hurt my eye. [no comma]

7. A cab driver, train engineer, or pilot must be able to distinguish colors in traffic signals.

8. Color blindness would be a serious, annoying problem for an artist or fabric designer.

9. The vision of color-blind people is usually not limited in any other way. C

10. The test for color blindness involves detecting a figure in a field of dots, squares, and other shapes.

EXERCISE 4 Proofreading Sentences

Insert all missing punctuation marks, including end marks.

1. A tall, red-haired young woman waited outside the stage door.

2. She huddled under an enormous umbrella printed with cats, dogs, and fish.

3. Three young actors, two dancers, and several musicians left the theater.

4. They glanced at her, turned away, and continued their conversations.

5. More actors, stagehands, and musicians emerged and hurried away.

6. She waited, she paced, and she looked at her watch.

7. A strong, wet, icy wind blew her umbrella inside out.

8. The young woman's program fell from her hand and landed in a puddle.

9. Finally, the show's star emerged along with her personal secretary, her dresser, and her understudy.

10. The starstruck young woman rushed forward with her wet program and pen and begged for an autograph.

EXERCISE 5 Proofreading a Paper

Take a paper you have written recently or one you wrote last year, and proofread it carefully. Focus particularly on end marks and commas. Check to see whether you have used these punctuation marks correctly. If you decide to make any punctuation changes, be ready to explain why you made each change.
Students should share their papers with partners.

Compound Sentences and Phrases

▐▐▐▶ Use a comma before a coordinating conjunction (*and, but, or, nor, for, so,* and *yet*) that joins two independent clauses.

> After dinner, Dave washed the pile of dishes **,** and Sara dried them and put them away.

▐▐▐▶ Use a comma after an introductory participle or participial phrase.
> **Terrified,** the kitten hid under the bed.
> **Terrified by the thunder,** the kitten hid under the bed.

▐▐▐▶ Use a comma after an introductory prepositional phrase or a series of introductory prepositional phrases.
> **In short,** no one was prepared.
> **At 2 A.M. on February 3,** a series of tornadoes struck town.

P.S. A comma after a short prepositional phrase, as in the first example above, may not be necessary, but it's never wrong. If you get in the habit of adding a comma after all introductory prepositional phrases, you'll be sure your meaning is clear.

When the subject follows the verb, as in the following sentence, do *not* use a comma after the introductory prepositional phrases.

> V   S
> Behind the mirror in the front hall **is** a treasure **map**.

▐▐▐▶ Use a comma after an introductory adverb clause.
> **If you look at the moon with binoculars,** you'll see craters.

For more on commas after introductory words, see Lesson 13.5.

EDITING TIP

Don't confuse a compound sentence with a sentence that has a compound subject or a compound verb. You don't need a comma between parts of a compound subject or compound verb.

COMPOUND VERB
Hana made the bread into loaves and let it rise near the oven. [no comma]

COMPOUND SENTENCE
Hana made the bread, and we ate it for dinner. [comma]

EXERCISE 6 Revising Sentences

On a separate piece of paper, revise each sentence so that it begins with an introductory element. Add commas where necessary. **Hint:** You may have to add, drop, or change some words.
See Answer Key at www.grammarforwriting.com.

1. The brothers Orville and Wilbur Wright owned a bicycle repair shop in Dayton, Ohio, from 1892 to 1904.

2. The brothers experimented with different designs for an airplane, using the tools in their shop.

3. No one had flown a craft that was heavier than air, although people had flown balloons and gliders successfully.

WRITING HINT

When you write paragraphs and essays, try to vary your sentences to avoid singsongy repetition. Use an introductory word, phrase, or subordinate clause to vary sentence beginnings.

4. The Wright brothers designed a power-driven biplane by attaching a homemade engine to a glider.

5. Orville Wright flew the plane 120 feet on December 17, 1903, at Kitty Hawk, North Carolina.

6. The Wright brothers made four flights that day, setting new aviation records.

7. The Wrights became world famous as they made longer flights during the next few years.

8. They founded the Wright Company in 1909, when the U.S. government ordered army planes.

9. You can visit the restored house where Orville was born as well as the Wrights' bicycle shop if you go to Greenfield Village, Michigan.

10. The government established the Wright National Monument in 1927 on more than four hundred acres in Kitty Hawk.

Working Together

EXERCISE 7 Writing a Paragraph

Work with a partner or small group to write a paragraph of at least five sentences. The paragraph should be based on the following notes. Proofread your paragraph to make sure you've used commas correctly.
Students' paragraphs may vary.

1910—Baroness Raymonde de la Roche of France = 1st licensed woman pilot

1911—1st licensed U.S. woman pilot = Harriet Quimby, magazine writer

April 16, 1912—1st woman to fly across English Channel: Harriet Quimby

July 1, 1912—Quimby killed in crash during Harvard-Boston aviation meet

June 15, 1921—1st licensed African American woman pilot: Bessie Coleman; killed in air crash in 1926

May 20–21, 1932—Amelia Earhart, 1st woman transatlantic solo, Newfoundland to Ireland, 15 hours

1932—1st woman commercial airline pilot: Ruth Rowland Nichols; held three international records: speed, distance, altitude

1973—Frontier Airlines hires Emily H. Warner, 1st female pilot of U.S. large airline

Dec. 14–23, 1986—Jeanna Yeager with Dick Rutan set records for speed & distance around world nonstop & nonrefueled

---

Sentence Interrupters and Nonessential Elements

Sentence interrupters are parts of a sentence that interrupt the main thought. At the end or beginning of a sentence, use a single comma to set off an interrupter. In the middle of a sentence, use a pair of commas.

▐▶ Use commas to set off a noun of direct address, the name of the person being spoken to.

> **Sondra,** did you know that the Bahamas became independent in 1973?

▐▶ Use commas to set off nonessential appositives and appositive phrases.

> The Bahamas are made up of 700 islands and 2,400 cays**, or small islands**.
> Nassau**, the capital,** is on New Providence Island.

▐▶ Use commas to set off parenthetical expressions and transitional expressions that interrupt a sentence.

> Christopher Columbus's first stop**, incidentally,** was in the Bahamas.

▐▶ Use commas to set off a nonessential adjective clause. Do not use commas with an essential adjective clause.

Every adjective clause is either essential or nonessential. An **essential adjective clause** is necessary to make the meaning of the sentence clear. Usually, it answers this question: "Which one(s)?" (A clause that begins with the word *that* is usually an essential clause.) A **nonessential adjective clause**, on the other hand, adds information, but the sentence makes sense without it.

ESSENTIAL	Blackbeard was one of the pirates **who frequented Bahamian waters**.
NONESSENTIAL	Blackbeard**, whose real name was Edward Teach,** died in 1718.
ESSENTIAL	The Americans **who invaded Nassau in 1776** held it briefly.
NONESSENTIAL	You can visit the forts on Nassau**, which were built to defend against a Spanish invasion**.

Some Common Parenthetical and Transitional Expressions
as a result
by the way
for example
for instance
furthermore
on the other hand
incidentally
in fact
moreover
nevertheless
of course

STEP BY STEP

The Comma Test

To decide if an adjective clause should be set off with commas:

1. Try saying the sentence aloud without the adjective clause.

2. If the sentence makes sense without the adjective clause, that clause is *nonessential*. Use commas to set off the clause.

3. If the sentence doesn't make sense without the clause, that clause is *essential*. Do not use commas.

EXERCISE 8 Proofreading Sentences

Proofread the following sentences, adding commas where they are needed. Write *C* if the sentence is correct.

1. Australia, which is between the Indian Ocean and the Pacific, is the smallest continent.

2. Bangladesh, a nation in southern Asia, became independent in 1971.

3. Did you know, Harold, that the Arctic Ocean has ice year-round?

4. Anchorage is Alaska's largest city, but not its capital.

5. Santa Fe, the capital of New Mexico, attracts many artists.

6. The Rio Grande is the river that forms our border with Mexico. C

7. Nova Scotia, which French settlers called Acadia, is one of the Canadian Maritime Provinces.

8. Iceland, a large island in the North Atlantic, has geysers.

9. Ms. Wu, how can we find out which cities have the most smog?

10. The Hague, of course, hosts the International Court of Justice.

EXERCISE 9 Revising Sentences

On a separate piece of paper, revise each sentence by inserting at the caret mark (∧) the words in parentheses. Use commas correctly.

EXAMPLE   The river ∧ is the Seine River. (that flows through Paris)

The river that flows through Paris is the Seine River.

1. The Sahara Desert ∧ is the world's largest desert. (which is in northern Africa) [, which is in northern Africa,]

2. French is the main language ∧. (that is spoken in Quebec) [that is spoken in Quebec]

3. Florence is the city ∧. (where da Vinci and Raphael lived) [where da Vinci and Raphael lived]

4. Many ships have disappeared in the Bermuda Triangle ∧. (a region in the Atlantic Ocean) [, a region in the Atlantic Ocean]

5. The Arctic and Antarctic circles are imaginary ∧. (of course) [, of course]

6. Algiers ∧ is a port city on the Mediterranean Sea. (which is the capital of Algeria) [, which is the capital of Algeria,]

7. The Nile River ∧ is the longest river in the world. (which flows north from central Africa to the Mediterranean) [, which flows north from central Africa to the Mediterranean,]

8. ∧ what part of Norway were your grandparents born? (John) [John, in]

9. New Delhi ∧ replaced Calcutta as India's capital. (in fact) [, in fact,]

10. Both Paul Gauguin and Robert Louis Stevenson chose to live in Tahiti ∧. (a south Pacific island) [, a south Pacific island]

Other Comma Uses

▐▐▐➡ Use commas to set off *well*, *yes*, *no*, and single-word adjectives that begin a sentence.

Well, did you hear the good news?

Yes, I did.   No, I didn't.

Anxious, she looked at her watch for the twentieth time.

Excited and happy, we waited to meet the adopted baby.

▐▐▐➡ Use commas to separate the date and year. No comma is needed between the month and date or between the month and year.

Malcolm X (then Malcolm Little) was born on May 19, 1925.

He was born on May 19.

Malcolm X was assassinated on February 21, 1965.

He was assassinated in February 1965.

▐▐▐➡ Use commas following the greeting and closing of a friendly letter.

Dear Maya,   Sincerely,

With love,   Best wishes,

Note: A comma may also be used to introduce some short, informal quotations. See Lesson 14.5 for the rules that govern the use of commas and colons in quotations.

WRITING HINT

A business letter's form differs from that of a friendly letter (see page 232). Friendly letters have no heading (usually, the writer gives only the date of the letter) and no inside address. In a friendly letter, a comma (not a colon) follows the greeting. The signature is always handwritten instead of typewritten.

EXERCISE 10 Using Commas Correctly

Circle the letter of *all* the correct answers for each question.

1. Which of the following is an appropriate greeting for a friendly letter? (a) Dear Mr. Tannenbaum: (b) Dear Leila, (c) To whom it may concern: (d) Dear Grandma,

2. Which is an appropriate closing for a friendly letter? (a) Sincerely, (b) Love, (c) Sincerely yours: (d) Yours sincerely:

3. Which of the following sentences is correctly punctuated? (a) Mary Shelley, the author of *Frankenstein*, was born on August 30, 1797. (b) Mary Shelley, the author of *Frankenstein*, was born in August, 1797. (c) Mary Shelley, the author of *Frankenstein*, was born on August, 30, 1797.

4. Which of the following sentences is correctly punctuated? (a) Yes we have no bananas. (b) Yes, we have no bananas. (c) Yes, we have no bananas

Enriching Your Vocabulary

The adjective *apt* comes from the Latin *aptus*, which means "suited, fitted, or appropriate." The class valedictorian offered *apt* advice to the new graduates. *Aptitude*, used in Exercise 11, is derived from *aptus* and the suffix *–tudo* ("condition or quality"). Do you have an *aptitude* for a particular sport?

5. Which date line for a friendly letter is correctly punctuated?
   (a) September 19 1975 (b) May 8, 1986.
   (c) July 1, 1779 (d) November, 18, 1995

EXERCISE 11 Editing and Proofreading a Friendly Letter

Proofread the friendly letter below. Add commas, periods, and other end punctuation marks where necessary. Correct any run-on sentences and sentence fragments. Be sure to check the spelling, too.

December 18, 2000

Dear Aunt Bea,

Wow! Thanks very much for the new dictionary. What a good birthday present. It's something I've wanted for a long time but haven't been able to buy for myself. It's certainly a great improvement over Mom's old dictionary, which was printed in something like the Dark Ages.

I'll make good use of the dictionary because I'm trying to study a little for the PSAT exam later this year even though everyone says you can't really study for it. PSAT stands for Preliminary Scholastic Aptitude Test; it's a kind of practice test for the Scholastic Aptitude Test. The SAT is important when I apply for college.

Well, how are you? I hope that you, Uncle Rob, Rhea, and Mike have all been well. I know you're always busy, Aunt Bea, and I really admire your ability to work full time and run a house. What's new at work?

Yes, we're all looking forward to seeing you and the family on New Year's Day. I can't wait to impress you with my new vocabulary from the dictionary you sent me.

Much love,
Nina

EXERCISE 12 Writing a Friendly Letter

Write a letter to a friend, relative, or pen pal who lives far away. Tell the person about one or two experiences that you are willing to share with the class. Be sure to ask some questions, too, so that the person you're writing to will write back. Students' letters will vary.

Correcting Run-on Sentences and Sentence Fragments

▐▐▐▶ A **run-on sentence** incorrectly combines two or more sentences. Use the following three strategies to correct run-on sentences.

1. Add end punctuation and a capital letter to break up the run-on.

RUN-ON   The earliest people were hunters and gatherers, agriculture came later.

CORRECTED   The earliest people were hunters and gatherers. Agriculture came later.

2. Change the run-on into a compound sentence. Note the different corrections that are possible.

RUN-ON   Hunters and gatherers roam freely, farmers stay in one place.

CORRECTED   Hunters and gatherers roam freely, **but** farmers stay in one place.

CORRECTED   Hunters and gatherers roam freely; **farmers** stay in one place.

3. Turn one of the sentences into a subordinate clause.

CORRECTED   **Although hunters and gatherers roam freely,** farmers stay in one place.

▐▐▐▶ To correct a **sentence fragment**, use these three strategies.

1. Add the missing subject, verb, or both.

FRAGMENT   With the cultivation of wild plants.

CORRECTED   Agriculture began with the cultivation of wild plants.

2. Attach the fragment to a complete sentence before or after it.

FRAGMENT   Some early farms were in the Southwest. In the land surrounding mesas.

CORRECTED   Some early farms were in the Southwest in the land surrounding mesas.

3. Drop a subordinating conjunction.

FRAGMENT   Because the women carried water to mesas.

CORRECTED   The women carried water to mesas.

EXERCISE 13 Editing and Proofreading a Paragraph

Proofread the paragraph on the following page to correct run-ons and fragments. Read your corrected paragraph aloud to see that the sentences sound smooth together.

Use **Grammar** Lesson 6.3 for practice in fixing sentence fragments. Use Lesson 6.5 for run-ons.

TEST-TAKING TIP

If you are asked on a standardized test to correct a run-on sentence, consider using a semicolon, providing that the two independent clauses are clearly and closely related. See item 4 on page 294 for an example.

WRITING HINT

If you always correct a fragment or run-on in the same way, your paragraphs may sound monotonous and singsongy. In a paragraph or essay, read the sentences aloud. See how they sound together. Aim for variety.

¹What happened to American farms during the last half of the twentieth century? ²Take a look at the graphs in Exercise 14. As ~~as~~ the number of American farms decreased, the average size of American farms increased. ³According to the first graph, there were more than six million farms in the United States in 1940. Now ~~now~~ there are about two million. ⁴Where did the farms go? ⁵Some family farms did disappear. as ~~As~~ cities, suburbs, towns, and malls grew in what once were fields. ⁷Most of America's farms, however, just got a lot bigger. ⁸The second graph shows the acreage of the average farm. ⁹There has been a ~~A~~ steady increase in farm size from 1940 to 1997. ¹⁰In 1940, the average American farm was 174 acres; in 1997 the average farm was 470 acres.

EXERCISE 14 Writing a Paragraph

Working with a partner, use the graphs below to write at least five sentences. Proofread your sentences to check for the correct use of commas and to eliminate fragments and run-ons. Then exchange sentences with another pair of classmates, and compare what you've written. Students' sentences will vary.

U.S. Farms, 1940-1997

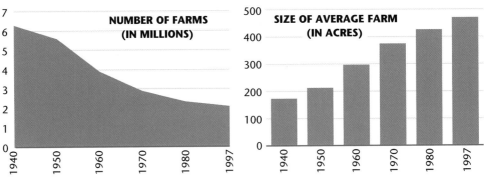

Source: National Agriculture Statistics Service, U.S. Dept. of Agriculture

Write What You Think

Work with a small group to make two separate charts listing what you think are the advantages and disadvantages of living (1) on a farm and (2) in a city. Write at least one paragraph, clearly stating your opinion about where you would rather live and supporting your opinion with reasons. When you've finished revising, proofread your paragraph to make sure there are no sentence fragments or run-on sentences. Check for correct commas. Answers will vary. Give students full credit if they have stated an opinion and attempted to support their opinions. They should also have written grammatically complete sentences that begin with a capital letter and end with an appropriate end punctuation mark.

Editing and Proofreading Worksheet 1

Edit the draft for errors in spelling, capitalization, punctuation, and usage. Write your edited version on a separate piece of paper. Compare your changes with those of a writing partner.

[1]In many cultures around the world**, there** ~~their~~ are myths about a trickster hero. [2]The Native Americans of the Pacific Northwest**,** for example**,** have many stories about Raven. [3]**He is their** ~~Their~~ trickster hero**,** who can change his shape through magic.

[4]Long ago at the beginning of the world**,** [5]Raven brought the Indian people the sun**,** the moon**,** and fire. [6]In the dark**,** cold world of earliest times**,** the people had no fire. [7]All of the people ate raw food and shivered in the cold. [8]Because Raven knew that there was fire up in the sky**, one** ~~One~~ night he flew up through a hole in the sky to the tent of the sun. [10]He transformed himself into a baby boy and lay outside the tent. [11]The daughter of the skies found him~~,~~ and brought him into the sun's tent. [12]The baby boy grew quickly**, and became** ~~Became~~ a toddler in four days. [14]Although everyone was kind to the little boy**,** he cried because he wanted to play with the sun's fire. [15]Raven cried and cried**, until** finally the sun said he could play with a small stick of firewood.

[16]As soon as he got the fire**,** the little boy transformed himself into his real shape**.** Raven held the firestick in his beak **and** escaped ~~threw~~ **through** a smoke hole in the sun's tent. **(** [17]The smoke dyed all his feathers black **, which is why** ~~and~~ Ravens are still black to this day. **)** [18]The people who lived in the sky were furious**. They** ~~they~~ chased Raven**,** but they could not catch him. [19]Raven found the hole in the sky**,** dived down to Earth**,** and carefully lay the stolen fire on dry wood**. It** ~~it~~ was the first fire on Earth. [20]**Raven also** ~~Also~~ taught the people how to start a fire by rubbing two sticks together.

Edit the draft for errors in spelling, capitalization, punctuation, and usage. Write your edited version on a separate piece of paper. Compare your changes with those of a writing partner. Students' corrected paragraphs may vary. A sample revision is given.

¹Have you ever taken care of a baby or young child if you have you know how exhausting babies can be a baby is totally helpless. ²And dependent for survival on a parent or caregiver ³One of the most difficult problems caregivers face is a baby who seems to cry endlessly. ⁴Its difficult to listen. ⁵To a crying baby who can't tell you what's wrong.

⁶When babies cry? ⁷Child care experts advise a process of elimination. ⁸To try to find out what's wrong first check the baby's diaper, some babies object to being wet or in soiled diapers, then see if the baby is hungry, doctors don't recommend that caregivers try to put newborns and very young babies on a feeding schedule, they should be fed whenever they are hungry. ⁹If a baby feels hot or seems sick take his or her temperature of course and call a doctor.

¹⁰Babies learn to trust the world when they are fed and changed. ¹¹And gently held and cuddled. ¹²Its a good idea to talk, sing or even read to young babies they learn from the sound of your voice. ¹³Some babies fall asleep. ¹⁴When they are gently rocked or rolled in a carriage.

¹⁵It takes a lot of patience kindness and energy to raise a baby into a child. ¹⁶It also takes someone to ask for advice, many child-care experts have written guidebooks on baby care ¹⁷If you can buy or borrow one. ¹⁸There are television programs, too ¹⁹Remember that a newborn human is totally helpless and completely dependent. ²⁰be glad when he or she is old enough to tell you what's wrong.

Chapter Review

EXERCISE A Proofreading Sayings

Proofread the following sayings. Add commas and end punctuation marks as needed.

EXAMPLE   Too many boatmen will drive the boat up the mountain.

1. Deal with the faults of others as gently as you do your own.

2. A people without history is like wind on the buffalo grass.

3. What does a frog in the well know about the ocean?

4. If you want to get on in the world, first help others to get on.

5. Yes, Virginia, there is a Santa Claus.

6. When the tiger is away, the rabbit is master.

7. So long as there is bread to eat, water to drink, and a bended arm to sleep on, happiness is not impossible.

8. Who knows this morning what will happen tonight?

9. Oh, the good times when we were so unhappy!

10. If two people keep a horse between them, it will be thin. If two people share a boat, it will leak.

EXERCISE B Using Commas and End Marks Correctly

In the following sentences, insert all missing commas, periods, and other end marks.

1. Citrus fruits, tomatoes, and broccoli are sources of Vitamin C.

2. Broccoli, in fact, also contains Vitamin A, calcium, and potassium.

3. Jorge, did we plant the grapefruit tree in May 1996?

4. Yes, it bears grapefruit from about October through March.

5. I like picking strawberries and tomatoes, for instance.

6. Did you know that strawberries are really false fruits?

7. The real fruits of a strawberry are those tiny black specks.

8. When you julienne a raw vegetable, you cut it into thin strips.

9. Parmesan and Romano, for example, are hard cheeses but mozzarella and Monterey Jack are soft cheeses.

10. How lucky we are to have summer fruits available all year! *or* .

You may wish to have students write ten sayings that they know. If they are in a language other than English, translate them into English, and identify the original language in parentheses. Have students check for the correct use of commas and end punctuation marks. Encourage students to invent their own sayings if they don't know any.

EXERCISE C Revising Sentences

Revise each sentence by inserting the words shown in parentheses at the caret mark. Add commas and end punctuation where necessary. Check to see that your sentences are punctuated correctly.

1. A trio is a group of three; a quartet , of course , has four . (of course)

2. Captain Ahab , who commanded the *Pequod* , was obsessed with killing the white whale . (who commanded the *Pequod*)

3. Harriet Beecher Stowe's *Uncle Tom's Cabin* , which appeared in 1851 , is a powerful antislavery novel . (which appeared in 1851)

4. When was the Bill of Rights added to the Constitution , Maxine ? (Maxine)

5. How did Beowulf , hero of the English epic poem , kill the monster Grendel ? (hero of the English epic poem)

6. *Gulliver's Travels* by Jonathan Swift is a satire that ridicules human weaknesses . (that ridicules human weaknesses)

EXERCISE D Proofreading a Paragraph

The following mess of words is a puzzle for you to figure out. Make it into a paragraph by separating it into sentences. Add commas, periods, and other end marks. Be sure to begin each sentence with a capital letter.

when you're looking for a quotation to begin or end an essay, you may find exactly what you're looking for in a book of quotations. you can usually find several books of quotations in a library or bookstore. for example, *Bartlett's Familiar Quotations*, which is in its seventeenth edition, contains more than 25,000 quotations by 2,500 authors. you can look up a quotation in two ways in *Bartlett's*. if you already know the quotation but want to check the exact wording, you can look up one of its main words in the alphabetical index at the back of the book. if you're looking for quotations by a specific author, check the alphabetical list of authors at the beginning of the book. for instance, you can find twelve different quotations by Dr. Martin Luther King, Jr. the entry for every author lists his or her birth and death dates as well as the source and date for every quotation. other books of quotations are organized by theme, or and some books contain only quotations by women, African Americans, or other special sources.

Punctuation: All the Other Marks

STUDENT WRITING
Expository Essay

An Important Lesson
by Mandy Kiaha
high school student, Kamehameha, Hawaii

Growing up, I never fully realized the importance of failure, and I never saw it as being something good. If my basketball team lost a game or if I got a bad grade on a test, I would get down on myself for failing. Not only did blaming myself for the failure prevent me from learning from it and improving, it also hurt my confidence and hindered my development even more. Then, I read *I Can't Accept Not Trying* by Michael Jordan. The author, a well-known athlete, as well as a role model of mine, said it best in this book when he [wrote], "I can accept failure, but I can't accept not trying."

This book has helped me see things from a different perspective—a better one at that. Michael Jordan took failure and transformed it into something good, something useful. He suggested that as long as we try our best in whatever it is we choose to pursue, failure is acceptable. In this respect, failure shapes us into stronger people who learn from and grow as a result of these experiences. As we become stronger and smarter individuals, we become successful in life. When I was cut from my high school's varsity basketball team my sophomore year, I realized that I never wanted to feel that way again, to have that hole in my heart. The following week, I remembered Michael Jordan's words and looked at my failure from a different perspective. Instead of wallowing in sorrow and blame, I vowed to work on my game all summer and to set new goals for myself. The lesson that I learned from this experience is that failure is acceptable as long as an earnest attempt is made toward the goal.

> The purpose of the essay above is to explain how the author learned to accept failure. She names an important book that helped her, but the essay is effective because the author relates an anecdote that shows how the lessons of the book influenced her. Facts, statistics, and anecdotes are all types of evidence that will make your writing more effective and interesting to readers.
>
> As you learn more ways to use punctuation accurately in this chapter, think about using anecdotes like this one to support your thesis statements.

Allow time for students to discuss the student writing. Suggest that they identify its strengths and propose possible improvements. Use the model to introduce the concepts in the chapter.

Colons

A colon (:) signals that something will follow: a list, a long quotation, or a formal statement.

▐▌▶ Use a **colon** before a list of items, especially after the words *the following* or *the following items*.

> COLON   Among Dickens's most popular novels are the following: *A Christmas Carol*, *Great Expectations*, and *A Tale of Two Cities*.

Exception: Do not use a colon when the list follows the main verb of a sentence or a preposition.

> NO COLON   The main characters in *A Tale of Two Cities* are Sydney Carton, Lucie Manette, and Charles Darnay.

EDITING TiP

Many people confuse colons and semicolons. Although these two punctuation marks look similar and their names are similar, they are *not* interchangeable. Colons and semicolons do totally different work. Lesson 14.2 gives the rules for using semicolons.

▐▌▶ Use a colon before a formal statement or quotation and before a long quotation that is set off as a block (any quotation of more than three lines).

> The editor points out why *A Tale of Two Cities* is unique among Dickens's novels: "It is the one work in the whole series that fully merits the title of a 'historical' novel."

When a long quotation (more than three lines) is set off as a block, indent the quotation, and don't use quotation marks.

> *A Tale of Two Cities* begins with a long run-on sentence that states a series of **paradoxes:**
>
> > It was the best of times, it was the worst of times, it was the age of wisdom, it was the age of foolishness, it was the epoch of belief, it was the epoch of incredulity, it was the season of Light, it was the season of Darkness, it was the spring of hope, it was the winter of despair. . . .

WRITING HiNT

You can also use a comma to introduce a short quotation, but always use a colon before a long quotation and in formal writing.

▐▌▶ Use a colon to emphasize a word or a phrase.

> Madame Defarge and her husband resemble two of Shakespeare's most famous characters: Lady Macbeth and Macbeth.

▐▌▶ Use a colon in these situations: (1) between the hour and minutes, (2) between the chapter and verse in a reference to the Bible, and (3) after the greeting of a business letter.

> 8:30 A.M.   Genesis 12:1–3   Dear Accounting Department:

Enriching Your Vocabulary

The noun *paradox* closely resembles the Greek word *paradoxos*, which means "unbelievable" or "beyond what is thought." In a country as wealthy as the United States, hunger is a *paradox*.

EXERCISE 1 Adding Colons to Sentences

Insert colons where they are needed in the following sentences. **Hint:** Not every sentence requires a colon. In sentences 8 and 9, accept a comma or a dash as well as a colon.

1. The two cities in Dickens's tale are Paris and London.

2. The novel deals with these issues: love, justice, mercy, and loyalty.

3. In the preface, Dickens acknowledges Thomas Carlyle's *History of the French Revolution.*

4. A maid accidentally destroyed Carlyle's manuscript of that history by throwing it into a fire.

5. Here is Dickens's stated purpose: "It has been one of my hopes to add something to the popular and picturesque means of understanding that terrible time. . . ."

6. Chapter 3 opens with this line: "A wonderful fact to reflect upon, that every human creature is constituted to be that profound secret and mystery to every other."

7. Among the novel's memorable minor characters are Miss Pross and Jerry Cruncher.

8. Cruncher holds two jobs: an odd-job man by day and a body snatcher by night.

9. Readers can never forget Madame Defarge's hobby: knitting.

10. The novel ends with Carton's words: "'It is a far, far better thing that I do, than I have ever done; it is a far, far better rest that I go to, than I have ever known.'"

EXERCISE 2 Writing a Journal Entry

What is your schedule for Monday, a typical school day? Tell what you do during the day; begin each entry with the time. Write complete sentences.

EXAMPLE   *7:15 A.M. I wake up, eat breakfast, and get dressed.*
Students' answers will vary.

Semicolons

A **semicolon** (;) signals a pause that is longer than a comma's pause but shorter than a period's.

▥▶ Use a semicolon to join independent clauses in a compound sentence when you are not using a coordinating conjunction.

SEMICOLON   For more than fifty years, Ellis Island was an immigration station; it was closed in 1954.

COMMA   For more than fifty years, Ellis Island was an immigration station, **but** it was closed in 1954.

▥▶ Use a semicolon before a conjunctive adverb or transitional expression that joins independent clauses. Use a comma after the conjunctive adverb or transitional expression.

Ellis Island was abandoned for decades; **however,** some of the buildings have been carefully restored.

▥▶ Use a semicolon to separate items in a series when one or more of the items contains a comma.

Uncle Ned's grandfather from Kiev, Russia; Frank's great-grandmother from County Cork, Ireland; and JoAnn's great-grandparents from Naples, Italy, all passed through Ellis Island.

EXERCISE 3 Using Semicolons and Colons

Some of the following sentences need a semicolon; others require colons. Review the rules for colons in Lesson 14.1, and then add the proper punctuation marks. If a sentence is correct, write *C*.

1. Samuel Ellis, a farmer, owned Ellis Island in the early 1700s; the U.S. government bought it in 1808.

2. Ellis Island is in New Jersey waters; however, an 1834 agreement brought it under New York jurisdiction.

3. The first stop for twelve million immigrants was Ellis Island; 98 percent of them entered the United States.

4. They came for many reasons: to escape religious persecution or starvation, to find a better way of life, and to be reunited with family.

5. Steerage passengers went through Ellis Island; first-class passengers did not.

6. Doctors examined new arrivals for infectious diseases; some were sent back home.

Some Common Conjunctive Adverbs

accordingly	meanwhile
also	moreover
besides	nevertheless
consequently	otherwise
furthermore	still
however	then
indeed	therefore

Some Common Transitional Expressions

as a result	in other
for example	words
for instance	on the other
in addition	hand
in fact	that is

EDITING TIP

When these same words (conjunctive adverbs and transitional expressions) are sentence interrupters, they're set off on both sides by commas.

Our view, however, was blocked by a steel beam.

We couldn't, as a result, see home plate.

Enriching Your Vocabulary

The Latin roots of the noun *jurisdiction* are *juris* ("law or right") and *dictio* ("the act of saying"). Thus, *jurisdiction* means "the legal power to rule on a matter" or "the power to exercise authority." The approval of a nominee to the Supreme Court falls within the *jurisdiction* of the U.S. Senate.

7. Government officials denied entrance to the following: criminals and the insane.

8. At its busiest, Ellis Island had thirty-five buildings: the main building has been carefully restored.

9. President Johnson declared Ellis Island a National Historic Site in 1964. In 1989, the Museum of Immigration opened. C

10. There you can see photographs, passports, and other documents; you can listen to tapes of immigrants' Ellis Island memories.

EXERCISE 4 Using Punctuation in Compound Sentences

On a separate piece of paper, combine each set of independent clauses into a compound sentence. Do *not* use coordinating conjunctions. Check your combined sentences for proper punctuation. See Answer Key at www.grammarforwriting.com.

1. An immigrant is someone who comes to live in a new country. An emigrant is someone who leaves a country.

2. American Indians are Native Americans. Many other Americans are immigrants or descendants of immigrants.

3. The first colonists were English. Later immigrants came from other Western European countries.

4. Some came to escape religious persecution. However, most sought a better economic opportunity.

5. As the country expanded, immigrants moved west to find land. For instance, Danes, Norwegians, and Swedes staked out farms on the Great Plains.

6. During the 1840s and 1850s, about 1.5 million Irish arrived. They came to escape the potato famine.

7. From the 1880s to the 1920s, 4.5 million Italians arrived. During the same period, 2.5 million Jews immigrated.

8. Communists took over Cuba in 1959. As a result, about 700,000 Cubans moved to the United States.

CONNECTING
Writing & Grammar

Write What You Think

Some people think the government should allow more legal immigrants to enter the United States. Others feel that there should be fewer legal immigrants.

Write what you think about the number of legal immigrants. State your opinion clearly, and support it with reasons and evidence. Be sure to revise and edit your writing. Answers will vary. Give students full credit if they have stated an opinion on one of the issues and attempted to support the opinion. They should also have written gramatically complete sentences that begin with a capital letter and end with an appropriate punctuation mark.

Underlining (Italics)

If you're writing by hand or on a typewriter, use underlining to indicate italics. But if you're writing on a computer, you can actually use italic type. (*Italic type is the slanted type that looks like this.*) Use underlining or italics, not both.

▐▐▐▶ Use underlining (or italics) for the following kinds of titles and names:

BOOKS	*The Odyssey Up from Slavery Pride and Prejudice*
MAGAZINES	*Sports Illustrated Scientific American*
NEWSPAPERS	*USA Today The Washington Post The Los Angeles Times*
PLAYS	*The Piano Lesson Romeo and Juliet The Miracle Worker*
MOVIES	*2001: A Space Odyssey The Empire Strikes Back E.T.*
TV/RADIO SERIES	*60 Minutes Masterpiece Theatre*
WORKS OF ART	Georgia O'Keeffe's *Red Poppy*
	Vincent van Gogh's *The Starry Night*
SHIPS, PLANES,	*H.M.S. Titanic Spirit of St. Louis*
SPACECRAFT	*Apollo 13* the space shuttle *Atlantis*

▐▐▐▶ Use italics for foreign words and expressions that are not commonly used and for words, letters, and numbers referred to as such.

FOREIGN WORDS	*E pluribus unum* means "out of many, one."
	I listed my studies at the *Instituto Internacional* on
	my résumé. [The word *résumé* is French but is
	commonly used and should not be italics.]
WORDS AS WORDS	Is *advice* or *advise* the right word for this sentence?
LETTERS	How many *s*'s are there in your name?
NUMBERS	What is the next ordinal number after the number *9*?

> **EDITING TIP**
>
> Not all titles are italicized. Many kinds of titles (short stories, poems, songs, and others) belong in quotation marks (see Lesson 14.4).

EXERCISE 5   Editing and Proofreading a Report

Read the following review. Add underlining to indicate italics.

[1]The Disney studio's animated movie The Lion King was a box office hit, but the Broadway musical is an even bigger hit. [2]The Broadway show, The Lion King, got all A's from reviewers; magical is the word they use most often to describe the show. [3]It's such a sellout that a cartoon in The New Yorker magazine suggests a ticket to the show as an appropriate

gift for a newborn baby. ⁴In The New York Times and other newspapers, scalpers advertise tickets for three hundred dollars and up.

⁵The Lion King on Broadway adds gorgeous African music and dance plus highly imaginative staging and costumes. ⁶Perhaps someday there'll be a movie version of this Broadway version of the Disney movie. ⁷(Where will it all end?)

⁸The concept of talking animals with human emotions, so basic to both versions of the hit, isn't new. ⁹It's found in Rudyard Kipling's The Jungle Book (talking tropical animals), in Richard Adams's Watership Down (talking rabbits), and even in Beatrix Potter's The Tale of Peter Rabbit (more talking rabbits).

¹⁰Adaptations of books are sometimes—but not always—a winning formula for stage and screen. ¹¹Consider these big winners: West Side Story (based on William Shakespeare's The Tragedy of Romeo and Juliet), My Fair Lady (based on George Bernard Shaw's play Pygmalion), Les Misérables (based on a novel by Victor Hugo), and Mary Poppins (based on a series of children's books by P. L. Travers). ¹²In contrast with the musical and movie based on the sinking of the Titanic, an event that actually occurred, all of these hit plays sprang from the writers' imaginations.

EXERCISE 6 Writing Brief Reviews

On a separate piece of paper, write a brief review of (1) your favorite movie, (2) your favorite television series, and (3) your favorite book. Explain as specifically as you can why you've chosen each one as the best. Write one or more paragraphs for each of the three works. Share your reviews to see if anyone else has named your favorites. Check each other's paragraphs for the correct use of italics and other punctuation marks. Reviews will vary. Each student should write one or more paragraphs for all three reviews.

Quotation Marks

▐▶ Use **quotation marks** for titles of short works.

POEMS	"Courage" "Mending Wall" "The Road Less Traveled"
SHORT STORIES	"The Most Dangerous Game" "Through the Tunnel"
ARTICLES	"Michigan Starts the New Year in Style" "An Interview with Maya Angelou"
SONGS	"Lift Ev'ry Voice and Sing" "Candle in the Wind"
SINGLE TV PROGRAMS	"Shirley Temple: The Biggest Little Star"
PARTS OF BOOKS	Chapter 3, "A New Nation"

P.S. It isn't easy to remember which kinds of titles are italicized and which go in quotation marks. If you're not sure about which one to use, check a punctuation guide such as this book or a book such as *The Chicago Manual of Style* or *Words into Type*.

▐▶ Use quotation marks at the beginning and end of a direct quotation.

When a direct quotation is an entire sentence, begin with a capital letter. Introduce a short, one-sentence quotation with a comma. When only a word or two is quoted, use a lowercase letter if the quoted words do not begin the sentence.

> Of the Louisiana Purchase, H. W. Elson writes, "The bargain was a great one for America."
>
> H. W. Elson called the bargain that America got "a great one."

> For placement of quotation marks in dialogue, see Lesson 14.5.

Quotation Marks with Other Punctuation Marks

- **Periods** and **commas** always go inside closing quotation marks.

- **Semicolons** and **colons** always go outside closing quotation marks.

- **Question marks** and **exclamation points** go inside closing quotation marks if the quotation is a question or an exclamation. They go outside if the whole sentence is a question or an exclamation.

EXERCISE 7 Punctuating Sentences

Add or change punctuation marks in the following sentences. If a sentence is punctuated correctly, write *C*.

1. Tennyson's poem "The Eagle" contains this memorable image: "The wrinkled sea beneath him crawls. . . ."

2. "My candle burns at both ends; / It will not last the night, . . ." wrote the American poet Edna St. Vincent Millay.

3. Edgar Allan Poe's raven keeps repeating one word: "Nevermore."

4. In her essay "Choice: A Tribute to Dr. Martin Luther King, Jr.," Alice Walker writes, "He gave us back our heritage."

> **EDITING TIP**
>
> Do not use quotation marks for an indirect quotation.
>
> **DIRECT**
> "Please close the door," she said.
>
> **INDIRECT**
> She asked me to close the door.

5. "The Dynasty: The Nehru–Gandhi Story" is a TV documentary about India's independence.

6. Anne Morrow Lindbergh wrote: "The wave of the future is coming and there is no fighting it."

7. What do you think "the pursuit of happiness" means? C

8. I really enjoyed reading Anton Chekhov's short story "The Bet."

9. "Song of Myself," Walt Whitman's poem, begins with this line: "I celebrate myself, and sing myself. . . ."

10. In *The Way to Rainy Mountain*, N. Scott Momaday writes: "Tai-me came to the Kiowas in a vision born of suffering and despair."

EXERCISE 8 Write Your Own Exercise

On a separate piece of paper, write one or more complete sentences on each topic in the numbered items below. Leave out all punctuation marks. Then exchange papers with a classmate, and see if you agree on how to punctuate each sentence. See the summary on page 247 about where to place other punctuation marks in relation to quotation marks. See Answer Key at www.grammarforwriting.com.

1. a song that's popular now (Mention the title and the performer.)

2. a direct quotation (an actual quotation or a made-up one) at the beginning of a sentence

3. a chapter title from a book and a summary of what's in the chapter (Use this book if you wish.)

4. a poem you've read and your thoughts about it (Mention the poem's title and author.)

5. a song that's been around a long time and the reason for its popularity

6. a newspaper or magazine article and your thoughts about it (an actual article or a made-up title)

7. a short story you've read and your thoughts about it (Mention the title and author.)

8. a TV program (a single episode, not a series) you watched last week and your thoughts about it (Make up a title for the program if you can't remember it.)

9. an indirect quotation

10. a direct quotation that's not a whole sentence (Make one up, and use it within a complete sentence.)

Punctuating Dialogue

Dialogue is the words the characters in a novel say. The words that identify the speaker (*he said, she said*) are called a **dialogue tag**. Follow these rules for punctuating dialogue and direct quotations.

▶ Begin a new paragraph every time the speaker changes.

▶ Place quotation marks at the beginning and end of a speaker's exact words.

    "Nori, it's time for you to learn some origami**,**" Mrs. Muro suggested.

▶ When a dialogue tag interrupts a quoted sentence, begin the second part of the quotation with a lowercase letter.

    "Maybe**,**" Nori asked, "you can teach me how to make a paper crane?"

If the second part of a divided quotation is a complete sentence, it should begin with a capital letter.

    "Do your homework," Nori's mother said. "Grandmother might teach you when you're through."

▶ When a direct quotation comes at the beginning of a sentence, use a comma, question mark, or exclamation point—but *not* a period—to separate it from the dialogue tag that follows.

    "Of course, I will**,**" Mrs. Muro answered.

▶ Commas and periods always go *inside* the closing quotation marks.

    "While you wash the dishes, I'll get my papers**,**" Grandma said.

▶ When the speaker's words are a question or an exclamation, place the question mark or exclamation point *inside* the closing quotation marks.

    "Do you remember how you cried when the paper cranes got wet**?**"
    "Yes**!**" laughed Nori, remembering.

▶ When the quotation itself isn't a question or exclamation, place the question mark or exclamation point *outside* the closing quotation marks.

    Who said, "I have but one life to give for my country"**?**
    Please stop saying "It's all your fault"**!**

▶ When the quotation is a question use a question mark inside the closing quotation mark. Place a period after the dialogue tag that follows.

    "Didn't you think they were beautiful**?**" she asked**.**

Enriching Your Vocabulary

The noun *dialogue* comes from a Greek verb, *dialegesthai*, meaning "to converse." The prefix *dia* tells us that at least two individuals are involved. A *monologue*, on the other hand, is spoken by one person. Hamlet's most famous *monologue* begins "To be, or not to be."

WRITING HINT

To write natural-sounding dialogue, use sentence fragments, contractions, and slang words and expressions. Also, don't overuse *said*. Try to use verbs that express the speaker's tone of voice, such as *whispered, laughed, complained,* and *insisted.*

EXERCISE 9 Writing a Dialogue

Work with a partner or small group to create one or more of the following dialogues. Write the dialogue on a separate sheet of paper, following the conventions for punctuating dialogue. Find a partner or partners to role-play your dialogue for a small group or the whole class. Students' answers will vary.

1. Write a conversation between two space visitors watching a football game (or any other sport) for the first time.

2. Write a dialogue in which two people are in conflict. Some possibilities include: a brother and sister, a boyfriend and girlfriend, two good friends.

3. Write a conversation involving three friends that you might overhear in a store, on a bus, in the school cafeteria, or after school.

EXERCISE 10 Punctuating Dialogue

On a separate piece of paper rewrite the following dialogue. Add all the appropriate punctuation marks. See Answer Key at www.grammarforwriting.com.

¹Tina and Lou are waiting for the school bus. ²Last night I read an article about a girl who's the kicker on her high school football team Tina told Lou. ³Really! he exclaimed. ⁴I don't believe you! ⁵Really, Tina insisted. ⁶Her name is Anna Lakovitch, and she goes to a private high school. ⁷She's the captain of the school soccer team, too, which is probably why she's such a good kicker. ⁸Hmphhh! Lou snorted. ⁹I can't believe they'd let girls play on a school varsity team. ¹⁰Tina's voice rose And why not, Lou? ¹¹If girls want to play football, they should play with other girls, not guys. ¹²They don't belong on a guy team, he growled. ¹³Well, her teammates like having her there. ¹⁴She scores points for them. ¹⁵And do you know what? she asked. ¹⁶Lou grunted What? ¹⁷Her football team nominated her as homecoming queen Tina announced and she won. ¹⁸She was crowned during half-time—wearing her football uniform!

Write What You Think

Write one or more paragraphs in which you state your opinion clearly on these three questions. Support your opinion with well-developed reasons and evidence. Be sure to revise and edit your writing.

• Should girls and boys play on the same varsity high school team?

• Should laws be passed enforcing a girl's right to try out and play for a school's varsity team?

• Is it inappropriate in some sports to have girls and boys on the same team? If so, which ones? Answers will vary. Give students full credit if they have stated an opinion on each of the three questions and attempted to support their opinions. They should also have written grammatically complete sentences that begin with a capital letter and end with an appropriate end punctuaton mark.

Apostrophes

Apostrophes (') are used in contractions, in the possessive forms of nouns and indefinite pronouns, and in three kinds of plurals.

▶ Use an apostrophe to show where letters, words, or numbers have been omitted.

you're   I'd   who'll   they're   we've   class of '99
o'clock   o'er   goin'

▶ Add an apostrophe and -s ('s) to a singular noun to show possession.

an hour's wait   our neighbor's dog
Charles's report   the bus's ignition

Exception: To make pronunciation easier, add only an apostrophe after ancient Greek names of more than one syllable with an unaccented ending pronounced *eez*. Do the same after the names *Moses* and *Jesus*.

Hercules' labors   Moses' brother   Jesus' sermon

▶ To show possession in a plural noun that ends in -s, add only an apostrophe (').

students' reports   two dollars' worth
the neighbors' dogs   the Fernandezes' car

▶ Add an apostrophe and -s ('s) to show possession in a plural noun that does not end in s.

women's wages   children's drawings
geese's feathers

▶ Use an apostrophe and -s ('s) to show the possessive form of indefinite pronouns.

everyone's papers   someone's wallet   anybody's turn

▶ Use an apostrophe and an -s ('s) to show a plural in three special cases: (1) to form the plurals of letters, (2) to form the plurals of numbers, and (3) when words are referred to as words.

The word *accommodate* has two *c*'s and two *m*'s.
Laura's phone number has five *6*'s and two *7*'s.
That sentence uses too many *and*'s.   When you write about decades, both 1990s and 1990's are acceptable.

> **EDITING TIP**
>
> One of the most common spelling mistakes is to put apostrophes in possessive personal pronouns. Don't! These pronouns show possession *without* an apostrophe.
>
> hers   his   yours
> its   ours   theirs

EXERCISE 11 Using Apostrophes

Write the contraction for these words.

1. I would _____I'd_____   6. they are _____they're_____

2. you are _____you're_____   7. who is _____who's_____

3. we will _____we'll_____   8. I am _____I'm_____

4. she would _____she'd_____   9. is not _____isn't_____

5. it is _____it's_____   10. will not _____won't_____

EXERCISE 12 Correcting Apostrophes

Read the following paragraphs. Correct all errors in the use of apostrophes. Also correct spelling mistakes. **Hint:** Not every sentence contains an error; some sentences have more than one.

¹One of the most popular winter ~~sport's~~ ^{sports} is skiing. ²(Note, by the way, that the word *skiing* has two ~~is~~ ^{i's} but *skier* has only one.) ³The latest "snow toy" on ski ~~resorts~~ ^{resorts'} slopes is the skiboard. ⁴Skiboards come in pairs (one for each foot), and they're hardly longer than a ~~skiers~~ ^{skier's} boots. ⁵~~Theyre~~ ^{They're} not ~~everyones~~ ^{everyone's} idea of what to do on a mountain; in fact, skiboarders endure many skiers wisecracks. ⁶But ~~theyre~~ ^{they're} just plain fun, one writer reports, and can improve a ~~skiers~~ ^{skier's} balance. ⁷~~Heres~~ ^{Here's} how to turn: Just tip a skiboard on ~~it's~~ ^{its} edge a tiny bit. ⁸You can do practically anything on skiboards you can do on skates: ~~trick's~~ ^{tricks} such as skiing backward, spinning, even dancing.

⁹An older "snow toy" is the snowboard (both feet on a single board), which has been around for many years. ¹⁰A ~~snowboarders~~ ^{snowboarder's} movements resemble a ~~surfers~~ ^{surfer's} or a ~~skateboarders~~ ^{skateboarder's} balancing act. ¹¹In fact, a snowboard looks like a longer, foot-wide version of a skateboard minus ~~it's~~ ^{its} wheels. ¹²One seventy-three-year-old snowboard manufacturer says that "boarding" is easy. ¹³"I tell people that if they ~~cant~~ ^{can't} learn in two hours, they should forget it."

Editing and Proofreading Worksheet 1

Edit the draft for errors in spelling, capitalization, punctuation, and usage. Write your edited version on a separate piece of paper. Compare your changes with those of a writing partner. (In this retelling of a myth, the word *Thunders* and the names of animals function as proper nouns and are therefore capitalized.)

[1]Do you know the Cherokee myth about the origin of fire? [2]Before there was fire,

the animals complained they ~~was~~ *were* very cold. [3]The Thunders sent lightning to make

the first fire in the base of a hollow tree, which was on an island far, far away.

[4]"I will go get fire," said Raven, "because I am so strong and I can fly far. [5]But the fire

in the base of the tree scorched Raven and blackened his feathers," so [6]Raven ~~flyed~~ *flew*

home without the fire.

[7]Then Screech Owl volunteered, but the fire and smoke burned his eyes. [8]Hooting

Owl and Horned Owl each tried, but neither could reach the fire; they both came

back with ashy circles around their eyes.

[9]Next, these two snakes tried: tiny Black Racer and huge Blacksnake. [10]They failed

, too to. [11]"I will succeed where all of you have failed," Blacksnake boasted. [12]But he fell into

the burning tree, [13]~~Barely~~ *barely* managing to escape.

[14]Now all of the other birds, other snakes, and four-footed animals refused to go.

[15]"I will bring back fire," announced Water Spider quietly. [16]From her spidery silk,

she ~~weaved~~ *wove* a tiny bowl and tied it to her back. [17]Then she walked on the water to

the island. [18]From the grass around the tree, she picked up one coal of fire, put it in

her bowl, and came back. [19]That's how fire entered our world.

[20]"Hooray!" they cheered, ~~welcomeing~~ *welcoming* Water Spider home. [21]"At last, we can stay

warm in this freezing world."

Editing and Proofreading Worksheet 2

Edit the draft for errors in spelling, capitalization, punctuation, and usage. Write your edited version on a separate piece of paper. Compare your changes with those of a writing partner.

¹Lets hurry Margo urged Bill or well miss the beginning. ²Dont worry Bill reassured her. ³It doesnt start till 730. ⁴You know therere at least fifteen minutes of previews.

⁵But I love the music from The King and I! ⁶Did you know it was based on a real governess autobiography, a book called Anna and the King of Siam? ⁷Besides, I'll bet therell be lots of people in line. ⁸Its opening night, parking will be a problem, and I dont want to sit in the front row.

⁹Not to worry, Margo. ¹⁰What's your favorite song from the movie? Bill asked. ¹¹Before she could answer, Bill boomed the songs first lines Shall we dance? On a bright cloud of music, shall we fly? ¹²Margo joined him with the rest of the song. ¹³Bill laughed, turning to look at her.

¹⁴Bill! she yelled. Watch out! ¹⁵A car was backing out of a driveway just ahead of them. ¹⁶We're going to hit it! she shouted. ¹⁷Bill slammed on his brakes and leaned on the horn. ¹⁸He wrestled with the steering wheel as Margo braced for the crash. ¹⁹They're car jumped the curb and bumped to a stop against a hedge. ²⁰The other car kept going and drove away.

²¹Wow, that was close! Bill breathed. ²²Are you OK, Margo? ²³I think so Margo answered her voice quavered and her hands shook.

You may wish to have students complete the story.

Chapter Review

EXERCISE A Using Colons and Semicolons

Insert colons and semicolons where they belong in the following sentences.
Hint: Some sentences need more than one punctuation mark.

1. Jana has lived in three cities:Budapest, Hungary,;New York City,
New York;and San Diego, California.

2. Hemingway's title comes from these lines by John Donne:"Do not ask for whom
the bell tolls;it tolls for thee."

3. The bus will leave promptly at 7:00 ~~700~~ A.M.;don't be late.

4. Egg prices vary from state to state;they also vary according to demand.

5. Sound travels faster at higher elevations;in fact, at 36,000 feet, sound travels
eighty miles an hour faster than at sea level.

6. Two of the earliest American Indian cultures include the following:the Clovis
Culture (about 11,200 years ago) and the Folsom Culture (about 10,900
years ago).

7. In 1932, Amelia Earhart became the first woman to fly solo across the Atlantic;it
took her about fifteen hours.

8. What comes after this line from Isaiah 2:4 in the Bible:"And they shall beat
their swords into plowshares. . ."?

9. Betsy Ross supposedly designed the first American flag;however, no one knows
if this is true.

10. The world's busiest airports include O'Hare in Chicago, Illinois,;Harts Field in
Atlanta, Georgia,;and Dallas/Ft. Worth Airport in Texas.

EXERCISE B Using Italics and Quotation Marks

Should you use underlining (italics) or quotation marks? Insert the appropriate
punctuation for each item. Make sure you place quotation marks in the right place
in relation to other punctuation marks. Before you start, review the summary in the
side column on page 247. Underlined words or phrases indicate italics.

1. Have you read Marjorie Kinnan Rawling's novel The Yearling?

2. My favorite song from the Broadway play Oklahoma! is "People Will Say
We're in Love."

3. "The Pedestrian," a short story by Ray Bradbury, is set in a frightening future.

4. The movie Apollo 13 is based on the near-disaster of the Apollo 13 spacecraft.

5. Mark Hamill is the actor who played the young hero in the 1977 movie Star Wars.

6. Every Sunday morning, reporters on Meet the Press interview someone famous.

7. In his essay "Shooting an Elephant," George Orwell tells about an experience he had as a police officer in Burma.

8. In the chapter entitled "Pulling Up Roots" from her book Passages, Gail Sheehy writes that before the age of eighteen, teenagers have a clear motto: I have to get away from my parents.

9. Richard Wright's autobiography Black Boy appeared in 1945.

10. "Ice" is the title of my favorite episode of The X-Files TV series.

EXERCISE C Adding Punctuation to Dialogue

Read the following dialogue. Insert quotation marks, other punctuation marks, and paragraph symbols (¶) where they are needed. See Answer Key at www.grammarforwriting.com.

¹Have you seen my sneakers? Laura asked. ²No, I haven't seen them, her younger brother Gabe answered. ³Why? he added sarcastically. ⁴Do you think I've hidden them? ⁵Don't be so smart, Gabe, she sighed. ⁶I know I left them right here by the couch. ⁷So, Laura, he asked why don't you put your shoes in the closet when you take them off—like I do? ⁸Everyone can't be as neat and perfect as you are, Gabe. ⁹Laura's voice had an edge to it. ¹⁰How did Gabe always manage to be so annoying? ¹¹Will you two please stop arguing all the time! Mom called from the kitchen. ¹²You left your sneakers under the kitchen table, Laura. ¹³And Gabe's right. ¹⁴Stop leaving your clothes all over this apartment.

On a separate piece of paper, continue the dialogue between Laura and her brother Gabe.

Capitalization

STUDENT WRITING
Research Paper

Jefferson Davis, Abraham Lincoln, and the American Revolution
by Greg Ruttan
high school student, Lake Oswego, Oregon

Direct students to www.grammarforwriting.com for chapter-specific portfolio projects.

The Civil War can be seen, in part, as a debate over what the Founding Fathers would have wanted. Neither the North nor the South rejected America's revolutionary heritage. Both Lincoln and Davis saw themselves as [men] following in the Founding Fathers' footsteps, and both of their positions would have [found] support among some of America's Founding Fathers. However, Lincoln supported more the Federalist point of view with his insistence on the power of the federal government, while Davis took the traditional Anti-Federalist view of the federal government being subordinate to the states. Prior to the Civil War, this clash of philosophies had been a part of American politics, even before the death of the Founding Fathers. The conflict between Andrew Jackson and South Carolina over nullification is a good example of this conflict. However, after the Civil War, the debate between the Federalist and Anti-Federalist philosophies ceased. The federal government was supreme. Lincoln and Davis not only alluded back to the Founding Fathers, but through military means they [also] settled the debate the Founding Fathers had been unable to resolve between the Federalists and the Anti-Federalists.

This excerpt is the concluding paragraph from a research paper that identifies the political and ideological similarities between the government leaders of the Revolutionary War and those of the Civil War. This paragraph summarizes the writer's main arguments and restates the paper's thesis statement.

You will learn about the use of capital letters in this chapter. The excerpt above is a good example of how frequently you may be called on to use these rules in your own writing.

Allow time for students to discuss the student writing. Suggest that they identify its strengths and propose possible improvements. Use the model to introduce the concepts in the chapter.

Proper Nouns and Proper Adjectives

Remember that a **proper noun** (Lesson 5.1) names a particular place, person, thing, or idea and that a **proper adjective** (Lesson 5.4) is the adjective form of a proper noun. Both proper nouns and proper adjectives begin with a capital letter.

▶ Capitalize the names of people.

    Marie Curie   Albert Einstein   George Washington Carver

▶ Capitalize geographic names.

PLANETS, CONSTELLATIONS	Earth Mars the constellation Big Dipper
CONTINENTS	North America Asia Australia Antarctica
ISLANDS	Haiti Hawaiian Islands Sicily Manhattan
COUNTRIES	United States Mexico India Israel Italy
STATES	Texas California New York Maine
CITIES	Los Angeles El Paso Detroit
BODIES OF WATER	Caribbean Sea Nile Lake Erie
LOCALITIES, REGIONS	Mount Rainier the Northeast the Far West the South
STREETS, HIGHWAYS	Speedway Overlook Road Fifth Avenue
BUILDINGS	the Eiffel Tower Rockefeller Center
PARKS, MONUMENTS	Lincoln Memorial Grand Canyon

Note: Articles (*the*) and short prepositions (*of*) that are part of the name are *not* capitalized.

▶ Capitalize proper adjectives formed by proper nouns.

    European   Shakespearean   Danish   French   American

EXERCISE 1 Proofreading Sentences

Insert capital letters where they belong in the following sentences. To indicate a capital letter, use the proofreading symbol of three underscores beneath the letter (t̲).

    EXAMPLE   Tornado warnings are in effect throughout the northeast.

1. Look for the bright stars in the belt of the constellation orion.

2. The danube river bisects the city of budapest, hungary.

3. Is madras on india's eastern or western coast?

4. An ocean liner on the st. lawrence seaway passes through many locks.

EDITING TIP

Don't capitalize words such as *north*, *south*, *east*, and *west* when you're talking about compass directions. Capitalize these words only when they refer to regions of a country.

Look toward the **northeast** after sunset.

A blizzard is expected in the **Northeast**—specifically, in Vermont and New Hampshire.

Also, don't capitalize a common noun that refers to a proper noun.

We hiked for a day in the **Rocky Mountains**. Below the frost line, the **mountains** were covered with wildflowers.

5. In 1911, the american explorer hiram bingham discovered machu picchu, a ruined incan city in peru.

6. Through a telescope, you can easily observe saturn's rings.

7. Which city is the capital of new mexico: albuquerque or santa fe?

8. Glacier national park spans both sides of the canadian border.

9. How does a shakespearean sonnet differ from an italian sonnet?

10. Settlers in the south and west supported jacksonian democracy.

 Working Together

EXERCISE 2 Writing a Biography

Work with a partner or small group to write a one-paragraph biography based on the following notes. You do not have to use all of the information. First, capitalize all the words on the note card that should be capitalized. Then write your biography on a separate piece of paper. Proofread it carefully to make sure that you've written complete sentences and that you've capitalized all the words that need capitalizing. Students' paragraphs will vary.

> herman melville [1819-1891]—american novelist & short story writer
>
> born new york city; dutch and english ancestry
>
> father died when melville was 12; quit school at 15; worked at odd jobs
>
> 1839–1844 mostly at sea: first as cabin boy on ship to liverpool, england; then 2 years on whaling ship; spent time in tahiti & other islands in pacific ocean
>
> wrote several novels based on sea experiences
>
> married & bought farm near pittsfield, massachusetts
>
> worked for 19 years as inspector in u.s. customs house in battery park, new york city
>
> died in poverty

EXERCISE 3 Writing Paragraphs

For a geography project, you've been asked to trace your "life route" on a map. Write two or more paragraphs that include all of the following information:

• the city, state, and country where you were born
• cities, states, and countries where you have lived
• where you have traveled and where you would like to travel
• where you would like to live someday

You may wish to have students exchange papers with a partner and check to see that the partner has written complete sentences and correctly capitalized words.

Titles

▐▶ Capitalize titles and abbreviations of titles only when they are used before names. Also capitalize abbreviations of academic degrees after a name.

Senator John Glenn a United States senator
Howard Esquinez, M.D. a family practice doctor

A few important titles are generally capitalized even without a person's name: *the President of the United States, the Prime Minister, the Pope, the Chief Justice of the Supreme Court.*

▐▶ Capitalize a word that shows a family relationship only when it is used before a name or when it is used as a name.

Grandpa Max   Aunt Ada   his stepfather   my aunt
"How does my pie taste, Grandmother?"

▐▶ Capitalize the first and last words and all important words in the titles of works.

Note: Unless they appear as the first word in a title, do not capitalize the following small words: articles (*a, an, the*), coordinating conjunctions, and prepositions with fewer than five letters.

BOOKS	*The Catcher in the Rye*	*Julie of the Wolves*
PERIODICALS	*The Washington Post*	*National Geographic*
STORIES, ESSAYS	"Through the Tunnel"	"On Civil Disobedience"
POEMS	"Stopping by Woods on a Snowy Evening"	
PLAYS	*The Skin of Our Teeth*	*The Tragedy of Romeo and Juliet*
TV SERIES	*I Love Lucy* *Live from the Met*	*Meet the Press*
WORKS OF ART	*Sunflowers* *Madame Cézanne in a Red Dress*	
MUSICAL WORKS	Brahms's First Symphony	"Michelle"
MOVIES	*Beauty and the Beast*	*It's a Wonderful Life*

EXERCISE 4 Proofreading Sentences

Insert capital letters where they belong in the following sentences. To indicate a capital letter, use the proofreading symbol of three underscores beneath the letter (m̲).

1. Delores read aloud Robert Frost's "the death of the hired man."

2. We watched an incredible game on Channel 3's *monday night football* broadcast.

Enriching Your Vocabulary

Credere is a Latin verb with several meanings, including "to have trust in" and "to believe." The prefix *in-* means "not." The combination of these word parts gives us *incredulous*, or "not inclined to believe," and *incredible*, as used in Exercise 4, meaning "hard to believe to be true." The jury was *incredulous* of the defendant's alibi. Similarly, you may find the plot of a movie *incredible*.

EDITING TIP

Remember that forms of *be* are verbs. They require capitals in titles of works.

Do you know the poem "No Man is an Island"?

3. I remember how uncle max piled too much food on everyone's plates.

4. The mayor appointed commissioner estella brown as chairperson.

5. The musical *kiss me, kate* is based on Shakespeare's *the taming of the shrew*.

6. During the seventh-inning stretch, fans sing, "take me out to the ball game."

7. The *nightly business report* analyzes the day's financial news.

8. In the original *star trek* series, James Kirk was captain of the *enterprise*.

9. The pair of skaters from Quebec skated to the theme from *gone with the wind*.

10. One of the Beatles' most popular songs is "yesterday."

EXERCISE 5 Editing and Proofreading a Paragraph

Work with a partner to insert capital letters where they belong in the following paragraph. To indicate a capital letter, use the proofreading symbol of three underscores beneath the letter (p).

> [HINT]
>
> Some sentences do not require any letters to be marked for capitalization.

¹Leslie went to the library to look for sources for her research paper, "the cuban missile crisis." ²First, she checked for articles in the *encyclopedia britannica*. ³She also looked at the "cuba" entry in the *encyclopedia americana*. ⁴Next, she checked the *reader's guide to periodical literature*. ⁵Using a microfilm machine, she took notes from "a new resolve to save the old freedoms" in the November 2, 1962, issue of *life* magazine. ⁶"the lessons learned" in the November 12, 1962, issue of *newsweek* contained several good quotations. ⁷In the library's online catalog, Leslie discovered two promising books. ⁸The first, *thirteen days* by u.s. attorney general robert f. kennedy, provided an eyewitness account of the crisis. ⁹She also took some notes from *force and statecraft* by gordon a. craig and alexander l. george. ¹⁰When she explored the Internet for information, Leslie couldn't tell which sources were biased and which were objective.

EXERCISE 6 Writing About Relatives

On a separate piece of paper, write two paragraphs. Each paragraph should focus on a different relative. You can write about a relative you know or an ancestor who is no longer living. Tell some important facts or a brief story about each relative. Be sure to explain how each person is related to you. When you have finished writing, proofread your paragraphs carefully to make sure you've used capital letters correctly. Students' paragraphs will vary.

First Words, Organizations, Religions, School Subjects

▸ Capitalize the first word in every sentence. Capitalize the first word in a direct quotation when the quotation is a complete sentence. But do not capitalize the first word in an indirect quotation.

DIRECT	Ms. Weil said, "Now we'll play Scott Joplin's 'Maple Leaf Rag.'"
INDIRECT	Ms. Weil said that now the band would play.

If a quoted sentence is interrupted, begin the second part with a lowercase letter.

"Now," said Ms. Weil, "let's play Scott Joplin's music."

Note: When you're quoting lines of poetry, follow the poet's style. Some modern poets, notably the American E. E. Cummings, don't follow the usual rules for using capital letters.

▸ Capitalize the names of languages, nationalities, peoples, races, and religions.

Schools in Bhutan teach English as the official language.
The three Tibetan Buddhist monks are creating a sand painting.

▸ Capitalize the names of groups, teams, businesses, institutions, and organizations.

Save the Children   New York Jets   University of Illinois

▸ Capitalize the names of school subjects that are followed by a number. Capitalize the names of all languages.

Tara is taking Algebra 2, English, world history, and journalism.

Some style books capitalize the terms *Black* and *White* when referring to people's race; some do not. Whichever style students follow, have them use it consistently.

EXERCISE 7 Proofreading Sentences

Insert capital letters where they belong in the following sentences. To indicate a capital letter, use the proofreading symbol of three underscores beneath the letter (w̲̲).

1. do you know who said "all's fair in love and war"?

2. at ohio state university, she majored in english and french.

3. patrick henry said, "it is natural for man to indulge in the illusions of hope."

4. the american league and national league baseball teams that train in florida play each other in the grapefruit league.

5. after graduating from college, amy plans to join the peace corps.

6. christopher columbus introduced the hammock, a native american invention, to europeans.

7. in *the power of myth*, joseph campbell advises, "follow your bliss."

8. for generations, people of croatian descent have been fishing in louisiana oyster beds.

9. the canadian eskimos prefer to be called inuit, which means "the people."

10. valentine's day is the feast day of st. valentine, a catholic saint.

EXERCISE 8 Create Your Own Exercise

On a separate piece of paper, write one or more complete sentences in response to each numbered item. When you've finished writing, exchange your sentences with a partner. Proofread each other's sentences for correct use of capital letters.
See Answer Key at www.grammarforwriting.com.

1. Tell what school subjects you plan to take next year.

2. Tell which sports you like to watch on TV and who your favorite teams are.

3. Define a word or expression that comes from a language other than English, and identify the language.

4. Name three charities that you would donate money to if you could.

5. Name two teams that you follow, and give your opinion of their abilities.

6. Tell something about your ancestry (your grandparents and great-grandparents). If you can, tell where your ancestors were born.

7. Write a sentence in which you quote a speaker or writer. You may quote someone you know (a friend or relative) or someone famous.

8. Take the same quotation that you wrote in question 7, and turn it into an indirect quotation.

9. Write one fact about a religious holiday (how or when it's celebrated), and identify the religion.

10. As part of the United States census every ten years, people are asked to identify their race. Write a sentence telling which categories (or choices) you think should be listed on the census form.

I and *O*; Historical Events, Documents, and Periods; Calendar Items; Brand Names

�▶ Capitalize the words *I* and *O*.

The first-person pronoun *I* is always capitalized. So is the poetic interjection *O*, which is rarely used today. The modern interjection *oh* isn't capitalized unless it's the first word in a sentence.

> One of Walt Whitman's poems about Lincoln is titled "**O** Captain! My Captain!"
> **Oh** dear, this book is overdue and, **oh**, the fine is twenty-five cents.

▶ Capitalize the names of historical events, documents, and periods.

HISTORICAL EVENTS	World War II Battle of Gettysburg D-day
SPECIAL EVENTS	Superbowl Sunday Mardi Gras
DOCUMENTS	Bill of Rights Emancipation Proclamation
PERIODS	the Middle Ages the Mesozoic Era the Renaissance

▶ Capitalize calendar items but not seasons.

CALENDAR ITEMS	Chinese New Year St. Patrick's Day Tuesday, October 6
SEASONS	spring semester autumn leaves a mild winter

When you refer to a century, however, do not use capital letters.

> twenty-first century architecture   music of the sixteenth century

▶ Capitalize brand names for manufactured products.

> Netscape Navigator   Ford Taurus

But do *not* capitalize the common noun that follows a brand name.

> a bar of Ultra-clean soap   a tube of Sparkle toothpaste

EXERCISE 9   PROOFREADING A PARAGRAPH

Insert capital letters where they belong in the following sentences. To indicate a capital letter, use the proofreading symbol of three underscores beneath the letter (f).

¹Mara has to write a research paper about some aspect of the french revolution. ²She's trying to limit her topic by exploring the Internet, using microsoft internet explorer. ³When she searched for the french revolution, she found thousands of articles. ⁴To narrow her search, she

added other key words: declaration of the rights of man and citizen, committee of public safety, and the revolutionary tribunal. ⁵she checked *encarta*, a CD-ROM encyclopedia, for information about the reign of terror, the name given to the period when thousands were guillotined. ⁶Exploring further, she discovered that bastille day on july 14 marks the beginning of the french revolution. ⁷She considered writing about the influence of the american revolution but decided that was too complicated. ⁸Somewhere in her paper, she wants to use this quotation by the frenchman Alexis de Tocqueville: "Never was any such event . . . so inevitable yet so completely unforeseen." ⁹Mara is writing her first draft on a dell computer, and she is using a hewlett packard printer. ¹⁰She's using microsoft word 2003 as her word-processing program and copying her draft on a xerox copier.

EXERCISE 10 Writing a Paragraph

Work with a partner to write one or more paragraphs on a separate piece of paper. Itemize the food you'd buy to feed ten of your friends at a birthday party. Mention the brand names of products. Be sure to write in complete sentences. Proofread your paragraphs for complete sentences and for the use of capital letters. Compare the foods you've chosen with the foods chosen by your classmates. Students' paragraphs will vary.

EXERCISE 11 Proofreading Sentences

Proofread the following sentences for the correct use of capital letters. Use these proofreading symbols: a slash (to indicate lowercase) and three underscores (to indicate a capital). In sentence 3, lowercase *fourth* is also acceptable.

Winter = lowercase letter   kraft cheese = capital letter

1. Lara bought a dozen Eggs and a package of Sabrett Hot Dogs.

2. Tony wrote, "i always buy a lot of fresh fruit in the Summer."

3. Every fourth of july, the supermarket runs out of hot dog buns.

4. Kevin buys Water and Juices instead of pepsi or other soft drinks.

5. For memorial day, Julio bought chicken to barbecue.

Editing and Proofreading Worksheet 1

Edit the draft for errors in spelling, capitalization, punctuation, and usage. Write your edited version on a separate piece of paper. Compare your changes with those of a writing partner.

¹william carlos williams, m.d., was a rare combination—a poet and a member of the american medical association. ²he was born in 1882 in rutherford, new jersey. ³williams was an ~~averege~~ average student at the horace mann school in new york city. ⁴he graduated from the university of pennsylvania in philadelphia. ⁵after graduating from college, he enrolled in a school of dentistry but later switched to a medical school.

⁶at nineteen, williams met fellow college freshman ezra pound, who would become an important poet. ⁷when he was a medical intern in 1909, williams ~~payed~~ paid to publish his first book of poems. ⁸ezra pound criticized williams's poems for their old-fashioned rhythm. ⁹williams never reprinted them; he called them "artificial."

¹⁰young dr. williams married florence (flossie) herman in 1912 after flossie's sister turned him down. ¹¹the couple settled in rutherford, where williams had his home and office at 9 ridge road for forty years. ¹²he delivered babies, tended the sick, and wrote poems about everyday things and people.

¹³in *the autobiography of le roi jones*, the african american poet, amiri baraka, praised williams's natural rhythms: "he knew american life had outdistanced the english rhythms and their formal meters. . . ." ¹⁴baraka went on to praise williams's use of "the language of this multinational land."

¹⁵two of williams's most famous poems are "the red wheelbarrow" and "spring and all." ¹⁶*paterson* (1945), his book about a small new jersey city, includes not only history but also poems, documents, newspaper clippings, and letters.

Editing and Proofreading Worksheet 2

Edit the draft for errors in spelling, capitalization, punctuation, and usage. Write your edited version on a separate piece of paper. Compare your changes with those of a writing partner. **Hint:** All the place names in this exercise are spelled correctly.

[1]during world war II, german nazi troops invaded many european nations, including austria, czechoslovakia, poland, denmark, holland, luxembourg, and france. [2]in may 1940, retreating british, belgian, and french soldiers huddled on the beach at dunkirk, a small french seaport on the english channel. [3]they were waiting to be evacuated. [4]german troops surrounded dunkirk; german planes bombed the city and the soldiers.

[5]from may 16 to june 14, more than 850 ships came to the soldiers' rescue. [6]some were british navy ships, but most were small boats. [7]british civilians sailed across the english channel to dunkirk, a vast armada of barges, ferries, fishing boats, tugboats, lifeboats, rowboats, yachts, and motorboats. [8]Even a thames river sightseeing boat made the trip. [9]ordinary british citizens who owned these small vessels risked their ~~lifes~~ lives. [10]some were killed when german planes sank their boats. [11]the rescuers brought more than 338,000 allied soldiers safely back to england. [12]"operation dynamo," as the rescue mission was called, ended on june 14, when the germans captured dunkirk and the remaining soldiers.

[13]in a speech to the british parliament, which is like the united states congress, prime minister winston churchill said that the evacuation of dunkirk must not be thought a victory. [14]"wars are not won by evacuations," churchill said. [15]he vowed, however, that britain would continue fighting germans ~~everywheres~~ everywhere and would never surrender.

Motivated students may wish to learn more about Operation Dynamo by reading *Dunkirk: The Complete Story of the First Step in the Defeat of Hitler* by Norman Gelb. It was published in 1989 by Morrow Publishing Company in New York City.

Chapter Review

EXERCISE A Proofreading Sentences

Insert capital letters where they belong in the following sentences. To
indicate a capital letter, use the proofreading symbol of three underscores
beneath the letter (b).

1. which of these great lakes is larger—lake erie or lake superior?
2. Like many other state capitols (the building in which state legislatures meet),
   the state house in boston, massachusetts, has a gold dome.
3. mount vernon, george washington's home, is on the potomac river in virginia.
4. niagara falls has two parts: the american horseshoe falls and the canadian falls.
5. if you fly over mount whitney, you are above the highest peak of the sierra
   madres in northern california.
6. the shoshones, a native american people, live mostly in idaho, nevada, utah,
   wyoming, and california.
7. during the precambrian era, what's now the state of florida was underwater.
8. the sears tower in chicago was once the world's tallest building.
9. which four united states presidents have their faces carved on
   mt. rushmore national memorial in the black hills of south dakota?
10. the mississippi river flows from northern minnesota to the gulf of mexico.

EXERCISE B Proofreading a Paragraph

Proofread the following sentences for the correct use of capital letters. Use the
proofreading symbol of three underscores to indicate a capital (s).

¹the scottish novelist and poet robert louis stevenson created a fictional island.
²he named it treasure island. ³in stevenson's novel, it is a small island off the coast
of mexico. ⁴on the island are three hills: foremast hill, mizzenmast hill, and spyglass
hill. ⁵a pirate, captain flint, buries his treasure on the island. ⁶bill bones, his first
mate, draws a map to show where it's buried. ⁷years later, someone discovers the
treasure map at the admiral benbow inn in black hill cove in western england. ⁸jim
hawkins (the narrator), squire trelawney, and dr. livesey set sail on the *hispaniola* to
find the island and the buried treasure. ⁹aboard ship are one of captain flint's crew
members—long john silver—and some other old pirates. ¹⁰to find out what
happens, read stevenson's classic novel, *treasure island*.

EXERCISE C Proofreading Paragraphs

Insert capital letters where they belong in the following sentences. To indicate a capital letter, use the proofreading symbol (h).

¹during world war II, carl gorman was one of four hundred navajo code talkers in the united states marines. ²gorman was born on the navajo reservation in chinle, arizona. ³like many native americans, he'd been forced to attend a government boarding school as a boy. ⁴there, he was forbidden—even punished—for speaking his native language. ⁵when the united states entered world war II, gorman was thirty-four. ⁶he was too old to serve in the military. ⁷in 1942, the marines were recruiting native americans who could speak both english and navajo fluently. ⁸the navajo language has no alphabet and is extremely complex. ⁹military experts had determined that only about thirty people in the world besides the fifty thousand or so navajos knew how to speak the language. ¹⁰mr. gorman lied about his age to enlist in the marines. ¹¹he became the oldest of the navajo code talkers. ¹²since the language has no words for modern weapons, the navajos used native words to stand for weapons. ¹³a bomber was *jay-sho*, or "buzzard," for example, and a fighter plane was *da-he-tih-hi*, or "hummingbird."

¹⁴throughout the war, the code talkers served on the front lines. ¹⁵when the Marines invaded guadalcanal in august 1942, gorman and other navajo volunteers relayed orders and reported troop movements by radio. ¹⁶the japanese code breakers could never figure out what the guttural sounds of the navajo language meant. ¹⁷on iwo jima, saipan, taiwan, and other islands in the pacific ocean, the navajo marines used the only american military code that was never broken.

Accept the word *marines* as either capitalized or lowercase. It appears throughout the exercise.

Spelling

STUDENT WRITING
Persuasive Essay

Computer Course Should Be Optional
by Leslie Miller
high school student, Pottsville, Pennsylvania

Although some students could benefit from taking computer courses in school, these classes should remain electives and not become requirements for receiving a high school diploma.

One main reason for this is that not all students have the need for a basic computer course. Unlike the material in the English, math, and science departments, many students already know many of the concepts that would be taught in one of these computer classes. This would make such classes boring and pointless for these students. Such a situation may lead to an undesirable scenario, one in which students who really do need the basic knowledge find themselves being disturbed and distracted by their peers.

Also, the fact that some students have prior knowledge of computers may force the teacher to accelerate the pace of the class. This also may lead to certain students not receiving all the training they need to use the computer.

Another negative effect of basic computer courses becoming mandatory for graduation is the time they would take up in the schedule of the student who wants to take more academic courses. Many courses, especially AP and advanced courses, are only offered during certain periods of the day. If a student were forced to choose between a computer course and an academic course, [he or she] would obviously have to choose the computer class, because it would be a required course. This would mean that the student would miss out on other challenging academic work merely to take a basic computer course.

Finally, requiring computer courses would force out some of the other programs and classes which use computer labs. In order to get all the students in who need the basic class, certain classes might have to be canceled or reduced to only one period a day. This would limit opportunities for students who want to take advanced computer classes, computer art classes, and other courses in which computers are needed on a daily basis. . . .

Some may say that classes must be mandatory to advance students in this world where technology is rapidly progressing. However, students have already proven that they can and will learn this technology without school courses. Most youths can grasp the concept quickly and can easily operate these machines. Therefore, requiring computer classes would simply waste students' precious class time.

The persuasive essay above is clearly organized. The first paragraph states the writer's opinion; then each following paragraph states a reason that supports the opinion. Transition words (*one*, *also*, *another*, and *finally*) lead a reader through the argument. The writer ends the essay with a restatement of her position.

Part of the power of this or any essay is the accuracy of the spelling. As you do the exercises in this chapter, use the spelling rules to make your own writing powerful.

Using a Dictionary

You may never compete in a spelling bee, but in school and in the world of work, spelling counts! One way to improve your spelling is to read a lot; another way is to refer to a dictionary often.

⫸ If you're in doubt about how to spell a word, use a dictionary.

Besides showing each entry word's definition and etymology (word history), a dictionary gives many kinds of spelling help:

Entry word — Irregular noun plural

deer \'dir *n, pl* **deer** *also* **deers**

Irregular comparative and superlative forms

ill \'il \ *adj* **worse**; **worst**

Syllable breaks in entry word — Part of speech

me·thod·i·cal \mə-'thä-di-kəl \ *also* **me·thod·ic** *adj* (1570)
1 : arranged, characterized by, or performed with method or order <a~treatment of the subject> **2** : habitually proceeding according to method : SYSTEMATIC <~in his daily routine> —
Related words
me·thod·i·cal·ly *adv* — **me·thod·i·cal·ness** *n.*

Pronunciation — Alternate plural form

Past, past participle with alternative past participle, and present participle

mil·len·ni·um \mə-'le-nē-əm \ *n., pl* **-nia** *or* **-niums**

prove \'prüv \ *vb* **proved; proved** *or* **prov·en; prov·ing**

—from *Merriam Webster's Collegiate Dictionary*, Eleventh Edition

In doing the following exercises, use a college dictionary to find or check your answers.

P.S. You may not be sure of the spelling of a word, but you probably have a good idea. Look in the dictionary for what you think the spelling of the word is. If the word isn't there, try looking up other possible ways of spelling it. Ask yourself, "What other letter or letters make the sound I'm looking for?" If you can't find a word after several tries, ask someone for help.

EXERCISE 1 Using a Dictionary to Check Spelling

Write the letter of the correct spelling in the blank. If you're not sure of the correct spelling of a word, look up the item in a dictionary.

_____c_____ 1. (a) simillar   (b) similer   (c) similar   (d) simmilar

_____c_____ 2. (a) unecessary   (b) unnecesary
                 (c) unnecessary   (d) unecesary

_____c_____ 3. (a) accidently   (b) acidentally
                 (c) accidentally   (d) accidentaly

_____d_____ 4. (a) embarass   (b) embarras   (c) embaras   (d) embarrass

_____c_____ 5. (a) believible   (b) beleivable   (c) believable   (d) believeable

_____a_____ 6. (a) disappearance   (b) disappearence
                 (c) dissapearance   (d) disapearance

_____a or b_____ 7. (a) judgement   (b) judgment   (c) judgemint   (d) judgmint

_____a_____ 8. (a) preferred   (b) prefered   (c) prefferred   (d) preffered

_____b_____ 9. (a) responsability   (b) responsibility
                 (c) responsiblety   (d) responsabilty

_____a_____ 10. (a) accommodate   (b) acommodate   (c) accomodate   (d) acomodate

EXERCISE 2   Using a Dictionary

Answer the following questions on a separate piece of paper. If you're not sure about how to spell your answer, look the word up in a college dictionary.

1. What is the plural of *datum*?   data

2. Assume that you have to hyphenate the word *sufficient* at the end of a line. Show all the points where you could place a hyphen.   suf- or suffi-

3. How do you spell the plural of *sheep*?   sheep

4. How do you spell the two-bladed tool that you use to cut paper or cloth?   scissors

5. How do you spell the word that describes two lines that never meet?   parallel

6. If you are measuring a room to buy a new carpet or rug, what are the two dimensions you need to measure?   length and width

7. How do you spell the past tense and past participle of the verb *pay*?   paid

8. When a word has alternate spellings, the one listed first in a dictionary is the preferred form. Write the spelling that is preferred in the United States.

     a. catalog *or* catalogue   d. theatre *or* theater
     b. traveler *or* traveller   e. cooperate *or* co-operate
     c. indexes *or* indices   f. grey *or* gray

9. If you have three brothers and they're all married, what do you call their wives when you refer to them as a group?   sisters-in-law

10. How do you spell the long, thin pasta that is not linguine and is often served with tomato sauce and meatballs?   spaghetti

Spelling Rules

English spelling is so irregular that it's useful to learn the few rules you can depend on—even though these rules have exceptions.

▶ Write *i* before *e* except after *c*.

Note that most of these words have a long *e* sound.

FOLLOW RULE	achieve	believe	chief
	niece	piece	
AFTER C:	ceiling	conceit	deceive
	receive	receipt	
EXCEPTIONS:	either	neither	leisure
	seize	weird	

▶ Write *ei* when these letters are not pronounced with a long *e*, especially when the sound is a long *a* as in *neighbor* and *weigh*.

	height	their	foreign	forfeit
SOUNDS LIKE *AY*:	eight	freight	neighbor	reign
	sleigh	veil	weigh	

▶ Watch out for words with more than one syllable that end with the sound *seed*. Only one word is spelled with *-sede*. Three words end in *-ceed*. All other words end in *-cede*.

-SEDE	supersede				
-CEED	exceed	proceed	succeed		
-CEDE	concede	intercede	precede	recede	secede

EXERCISE 3 Remembering Spelling Rules

Work with a partner or small group to complete each item below. Then compare your answers with those of others in your class.
See Answer Key at www.grammarforwriting.com.

1. Write a mnemonic device (see the Writing Hint) to help you remember the three words that end in *-ceed*.

2. Write all of the one-syllable words that end with *-eed*. How many can you think of? Check your list with a partner or small group.

3. Write a definition for each of the words that ends with *-cede*: *concede, intercede, precede, recede, secede*. Then use each word in a sentence.

Enriching Your Vocabulary

The Latin verb *intercedere* comes from *inter*, or "between," and *cedere*, or "to move or go." It is the source of the English verb *intercede*. Have you ever tried to *intercede* in an argument between friends?

WRITING HINT

A good way to remember something is to make up a mnemonic, or memory, device. Here's a nonsense sentence to help you remember the exceptions to the *i*-before-*e* rule:

"**Either weird** sister can **seize** a lizard at **leisure**, but **neither** ever tries."

EXERCISE 4 Proofreading a Newspaper Column

The newspaper that published the following letter needs a better proofreader. Find and correct all of the spelling mistakes in the two letters below. **Hint:** You should find 23 errors.

Dear Doctor Diet:

conceit   niece
¹Is it ~~conciet~~ that motivates my ~~neice~~, who's always on a diet? ²Can she

believe
really ~~beleive~~ that if she wears a size eight dress, she's too fat?

Worried in Wisconsin

Dear Worried in Wisconsin:

                                         their weight
³Many teenagers are unduly concerned with ~~thier~~ ~~wieght~~, but others who

chief   weigh
aren't concerned should be. ⁴The ~~cheif~~ worry for dieters is that they ~~wiegh~~ too

their height
much for ~~thier~~ ~~hieght~~, and often they do. ⁵Unfortunately, many dieters

deceive   achieve
~~decieve~~ themselves by thinking they can ~~acheive~~ popularity, happiness, and

success if they look like the models on TV and in magazine ads.

weight   neither
⁶The key to a healthy body ~~wieght~~ is ~~niether~~ dieting nor diet aids. ⁷I've been

pieces   patients   succeed
giving these same two ~~peices~~ of advice to my ~~pateints~~ for years. ⁸To ~~succede~~ in

reaching your ideal weight, eat a diet that is long on fruits, vegetables, and

grains and short on fats; and equally important, get out and exercise during

leisure   Weird
your ~~liesure~~ time. ⁹~~Wierd~~ crash diets—including the currently popular high-

protein   weight
~~protien~~ diet—play havoc with the body, and often the ~~wieght~~ loss is only

niece   seize
temporary. ¹⁰So tell your ~~neice~~ to put down that piece of cake or pie, ~~sieze~~ her

friend
sneakers, and go for a walk or bicycle ride or play tennis with a ~~freind~~.

Doctor Diet

Prefixes and Suffixes

Prefixes and suffixes are groups of letters that change a word's meaning. A **prefix** (such as *dis-*, *il-*, *mis-*, and *un-*) is added to the beginning of a word; a **suffix** (such as *-er*, *-ly*, *-ment*, and *-ness*) is added to the end.

▷ Adding a prefix does not change the spelling of the original word.
disappear   illegible   mistrust   unusual

▷ If a word ends in *-y* preceded by a consonant, change the *-y* to *i* before adding a suffix.

| | pettiness | carrier | happiness | loneliest | tried |
| EXCEPTIONS: | dryness | trying | flying |

▷ If a word ends in *-y* preceded by a vowel, keep the *-y*.

| | joyous | **buoyant** | employer | stayed |
| EXCEPTIONS: | laid | said |

▷ Adding the suffix *-ly* or *-ness* does not change the spelling of the original word.

carefully   lateness   really   stillness

If a word ends in two *-l*'s, drop one of the *l*'s before adding *-ly*:
dull + ly = dully.

▷ Drop a word's final silent *-e* before adding a suffix that begins with a vowel. **Note:** American dictionaries give *likable*, *lovable*, *movable*, and *sizable* as preferred spellings but do also include *likeable*, *loveable*, *moveable*, and *sizeable*.
creative   likable   loving   provider   mistaken   Students should be consistent in whichever spelling they choose.

▷ Keep the final silent *-e* if the word ends in *-ge* or *-ce* and the suffix begins with *a* or *o*.
changeable   courageous   noticeable   outrageous

▷ Keep the final silent *-e* before adding a suffix that begins with a consonant. **Note:** American dictionaries give *judgment* as the preferred spelling but also include *judgement*.

| | amazement | boredom | hopeful | placement | statehood |
| EXCEPTIONS: | argument | ninth | truly | wisdom |

▷ Double the final consonant in some one-syllable words when the suffix begins with a vowel. Doubling occurs when the word ends in a consonant preceded by a single vowel.
hopping   planning   redder   shopping   sitter   winner

▷ Double the final consonant in some words of more than one syllable. Doubling occurs if the word ends in a single consonant

Some Prefixes and Their Meanings

Prefix	Meaning
circum-	around
dis-, un-	the opposite
il-, im-, in-, ir-	not
post-	after
pre-	before
re-	again
sub-	below
super-	above, beyond

Some Suffixes and Their Meanings

Suffix	Meaning
-able	capable of being
-ate, -en, -fy	become, make
-dom, -hood	state of being
-er, -or	a person who
-less	without
-ment	state or condition of
-ous, -ful	full of

Enriching Your Vocabulary

The adjective *buoyant* is derived from the Spanish verb *boyar* ("to float"). In addition to its literal meanings of "floating" or "capable of keeping something afloat," *buoyant* may be used in the figurative sense of "cheerful" or "light." The *buoyant* snorklers bobbed in the waters of the bay. The party guests were in a *buoyant* mood.

preceded by a single vowel *and* the new word is accented on the second syllable.

controller   occurrence   referral   submitted

Do *not* double the final consonant when the new word is not accented on the second syllable: *preference, reference.*

P.S. You don't have to memorize all of these rules and their exceptions. When in doubt about how to spell a word, check your dictionary.

Exercise 5   Adding Prefixes and Suffixes

Write the word that results when the following prefixes or suffixes are added.

1. occur + -ing	occurring		11. encourage + -ment	encouragement
2. pay + -able	payable		12. careful + -ly	carefully
3. il- + legal	illegal		13. submit + -ed	submitted
4. im- + mobile	immobile		14. luxury + -ant	luxuriant
5. note + -able	notable		15. full + -ly	fully
6. occasion + -al	occasional		16. dis- + appear	disappear
7. argue + -ment	argument		17. un- + necessary	unnecessary
8. sincere + -ity	sincerity		18. nine + -ty	ninety
9. pre- + caution	precaution		19. ir- + responsible	irresponsible
10. mean + -ness	meanness		20. love + -able	lovable

Working Together

Exercise 6   Create Your Own Exercise

Write ten sentences in which you use at least ten words that contain prefixes or suffixes or both. Spell some of these words incorrectly. Then exchange papers with a classmate. Proofread each other's sentences to find and correct all of the spelling errors. Students' sentences will vary.

Exercise 7   Writing New Words

Hold a contest. In ten minutes, write as many words as you can that contain one of the prefixes or suffixes (or both) that are listed in the side column on page 277. Get together with a small group to compare your lists. See if you can define all of the words you've listed. **Hint:** Look up the prefix or suffix in a college dictionary for help. Students' answers will vary. Give full credit if they write 10 new words.

Noun Plurals

For any noun, start with the singular form, and follow the directions below to form the plural.

Making Nouns Plural		
KINDS OF NOUNS	**WHAT TO DO**	**EXAMPLES**
Most nouns	Add -s to the singular.	computers, towers, landslides
Nouns that end in -s, -x, -z, -ch, -sh	Add -es to the singular.	buses, kisses, foxes, waltzes, inches, dishes
Family names	Follow the two preceding rules.	the Washingtons, the Foxes, the Churches, the Horowitzes
Nouns that end in -y preceded by a consonant	Change the -y to i, and add -es.	babies, worries, ladies, flurries
Nouns that end in -y preceded by a vowel	Add -s.	monkeys, turkeys, toys, boys, valleys
Most nouns that end in -f	Add -s.	chiefs, roofs, beliefs, proofs, tariffs
A few nouns that end in -f or -fe	Change the -f to v and add -s or -es.	thieves, shelves, leaves, lives, wives
Nouns ending in -o preceded by a vowel	Add -s.	radios, zoos, patios
Most nouns ending in -o preceded by a consonant	Add -es.	heroes, tomatoes, potatoes, tornadoes
Most musical terms ending in -o	Add -s.	sopranos, altos, solos, cellos, pianos
Compound nouns	Make the most important word plural.	attorneys general, **men**-of-war, passersby, sisters-in-law
Letters, numbers, and words referred to as words	Use an apostrophe ' + -s.	A's, 3's, no if's, and's, or but's
Irregular plurals, foreign plurals, and words that stay the same for both singular and plural	No rules apply! Memorize these forms.	children, mice, women, men, feet, teeth, geese, series, oxen, data, alumni, sheep, deer, species

EDITING TIP

Even if you're writing on a computer, you still need to proofread your papers carefully because a spell check program won't catch *every error*. For instance, it won't point out that you've written *there* when you should have written *their*, and it won't catch proper nouns that are misspelled.

Exceptions:
A few nouns have two acceptable forms:
hoo**fs** or hoo**ves**,
scar**fs** or scar**ves**,
dwar**fs** or dwar**ves**.

Exceptions:
memos, silos
A few nouns have two acceptable forms:
volcano**s** or volcano**es**,
mosquito**s** or mosquito**es**,
flamingo**s** or flamingo**es**.

EXERCISE 8 Forming Noun Plurals

Write the plural form of each noun. If you're unsure of the correct form, check a dictionary to see if it lists irregular plurals or alternate plural forms. If no plural form is listed, follow the rules in the chart on page 279.

1. video _____videos_____
2. child _____children_____
3. rodeo _____rodeos_____
4. Willis _____Willises_____
5. great-grandmother _____great-grandmothers_____
6. finch _____finches_____
7. half _____halves_____
8. studio _____studios_____
9. strawberry _____strawberries_____
10. ox _____oxen_____
11. brother-in-law _____brothers-in-law_____
12. Gutierrez _____Gutierrezes_____
13. woman _____women_____
14. waltz _____waltzes_____
15. adviser _____advisers_____
16. ditch _____ditches_____
17. cargo _____cargoes or cargos_____
18. soccer ball _____soccer balls_____
19. referee _____referees_____
20. tape recorder _____tape recorders_____
21. volcano _____volcanoes or volcanos_____
22. kilometer _____kilometers_____
23. Chefitz _____Chefitzes_____
24. secretary of state _____secretaries of state_____
25. square foot _____square feet_____

EXERCISE 9 Writing with Noun Plurals

You have just won an essay contest. The first prize is a ten-minute spending spree in the store of your choice. There's no dollar limit. You can buy as many items as you can gather up during the ten minutes, but there's only one catch: You have to buy two of every item you choose.

Write several paragraphs in which you give the following information:

1. what kind of store you'll shop in

2. what you'll put into your shopping cart

3. what you'll go for first, second, and third

Remember to choose two of every item. When you've finished writing, check to see that all noun plurals are spelled correctly. Students' paragraphs will vary. Make sure that they've spelled noun plural forms correctly.

Editing and Proofreading Worksheet 1

Correct all of the spelling and punctuation errors that you find in the following e-mail. Follow the form and punctuation for a friendly letter shown on page 232, and add today's date and your full name as the signature. Write your edited e-mail on a separate piece of paper. Revisions will vary. A sample revision is given. Students should correct all spelling and punctuation errors.

Dear Mrs. Eliot:

[1]I would like to ~~recieve~~ receive some information about the ~~posibility~~ possibility of a summer job in your company. [2]I am ~~hopeing~~ hoping to apply for one of your internship positions. [3]I read about your company in ~~todays~~ today's newspaper and about ~~it's~~ its special summer program for students interested in science. I understand that you are the person who is in charge of ~~hireing student's~~ hiring students to work during ~~there~~ their summer vacations.

[4]Can you tell me when the summer internship begins. ~~And~~ please and when it will end? [6]I ~~beleive~~ believe I'm ~~exceptionaly good~~ exceptionally well qualified to work in your office. [7]I have had a year of ~~typeing, my~~ keyboarding. My teacher says my handwriting is ~~legable~~ legible and my ~~typing~~ keyboarding skills are excellent.

[8]I have had a lot of ~~expereince~~ experience working with photocopying and fax machines. ~~Computers~~ computers, and ~~electrics typewriter~~ electric typewriters. [10]I ~~designd~~ designed a new ~~fileing~~ filing system for the student council this year. [11]I can give you several ~~recomendations~~ recommendations. [12]I am confident I have the skills ~~your~~ you're seeking in a summer intern.

[13]Are ~~their applicationes~~ there applications I should complete? [14]Please write or call. ~~you~~ You can reach me at home during the day or evening at 954-555-9706. [15]Thank you for considering me for a summer internship, and I look forward to hearing from you soon.

Yours ~~sincerly,~~ sincerely,

Add typed name.

Editing and Proofreading Worksheet 2

Edit the draft for errors in spelling, capitalization, punctuation, and usage. Write your edited version on a separate piece of paper. Compare your changes with those of a writing partner. **Hint:** You should find 28 spelling errors.

¹Beatrix Potter is famous for ~~writeing~~ *writing* and illustrating books for ~~childs~~ *children*. ²Growing up in one of London's wealthy families, ³Beatrix had no ~~freinds~~ *friends* and did not go to school. ⁴A governess taught her lessons in a schoolroom at home. ⁵Her younger brother, Bertram, ~~he~~ was the only child she ever saw. ⁶Beatrix and Bertram amused ~~themselfs~~ *themselves*. ⁷They kept pets and ~~carefuly~~ *carefully* observed and drew them.

⁸The ~~Potteres~~ *Potters* spent their summers *in the country* outside of London. ⁹First they went to Scotland *and* later to the ~~beautyful~~ *beautiful* Lake District in northern England. ¹⁰By the time she was twelve, ¹¹Beatrix was ~~recieving~~ *receiving* private drawing lessons. ¹²She made ~~sketchs~~ *sketches* of ~~foxs~~ *foxes*, rabbits, ~~mouses~~ *mice*, ~~cockroachs~~ *cockroaches*, and other ~~animales~~ *animals*. ¹³~~She~~ was ~~happyest~~ *happiest* when she was drawing.

¹⁴As she grew older, ¹⁵~~She~~ *she* pursued her interests in art, geology, botany, and archaeology. ¹⁶She was in her ~~twentys~~ *twenties* when she sold her first drawings to a publisher. ¹⁷That was her first ~~sucess~~ *success*. ¹⁸~~Unusual~~ for ~~womans~~ *women* in wealthy English ~~familys~~ *families*. ¹⁹She ~~supplyed~~ *supplied* additional drawings, *which* ²⁰~~Which~~ the company published as ~~greating~~ *greeting* cards and book ~~ilustrations~~ *illustrations*.

²¹In 1893, Beatrix wrote to the five-year-old son of her former governess. ²²Her letter began, "My dear Noel, I don't know what to ~~right~~ *write* to you, so I shall tell you a story about four little rabbits whose names were Flopsy, Mopsy, Cottontail, and Peter." ²³The letter contained drawings, ~~two~~ *too*. ²⁴Five years later, Beatrix borrowed the letter from young Noel. ²⁵From the letter's story, she wrote and ~~ilustrated~~ *illustrated* her ~~extremly~~ *extremely* ~~successfull~~ *successful* first book, *The Tale of Peter Rabbit*. ²⁶If you ~~havent~~ *haven't* met Peter Rabbit yet, try reading aloud his story (or a different one from Potter's ~~serieses~~ *series* of little books) to a young child.

Chapter Review

EXERCISE A Spelling with Prefixes and Suffixes

On a separate piece of paper, create fifteen new words from the following prefixes, words, and suffixes. See Answer Key at www.grammarforwriting.com.

PREFIXES		WORDS		SUFFIXES	
dis-	re-	imagine	appear	-ment	-ing
un-	mis-	form	like	-ed	-ance
pre-	in-	amaze	excite	-able	-ation

EXERCISE B Spelling Noun Plurals

In the space provided, write the plural form of each of the nouns listed below.

1. memory _____ memories _____
2. leaf _____ leaves _____
3. belief _____ beliefs _____
4. series _____ series _____
5. species _____ species _____

6. silo _____ silos _____
7. monkey _____ monkeys _____
8. cliff _____ cliffs _____
9. hero _____ heroes _____
10. tomato _____ tomatoes _____

EXERCISE C Choosing the Correct Spelling

Look carefully at each choice, and then choose the correct spelling of each word. Write the letter of the correct spelling in the blank.

___a___ 1. (a) grammar   (b) grammer   (c) gramar   (d) gramer

___c___ 2. (a) privelege   (b) privalege   (c) privilege   (d) privalige

___c___ 3. (a) prefered   (b) preffered   (c) preferred   (d) prefferred

___b___ 4. (a) receed   (b) recede   (c) riseed   (d) resede

___a___ 5. (a) recommendation   (b) reccommendation
            (c) reccomendation   (d) recomendation

___c___ 6. (a) dissapearance   (b) disapearance
            (c) disappearance   (d) disappearence

___b___ 7. (a) temperment   (b) temperament
            (c) tempermant   (d) tempermint

___c___ 8. (a) liesure   (b) leizure   (c) leisure   (d) liezure

___a___ 9. (a) separate   (b) seperate   (c) seperit   (d) separrate

___d___ 10. (a) imediately   (b) imediatly
             (c) immeditely   (d) immediately

EXERCISE D Proofreading Paragraphs

Proofread the following paragraphs to correct all spelling errors. **Hint:** The word *résumé* is spelled correctly. You should find 25 spelling errors.

¹When you're looking for or applying for a job, one of the things you'll need is a résumé. ²A résumé lists information about you and about your work history. ³Here is the kind of information you should include: your name, ~~adress~~ [address], and ~~telefone~~ [telephone] number; your education; your work history, including the ~~companys~~ [companies] or persons you've worked for. ⁴You should also include two references. ⁵These are names and phone numbers of people who know you ~~personaly~~ [personally] and can ~~recomend~~ [recommend] you.

⁶It used to be that résumés were ~~allways~~ [always] on ~~peices~~ [pieces] of paper that you would mail to a company or take in person to a job ~~interveiw~~ [interview]. ⁷Some résumés still are paper ones, but more and more of them are electronic. ⁸The Internet is used increasingly by employers to ~~advertize~~ [advertise] jobs. ⁹Job seekers e-mail ~~there~~ [their] résumés to companies.

¹⁰More than half of the ~~bigest~~ [biggest] companies in the United States use computers to scan the ~~thousends~~ [thousands] of résumés they ~~recieve~~ [receive]. ¹¹The computers search for keywords to find job hunters who have the ~~experiance~~ [experience] and education the company is looking for. ¹²Also, there are employment ~~agencys~~ [agencies] that ~~specialise~~ [specialize] in finding jobs for clients by ~~useing~~ [using] the Internet.

¹³~~Heres~~ [Here's] some advice from these employment agencies. ¹⁴Use light-colored paper; avoid graphics. ¹⁵Spell every word ~~corectly~~ [correctly]. ¹⁶Describe your ~~personel~~ [personal] characteristics, such as "good memory," "high energy," or "~~responsable~~ [responsible] and dedicated." ¹⁷List the specific skills that will make you a good ~~candadate~~ [candidate] for the job. ¹⁸~~Eventualy~~ [Eventually], if you are chosen for an interview, a real person—a ~~hireing~~ [hiring] manager—will talk to you in person. ¹⁹An ~~efective~~ [effective] résumé can help you get that interview.

Cumulative Review

EXERCISE A Punctuation Marks

Add end marks and commas where they belong in the following paragraphs, and correct any spelling errors. Use the proofreading symbols shown below.

capital ≡	question mark ?	comma ⌄	semicolon ⨀
period ⊙	exclamation point !	colon ⊙	apostrophe ⌄
quotation marks ⌄ ⌄		italics <u>tête-á-tête</u>	

¹Every year at the Santo Domingo Pueblo near Santa Fe, New Mexico, the Pueblo Indians celebrate an ancient ritual. ²The Corn Dance lasts a ~~hole~~ whole day. ³About a thousand dancers chant, pray, and dance to complex drum rhythms. ⁴The Corn Dance is an ancient, sacred ceremony during which the Pueblo Indians pray for rain and a good harvest. ⁵At least one adult from each family participates in the dance, and ~~childs~~ children are taught the dance steps in school. ⁶Some dancers wear ~~strikeing~~ striking costumes. ⁷A few men are covered with white body paint and have corn husks standing on top of ~~there~~ their heads. ⁸These dancers, who represent dead spirits, weave in and out of the other dancers. ⁹The others ignore the spirit dancers, for ~~theyre~~ they're supposed to be invisible. ¹⁰Each dancer wears shell jewelry and holds or wears an evergreen bough, which symbolizes rebirth. ¹¹Young ~~womans~~ women wear flat blue wooden headdresses that symbolize the mesas and the rain-giving clouds.

EXERCISE B Capitalization

Add capital letters where they are needed in the following expressions. To indicate a capital letter, use the proofreading symbol of three underscores beneath the letter (f̲̲̲).

1. this year's spring vacation
2. *the los angeles times*
3. dr. janice beckerman
4. english, math, and art
5. the american red cross
6. the united nations
7. the french ambassador
8. in the city of victoria on vancouver island
9. a paint store on euclid avenue
10. the rio grande
11. world history 101 and algebra
12. the world's tallest building
13. uncle leo, aunt dora, and sam

14. a ski resort in new mexico
15. the best restaurant in town
16. the middle ages
17. the song "over the rainbow"
18. charley's hamburger heaven, my favorite café
19. st. patrick's day
20. the bill of rights at the end of the constitution

EXERCISE C Spelling

On a separate piece of paper, rewrite each sentence, correcting the misspelled words.

1. Five ~~foriegn frieghters~~ [foreign freighters] achieved ~~unbeleivable~~ [unbelievable] speeds despite the fact that their cargos ~~wieghed~~ [weighed] two thousand tons.
2. The police chief's niece has few ~~freinds~~ [friends] because she's ~~to concieted~~ [too conceited].
3. ~~Ninty~~ [Ninety]-eight ~~sliegh~~ [sleigh] dogs sledded to the North Pole.
4. The seven ~~sister-in-laws suceeded~~ [sisters-in-law succeeded] in ~~seceeding~~ [seceding] from serious squabbles.
5. In the hospital's newborn nursery, ~~beautyfull babys~~ [beautiful babies] bawl and babble.

EXERCISE D Editing and Proofreading a Passage

Add all of the missing punctuation marks and capital letters to the words below. Use the proofreading symbols shown on page 285, and write the correctly punctuated and capitalized passage on a separate piece of paper.

one of robert frost's most popular poems is "stopping by woods on a snowy evening" when i first read this poem in *the poetry of robert frost*, i thought it was perfectly easy and simple. its about a horse and a person who stop to watch some woods on a snowy evening. on looking at the poem more closely, however, i found that there's much more than just the poem's literal meaning. for example, in the final stanza, what promises does the speaker have to keep, and what does the word sleep mean? i think that the dark woods and the snow symbolize death and that the promises symbolize the speaker's commitment to life. do you agree or disagree with this interpretation?

Standardized-Test Practice: Grammar and Usage

In addition to an essay component, standardized writing tests include a multiple-choice component that tests your understanding of standard written English. In this section of Level Blue, you will find four multiple-choice formats in four different sections. (For additional practice in standardized-test formats with grammar feedback, go to www.grammarforwriting.com.) The four formats include:

- SAT Practice: Identifying Sentence Errors
- SAT Practice: Improving Sentences
- SAT Practice: Improving Paragraphs
- ACT Practice

Following these four sections is a practice test in which items from three formats are combined.

IDENTIFYING SENTENCE ERRORS

In this type of multiple-choice item, a sentence will have four words or phrases underlined and labeled **A** through **D**. Your task will be to identify an error, if there is one, and fill in the corresponding answer oval. If there is no error, your answer choice will be **E**, which is "No Error."

IMPROVING SENTENCES

In this section, your task will be not only to spot mistakes but fix them, too. In each test item, a sentence will be all or partly underlined. You must spot and fix an error, if there is one, within the underlined portion. Choices **B** through **E** each rephrase the underlined portion, serving as a possible replacement for it. Choice **A** repeats the underlined portion exactly as it is originally given. Choose **A** if you think the item is correct as is.

IMPROVING PARAGRAPHS

The test items in this section have the same structure as the ones in the Improving Sentences section but are keyed to a passage instead of an individual sentence. The items test your ability to revise and combine sentences within the context of an essay and improve its unity, organization and coherence, and word choice.

ACT PRACTICE

As its title suggests, this section is standardized-test practice in ACT format. It includes two passages with grammar and usage items keyed to them. Like the Improving Paragraphs section, the test items ask you to revise and combine sentences within the context of an essay and improve its unity, organization and coherence, and word choice.

ONLINE COMPONENTS
www.grammarforwriting.com
SAT and ACT practice worksheets
with grammar feedback are available online.

Directions: In each item, one of the underlined words or phrases may contain an error in grammar, usage, word choice, or idiom. If there is an error, choose the underlined part that must be changed to make the sentence correct, and fill in the corresponding oval. If the sentence has no error, fill in oval E. In selecting answers, follow the requirements of standard written English.

Example

One of the really <u>difficult</u> problems that people everywhere
               A

<u>must contend</u> with <u>are</u> preserving <u>their</u> food supply. <u>No error</u>
       B   C   D   E

Ⓐ Ⓑ ⬤ Ⓓ Ⓔ

The correct choice is **C**. The subject of the sentence is *One*, and requires a singular verb such as *is*, not *are*.

1. The myth of Daedalus and Icarus <u>are</u> one of the <u>most famous</u> Greek
                                      A   B

   <u>myths; it is</u> the story of a boy <u>who</u> ignores his father's advice. <u>No error</u>
        C   D   E

   ⬤ Ⓑ Ⓒ Ⓓ Ⓔ

2. My <u>best</u> choice, I <u>decided</u>, is to vote for the incumbent, but not
      A   B

   because he <u>is</u> the <u>unequivocally</u> favorite. <u>No error</u>
             C   D   E

   Ⓐ Ⓑ Ⓒ ⬤ Ⓔ

3. <u>Neither</u> she nor her parents <u>prefers</u> rock-and-roll music to the <u>kinds</u> of
      A   B   C

   music Jessica plays <u>when</u> she's practicing her flute lessons. <u>No error</u>
                         D   E

   Ⓐ ⬤ Ⓒ Ⓓ Ⓔ

4. Everyone in the marching band <u>is</u> responsible for <u>his or her</u> own
                                   A   B

   instrument, <u>so</u> when Kevin lost his tuba, he <u>had</u> to pay for it. <u>No error</u>
               C   D   E

   Ⓐ Ⓑ Ⓒ Ⓓ ⬤

STANDARDIZED TEST PRACTICE

5. Alexis and her brother Aaron <u>are</u> the two student council members
A

<u>whom</u> are <u>most outspoken</u> about <u>replacing</u> block scheduling with
  B   C   D

traditional fifty-minute periods. <u>No error</u>
E

6. <u>Both</u> Mihal and Gina <u>know</u> more about computers than <u>anyone</u> in
   A   B   C

<u>their</u> class. <u>No error</u>
 D   E

7. Laura <u>had searched</u> everywhere but <u>couldn't find</u> her new backpack,
        A   B

until, finally, she <u>found</u> it <u>laying</u> on the porch in the rain. <u>No error</u>
                  C   D   E

8. Native Americans dried ears of corn for winter <u>food. Just</u> as <u>the earliest</u>
                                                  A   B

people <u>who lived in Scotland</u> <u>dried oats</u> for oatmeal. <u>No error</u>
              C   D   E

9. The sun's corona, a halo of hot gases <u>surrounding the sun</u> that
A

<u>reaches</u> temperatures of about 3,600,000 degrees Fahrenheit, <u>are</u>
 B   C

visible <u>during a solar eclipse.</u> <u>No error</u>
              D   E

10. The Portuguese explorer Vasco da Gama <u>was</u> the first European
A

explorer <u>discovering</u> the sea route to India when he led an expedition
         B

in 1497 that <u>sailed</u> around the Cape of Good Hope on the coast of
               C

what <u>is now</u> South Africa. <u>No error</u>
      D   E

11. <u>Among the world's largest islands</u> <u>is</u> Greenland, with an area of
  　　　　　A　　　　　　　　　　　　B

840,000 square miles, and Great Britain, with 88,795 square miles;

Australia <u>is not considered</u> an island <u>but</u> a continent. <u>No error</u>　　　Ⓐ Ⓑ Ⓒ Ⓓ Ⓔ
  　　　　　　C　　　　　　　　　　　D　　　　　　E

12. <u>Prized</u> for <u>its</u> ability to kill snakes, the mongoose can be found either
  　　A　　　B

in the wild <u>and</u> as a <u>tame</u> animal, like Rikki-tikki-tavi in the story by
  　　　　　C　　　　　D

Rudyard Kipling. <u>No error</u>　　　　　　　　　　　　　　　Ⓐ Ⓑ Ⓒ Ⓓ Ⓔ
  　　　　　　　　　E

13. In 1962, James Watson, an American biologist, and Francis Crick, a

British molecular biologist, <u>were awarded</u> the Nobel Prize for <u>their</u>
  　　　　　　　　　　　　A　　　　　　　　　　　　　B

research on the structure of DNA, <u>which contains</u> the genetic code
  　　　　　　　　　　　　　　　C

needed for building and <u>to maintain</u> living organisms. <u>No error</u>　　　Ⓐ Ⓑ Ⓒ Ⓓ Ⓔ
  　　　　　　　　D　　　　　　　　　　　　E

14. On June 16th, in cities around the world, devotees of the Irish writer

James Joyce <u>celebrate</u> Bloomsday, the anniversary of the day Joyce
  　　　　　A

<u>depicts</u> in his novel *Ulysses*, by gathering <u>to read</u> from the book, eat
  B　　　　　　　　　　　　　　　C

typically Irish foods, and <u>talking</u> about the author. <u>No error</u>　　　Ⓐ Ⓑ Ⓒ Ⓓ Ⓔ
  　　　　　　　　D　　　　　　　　　E

15. Each man <u>puts</u> on <u>their</u> wings, and Daedalus warns Icarus to
  　　　　　A　　　B

follow <u>him</u> and not <u>to set</u> his own course. <u>No error</u>　　　Ⓐ Ⓑ Ⓒ Ⓓ Ⓔ
  　　　C　　　　　D　　　　　　　E

16. There <u>is</u> about 700 different versions of the Cinderella story, <u>in which</u>
      A   B

a young woman <u>who</u> is ill-treated by her stepmother goes to a ball,
               C

loses a slipper, and <u>ends up marrying</u> a prince. <u>No error</u>   Ⓐ Ⓑ Ⓒ Ⓓ Ⓔ
                         D   E

17. A kiwi is both a flightless bird found <u>only in New Zealand</u> <u>and</u> a small,
                                              A   B

<u>commercial</u> <u>grown</u> oval-shaped fruit that is brown and fuzzy on the
    C   D

outside. <u>No error</u>   Ⓐ Ⓑ Ⓒ Ⓓ Ⓔ
            E

18. Smoking, a drying method <u>used for meat and fish</u>, <u>preserves</u> food,
                               A   B

<u>adds</u> a pleasant, smoky flavor, and <u>will please</u> many people. <u>No error</u>   Ⓐ Ⓑ Ⓒ Ⓓ Ⓔ
  C   D   E

19. When someone <u>says</u> that a real-life event is Kafkaesque, <u>they were</u>
                    A   B

alluding to the <u>surreal, nightmarish qualities</u> of the novels by
                 C

twentieth-century Czech writer Franz Kafka, <u>such as</u> The Castle.
                                              D

<u>No error</u>   Ⓐ Ⓑ Ⓒ Ⓓ Ⓔ
   E

20. Mary Cassatt (1845-1926), <u>who</u> is <u>best known</u> for her prints and
                                 A   B

paintings of mothers and children, <u>is</u> the only American <u>to have</u>
                                     C   D

<u>exhibited</u> with the French Impressionist painters in 1886. <u>No error</u>   Ⓐ Ⓑ Ⓒ Ⓓ Ⓔ
   D   E

21. You may think the English novelist George Eliot was a man;

however, Eliot actually was a woman, Mary Ann Evans, whose
   A   B

most popular novels include *Silas Marner*. No error   Ⓐ Ⓑ Ⓒ Ⓓ ●
       C   D   E

22. Experts in the health fields agree that among the most important
                                 A   B

elements in a healthy life style is a low-fat diet and regular physical
                                   C

exercise, such as bicycling, running, and swimming. No error   Ⓐ Ⓑ ● Ⓓ Ⓔ
                         D   E

23. The Maya, a highly developed civilization, flourished in the Yucatan
             A

and Guatemala until the Spanish have arrived in the 1560s; you can
                                 B

still, however, find Mayan people today, many of whom speak their
                                          C   D

ancient language. No error   Ⓐ ● Ⓒ Ⓓ Ⓔ
             E

24. Of the many types of blue, green, and brown seaweed found in oceans
                                              A

and freshwater, some are edible; others yield products used in the
                        B   C

manufacture of ice cream, toothpaste, and making soap. No error   Ⓐ Ⓑ Ⓒ ● Ⓔ
                                 D   E

25. Morse code, invented by the American Samuel F. B. Morse, is a
              A   B

system of long and short signals (the most famous of which is SOS)
                                        C

for relaying messages by either telegraph and radio. No error   Ⓐ Ⓑ Ⓒ ● Ⓔ
                             D   E

STANDARDIZED TEST PRACTICE

SAT Practice: Improving Sentences

Directions: In each of the following items, all or part of the sentence is underlined. Beneath each sentence are five ways of phrasing the underlined part. Choice (A) is the same as the original; the other four choices are different. Select the answer choice that best expresses the meaning of the original sentence. Your goal is to produce the most effective sentence, one that is clear and not wordy. Choose (A) if the original sentence is better than any of the other answer choices.

Example

I read in an <u>encyclopedia. That a giant clam can grow as wide as a yardstick and can live for fifty years and weighing</u> a thousand pounds.

(A) encyclopedia. That a giant clam can grow as wide as a yardstick and can live for fifty years and weighing

(B) encyclopedia that a giant clam can grow as wide as a yardstick and can live for fifty years and weighing

(C) encyclopedia: that a giant clam can grow as wide as a yardstick and can live for fifty years and weigh

(D) encyclopedia that a giant clam can grow as wide as a yardstick, live for fifty years, and weigh

(E) encyclopedia that a giant clam can grow as wide as a yardstick in spite of the fact that it lives for fifty years and weighs

Ⓐ Ⓑ Ⓒ ● Ⓔ

The best choice is **D**. The fragment ("That a giant clam ... pounds.") is an error that can be combined into a larger sentence with a series of verbs that have parallel structure: *grow, live,* and *weigh.* Choice **B** corrects the fragment error but not the verb problem, as *weighing* is not in the same form as *grow* and *live.* **C** uses a colon improperly. **E** is correct grammatically but "in spite of the fact" incorrectly suggests a contradictory relationship between the idea that precedes it and the one that follows.

1. Neither Jed <u>nor his sister take the time</u> to read the directions before putting together a new computer or fax machine.

   (A) nor his sister take the time

   (B) nor his sister takes the time

   (C) or his sister takes the time

   (D) or his sister take the time

   (E) and his sister take the time

   Ⓐ ● Ⓒ Ⓓ Ⓔ

STANDARDIZED TEST PRACTICE

2. The ancient Inca city of Machu Picchu, high in the mountains of Peru, was discovered in 1911 by the American explorer Hiram <u>Bingham. Later becoming</u> governor of Connecticut and a United States senator.

   (A) Bingham. Later becoming

   (B) Bingham, later becoming

   (C) Bingham, and he later became

   (D) Bingham, who later became

   (E) Bingham, although he later became

3. <u>Taken from high above the earth</u>, the ozone layer above Antarctica appears to have a "hole."

   (A) Taken from high above the earth,

   (B) If you could view Antarctica from high above the earth,

   (C) In satellite images taken from high above the earth,

   (D) Viewing the ozone layer taken from high above the earth,

   (E) Unless anyone can see it from high above the earth,

4. The turtle lumbered awkwardly out of the <u>sea, then it dug a hole, then it laid its eggs in the hole, then it carefully covered them</u> with sand.

   (A) sea, then it dug a hole, then it laid its eggs in the hole, then it carefully covered them

   (B) sea, then it dug a hole in which it laid its eggs in, then it covered them carefully

   (C) sea; then it dug a hole where it laid its eggs and carefully covered them

   (D) sea; then it dug a hole, lay its eggs in the hole, and carefully covered them

   (E) sea because it dug a hole, laid its eggs, and covered them

5. <u>Slowly crossing the street, the speeding car, going at least fifteen miles above the speed limit, just missed the little dachshund.</u>

   (A) Slowly crossing the street, the speeding car, going at least fifteen miles above the speed limit, just missed the little dachshund.

   (B) Slowly crossing the street, the speeding car, which was going at least fifteen miles above the speed limit, just missed the little dachshund.

   (C) The little dachshund, going at least fifteen miles above the speed limit, just missed the speeding car, which was slowly crossing the street.

(D) The speeding car, which was going at least fifteen miles above the speed limit, just missed the little dachshund slowly crossing the street.

(E) The speeding car, slowly crossing the street, just missed the little dachshund, which was going at least fifteen miles above the speed limit.

6. Sometimes a mathematical equation can have more than one correct <u>solution; in this case, either of the two answers are correct</u>.

   (A) solution; in this case, either of the two answers are correct

   (B) solution; so either of the two answers are correct

   (C) solution so that either of the two answers is correct

   (D) solution; in this case, either of the two answers is correct

   (E) solution, but in this case, either of the two answers is correct

7. Although cutbacks are <u>imminent, few of the staff feels</u> hostility toward management, as the budget problem originates elsewhere.

   (A) imminent, few of the staff feels

   (B) imminent, few of the staff is feeling

   (C) imminent, few of the staff has been known to feel

   (D) imminent, merely a few on the staff have been known to feel

   (E) imminent, few of the staff feel

8. To even be considered for the job, you need <u>an impeccable resume, two laudatory letters of reference, and you should retain a knowledgeable headhunter</u>.

   (A) an impeccable resume, two laudatory letters of reference, and you should retain a knowledgeable headhunter

   (B) a resume that is impeccable, two letters of reference that are laudatory, and to hire a headhunter that is knowledgeable

   (C) a resume of an impeccable nature, two laudatory letters of reference, and to retain a knowledgeable headhunter

   (D) an impeccable resume, two laudatory letters of reference, and a knowledgeable headhunter

   (E) besides an impeccable resume, two laudatory letters of reference and to retain the aid of a knowledgeable headhunter

9. The <u>statistics, changing at an alarming rate because</u> the number of people diagnosed with Type 2 diabetes has increased exponentially.

(A) statistics, changing at an alarming rate because

(B) statistics, having changed at an alarming rate because

(C) statistics, continuing to change at an alarming rate because

(D) statistics are changing at an alarming rate where

(E) statistics are changing at an alarming rate because

10. <u>In his Second Inaugural Address, President Lincoln urged the nation to act "with malice toward none, with charity for all," he gave the Second Inaugural Address a month before the end of the Civil War.</u>

(A) In his Second Inaugural Address, President Lincoln urged the nation to act "with malice toward none, with charity for all," he gave the Second Inaugural Address a month before the end of the Civil War.

(B) In his Second Inaugural Address, President Lincoln urged the nation to act "with malice toward none, with charity for all" because the Second Inaugural Address was delivered a month before the end of the Civil War.

(C) Although he urged the nation to act "with malice toward none, with charity for all," President Lincoln delivered the Second Inaugural Address a month before the end of the Civil War.

(D) In his Second Inaugural Address, which he delivered a month before the end of the Civil War, President Lincoln urged the nation to act "with malice toward none, with charity for all."

(E) Urging the nation to act "with malice toward none, with charity for all," the Second Inaugural Address was delivered by President Lincoln a month before the end of the Civil War.

11. The rising cost of health insurance premiums, <u>an issue troubling many citizens, remain</u> a hot-button ticket item for any presidential candidate.

(A) an issue troubling many citizens, remain

(B) an issue already troubling many citizens, remain

(C) an issue troubling many citizens, remains

(D) an issue for many and troubling for many citizens, remains

(E) one issue that has been made troubling for many citizens, remains

STANDARDIZED TEST PRACTICE

12. Queen Elizabeth I, <u>whom is known as the Virgin Queen, reigned for</u> <u>seventy years, from 1533–1603, and she never married.</u>

(A) whom is known as the Virgin Queen, reigned for seventy years, from 1533–1603, and she never married

(B) who is known as the Virgin Queen, reigned for seventy years, from 1533–1603, while she never married

(C) whose known as the Virgin Queen, reigned for seventy years, from 1533–1603, in spite of the fact that she never married

(D) who is known as the Virgin Queen, reigned for seventy years, from 1533–1603, and that happened despite the fact that she never married

(E) who is known as the Virgin Queen because she never married, reigned for seventy years, from 1533–1603

13. Superstitious actors won't refer to Shakespeare's *Macbeth*, <u>it is a tragedy</u> <u>of murder and ambition, by name, they call it</u> "the Scottish play."

(A) *Macbeth*, it is a tragedy of murder and ambition, by name, they call it

(B) *Macbeth*, a tragedy of murder and ambition, by name because they call it

(C) *Macbeth* by name. It is a tragedy of murder and ambition, and so they will call it

(D) *Macbeth*, which is a tragedy of murder and ambition, by name, they call it

(E) *Macbeth*, a tragedy of murder and ambition, by name; instead they call it

14. The polygraph, or lie detector, measures <u>changes in a person's</u> <u>breathing rate,</u> blood pressure, pulse rate, and sweat gland activity.

(A) changes in a person's breathing rate,

(B) a person who changes his or her breathing rate,

(C) how a person changes their breathing,

(D) if a person changes their breathing rate,

(E) when the breathing rate of a person changes, along with their

15. "The Song of Myself" is the longest poem in Walt Whitman's *Leaves of Grass, it's written in free verse, it has* no regular rhyme or meter.

(A) *Grass*, it's written in free verse, it has

(B) *Grass* because it's written in free verse and has

(C) *Grass*, it's written in free verse and has

(D) *Grass*; it's written in free verse, which means that it has

(E) *Grass*; and it's written in free verse, and it has

16. My supervisor outlined my job duties for a new project, and I started working on it immediately, and I didn't stop until I thought it was perfect.

(A) My supervisor outlined my job duties for a new project, and I started working on it immediately, and I didn't stop

(B) Because my supervisor outlined my job duties for a new project, I started working on it immediately and didn't stop

(C) I immediately started working on the project whose duties were outlined to me by my supervisor, and didn't stop

(D) After my supervisor outlined my job duties for a new project, I started working on it immediately and didn't stop

(E) It was after my supervisor's outlining of my job duties for a new project that I began to immediately work on it, not stopping

17. Hoping to finish her assignment before the due date, the new contract didn't arrive until three days before the final deadline.

(A) Hoping to finish her assignment before the due date,

(B) Because she hoped to finish her assignment before the due date,

(C) She had been hoping to finish her assignment before the due date, but

(D) Despite hopes to finish the assignment before the due date,

(E) The fact that she hoped to finish her assignment before the due date didn't help,

SAT Practice: Improving Paragraphs

ONLINE COMPONENTS
www.grammarforwriting.com

SAT and ACT practice worksheets with grammar feedback are available online.

Directions: The passage that follows is an early draft of an essay. Some parts need to be rewritten. Read the passage carefully and answer the questions that follow. Choose the answer that most clearly and effectively expresses the writer's intended meaning. In making your decisions, follow the conventions of standard written English. After you have chosen your answer, fill in the corresponding oval.

(1) Before Whitman began writing his poetry in the simple, natural rhythms of speech, American poetry looked and sounded very much like British poetry. (2) American poets never strayed from using traditional meters, rhyme schemes, and stanza forms. (3) After Whitman published his poetry, American poets were freed from these constraints.

(4) Walt Whitman was born in 1819 and grew up on his father's farm in West Hills, Long Island, with eight brothers and sisters. (5) In 1823, Whitman's family moved to Brooklyn, it was then a separate city just across the East River from New York. (6) When he was eleven, Whitman dropped out of school and got a job as an office boy. (7) For ten years, he worked as a journalist; then he left to travel to New Orleans, the Great Lakes, and Niagara Falls. (8) He returned to Brooklyn. (9) He became the editor of a newspaper, it was called *The Freeman*.

(10) Whitman loved to walk on the beaches of Long Island and to roam the woods and fields. (11) Although he never went to college, he read a lot, including the Bible, Shakespeare's plays, and the poetry of Homer and Dante. (12) His main activity, however, was writing poems. (13) He filled many notebooks with his poems. (14) In 1855, he paid out of his own pocket to publish a collection of his poems, which he titled *Leaves of Grass*. (15) For the rest of his life, Whitman kept revising his book through nine editions. (16) Not everyone who saw his book realized its worth, but the great American essayist Ralph Waldo Emerson did. (17) *Leaves of Grass*, Emerson wrote to Whitman, is "the most extraordinary piece of wit and wisdom that America has yet contributed."

1. In context, which of the following would make the best introductory sentence (inserted before sentence 1)?

(A) Walt Whitman had a great influence on American poetry.

(B) Walt Whitman is a famous nineteenth-century American poet.

(C) Without Walt Whitman, what would American poetry be like today?

(D) In 1855, Walt Whitman burst upon the American literary scene with a dynamic new kind of poetry.

(E) If you're one of those people who dislike reading poetry because you think it's too hard, try reading Walt Whitman's poetry.

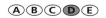

2. Which of the following is the best revision of the underlined portion of sentence 5 (reproduced below)?

In 1823, Whitman's family moved to <u>Brooklyn, it was then</u> a separate city just across the East River from New York.

(A) (As it is now)

(B) Brooklyn; Brooklyn was then

(C) Brooklyn because it was then

(D) Brooklyn, which was then

(E) Brooklyn, being that it was

3. In context, which of the following is the best way to revise and combine sentences 8 and 9 (reproduced below)?

He returned to Brooklyn. He became the editor of a newspaper, it was called The Freeman.

(A) He returned to Brooklyn, and he became the editor of a newspaper, and it was called *The Freeman*.

(B) He returned to Brooklyn, editing a newspaper, *The Freeman*.

(C) He returned to Brooklyn, where he became the editor of a newspaper called *The Freeman*.

(D) Becoming the editor of a newspaper called *The Freeman*, he later returned to Brooklyn.

(E) He returned to Brooklyn; he became the editor of a newspaper called *The Freeman*.

4. To improve the third paragraph, what should be done with sentence 11 (reproduced here)?

Although he never went to college, he read a lot, including the Bible, Shakespeare's plays, and the poetry of Homer and Dante.

(A) Nothing. Leave it as it is.

(B) Delete it.

(C) Add "and many other poets" at the end of the sentence.

(D) Delete "read a lot" and insert "was self-educated and read great works".

(E) Change "Although" to "As a result".

5. In context, which of the following is the best way to revise and combine sentences 12 and 13 (reproduced below)?

His main activity, however, was writing poems. He filled many notebooks with his poems.

(A) However, his main activity was filling notebooks.

(B) His main activity, however, was writing poems in many note-books, which he filled completely.

(C) Writing many notebooks, however, with his poems was his main activity.

(D) Writing poems, however, was his main activity, and he filled many notebooks with them.

(E) However, writing notebooks in which there were poems was his main activity.

6. The writer of this draft uses all of the following strategies EXCEPT

(A) imaginative description

(B) direct quotation

(C) biographical details

(D) literary background

(E) evaluation of the subject's importance

7. In context, what should be done to improve the underlined portion of sentence 16 (reproduced below)?

Not everyone who saw his book realized its worth, <u>but the great American essayist Ralph Waldo Emerson did</u>.

(A) Nothing. Leave it as is.

(B) Change "did" to "enthusiastically admired Whitman's work".

(C) Change the period to an exclamation mark.

(D) Insert "(1803-1882)" after the name *Emerson.*

(E) Insert "who wrote 'The Rhodora,'" after the name *Emerson.*

ACT Practice

ONLINE COMPONENTS
www.grammarforwriting.com

SAT and ACT
practice
worksheets
with grammar
feedback are
available online.

STANDARDIZED TEST PRACTICE

DIRECTIONS: You will find two reading passages in the left column and questions in the right column. In each of the passages, some words and phrases are underlined with a number underneath. The numbers refer to the questions at the right. Most questions ask you to choose the answer that best expresses the idea in standard written English or in the style of the passage. If you think the original wording is best, choose answer A, "NO CHANGE."

Other questions, indicated by a small number in a box, ask questions about the passage as a whole or about a particular section of the passage.

For each question, choose what you think is the best answer, and fill in the corresponding oval at the bottom of the page. Sometimes you will need to read several sentences beyond the numbered point in the passage to answer the question correctly.

Passage I

Homer's *The Iliad*

[1]

Not many details <u>is known</u> about
                          1
Homer, the ancient Greek poet. He is said to have been a blind man living during the eighth century B.C. and the author of two great epics, *The Iliad* and *The Odyssey*. Literary scholars speculate that Homer was one of ancient Greece's many <u>*rhapsodes,* they</u>
                                        2
<u>were storytellers</u> who moved from town to
     2
town reciting the much-loved tales of gods and heroes.

[2]

③ Scholars believe that the war actually did take place during the twelfth

1. **A.** NO CHANGE
   B. have been known
   C. are known
   D. was known

2. **F.** NO CHANGE
   G. *rhapsodes,* storytellers
   H. *rhapsodes,* and they were story-tellers
   J. *rhapsodes,* being that they were storytellers

1. Ⓐ Ⓑ ⬤ Ⓓ

2. Ⓕ ⬤ Ⓗ Ⓙ

century B.C. because of trade disputes. According to legend, the war began when the Greek kings and their armies sailed to Troy to rescue King Menelaus's wife, Helen, said to be the most beautiful woman in the world. She had been abducted and taken to Troy by Paris, son of the Trojan king.

[3]

Homer's *Iliad*, begins, neither at the beginning of the war nor with the back story of the beauty contest that calls for Paris to choose the most beautiful of three goddesses. *The Iliad* begins right smack dab in the middle of the story. The Greeks have laid siege to Troy for almost ten years. A plague has struck the Greek army, and after ten days Achilles, the Greeks' best warrior, calls a meeting to explore the cause of the plague. During that meeting, something happens that causes a bitter quarrel between Achilles and King Agamemnon of Mycenae, whose commander of the Greek army.

3. Which of the following is the best sentence to insert at the beginning of paragraph 2 to connect the ideas in paragraphs 1 and 2?
   A. Both *The Iliad* and *The Odyssey* are spin-offs of the legend of the Trojan War.
   B. The events of *The Iliad* take place inside and outside of the walled city of Troy.
   C. No one knows the cause of the Trojan War.
   D. What is the background for Homer's story?

4. **F.** NO CHANGE
   G. legend, therefore, the war
   H. legend, however, the war
   J. legend, as a result, the war

5. **A.** NO CHANGE
   B. Homer's *Iliad* begins
   C. Homer's *Iliad* begins,
   D. Homer's *Iliad* begins:

6. **F.** NO CHANGE
   G. begins
   H. began right smack dab
   J. is beginning

7. **A.** NO CHANGE
   B. years'; a plague
   C. years, but a plague
   D. years, and a plague

8. **F.** NO CHANGE
   G. who has been
   H. who is
   J. whom readers come to recognize as

3. Ⓐ Ⓑ Ⓒ Ⓓ
4. Ⓕ Ⓖ Ⓗ Ⓙ
5. Ⓐ Ⓑ Ⓒ Ⓓ

6. Ⓕ Ⓖ Ⓗ Ⓙ
7. Ⓐ Ⓑ Ⓒ Ⓓ
8. Ⓕ Ⓖ Ⓗ Ⓙ

[4]

Find a modern translation. Don't miss
the beauty and the power of Homer's tale.
As you read, be on the lookout for the
conventions, or characteristic features, of
an epic poem. For example, all epics begin
with an invocation, which is a poet's
calling on a god or muse for support and
inspiration. *The Iliad* begins with an invocation to the muse Calliope. Right away,
we see one of them: that the action
begins *in medias res,* which in Latin
means "into the middle of things." Other
conventions include extended similes,
sometimes called Homeric similes, that use
the words *like* or *as* to compare an image
of war with an everyday event that ordinary Greeks could ready understand.
Finally, look for the stock epithets like
"rosy-fingered Dawn," "gray-eyed
Athena," and "horse-taming Hector"
that Homer uses repeatedly throughout
the epic.

9. What is the best way to combine these
   two sentences?

   A. Find a modern translation, watch
   out not to miss the beauty and
   power of Homer's tale.

   B. In a good translation, don't miss
   the beauty and power of Homer's
   tale.

   C. Find a modern translation, but
   don't miss the beauty and power
   of Homer's tale.

   D. You can enjoy the beauty and
   power of Homer's tale by reading a
   modern translation.

10. **F.** NO CHANGE

    G. one of the conventions that

    H. another convention: that

    J. another one of the conventions;
    that

11. **A.** NO CHANGE

    B. could readily understood

    C. could readily understand

    D. would be ready to understand

Question 12 asks about Passage I as a whole.

---

12. The writer wishes to add the following
    sentence:

    The Iliad is a powerful tale of war and
    jealousy and rage.

    This sentence would most logically be
    placed at the end of:

    F. paragraph 1

    G. paragraph 2

    H. paragraph 3

    J. paragraph 4

---

9. Ⓐ Ⓑ Ⓒ ●   **11.** Ⓐ Ⓑ ● Ⓓ
10. Ⓕ Ⓖ ● Ⓙ   **12.** Ⓕ ● Ⓗ Ⓙ

Passage II

The Art of Camouflage

[1]

At the end of <u>Shakespeare's tragedy</u>
₁₃
<u>Macbeth</u>, enemy soldiers approach Macbeth's
₁₃
castle, each carrying a tree branch. They are
fulfilling the witches' prophecy that Macbeth
shall never be vanquished until Great
Birnam Wood comes to his castle. Like
those of the modern-day military, the soldiers are using the art of camouflage, or
<u>disguise. Which is a form</u> of defense they
₁₄
adapted from birds, insects, and other
animals.

[2]

In the animal world, camouflage has two
main purposes. The first purpose is to protect the animal from being seen by <u>either</u>
₁₅
<u>it's predators and it's</u> prey. 16 During
₁₅
winter, Arctic Foxes that are normally
gray or tan grow a whole new coat of
white fur to help make themselves invisible
against the snow and ice. The walking twig,
an insect, disguises itself as a twig, an object
its predators wouldn't think of eating. Even

13. A. NO CHANGE
    B. Shakespeares' tragedy *Macbeth*,
    C. Shakespeare's tragedy, Macbeth,
    D. Shakespeare's tragedy Macbeth

14. F. NO CHANGE
    G. disguise, that is a form
    H. disguise, which is a form
    J. disguise. A form

15. A. NO CHANGE
    B. either its predators and its
    C. either its predators or its
    D. either it's predators or it's

16. Which transitional word or phrase can
logically be inserted at the beginning
of this sentence?
    F. However,
    G. Consequently,
    H. For example,
    J. On the other hand,

13. Ⓐ Ⓑ Ⓒ Ⓓ   15. Ⓐ Ⓑ Ⓒ Ⓓ
14. Ⓕ Ⓖ Ⓗ Ⓙ   16. Ⓕ Ⓖ Ⓗ Ⓙ

birds' eggs that are on the ground and <u>laying right there out in the open</u> ₁₇ are colored tan and gray with mottled speckling to disguise them among pebbles, rocks, or soil.

[3]

[1] Mimicry is another purpose of <u>camouflage, if</u> you look like something ₁₈ dangerous, your enemies will avoid you. [2] Some caterpillars, butterflies, and moths are look-alike twins of foul-tasting, even poisonous creatures. [3] For example, the Viceroy butterfly, a perfectly palatable meal for predators, mimics the markings and coloring of the Monarch butterfly, an unpleasant tasting relative. [4] Mimics may taste <u>delicious, but there</u> predators ₁₉ don't bother them. [20] [5] Large under-water animals like sharks and dolphins and whales are bluish-gray in coloring, like the ocean water. [6] Smaller sea creatures that live on brightly colored coral reefs blend in by being brightly colored themselves.

17. **A.** NO CHANGE
    B. laying out in the open
    C. lying out in the open
    D. lying right there

18. **F.** NO CHANGE
    G. camouflage, and if
    H. camouflage because if
    J. camouflage although if

19. **A.** NO CHANGE
    B. deliciously, but their
    C. delicious, but their
    D. delicious, although their

20. What is the best thing to do with sentences 5 and 6 in paragraph 3?
    F. Leave them where they are.
    G. Insert them as additional examples in paragraph 2.
    H. Delete them.
    J. Move them to the end of the essay.

17. Ⓐ Ⓑ Ⓒ Ⓓ
18. Ⓕ Ⓖ Ⓗ Ⓙ

19. Ⓐ Ⓑ Ⓒ Ⓓ
20. Ⓕ Ⓖ Ⓗ Ⓙ

[4]

[21] [1] The patterns may change, but basically the standard mottled brown, khaki, green, and gold colors are designed to blend in with wooded areas and jungles. [2] Although the animal kingdom has been incorporating camouflage for eons, the American military just started using it for uniforms and equipment during World War I. [3] In winter during wartime, however, military personnel wear snow-country uniforms, just as starkly white as the Arctic Fox's winter coat.

21. What is the best sequence for the sentences in paragraph 4?
   A. NO CHANGE
   B. 3, 1, 2
   C. 2, 1, 3
   D. 3, 2, 1

Question 22 asks about Passage II as a whole.

22. What is the main purpose of paragraph 1?
   F. To support the main ideas expressed in paragraphs 2 and 3
   G. To grab the reader's attention and state the main idea of the essay
   H. To establish a connection between literature, biology, and the military
   J. To show that camouflage was used in seventeenth-century England

21. Ⓐ Ⓑ Ⓒ Ⓓ   22. Ⓕ Ⓖ Ⓗ Ⓙ

Practice Test

PART A

Time—25 Minutes (1 question)

You have 25 minutes to write an essay on the topic below.

DO NOT WRITE AN ESSAY THAT ADDRESSES ANY OTHER TOPIC. AN ESSAY ON A DIFFERENT TOPIC WILL NOT BE ACCEPTED.

Plan and write an essay on the assigned topic. Present your thoughts clearly and effectively. Include specific examples to support your views. The quality of your essay is more important than its length, but to express your ideas on the topic adequately, you will probably want to write more than one paragraph. Be sure to make your handwriting legible.

Consider the following statement. Then write an essay as directed.

"A strong America depends on its cities—America's glory, and sometimes America's shame."
—from John F. Kennedy, State of the Union address, Jan. 11, 1962

Assignment: Write an essay in which you agree or disagree with the statement above, using examples from history, current events, science, art, music, or your own experience to support your position.

WRITE YOUR ESSAY ON A SEPARATE SHEET OF PAPER.

PART B

Time—35 Minutes (47 questions)

Directions: In each item, one of the underlined words or phrases may contain an error in grammar, usage, word choice, or idiom. If there is an error, choose the underlined part that must be changed to make the sentence correct, and fill in the corresponding oval. If the sentence has no error, fill in oval E. In selecting answers, follow the requirements of standard written English.

Example

As his father did before him, the young, gifted songwriter
A   B
will have written one memorable song after another. No error
          C   D   E

1. Each member of the group gave their name and occupation to the
   A   B   C

   persistent interviewer. No error
      D   E

2. Either a play or a concert are being performed at the community
   A   B   C   D

   center tonight. No error
                    E

3. Whomever is in charge of our trip itinerary should make sure that
   A   B

   we get to visit all three national parks: Bryce Canyon, Zion, and
                          C   D

   Arches. No error
            E

4. Generally, <u>neither</u> rain <u>nor</u> snow <u>stop</u> mail carriers from
                A   B   C

delivering <u>everyone's</u> mail. <u>No error</u>
          D   E

Ⓐ Ⓑ Ⓒ Ⓓ Ⓔ

5. After the <u>sudden</u> downpour yesterday, in which I <u>became</u> soaked
           A   B

from head to toe, I decided that I <u>will always</u> <u>have taken</u> an
                                  C   D

umbrella with me when I go out. <u>No Error</u>
                             E

Ⓐ Ⓑ Ⓒ Ⓓ Ⓔ

6. The climbers slowly made <u>their</u> <u>dissent</u> into the cave along the steep
                          A   B

and <u>dimly</u> lit trail, <u>carefully</u> placing one foot after the other.
       C   D

<u>No error</u>
  E

Ⓐ Ⓑ Ⓒ Ⓓ Ⓔ

7. The exhibit of Winslow Homer's watercolors, <u>recently</u> put on display
                                          A

at the museum, <u>receive</u> more visitors <u>than</u> <u>any other</u> exhibit there.
             B   C   D

<u>No error</u>
  E

Ⓐ Ⓑ Ⓒ Ⓓ Ⓔ

8. On their <u>recent</u> trip to Tuscany, the Wilsons <u>saw</u> frescoes, paintings,
          A   B

<u>statues</u>, and <u>they saw</u> tapestries. <u>No error</u>
  C   D   E

Ⓐ Ⓑ Ⓒ Ⓓ Ⓔ

9. We <u>couldn't hardly</u> believe <u>it</u> when the congratulatory letter from
         A   B

the college <u>arrived</u>; we did not expect that I <u>would be</u> accepted there.
        C   D

<u>No error</u>
  E

Ⓐ Ⓑ Ⓒ Ⓓ Ⓔ

10. Exactly <u>whom</u> was responsible for the invention of eye glasses <u>has been</u>
           A   B

among the most <u>hotly</u> disputed <u>issues</u> in the history of science.
               C   D

<u>No error</u>
  E

Ⓐ Ⓑ Ⓒ Ⓓ Ⓔ

11. The coach had already <u>broke</u> the rules <u>when</u> he refused <u>to leave</u> the
                      A   B   C

court in a <u>timely</u> manner. <u>No error</u>
        D   E

Ⓐ Ⓑ Ⓒ Ⓓ Ⓔ

12. <u>Choosing</u> the perfect location for <u>her</u> new film was hard for the
     A   B

director, <u>who</u> struggled to choose from <u>among</u> several appealing
         C   D

possibilities. <u>No error</u>
          E

Ⓐ Ⓑ Ⓒ Ⓓ Ⓔ

13. Late in his life, Walt Whitman <u>expresses</u> regret that his book of poems,
                                A

Leaves of Grass, had not gained the acceptance he <u>had hoped</u> and
                                       B

<u>conveyed</u> his wish that it <u>would receive</u> more recognition in the
  C   D

future. <u>No error</u>
      E

Ⓐ Ⓑ Ⓒ Ⓓ Ⓔ

14. Songs in the contest <u>are judged</u> according to <u>lyrics</u>, <u>melody</u>, message,
                     A   B   C

and <u>if they are easy to dance to</u>. <u>No error</u>
        D   E

Ⓐ Ⓑ Ⓒ Ⓓ Ⓔ

15. <u>Although</u> I scored higher <u>then</u> Ben did on my first try, it was <u>really</u> a
     A   B   C

matter of <u>beginner's</u> luck more than anything else. <u>No error</u>
        D   E

Ⓐ Ⓑ Ⓒ Ⓓ Ⓔ

16. <u>Everybody</u> in the class, including <u>those</u> <u>who</u> commute, <u>want</u> to
　　　A　　　　　　　　　　　　　　　B　　C　　　　　　　D

postpone the due date for the term paper until after the break.

<u>No error</u>　　　　　　　　　　　　　　　　　　　Ⓐ Ⓑ Ⓒ ● Ⓔ
　E

17. I <u>first</u> read a novel by Wallace Stegner, <u>which</u> I <u>thoroughly</u> enjoyed,
　　　　A　　　　　　　　　　　　　　　　　B　　　C

<u>near</u> ten years ago. <u>No error</u>　　　　　　　　Ⓐ Ⓑ Ⓒ ● Ⓔ
　D　　　　　　　　E

18. Painters <u>need</u> a place in which to work on <u>their</u> art, and <u>you</u> also need
　　　　　　A　　　　　　　　　　　　　　　B　　　　　C

ample amounts of <u>good</u> light. <u>No error</u>　　　　Ⓐ Ⓑ ● Ⓓ Ⓔ
　　　　　　　　D　　　　　E

19. The annual sales of Scotch tape <u>totaled</u> only $33 when Richard Drew
　　　　　　　　　　　　　　　　　A

invented it in 1930; <u>now</u> enough tape <u>is sold</u> <u>each</u> year to wrap
　　　　　　　　　B　　　　　　　C　　D

around the earth 165 times. <u>No error</u>　　　　　Ⓐ Ⓑ Ⓒ Ⓓ ●
　　　　　　　　　　　　E

20. People <u>who</u> collect dolls and other <u>antique</u> toys <u>pays</u> thousands of
　　　　　A　　　　　　　　　　　B　　　C

dollars for <u>original</u> Raggedy Ann dolls. <u>No error</u>　　Ⓐ Ⓑ ● Ⓓ Ⓔ
　　　　　D　　　　　　　　　　　E

312 *Standardized Test Practice*

Directions: In each of the following items, all or part of the sentence is underlined. Beneath each sentence are five ways of phrasing the underlined part. Choice (A) is the same as the original; the other four choices are different. Select the answer choice that best expresses the meaning of the original sentence. Your goal is to produce the most effective sentence, one that is clear and not wordy. Choose (A) if the original sentence is better than any of the other answer choices.

Example

Accept for Bob, all those in our group were delighted with the outcome of the game.

(A) Accept for Bob,

(B) Accepting for Bob,

(C) Except for Bob,

(D) Accepting Bob,

(E) Excepting for Bob

21. It can get pretty cold in Juneau and in Anchorage, but neither city get as cold as Fairbanks does.

(A) get as cold as Fairbanks does

(B) get as cold as Fairbanks

(C) gets as cold as Fairbanks does

(D) get as cold as Fairbanks gets

(E) gets as cold as Fairbanks gets, which is pretty cold

22. Jesse James is remembered as an outlaw of the Old West, his exploits never took him west of the Mississippi River.

(A) Jesse James is remembered as an outlaw of the Old West, his exploits never took him west of the Mississippi River.

(B) Jesse James is remembered as an outlaw of the Old West, and his exploits never took him west of the Mississippi River.

(C) Jesse James is remembered as an outlaw of the Old West where his exploits never took him west of the Mississippi River.

(D) Although Jesse James is remembered as an outlaw of the Old West, his exploits never took him west of the Mississippi River.

(E) Jesse James is remembered as an outlaw of the Old West, so his exploits never took him west of the Mississippi River.

23. For soldiers, suffering from combat fatigue syndrome may be <u>as common as to get wounded</u>.

    (A) as common as to get wounded

    (B) as common as wounds

    (C) as common as wounds themselves

    (D) as common as getting wounded

    (E) as common as to getting wounded

24. The talented young ballplayer put up some very impressive hitting numbers in the minor leagues, <u>and he was not considered ready to perform successfully at the major league level.</u>

    (A) , and he was not considered ready to perform successfully at the major league level.

    (B) . He was not considered ready to perform successfully at the major league level.

    (C) , but he was not considered ready to perform successfully at the major league level.

    (D) because he was not ready to perform successfully at the major league level.

    (E) , despite the fact that he was not considered ready to perform successfully at the major league level.

25. <u>The runaway car crashed into a guardrail going 60 miles per hour.</u>

    (A) The runaway car crashed into a guardrail going 60 miles per hour.

    (B) Going 60 miles per hour, the runaway car crashed into a guardrail.

    (C) The runaway car crashed into a guardrail, which was going 60 miles per hour.

    (D) The runaway car crashed into a guardrail. They were going 60 miles per hour.

    (E) The runaway car crashed into a guardrail, and it was going 60 miles per hour.

26. Like many artists at the show, Ken's paintings received a considerable amount of attention from the critics.

(A) Like many artists at the show, Ken's paintings received a considerable amount of attention from the critics.

(B) Ken's paintings, like those of many other artists at the show, received a considerable amount of attention from the critics.

(C) Ken's paintings, like many other artists at the show, received a considerable amount of attention from the critics.

(D) Like many other artists at the show, Ken's paintings received a considerable amount of attention from the critics.

(E) Like many artists at the show, Ken received a considerable amount of attention from the painting critics.

27. When Claire introduced Charles to her father, he shook his hand with disinterest.

(A) When Claire introduced Charles to her father, he shook his hand with disinterest.

(B) When Claire introduced Charles to her father, he shook their hand with disinterest.

(C) When Claire introduced Charles to her father, they shook hands with disinterest.

(D) Claire introduced Charles to her father, but he shook his hand with disinterest.

(E) When Claire introduced Charles to her father, her father shook his hand with disinterest.

28. Owning an umbrella which is quite common today was once the exclusive privilege of the wealthy and powerful.

(A) Owning an umbrella which is quite common today was once the exclusive privilege of the wealthy and powerful.

(B) Owning an umbrella a quite common occurrence today was once the exclusive privilege of the wealthy and powerful.

(C) Owning an umbrella, which is quite common today, was once the exclusive privilege of the wealthy and powerful.

(D) Owning an umbrella is quite common today and was once the exclusive privilege of the wealthy and powerful.

(E) Owning an umbrella, is quite common today, once a very powerful privilege.

29. Since Gloria had been at every family event in recent years, <u>she felt badly when she could not make it to her cousin's graduation.</u>

(A) , she felt badly when she could not make it to her cousin's graduation.

(B) , she had felt badly when she could not make it to her cousin's graduation.

(C) . She felt bad that she could not make it to her cousin's graduation.

(D) , she felt bad when she could not make it to her cousin's graduation.

(E) she felt badly when she could not make it to her cousin's graduation.

30. As Harold Abrahams, the Olympic sprint champion depicted in *Chariots of Fire,* once did, <u>the skilled young runner was quickly seeking coaching help as soon as she recognized that her competitors were every bit as fast as she was.</u>

(A) the skilled young runner was quickly seeking coaching help as soon as she recognized that her competitors were every bit as fast as she was

(B) the skilled young runner sought coaching help as soon as she recognized that her competitors were every bit as fast as she was

(C) the skilled young runner quickly sought coaching help although she recognized that her competitors were every bit as fast as she was

(D) the skilled young runner, who quickly sought coaching help as soon as she recognized that her competitors were every bit as fast as she was

(E) the skilled young runner quickly sought coaching help when she suddenly recognized that her competitors who were every bit as fast as she was

31. <u>We would of spent less time in the Hall of Mammals</u> had we realized that the museum's closing time would soon be upon us.

(A) We would of spent less time in the Hall of Mammals

(B) We would of spent more time in the Hall of Mammals

(C) We would have spent less time in the Hall of Mammals

(D) We could of spent more time in the Hall of Mammals

(E) We would have been spending more time in the Hall of Mammals

32. Urban planners and architects learn their craft in graduate school, <u>but you can also get inspiration from studying the efforts of those in their field</u>.

    (A) but you can also get inspiration from studying the efforts of those in their field

    (B) but also getting inspiration from studying the efforts of those in their field

    (C) since you can also get inspiration from studying the efforts of those in their field

    (D) but they can also get inspiration from studying the efforts of those in their field

    (E) but also getting inspiration from studying the efforts of those in their field is another way you can learn

33. In ancient Egypt, when a new pharaoh ascended to the throne, <u>he would commission the enormous task of building his tomb, a challenge that would consume gangs of slaves for years</u>.

    (A) he would commission the enormous task of building his tomb, a challenge that would consume gangs of slaves for years

    (B) he would commission the enormous task of building his tomb; a challenge that would consume gangs of slaves for years

    (C) he would have commissioned the enormous task of building his tomb, a challenge that would consume gangs of slaves for years

    (D) he would commission the enormous task of building his tomb, this was a challenge that would consume gangs of slaves for years

    (E) commissioning the enormous task of building his tomb, a challenge that would consume gangs of slaves for years

34. Despite common perceptions, we now know from new historical research that the Americas at the time of Columbus were anything but thinly populated lands; the "new" world featuring cities that were larger than some European capitals.

(A) Despite common perceptions, we now know from new historical research that the Americas at the time of Columbus were anything but thinly populated lands; the "new" world featuring cities that were larger than some European capitals.

(B) Despite common perceptions, we now know from new historical research that the Americas at the time of Columbus were anything but thinly populated lands. The "new" world featuring cities that were larger than some European capitals.

(C) Despite common perceptions, we now know from new historical research that the Americas at the time of Columbus were anything but thinly populated lands; the "new" world featured cities that were larger than some European capitals.

(D) Despite common perceptions, we now know from new historical research that the Americas at the time of Columbus were anything but thinly populated lands, the "new" world featured cities that were larger than some European capitals.

(E) Despite common perceptions, we now know from new historical research that the Americas at the time of Columbus were anything but thinly populated lands the "new" cities were larger than some European capitals.

35. Upon arriving at my new school, the teacher greeted me warmly and introduced me to the class.

(A) Upon arriving at my new school, the teacher greeted me warmly and introduced me to the class.

(B) Upon arriving at my new school, the teacher greeted me with warmth and introduced me to the class.

(C) Upon arriving at my new school, the teacher greeted me warmly as she introduced me to the class.

(D) Arriving at my new school, the teacher greeted me warmly and introduced me to the class.

(E) When I arrived at my new school, the teacher greeted me warmly and introduced me to the class.

36. When she returned to the pool after recovering from her injury, <u>she swum several laps perfectly, surprising herself as well as her coach</u>.

   (A) she swum several laps perfectly, surprising herself as well as her coach

   (B) she swam several laps perfect, surprising herself as well as her coach

   (C) she swam several laps perfectly, surprising herself as well as her coach

   (D) she swam several laps perfectly, surprising herself as well as her coach, too

   (E) she swum several perfect laps, surprising herself as well as her coach

37. <u>Jessica, along with Ahmed, Tyson, and Miriam, eagerly seeks her classmates' votes.</u>

   (A) Jessica, along with Ahmed, Tyson, and Miriam, eagerly seeks her classmates' votes.

   (B) Jessica, along with Ahmed, Tyson, and Miriam, eagerly seek their classmates' votes.

   (C) Jessica, along with Ahmed, Tyson, and Miriam, are eagerly seeking their classmates' votes.

   (D) Jessica, along with Ahmed, Tyson, and Miriam, eagerly seeks their classmates' votes.

   (E) Jessica, who along with Ahmed, Tyson, and Miriam, eagerly seeks her classmates' votes.

Directions: The passage that follows is an early draft of an essay. Some parts need to be rewritten. Read the passage carefully and answer the questions that follow. Choose the answer that most clearly and effectively expresses the writer's intended meaning. In making your decisions, follow the conventions of standard written English. After you have chosen your answer, fill in the corresponding oval.

   (1) Is democracy the way of the future? **(2)** I have my doubts. **(3)** I, who live in a democracy, firmly believe in the democratic values of freedom, equal rights, and respecting dissimilar views. **(4)** Despite my feelings, I wonder whether democracy can take hold everywhere in the world, simply because it is viewed as a humane and fair way of governing.
   (5) People have been living in governed towns, cities, and countries for thousands of years, but democracy, in the form of representative

government, is quite new. **(6)** In fact, it is only about 200 years old. **(7)** I think of democracy as a baby taking their first steps, sometimes succeeding to walk at a steady clip and sometimes falling down. **(8)** In some of the world's fledgling democracies, for instance, dictators took over and forcefully ended freedoms, like Franco did in Spain. **(9)** Another example is when, in democracies, people get elected who are not the best leaders or who do more harm than good for their countries. **(10)** Hitler was elected to office in Germany.

(11) In the United States, democracy took hold among people who had had a history of self governing and who, for the most part, shared a common religious tradition. **(12)** But it still took a considerable effort by extraordinary people like Adams, Jefferson, Washington, and Hamilton to make democracy the law of the land. **(13)** It also took a bloody war, and so much compromise that not all Americans became free to enjoy the liberties that were fought for so valiantly.

(14) Let me say that I'm not by nature a pessimist. **(15)** I think that people are basically decent and peaceful, that they are interested in living full, free lives, and that they will pick the best path to provide themselves with this when given the choice. **(16)** Once again, however, democracy is a challenging kind of government to get going and to make work. **(17)** It may not take root without hardly any difficulties arising and, in some areas, may not take hold at all. **(18)** Democracy costs; if undertaken too quickly or carelessly, it can cost too much.

38. In context, which of the following is the best revision of sentence 3 (reproduced below)?

I, who live in a democracy, firmly believe in the democratic values of freedom, equal rights, and respecting dissimilar views.

(A) (As it is now)

(B) I, by living in a democracy, firmly believe in the democratic values of freedom, equal rights, and respecting dissimilar views.

(C) I, who live in a democracy, firmly believe in the democratic values of freedom, equal rights, and respect for dissimilar views.

(D) I, without question, believe in the democratic values of freedom, equal rights, and respect for dissimilar views, living in a democracy.

(E) Although I live in a democracy, I firmly believe in the democratic values of freedom, equal rights, and respect for dissimilar views.

39. Which of the following is the best revision of the underlined portion of sentence 7 (reproduced below)?

I think of democracy as a baby <u>taking their first steps</u>, sometimes succeeding to walk at a steady clip and sometimes falling down.

(A) (As it is now)

(B) who walks for the first time

(C) about to take their first steps

(D) taking his or her first steps

(E) taking its first steps

40. In context, which is the best way to revise and combine sentences 9 and 10 (reproduced below)?

Another example is when, in democracies, people get elected who are not the best leaders or who do more harm than good for their countries. Hitler was elected to office in Germany.

(A) It also happens in democracies that people get elected who are not the best leaders or who do more harm than good for their countries, Hitler getting elected to office in Germany is an example of this.

(B) People who get elected in democracies sometimes are not the best leaders or do more harm than good for their countries; Hitler was elected to office in Germany.

(C) And sometimes in democracies, people get elected who are not the best leaders or who are harmful rather than good for their countries; Hitler's election to office in Germany can be seen as an example of this.

(D) In democracies, people sometimes get elected who are not the best leaders or who do more harm than good for their countries; Hitler was elected to office in Germany.

(E) Sometimes, too, in democracies people get elected who are not the best leaders or who turn out to do more harm than good for their countries, which is what happened when Hitler was elected to office in Germany.

41. Which of the following best replaces the underlined portion of sentence 17 (reproduced below)?

It may not take root without hardly any difficulties arising and, in some areas, may not take hold at all.

(A) (As it is now)

(B) without difficulties arising

(C) without difficulties that are arising

(D) with difficulties hardly arising

(E) without difficulties that arise as a result of it being challenging

42. Which sentence best states the main idea of paragraph 2?

(A) sentence 5

(B) sentence 6

(C) sentence 8

(D) sentence 9

(E) sentence 10

43. Which of the following would make the most logical final sentence for the essay?

(A) However, it is always worth trying; I say, "Go for it at any price."

(B) It could cost billions of dollars.

(C) Therefore, I urge leaders to be mindful of the consequences and to move slowly and carefully in any effort to introduce democracy.

(D) Furthermore, people in many parts of the world live in places without any central government at all.

(E) This sums up what I have to say about democracy and its challenges.

Directions: In each item, one of the underlined words or phrases may contain an error in grammar, usage, word choice, or idiom. If there is an error, choose the underlined part that must be changed to make the sentence correct, and fill in the corresponding oval. If the sentence has no error, fill in oval E. In selecting answers, follow the requirements of standard written English.

Example

When Dawn <u>last</u> <u>spoke</u> with her mother, <u>she</u> was on
      A   B   C
vacation in Norway and in <u>great</u> spirits. <u>No error</u>
                    D   E

Ⓐ Ⓑ ⒸⒸ Ⓓ Ⓔ

44. When the retiree won the lottery he couldn't <u>hardly</u> believe <u>it</u>,
                                      A   B

  <u>especially</u> since he <u>had purchased</u> only one ticket. <u>No error</u>
     C   D   E

🅐 Ⓑ Ⓒ Ⓓ Ⓔ

45. Each <u>of the associates</u> of the intelligence chief <u>agrees</u> to keep the
          A   B

  <u>seriousness</u> of the <u>matter</u> a secret. <u>No error</u>
     C   D   E

Ⓐ Ⓑ Ⓒ Ⓓ 🅔

46. What was the mayor <u>inferring</u> with his <u>reference</u> to the <u>dwindling</u>
                    A   B   C

  attendance at school events and <u>at</u> parent-teacher meetings? <u>No error</u>
                               D   E

🅐 Ⓑ Ⓒ Ⓓ Ⓔ

47. The copper mine <u>had been</u> abandoned for years; <u>however, some</u> of
                  A   B

  the <u>town's</u> buildings, including the jail and schoolhouse, <u>is</u> still
       C   D

  standing. <u>No error</u>
         E

Ⓐ Ⓑ Ⓒ 🅓 Ⓔ

Commonly Confused Words

➤ **accept, except** *Accept* is a verb that means "to receive" or "to agree to." *Except* is a preposition that means "but."

> Everyone agreed to **accept** the judge's decision.
> Everyone **except** me stayed late.

➤ **affect, effect** *Affect* is a verb that means "to influence." The noun *effect* means "the result of an action." The verb *effect* means "to cause" or "to bring about."

> Crossing several time zones may **affect** your sleep.
> What are the **effects** of overcrowded schools?
> Timeouts are meant to **effect** changes in a child's behavior.

➤ **all right** Spell *all right* as two separate words. The word *alright* is not acceptable in formal written English.

> Are you feeling **all right** after so little sleep?

➤ **amount of, number of** Use *amount of* when you write about a general quantity of something. Use *number of* to refer to something that can be counted.

> The **amount of** popcorn sold at the theater was huge, even though only a small **number of** people saw the movie.

➤ **anywheres, everywheres, nowheres, somewheres** These words are spelled incorrectly. *Anywhere, everywhere, nowhere,* and *somewhere* have no *-s* at the end.

> We saw palm trees **everywhere.** I couldn't see snow **anywhere.**

➤ **bad, badly** Use *bad* as an adjective and as a predicate adjective after linking verbs. **Remember:** A predicate adjective describes the subject. Use *badly,* an adverb, to modify an action verb.

> Chris feels **bad** about missing the party.
> She sings **badly.**

➤ **beside, besides** *Beside* means "by the side of." *Besides* means "in addition to." *Besides* as an adverb means "moreover."

> We picnicked **beside** the river. **Besides** sandwiches, we brought fruit.
> It's too cold to swim; **besides,** we have no sunscreen.

between, among Use *between* to refer to two people or things being compared. You can also use *between* when discussing three or more items if you think only two will be compared at a time. Use *among* to refer to a group or to three or more people or things.

> Just **between** you and me, I can't stand cilantro.
> Can you tell the difference **between** a sonnet, a ballad, and a couplet?
> It's good to be back home **among** family and friends.

borrow, lend, loan, *Borrow* means "to take something temporarily that must be returned." *Lend,* the opposite of *borrow,* means "to give something temporarily." Don't confuse *loan* and *lend. Loan* is always a noun in formal written English; a loan is the thing that is lent.

> Howie wants to **borrow** five dollars
> Sheila **lent** him the money.
> He will repay her **loan** Saturday.

bring, take *Bring* refers to a movement toward or with the speaker. *Take* refers to a movement away from the speaker.

> Karl **brought** me a souvenir. Please **take** this package to him.

could (might, should, would) of Use *have,* not *of,* with these helping verbs.

> Avram **should have** brought his guitar to the party.

different from Use *from,* not *than,* after *different.*

> How is a square **different from** a rectangle?

farther, further *Farther* refers to physical distance. *Further* means "to a greater degree or extent."

> Which is **farther** from Earth—Neptune or Pluto?
> I will study the issue **further** and give you my opinion.

fewer, less *Fewer* refers to nouns that can be counted. *Less* refers to nouns that can't be counted.

> Sean buys **fewer** books. I should eat **less** chocolate.

good, well *Good* is always an adjective, never an adverb. *Well,* however, can be both. The adverb *well* means "done in a satisfactory way." The adjective *well* means "in good health."

> Sally has a **good** excuse.
> She wasn't feeling **well,** so she didn't do **well** on her exam.

▐▐▐▶ **had ought, hadn't ought** Drop the *had.* Use just plain *ought* and *ought not.*

> They ~~had~~ **ought** to start early to miss the rush
> hour traffic.

▐▐▐▶ **kind (sort, type) of a** Drop the *a.* Use *kind of, sort of,* or *type of.* But keep in mind that *kind (sort, type) of* can usually be omitted without changing the meaning of a sentence and should be avoided unless it is truly necessary.

> This **kind of** ~~a~~ squash tastes like sweet potato.
> This squash tastes like sweet potato.

▐▐▐▶ **learn, teach** Don't use *learn* when you mean *teach* or *instruct. Learn* is what a student does; *teach* is what a *teacher* does.

> I **learned** how to embroider from a Hmong woman who **taught** our class.

▐▐▐▶ **leave, let** *Leave* means "to depart" and "to place." *Let* means "to allow."

> When you **leave,** please **leave** the books on the table.
> Don't **let** them get lost.

▐▐▐▶ **lie, lay** *Lie* means "to rest or recline." *Lay* means "to place or put." The past tense of *lie* is *lay,* and the past participle is *lain.* Both the past tense and the past participle of *lay* is *laid.*

> LIE   Yesterday, Justin **lay** on the couch and fell asleep.
> LIE   The newspaper **had lain** in a puddle for weeks and was soaked.
> LAY   She **laid** the heavy package on the table.

▐▐▐▶ **like, as, as if, as though,** Don't use *like* to introduce a subordinate clause. Use *as, as if,* or *as though.* Use *like* to express a similarity.

> He looks **as if** he's really sorry.
> Carey arrived early, **as** she said she would.
> The mime looked **like** a statue.

▐▐▐▶ **of, off of** Don't use *of* after the prepositions *inside, outside,* and *off.* Also, use *from,* not *off* or *off of,* when you're referring to the source of something.

> I put the milk **inside** ~~of~~ the cooler.
> Please take the cooler **off** ~~of~~ the table.
> Is this the cooler we borrowed **from** Jee-Young?

▐▐▐▶ **real, really** *Real* is an adjective that means "actual." *Really* is an adverb that means "actually" or "genuinely."

> Your news was a **real** surprise. We are **really** disappointed.

▐▐▐▶ **rise, raise** *Rise* means "to stand up." *Raise* means "to lift or bring up." The past tense of *rise* is *rose,* and the past participle is *risen.* Both the past tense and the past participle of *raise* is *raised.*

RISE   Last week, Mrs. Kaplan **rose** to speak at the board meeting.

RAISE   She **raised** two very important points.

▐▐▐▶ **sit, set** *Sit* means "to rest oneself on a chair." *Set* means "to put." Both the past tense and the past participle of *sit* is *sat.* Both the past tense and the past participle of *set* is *set.*

SIT   Last night, we **sat** on the bench and watched the fireworks.

SET   On Friday, Jim **set** the table and cooked dinner.

▐▐▐▶ **some, somewhat** *Some* is an adjective. *Somewhat* is an adverb meaning "slightly." Don't use *some* as an adverb.

Let's think about cooking **some** food.

The rain has let up **somewhat.**

▐▐▐▶ **than, then** *Than* is a conjunction that introduces a subordinate clause. *Then* is an adverb meaning "therefore" or "next in order or time."

She lives closer to our school **than** I do. **Then** why don't we meet at her house? First, let's discuss your idea; **then** we'll vote.

▐▐▐▶ **that, which** Use *which* to introduce a nonessential clause. Use *that* in an essential clause.

Our math team is going to the state finals, **which** start next week. The team **that** wins the competition will get the trophy.

▐▐▐▶ **that, who** Use *who* in clauses that refer to people. Use *that* in essential clauses that refer to things.

Ms. Houlihan, **who** teaches algebra, coaches the math team.

The calculator **that** I use at school is solar-powered.

▐▐▐▶ **this here, that there** In standard written English, *this* and *that* are used alone. Drop the word *here* or *there.*

I'm trying to fix **this** ~~here~~ chair. Please hand me **that** ~~there~~ screwdriver.

▐▐▐▶ **when, where** When you define a word, don't use *when* or *is when. Where* refers to a place. Also, don't use *where* to mean "that."

INCORRECT   Squaring a number **is when** you multiply the number by itself.

CORRECT   To square a number, multiply the number by itself.

INCORRECT   I read **where** the Chinese New Year is this Friday.

CORRECT   I read **that** the Chinese New Year is this Friday.

Index

A

a, an, 95, 261
abbreviations, 223–24
  capitalization of, 261
  periods after, 223
abstract nouns, 89
accept, except, 324
acronyms, 223–24
action verbs, 93, 119
active voice, 173
adjective(s), 18, 95–96. *See also* adverb(s); modifiers
  versus adverbs, 97
  commas to separate two or more, 225
  commas to set off single-word, 231
  defined, 95
  degrees of comparison in, 207–8
  infinitive/infinitive phrases as, 137
  past participles as, 163
  predicate, 95, 121
  present participles as, 163
  proper, 95, 259
  using specific, 95
adjective clauses, 147–48
  in combining sentences, 44
  definition of, 147
  as essential, 147, 229
  introductory words for, 147
  setting off, with commas, 229
adjective phrase, 129
adverb(s), 18, 97–98. *See also* adjective(s); modifiers
  versus adjectives, 97
  conjunctive, 117, 243
  defined, 97
  degrees of comparison in, 207–10
  distinguishing between prepositions and, 129
  infinitive/infinitive phrases as, 137
  relative, 147
adverb clauses, 101, 149–50
  in combining sentences, 44, 101
  definition of, 149
  elliptical, 149
  introductory words for, 149
  setting off, with commas, 149
adverb phrase, 129
affect, effect, 324

agreement
  pronoun with antecedent, 201
  subject-verb, 179–80
    with compound subjects, 183–84
    with indefinite pronouns, 193–94
    with intervening phrase, 191
    in person and number, 179–80
    with special nouns, 185–86
ain't, 211
all right, 324
American English, 167
among, between, 325
amount of, number of, 324
an, a, 95, 261
analyzing in essay question, 68
anecdotes
  in persuasive writing, 29, 62
  in supporting main idea, 23
antecedent, 91
  agreement with pronoun, 201
anywheres, everywheres, nowheres, somewheres, 324
apostrophe(s), 251–52
  in contractions, 251
  in forming plurals of letters, numbers, or words referred to as words, 251
  in indefinite pronouns, 251
  in possessive nouns, 251
  to show omission of letters, words, or numbers, 251
  to show possession, 251
appositive(s), 139, 199
  in combining sentences, 139
  commas to set off, 139
  nouns as, 199
  pronouns as, 199
appositive phrase, 139
  in combining sentences, 139
  commas to set off, 139
argument in persuasive writing, 57
articles
  definite, 95
  indefinite, 95
artworks
  capitalization for titles of, 261
  italics for titles of, 245
  and subject-verb agreement, 185
as, as if, as though, like, 326
attention grabber in persuasive writing, 31

audience, 13, 81
autobiographical incident in narrative writing, 52–56

B

bad, badly, 324
be, forms of, 93, 121
  capitalization of, in titles, 261
beside, besides, 324
between, among, 325
Bible, use of colon between chapter and verse, 241
block method of organizing a compare and contrast essay, 64–65
body, 67
  in essay writing, 32–33
  in literary analysis, 73
books
  capitalization for titles of, 261
  italics for titles of, 245
  quotation marks for parts of, 247
borrow, lend, loan, 325
brainstorming, 10
brand names, capitalization of, 265
bring, take, 325
businesses, capitalization of names of, 263
business letters
  differences between friendly letters and, 231
  use of colon after greeting, 241

C

calendar items, capitalization of, 265
call to action in persuasive writing, 31, 60
capitalization
  of brand names, 265
  of calendar items, 265
  of first words of quotations, 247
  of first words of sentences, 263
  of geographic names, 259
  of groups, 263
  of interjection *O*, 265
  of names of groups, teams, businesses, institutions, and organizations, 263
  of names of historic events, documents, and periods, 265
  of names of people, 259
  of names of school subjects, 263
  of pronoun *I*, 265
  of proper adjectives, 95, 259–60

capitalization (*continued*)
of proper nouns, 89, 259–60
of religions, 263
of sentence beginning, 109
of titles, 261
of words that show family
relationships, 261
proofreading for, 18
cause and effect, transitional words
and expressions to show, 27
-cede, spelling rules for, 275
-ceed, spelling rules for, 275
centuries, 265
Character, by Arthur Ashe, 52
characters in literary analysis, 72
chronological order, 26
in narrative writing, 29
need for transition words in, 44
claim, 32
clause(s)
adjective, 44, 147–48
adverb, 101, 149–50
elliptical, 149
dependent, 44–45, 145
essential, 147, 229
independent, 145–46, 153
main, 145–46
nonessential, 147, 229
noun, 151–52
subordinate, 44–45, 145, 147,
149, 151
clause fragment, 145
clincher sentence, 21, 22
clustering, 10
coherence in writing, 26–28
collective nouns, 89, 185
colloquial speech, 211
colons, 241–42
after greeting of business letter,
241
before formal statement or
quotation, 241
before list of items, 241
between chapter and verse in
reference to Bible, 241
between hour and minutes, 241
to emphasize word or phrase,
241
to introduce long quotation,
241, 247
combining sentences, 46–47. *See
also* complex sentence;
compound-complex sentence;
compound sentences
with appositives, 139
appositives/appositive phrases
in, 139

compound subject and
compound verbs in, 38–39
coordinating conjunctions in,
40–41
inserting phrases in, 42–43
inserting single words, 46–47
subordinate clauses in, 44–45
commas
after abbreviations, 223
after introductory participle or
participial phrase, 227
after introductory prepositional
phrase, 133, 227
with compound sentences and
introductory elements, 227–28
following greeting and closing
of friendly letter, 231
to introduce short informal
quotations, 231, 247
with nonessential elements, 229
to prevent misreading, 133
with quotation marks, 249
with sentence interrupters, 229
to separate date, 231
to separate year, 231
in a series, 41, 225–26
to set off adverb clauses, 149
to set off appositive phrases,
139
to set off interjections, 101
to set off introductory
prepositional phrases, 133
to set off nonessential adjective
clauses, 44
to set off nonessential
appositives and appositive
phrases, 229
to set off noun of direct address,
229
to set off parenthetical
expressions and transitional
expressions, 229
to set off single-word adjectives
that begin sentence, 231
to set off *well, yes, no*, 231
comma splice, 117
common nouns, 89
comparative as degree of
comparison, 207–210
compare, 62
compare and contrast essay, 62–67
drafting, 66–67
prewriting, 63–66
proofreading, 67
publishing, 67
revising and editing, 67

compare and contrast in essay
question, 84
comparison(s), 67
avoiding double, 209
avoiding illogical, 209
avoiding unclear, 209
degrees of, 207–210
in supporting main idea, 23
transitional words and
expressions to show, 27
complement, subject, 121
complete predicate, 111
complete subject, 111
complex sentence, 153
independent clause in, 153
subordinate clauses in, 153
compound-complex sentence, 153
independent clause in, 153
subordinate clauses in, 153
compound nouns, 89, 225
compound prepositions, 99
compound sentences, 145, 153, 227
changing run-on sentences into,
233
commas in forming, 227–28
semicolons in forming, 243
compound subjects, 38–39, 183
agreement with, 183–84
in combining sentences,
38–39
compound verbs, 38–39, 227
in combining sentences, 38–39
conclusions, 67
in essay question, 85
in essay writing, 33
in literary analysis, 73
concrete nouns, 89
conjunctions, 101, 117
coordinating, 38, 40–41, 101,
117, 183, 225, 228, 261
correlative, 38, 101
subordinating, 44, 101, 149
conjunctive adverbs, 243
in correcting run-on sentences,
117
use of semicolons before, 243
construction, incomplete, 199
contractions, 211
apostrophes in, 251
contrast, 62
transitional words and
expressions to show, 27
controlling idea, 32
coordinating conjunctions, 40–41,
101, 225, 227, 261

coordinating conjunctions (*continued*)
in correcting run-on sentences,
117
in forming compound subject
or verb, 38, 183
correlative conjunctions, 101
in forming compound subject
or verb, 38
could of, 325
counterarguments, presenting and
demolishing, 60
criteria, 68

D

dangling modifier, 213
dates, commas to separate parts of,
231
declarative sentences, 109, 223
punctuation with, 109, 223
definite articles, 95
definitions
in expository writing, 30
in persuasive writing, 59
in supporting main idea, 23
degrees of comparison, 207–10
demonstrative pronouns, 91
dependent clause, 145
descriptive writing, 29
sensory details in, 29
spatial order in, 29
details
elaborating with supporting,
23–25
sensory, in descriptive writing, 29
specific, in narrative writing, 29
dialects, 167
dialogue, punctuating, 249–50
dialogue tag, 249
dictionary, 273–74
abbreviations in, 223
preferred spellings in, 277
principal parts of irregular verbs
in, 165
different from, 325
direction statement, 81
direct object, 93, 119, 195
noun clause as, 151
direct question, 223
direct quotations
capitalization of, 263
quotation marks at beginning
and end of, 247
discussion in essay question, 84
documents, capitalization of names
of, 265
double comparisons, 209
double negatives, 211–12

drafting
for compare and contrast essay,
66–67
defined, 13
for essay questions, 86
for expository writing, 82
for literary analysis, 72–73
for narrative writing, 56
for persuasive writing, 61
strategies in, 13–14

E

editing, 18–19
for persuasive writing, 61
Editing and Proofreading Worksheets,
235, 236, 253, 254, 267, 268, 281,
282
Editing Tip, 91, 117, 121, 133, 135,
145, 147, 163, 165, 169, 181, 183,
199, 211, 223, 225, 227, 241, 243,
245, 247, 251, 259, 261
effect, affect, 324
-ei, spelling rules for, 275–76
elaboration, 23
elements of fiction, 68
ellipsis points, 71
elliptical adverb clause, 149
emotional appeals, in persuasive
writing, 57, 60
emphasis, transitional words and
expressions to show, 27
emphatic form of verb, 169
Ending Child Hunger, by Bob Dole
and George McGovern, 57
English
American, 167
colloquial, 211
formal, 121
standard, 109, 167, 209
essays, 48. *See also* compare and
contrast essay; personal response
essay
body in, 32–33
capitalization for titles of, 261
conclusion in, 33
introduction in, 32
topic sentence in, 21
essay tests, 83–86
essential clauses, 147, 229
evaluation, 68
*everywheres, anywheres, nowheres,
somewheres*, 324
examples
in expository writing, 30
in persuasive writing, 31
in supporting main idea, 23
transitional words and
expressions to show, 27

except, accept, 324
exclamation points, 223
after abbreviations, 223
to end exclamatory sentence,
109, 223
with quotation marks, 249
to set off interjections, 101
exclamatory sentences, 109, 223
expert opinions in persuasive
writing, 59
explanation in essay question, 84
expository writing, 30
compare and contrast essay as,
62–67
logical order in, 30
research paper as, 74–82

F

facts
in expository writing, 30
difference between opinion
and, 66
in persuasive writing, 31, 59
in supporting main idea, 23
family relationships, capitalization
of words that show, 261
farther, further, 325
fewer, less, 325
fiction, elements of, 68
first person, 179
first words in sentences,
capitalization of, 263
5-W and How? questions, 11
foreign words and expressions,
italics for, 245
formal English, 121
fragments
clause, 145
sentence, 109, 113–14, 233
freewriting, 10
friendly letters
commas following greeting and
closing of, 231
differences between business
letters and, 231
further, farther, 325
future perfect tense, 169
future tense, 169

G

geographic names, capitalization
for, 259
gerund, 135–36
gerund phrase, 135
good, well, 325
Grant and Lee: A Study in Contrasts,
by Bruce Catton, 62–63

groups, capitalization of names of, 263

H

hadn't ought, had ought, 326
helping verbs, 93, 163
Hemingway's Ancient Mariner, by Carlos Baker, 68–69
historical events
    capitalization of, 265
    chronological order for, 26
historic periods, capitalization of names of, 265
hyphens in compound names, 89

I

I, capitalization of, 265
ideas and unity, 15
-ie, spelling rules for, 275–76
illogical comparisons, avoiding, 209
imperative sentences, 199, 223
    finding subject of, 115
    punctuation for, 199, 223
importance, transitional words and expressions to show order of, 27
incidents in supporting main idea, 23
incomplete construction, 199
indefinite articles, 95
indefinite pronouns, 91, 201
    apostrophes in possessive form of, 251
    singular and plural of, 193–94
independent clauses, 145–46, 153
    commas between, 225
    in complex sentence, 153
    in compound-complex sentences, 153
    in compound sentence, 153
indirect object, 119, 195
    noun clause as, 151
indirect question, 223
indirect quotation, capitalization of, 263
infinitive phrase, 137
infinitive(s), 137–38
    split, 137
institutions, capitalization of names of, 263
intensifiers, 97
intensive pronouns, 91
interjections, 101
    capitalization of *O,* 265
    punctuation after, 101
interpreting in essay question, 84
interrogative pronouns, 91
interrogative sentences, 109, 223.
 See also questions

end punctuation for, 109, 223
finding subject of, 115
intervening phrase, 179
introduction
    in essay question, 85
    in essays, 32, 67
    in literary analysis, 73
introductory participle or participial phrase, comma after, 227
introductory prepositional phrase, comma after, 133, 227
inverted sentence, 115
irregular degrees of comparison, 207
irregular verbs, 165–68
I-Search paper, 74
italics, 245–46
items in series
    commas to separate, 225–26
    semicolons to separate, 243

K

kind of a, 326

L

languages, capitalization of names of, 263
lay, lie, 165, 326
learn, teach, 326
leave, let, 326
lend, loan, borrow, 325
less, fewer, 325
let, leave, 326
letters. *See also* business letters; friendly letters
    apostrophes to form plurals of, 251
    italics for, 245
letter to editor
    in persuasive writing, 59–61
lie, lay, 165, 326
like, as, as if, as though, 326
linking verbs, 93, 119, 121
literary analysis, 68–73
    analyzing fiction, 68–73
    drafting, 72–73
    prewriting, 70–72
    proofreading, 73
    publishing, 73
    revising and editing, 73
literary present tense, 169
loaded words, 60
loan, borrow, lend, 325
logical appeals in persuasive writing, 57
logical order, 26
    in expository writing, 30, 32

M

magazines
    capitalization of titles of, 245
    italics for titles of, 245
    quotation marks for titles of articles in, 247
main clause, 145–46
main idea, stating, in expository writing, 30
mapping, 10–11, 55
might of, 325
misplaced modifier, 213–14
mnemonics, 275
Modern Language Association (MLA) style, 74, 80
modifiers. *See also* adjective(s); adverb(s)
    dangling, 213
    irregular, 207
    misplaced, 132, 213–14
movie titles
    capitalization of, 261
    italics of, 245
musical works, capitalization of titles of, 261

N

names of people, capitalization for, 259
narrative writing, 29–30
    autobiographical incident in, 52–56
    chronological order in, 26, 29
    details in, 29
    drafting in, 56
    prewriting in, 55
    proofreading in, 56
    publishing in, 56
    revising in, 56
nationalities, capitalization of names of, 263
negatives, double, 211–12
newspapers, italics for titles of, 245
no, commas to set off, 231
nominative, predicate, 121, 193
none, 181
nonessential adjective clause, 229
nonessential appositives and appositive phrases, commas to set off, 229
nonessential clauses, 147, 229
notes, taking, for research paper, 79
noun(s), 89–90
    abstract, 89
    agreement with special, 185–86
    appositive/appositive phrase as, 139, 199

noun(s) (*continued*)
    collective, 89, 185
    common, 89
    compound, 89, 225
    concrete, 89
    defined, 89
    gerund/gerund phrases as, 135
    infinitive/infinitive phrases as, 137
    plural, 279–80
    possessive, 135, 251
    proper, 89, 259
    using specific, 89
noun appositive, 199
noun clauses, 151–52
noun of direct address, comma to set off, 229
nowheres, somewheres, anywheres, everywheres, 324
number in subject-verb agreement, 179
number of, amount of, 324
numbers
    apostrophes to form plurals of, 251
    italics for, 245

O

O, capitalization of, 265
object
    direct, 93, 119, 195
    indirect, 119, 195
    of preposition, 151, 195
objective test, 83
object pronouns, 195–96
    as appositives, 199
    whom as, 197
observations in persuasive writing, 59
of, off of, 326
opinion, difference between fact and, 66
opinion statement, in persuasive writing, 31
order
    chronological, 26, 29, 40
    of importance, 26, 27, 31
    logical, 26, 30
    spatial, 26, 29
organization
    of compare and contrast essay, 64
    of essays, 32–33
    in revising, 15
organizations, capitalization of names of, 263
original research, 74
outline
    in essay question, 85

in expository writing, 80–81
in persuasive writing, 61
use of prewriting notes in creating, 13

P

paragraphs
    clincher sentence in, 21–22
    coherence in, 26–28
    topic sentence in, 21, 22
    types of, 29–31
    unity of, 21–25
    varying sentence beginnings and structure in, 36–37, 133–34
paraphrase, 79
parenthetical documentation, 80
parenthetical expressions and transitional expressions, commas to set off, 229
participial phrase, 131–32
    in combining sentences, 42–43
    commas after introductory, 227
participles, 131–32
    past, 131, 163
    present, 131, 163
part of speech. *See also* adjective(s); adverb(s); conjunctions; interjections; noun(s); prepositions; pronoun(s); verb(s)
    determining for word, 103
parts of books, quotation marks for titles of, 247
passive voice, 173
past participles, 131, 163
    as adjectives, 163
    as verbs, 163
past perfect tense, 169
past tense, 169
people, capitalization of names of, 263
perfect tense, 169
periodicals
    capitalization of titles of, 245, 261
    italics for titles of, 245
    quotation marks for titles of articles in, 247
periods
    after abbreviations, 223
    to end declarative sentence, 109, 223
    to end exclamation, 223
    to end imperative sentence, 109, 223
    to end indirect question, 223
    with quotation marks, 249

personal experiences in persuasive writing, 59
personal pronouns, 91
personal response essay, 68
person in subject-verb agreement, 179
persons, capitalization of names of, 259
persuasion in persuasive writing, 57
persuasive writing, 31
    attention grabber in, 31
    call to action in, 31
    clincher sentence in, 21
    drafting in, 61
    editing in, 61
    letter to editor as, 59–61
    opinion statement in, 31
    order of importance in, 31
    prewriting in, 60–61
    proofreading in, 61
    publishing in, 61
phrases
    adjective, 129
    adverb, 129
    colons to emphasize, 241
    in combining sentences, 42–43
    gerund, 135
    infinitive, 137
    intervening, 179
    participial, 131–32
    prepositional, 129
    verb, 93, 131, 179
place, transitional words and expressions to show, 27
plagiarism, 80
planes, italics for titles of, 245
play titles
    capitalization of, 261
    italics of, 245
plot in literary analysis, 71
plot summary in literary analysis, 70
plural nouns
    apostrophes in, 251
    spelling of, 279
plural pronouns, 201
plural subjects, 179
plural verbs, 179
poems
    capitalization in lines of, 263
    capitalization of titles of, 261
    quotation marks for titles of, 247
point-by-point method of organizing a compare and contrast essay, 64–65

point of view in literary analysis, 72

position statement in persuasive writing, 59

positive as degree of comparison, 207–10

possessive nouns, 135
    apostrophes in, 251

possessive pronouns, 91, 135

predicate(s), 111–12
    complete, 111
    simple, 111

predicate adjective, 95, 121

predicate nominative, 121, 193
    noun clause as, 151

prefix, 277–78

prepositional phrase, 129
    comma to set off introductory, 133, 227

preposition(s), 99–100
    compound, 99
    defined, 99
    distinguishing between adverbs and, 129
    ending sentence with, 99
    object of, 151, 195

present participles, 131, 163
    as adjectives, 163
    as verbs, 163

present perfect tense, 169

present tense, 169
    literary present, 169

prewriting
    brainstorming in, 10
    clustering in, 10–11
    for compare and contrast essay, 63–66
    defined, 9
    for essay questions, 85–86
    for expository writing, 80–81
    5-W and How? questions in, 11
    freewriting in, 10
    for literary analysis, 70–72
    mapping, 10–11, 55
    for narrative writing, 55
    for persuasive writing, 60–61
    Venn diagram in, 64
    webbing in, 10–11
    writer's notebook in, 9

primary source, 78

principal parts of verbs, 163, 165

problem-solution research report, 75

progressive form, 169

pronoun(s), 26, 91–92
    agreement with antecedent, 201

appositive/appositive phrase as, 139, 199
    capitalization of *I*, 265
    defined, 91
    demonstrative, 91
    indefinite, 91, 181–82, 201
    intensive, 91
    interrogative, 91
    object, 195–96
    personal, 91
    plural, 201
    possessive, 91, 135
    as predicate nominative, 121
    reflexive, 91
    relative, 147
    singular, 201
    subject, 193–94

proofreading, 18–19
    of compare and contrast essay, 67
    of essay questions, 86
    of expository writing, 82
    of literary analysis, 73
    of narrative writing, 56
    of persuasive writing, 61
    and spell checking, 279
    symbols for, 19

proofreading log, 273

proper adjectives, 95, 259

proper nouns, 89, 259

publishing
    of compare and contrast essay, 67
    of expository writing, 82
    of literary analysis, 74
    of narrative writing, 56
    of persuasive writing, 61

punctuation marks. *See* apostrophes; colons; commas; ellipsis points; exclamation points; hyphens; italics; periods; question marks; quotation marks; semicolons
    proofreading for, 18

purpose, 13, 81

Q

question marks
    after abbreviations, 223
    to end interrogative sentence, 109, 223
    with quotation marks, 249

questions. *See also* interrogative sentences
    5-W and How?, 11
    direct, 223
    indirect, 223

quotation marks, 247–48
    at beginning and end of direct quotations, 247–48
    at beginning and end of speaker's exact words, 249
    enclosing single words, phrases, and short sentences in, 71
    with other punctuation marks, 249
    for titles of short works, 245, 247

quotations
    capitalization for first words of, 247, 263
    colon to introduce, 241
    commas to introduce short informal, 231
    direct, 263
    ellipsis points to indicate omissions, 71
    in expository writing, 30
    indenting block, 241
    indirect, 263
    in persuasive writing, 31
    in supporting main idea, 23

R

raise, rise, 327

real, really, 326

reasons
    in persuasive writing, 59
    in supporting main idea, 23

reflexive pronouns, 91

relative adverbs, 147

relative pronouns, 147

religions, capitalization of names of, 263

repetition
    avoiding, 32
    eliminating, 48

research paper, 74–82. *See also* expository writing

revising, 15–17
    of compare and contrast essay, 67
    of essay questions, 86
    of expository writing, 82
    of literary analysis, 73
    of narrative writing, 56
    sentence variety, 15

Revising and Editing Worksheets, 50, 104, 123, 124, 140, 155, 156, 174, 187, 188, 202, 215, 216

rise, raise, 327

run-on sentences, 117–18
    correcting, 233

S

school subjects, capitalization of, 263
science research papers, 74
secondary source, 78
second person, 179
-sede, spelling rules for, 275
semicolons, 243–44
    before conjunctive adverb that joins independent clauses, 243
    in correcting run-on sentences, 117
    to join independent clauses in compound sentence, 243
    with quotation marks, 247
    to separate items in series when one or more of the items contains a comma, 243
    before transitional expression that joins independent clauses, 243
sentence(s). *See also* combining sentences
    clincher, 21, 22
    complex, 153
    compound, 145, 153, 227
    compound-complex, 153
    declarative, 109, 223
    defined, 109
    ending with prepositions, 99
    exclamatory, 109, 223
    imperative, 109, 223
    interrogative, 109, 223
    inverted, 115
    need for subject and predicate in, 111–12
    run-on, 117–18
    simple, 153
    testing for, 113
    topic, 21, 22, 32
    varying beginnings and structure of, 36–37, 133–34, 227
sentence fragments, 109
    correcting, 113–14, 233
sentence interrupters, commas with, 229–30
series
    commas in, 41, 225–26
    semicolons in, 243
set, sit, 327
setting in literary analysis, 71
ships, italics for names of, 245
short stories
    capitalization for titles of, 261

quotation marks for titles of, 247
should of, 325
simple predicate, 111
simple sentence, 153
simple subject, 111
simple tenses, 169
singular pronouns, 201
singular subject, 179
singular verb, 179
sit, set, 327
some, some what, 325
somewheres, anywheres, everywheres, nowheres, 324
songs, quotation marks for titles of, 247
sort of a, 326
source card, 78
spacecraft, italics for names of, 245
spatial order, 26
    in descriptive writing, 29
spell checking, 279
spelling, 275–80
    with *-cede, -ceed,* and *-sede,* 275
    to form plural nouns, 279
    of gerunds formed from verbs ending in *-e,* 135, 277
    getting information on, from dictionary, 273
    i before *e* except after *c,* 275–76
    of past participles, 163
    with prefixes, 277
    of present participles, 163
    proofreading for, 18
    with suffixes, 277
split infinitives, 137
standard English, 109, 167, 209
statistics
    in expository writing, 30
    in persuasive writing, 31, 59
    in supporting main idea, 23
Step by Step, 46, 59, 113, 115, 119, 183, 193, 195, 197, 207, 225, 229
steps in process, chronological order for, 26
story map, 55
subject, 111–12
    complete, 111
    compound, 38–39, 183
    finding, 115–16
    noun clause as, 151
    plural, 179
    simple, 111
    singular, 179
    understood, 115
subject complements, 121

predicate adjectives as, 121
predicate nominatives as, 121
subject pronouns, 193–94
    as appositives, 199
    who as, 197
subject-verb agreement. *See* agreement
subordinate clauses, 44–45, 145, 147, 149, 151. *See also* adjective clauses; adverb clauses; noun clauses
    in combining sentences, 44–45
    in complex sentences, 153
    in compound-complex sentences, 153
    in correcting run-on sentences, 117, 233
    in varying sentences, 36
subordinating conjunctions, 44, 101, 149
suffix, 277–78
summarizing, transitional words and expressions to show, 27
summarizing information, 79
superlative as degree of comparison, 207–8
synonyms, 26

T

take, bring, 325
teach, learn, 326
teams, capitalization of names of, 263
tense. *See* verb tense
Test-Taking Tip, 38, 113, 117, 137, 139, 145, 151, 169, 171, 181, 213
than, then, 327
that, which, 327
that, who, 327
that there, this here, 327
the, 95
theme in literary analysis, 72
then, than, 327
thesis statement
    in essay, 32
    in essay test, 85–86
    in expository writing, 80
    in literary analysis, 70
    in persuasive writing, 59
this here, that there, 327
time
    transitional words and expressions to show, 27
    use of colon between hour and minutes, 241
time order, 54

titles, 261–62
    capitalization in, 261
    italics for, 245
    quotation marks for, 245, 247
topic
    choosing, 10
    narrowing, 9
topic sentences, 21, 22, 32
transitions, 26, 63
    list of common, 27
    use of semicolons before, 243
    using clear, 64–65
transitive verbs, 119
TV/radio
    capitalization of titles of, 261
    italics for titles of series of, 245
    quotation marks for titles of
      programs on, 247
type of a, 326

U

unclear comparisons, avoiding, 207
underlining. *See* italics
understood subject, 115
unity, 21–25
    skills for maintaining, 22

V

Venn diagram, 64
verb(s), 16, 93–94
    action, 93, 119
    compound, 38–39, 227
    defined, 93
    emphatic form of, 169
    helping, 93, 163
    irregular, 165–68
    linking, 93, 119, 121
    past participle as, 163

plural, 179
present participle as, 163
principal parts of, 163, 165
regular, 163–64
singular, 179
transitive, 119
using vivid, 93
voice, 173–74
verbals, 131
    gerunds as, 135–36
    infinitives as, 137–38
    participles as, 131–32
verb phrase, 93, 131, 179
verb tense, 93, 169–70
    future, 169
    future perfect, 169
    literary present, 169
    past, 169
    past perfect, 169
    perfect, 169
    present, 70, 169
    present perfect, 169
    simple, 169
voice
    active, 173
    passive, 173

W

webbing, 10–11
well, commas to set off, 231
well, *good*, 325
when, *where*, 327
which, *that*, 327
who, *that*, 327
who/whom, 147, 197–98
wordiness, eliminating, 26, 33,
  48–49

words
    choice of, in revising, 15
    colons to emphasize, 241
    determining part of speech for,
      103
    inserting single, in combining
      sentences, 46–47
    loaded, 60
words as words
    apostrophes to form plurals of,
      251
    italics for, 245
Working with a Writing Partner, 16
Works Cited list, 80
would of, 325
writer's notebook, 9
Writing Hint, 13, 21, 29, 38, 48, 67,
  71, 89, 93, 95, 99, 109, 129, 131,
  137, 149, 167, 173, 193, 199, 201,
  227, 231, 233, 241, 249, 275
writing process
    drafting in, 13–14
    prewriting in, 9–12
    proofreading in, 18–19
    revising and editing in, 15–17
writing strategies
    for coherence, 26–28
    eliminating wordiness, 48–49
    for unity, 21–25
writing style, 13

Y

year, commas to separate, 231
yes, commas to set off, 231
you, as the understood subject, 115